GOD OF BATTLES

The Papal State under Martin V
A Short Political Guide to the Arab World
The Lands of St Peter: The Papal State
in the Middle Ages and the Early Renaissance
Renaissance Rome 1500–1559: A Portrait of a Society
The Murdered Magicians: The Templars and their Myth
Arab Voices: The BBC Arabic Service 1938–1988
The Pope's Men: The Papal Civil Service in the Renaissance

GOD OF BATTLES

❖

Holy Wars of
Christianity and Islam

PETER PARTNER

PRINCETON UNIVERSITY PRESS

PRINCETON, NEW JERSEY

Originally published in 1997 by HarperCollins*Publishers*, 77–85 Fulham Palace Road,
Hammersmith, London W6 8JB, and reprinted by arrangement with the publisher

Maps by Leslie Robinson

Library of Congress Cataloging-in-Publication Data

Partner, Peter.
God of battles : holy wars of Christianity and Islam / Peter Partner.
p.   cm
Originally published : London : Harper Collins. 1997.
Includes bibliographical references (p.   ) and index.
ISBN 0-691-00235-5 (pbk. : alk. paper)
1. War—Religious aspects—Christianity—History of doctrines.
2. War—Religious aspects—Islam—History of doctrines.
3. Christianity and other religions—Islam. 4. Islam—Relations—Christianity.
5. Crusades—History. 6. Jihad—History.
I Title.
BT736.2.P27   1998
291.1'7873'09—dc21   98-28813

Princeton University Press books are
printed on acid-free paper and meet the guidelines
for permanence and durability of the Committee
on Production Guidelines for Book Longevity
of the Council on Library Resources

First Princeton Paperback printing, 1998

http://pup.princeton.edu

Printed in the United States of America

1   3   5   7   9   10   8   6   4   2

To the memory of
Albert Habib Hourani
and of his niece
born Leila May Fadil

CONTENTS

ILLUSTRATIONS

A verse of the Qur'an is revealed to Muhammad during the Battle of Uhud. (*Eighteenth-century illustration from Erzeni's* Life of Muhammad, *Museum of Turkish and Islamic Art, Istanbul*)

The 'Son of Man', holding a sword between his teeth, leads his troops into battle in a fourteenth-century illustration to the Apocalypse. (*By permission of the British Library: Roy.19.B.XV*)

Illustration to the Book of Maccabees from the twelfth-century Winchester Bible. (*Courtesy of the Dean and Chapter of Winchester. Photograph © Murray Davison*)

The first crusade of Peter the Hermit, in 1096. (*Bibliothèque Nationale, Paris. Photograph © The Bridgeman Art Library*)

Christian and Muslim combat, supposed to represent Richard I and Saladin. (*By permission of the British Library: Add 42130*)

Godfrey de Bouillon assembles his company of crusaders. Illustration from *Historia rerum in partibus transmarinis gestarum*, by William of Tyre. (*Bibliothèque Nationale, Paris. Photograph © Edimedia*)

Capital from a lost crusader church in Nazareth, showing the devil as a Saracen warrior. (*Photograph © The Ancient Art and Architecture Collection*)

Fourteenth-century fresco depicting the assault of the Saracen king on Christian troops, Chapel of the Corporal, Orvieto Cathedral. (*Photograph courtesy of the Central Institute for Cataloguing and Documentation, Rome*)

Eleventh-century combat between Muslim and Christian ships, from 'De Passagiis', in *Venetian Chronologia Magna*. (*Biblioteca Nazionale Marciana, Venice. Photograph © Foto Tosto*)

Ambrogio Lorenzetti (active 1319–47), *Martyrdom of Franciscan Monks at Ceuta* (Morocco). Church of San Francesco, Siena. (*Photograph © Scala*)

Captured early-fourteenth-century Christian sword. (*By courtesy of the Board of Trustees of the Armouries*)

Chain mail and helmet of a Muslim warrior of the crusader period, Lebanon. (*Photograph © The Ancient Art and Architecture Collection*)

Cosmati mosaic of the vision of John of Matha, founder of the Trinitarian Order. Church of San Tommaso in Formis, Rome. (*Photograph courtesy of the Central Institute for Cataloguing and Documentation, Rome*)

Melchior Loritz, panorama of Constantinople, showing European trading ships in the harbour. (*Photograph © Leiden Universiteitsbibliotheek*)

Conquistadores massacre and enslave the Aztecs. Illustration to Las Casas, *Brief History of the Destruction of the Indies*. (*Photograph © Fotomas Index/Barnaby's Picture Library*)

Nicolas Poussin (1594–1665), *Rinaldo and Armida, oil on canvas*, 82.2 × 109.2 cms, probably painted 1625–30. (*By permission of the Trustees of Dulwich Picture Gallery*)

Gianbattista Tiepolo (1696–1770), *Rinaldo and Armida in her Garden*, oil on canvas, 186.9 × 259.5 cms, 1742. (*Bequest of James Deering, 1925.699. Photograph © 1997, The Art Institute of Chicago. All rights reserved*)

Frontispiece to the *Description de l'Egypte*, showing Napoleon's troops among the great Pharaonic monuments. (*Photograph by permission of the Warden and Scholars of Winchester College*)

Eugène Delacroix (1798–1863), *The Abduction of Rebecca*, oil on canvas, 105 × 81.5 cms, 1858. (*Musées du Louvre. Photograph © Lauros/Giraudon*)

Delacroix, *Entry of the Crusaders into Constantinople*, oil on canvas, 161 × 196 cms, 1840. (*Musées du Louvre. Photograph © Giraudon*)

Delacroix, *The Massacre of Chios*, oil on canvas, 164 × 139 cms, 1824. (*Musées du Louvre, Photograph © Giraudon*)

The Algerian holy war leader 'Abd al-Qadir in exile in Damascus in 1864. (*Photograph © The Mansell Collection*)

Hizbullah funeral procession in Beirut, June 1996. (*Photograph © El Dakhakhny/Rex Features*)

Hizbullah women, Beirut, 1996. (*Photograph © El Dakhakhny/Rex Features*)

MAPS

ACKNOWLEDGEMENTS

I am very grateful for the kindness shown me by Mme Shahira Mehrez in Cairo and by Mme Nuhad Makdissi in Beirut. Professor Kemal Salibi (American University of Beirut) was good enough to help me with the translation of some passages in a twelfth-century chronicle. Professor Ridwan al-Sayyid (Lebanese University of Beirut) gave me access to some published and unpublished writings of his on contemporary Islamist movements. For help with the revision of the text I am grateful to my editor, Robert Lacey, and to my son, Simon.

I am indebted to Joyce Hitchcock for more important things than encouragement to write books, but I nevertheless owe it to her that this book could be written.

I am grateful to Faber & Faber Ltd for permission to reproduce an extract from Chorus VIII of 'The Rock', from *Collected Poems 1909–1962* by T.S. Eliot.

INTRODUCTION

In the winter of 1861 the American author Julia Ward Howe visited a
Unionist military camp outside Washington DC, and wrote what came to
be known as 'The Battle Hymn of the Republic'. Drawing on the Biblical
vocabulary of her generation, she saw divine judgement in the battles of
the Civil War. The hymn, sung to the tune of 'John Brown's Body', became
one of that war's most emotive songs.

> Mine eyes have seen the glory of the coming of the Lord;
> He is trampling out the vintage where the grapes of wrath are stored;
> He hath loosed the fateful lightning of His terrible swift sword;
> His truth is marching on.
>
> I have seen Him in the watchfires of a hundred circling camps;
> They have builded Him an altar in the evening dews and damps;
> I can read His righteous sentence by the dim and flaring lamps;
> His day is marching on . . .
>
> In the beauty of the lilies Christ was born across the sea,
> With a glory in His bosom that transfigures you and me;
> As He died to make men holy, let us die to make them free,
> While God is marching on.

The early God of Israel (but the generation of Julia Ward Howe was
only beginning to see that He could be referred to as 'early') was a god of
war who, like many Semitic war gods, summoned wind and storm, thunder
and lightning, among other divine weapons, to the aid of the people He
protected. Like His counterparts, to the confusion of the battlefield He
was able to bring the added confusion of natural forces controlled by supernatural ones.

In the first Christian century the Revelation of John had drawn upon
the by then ancient imagery of holy war for his vision of the Son of Man,
crowned with a golden crown and holding a sharp sickle, presiding over

the angel whose sickle would gather the vine of the earth and cast it into the winepress of the wrath of God.[1] John's Apocalypse imagined the armies of God to march and destroy, or the armies of wicked angels and men being permitted by God to march and destroy: whether good or evil, the agents of divine anger were supernatural, and John did not say that the final holy wars were to be fought by the followers of Christ, whose duty it was to be faithful in other ways.

But the ambiguities of holy war, which have confused image with substance for several millennia, allowed Julia Ward Howe to borrow the vocabulary of a first-century Syrian visionary to describe an all-too-human war on the modern North American continent. She allowed herself to militarize the Christian faith in a manner that was more ancient than she knew. As Christ, she wrote, who was born and had died 'across the sea', had 'died to make men holy', so should Americans 'die to make them free'. Like many in the past, from both the Eastern and the Western regions and religions, she did not wait upon God's vengeance to be executed by others: men must participate in the holy wars. Julia Ward Howe was a woman of liberal sympathies. Less than ten years later she was launching her Congress of Women Throughout the World to promote the cause of international peace. But in her best-known poem she touched a theme that connected nineteenth-century America with ideas of godly bloodshed that were rooted in the Ancient Near East.

The history of holy war, from the Biblical Hebrews to our own times, is a history of texts belonging to scriptural religions; it is also a history of human behaviour. The violence that men do, they seek to justify. To turn to God, or to gods, is only one way of justifying war, and this has been acknowledged in the Hebrew and Hebrew-derived religions from their beginnings. Holy war is a special case; other wars may claim the benefit of divine approval, but holy war is one that God requires the faithful to fight. The holy warrior is marked out by God, distinguished from all other fighting men. He may fight only with the weapons of the spirit, but he may also fight with those of the flesh. Holy war may seem a strange way of imposing moral behaviour upon human relationships, but there have been times and places where it can be argued that this was so, particularly during the lifetime of Muhammad.

It is hard to know whether to be more impressed by the apparent continuity of holy war, or by its extraordinary interruptions. When Julia Ward Howe used the language of sacred violence, she was drawing upon a vocabulary that, in the form of crusading rhetoric, had been used in Christianity for many centuries. In her own day it was apparently dead: by the late nineteenth century the crusade was thought of in North America as being no more than a picturesque historical phenomenon of the long-past Catholic Middle Ages. Julia Ward Howe was not preaching a new holy war in a way that could be readily attached to the old holy wars. Her ideals and preoccupations were entirely modern. Yet she clothed her feelings in the same language as had been used by the medieval Catholic clergy to incite men to fight the infidel.

It is worth adding that the medieval Catholic clergy did not reserve their crusading zeal entirely for combat against the Saracens, but were quite ready to ask for bloody holy war sanctions against erring Christians. So the call for a godly war against Christian enemies had its medieval Christian precedents.

The use of ancient sacred texts by an American woman poet to find modern moral metaphors is not necessarily strange or archaic. It is quite close, although the familiarity of its language to people brought up in a Christian tradition obscures this, to what is often represented as the bloodthirsty medievalism of present-day Islamist radicals. By their 'holy flight' or by their armed struggle against oppression certain Muslims of the nineteenth and twentieth centuries have appeared, in their eyes at least, to be repeating the history of the prophet Muhammad in the seventh. Modern people outside the Islamic communities tend to accept at face value the assertions of such Islamists that their revival of Islamic holy war is a simple continuation of a millennial religious duty. But the case is quite otherwise. The underlying motives that incite 'fundamentalist' Islamists to proclaim a duty of waging holy war are rooted in the passions of modern politics, even if expressed in the archaic language of religion, just as were the motives that caused Julia Ward Howe to write 'The Battle Hymn of the Republic'.

Modern revivals of the language of holy war are not confined to Islam, nor do they end, outside Islam, with Julia Ward Howe. That a few Israeli zealots should in the late 1960s have begun to say that it was a religious duty to 'destroy Amalek', thus trying to revive an idea of religious war that had been dead in Judaism for nineteen hundred years, seems to be an alarming instance of the conjuring power of religious texts. But the dynamic that moves people to commit acts of war and terrorism is not some sort of cultural imperative that arises from the texts themselves. For both modern Islamism and modern Zionism, the moving power behind their sacred vocabulary is entirely of their own times.

The question of whether holy war is now a disused medieval idea that exerts no influence at all upon modern people who think of themselves as 'Westerners' is important when we consider the judgements that they make about people of other faiths, and about Muslim fundamentalists in particular.

Until the Christianization of the Roman Empire in the fourth and fifth centuries, Christians were not forbidden by their religion to serve in the army, but waging war for Christian purposes was not even considered. For some centuries after the adoption of Christianity by the Empire, the attitude of church leaders to war was hesitant and somewhat ambiguous. The adoption of holy war in the crusading movement of the late eleventh and early twelfth centuries broke with a long tradition of refraining from bloodshed in Christ's name.

Medieval Christianity thus embraced holy war after a millennium of eschewing it, and Reformation Christianity, after a further half-millennium, abandoned it. So, too, did Catholic Christianity, although only after a very long hesitation. In this sort of historical perspective the three or four centuries that have elapsed since the Protestant Reformation are not an inordinately long time. It might be that manifestations like holy war may characterize a religion at some historical points and not at others. And so we have to consider the possibility that holy war might under certain circumstances return as a Christian practice. A similar disruption of the holy war idea seems to have occurred in Judaism after the destruction of the Temple in Jerusalem in 60 AD, but the establishment of an armed Jewish state in the Middle East in the twentieth century means that the remote possibility of a new Jewish holy war, of a Maccabaean revival, cannot be entirely put aside.

Their abandonment of holy war does not mean, in spite of some commonly received notions, that the peoples of cultures that profess Christianity or Judaism are more pacific than others. The history of war down to the present time suggests nothing of the kind, although Judaism was, it is true, a pacific religion for a very long period. Christianity, on the contrary, has from the early Middle Ages been a warrior religion.

One rather less-known historical development should perhaps be emphasized by historians more than it has been in the past. Although crusading in the formal sense was abandoned by almost all governments in the modern period, its vocabulary and legal terminology were by no means without effect on the ways in which early modern colonial regimes conceived their relationship with non-Christian peoples. Without the crusades, the whole attitude of European empires to their subject peoples would have been different.

Now that Biblical language is no longer generally used in Western democratic countries to express political emotions, only a very tiny number of Christians think of the people of God as subject to the duty of waging holy war. A much larger number of people who do not immediately identify themselves as Christian, although they belong to a culture of Christian origin, think of holy war as a quite foreign and bizarre notion. Consequently, when some modern Islamists say that the policies of Christian states are still today dictated by the religious zeal of the crusades, modern Americans and Europeans are puzzled and resentful; they feel that they are being given a medieval label by people with medieval ideas. But Islamist denunciation of the crusading tradition is not as inexplicable, nor as archaistic, as is often thought.

Western civilization seems more or less conscious of its Christian cultural origins, but is unwilling to identify itself as Christian except in a very patchy and hesitant way. When the point of view of Westerners is linked by outsiders to that of medieval Christianity, they feel uneasy. This touchiness sits strangely with attitudes to other cultures that can only be described as aggressive. Many Westerners are quite willing to identify a supposed cultural entity, such as Islam, in a confident and dogmatic way, and to attach to the many nations and regions where Islam is the dominant faith a whole set of common attributes.

People refuse to be associated with such 'medieval' concepts as the crusade, but apply that label without hesitation to other religions. This presumption is not only due to ignorance. Less than half a century ago, unconscious of their own arrogance and inaccuracy, Westerners used to write confidently about something they called 'the Arab mind'. Today their successors attach to a supposedly identifiable entity called 'Islam' a questionable bundle of attitudes, beliefs and practices that recalls the mythical 'Arab mind' of the 1950s, and that goes back to comparable Western attitudes of the nineteenth century.

That Islamic nations today face ideological and social problems similar in many respects to the problems that confront modern Western nations never enters the heads of such people. The national, social and ethnic traditions of the Islamic states are so diverse as to forbid their being assigned a single cultural identity. But the divergence is inconvenient to those who want to argue that Islam is a 'cultural unit' that cannot avoid continual conflict with other 'cultural units'.

One especially evident difference between the Western and the Islamic-derived points of view is the distinction, supposed in the West to be basic and permanent, between the rights and duties assigned to the political order and those assigned to the religious order. This was the subject of great struggles in Europe and the Americas during the earlier modern period. That church and state could and should pursue their separate tasks, each undisturbed by the other, was the conviction of most Anglo-Saxon liberals. The rights of either party were often far from obvious, and clashes between church and state have, even in the past century, sometimes been brutal. And while no one in the West seriously advocates the sort of theocracy that was rife as a political theory in the Middle Ages, the differences between religious and secular interests about the way society should be organized are very far from over, as, for example, the disputes over abortion demonstrate.

Nevertheless, the naive brand of theocracy espoused by revivalist Islamist reformers in the past few years has been an easy target for Western critics. These critics normally pay no attention to the political realities of the modern world of nation states, and to the way in which these states are organized in the Muslim world. It is too often forgotten that most Islamist reformers represent minority groups – sometimes tiny minority groups – and not governments. In the Muslim world as elsewhere, nation states rule their own patches. Outside Iran there are no states containing Muslim majorities that pay more than lip-service to the theocratic principle, even if their principles are in theory 'fundamentalist'. Even in Iran the relationship between government and religion is infinitely more complex and subtle than it is popularly supposed to be. It is, for example, very questionable whether a genuine holy war in the proper legal Muslim sense has been fought by Iran since the regime of the ayatollahs began.

Because of the permanent situation of political crisis in the Middle East, and its occasional spill-over into terrorist acts elsewhere, a small number of desperate minorities in various parts of the Muslim world have become widely thought of as typical of a threatening, theocratic, terrorist current that is in some way broadly characteristic of a religion and of the peoples who profess it. In most cases, for example in Saudi Arabia, Egypt and Algeria, the extremists are rebelling against their own Muslim governments. But the feeling of a general threat against the West remains. The prejudice seems on the whole to have been encouraged by Western governments, who perhaps want to mobilize popular support for any drastic action they happen to decide on against Middle Eastern factions that obstruct their policies.

How far propagandist and media speculation about the religious connections of terrorism is justified is hard to say. There may be a real terrorist threat from certain groups, and these groups may perhaps have occasional support from governments in the Arab or Iranian world. But even in the best known 'holy war' cases, like Palestinian Hamas, there is not much evidence to prove that the 'fundamentalist' states (which in practice means Iran, with a glance at the Sudan) are always the conspiratorial culprits behind the terrorists. Secular Middle Eastern states have also been thought to have sponsored terrorism. Israel, a main party to denouncing terrorism, has been guilty of organizing violent acts against its enemies in neutral countries far from Israeli soil.

It is true that the major Western powers, to whom many Muslim governments are allied by preference or interest, always make a sharp public distinction between Islamist 'extremists' and Islamic 'moderates'. But the anti-Islamist prejudice is bound to affect Western public opinion as a whole, as it is intended to do. It may not be unconnected with the existence of substantial Muslim minorities in many Western countries, and with a certain distrust felt by the host communities towards the religious tendencies that they think can be detected in these minorities. Whether this distrust actually influences Western governments in their attitudes to 'fundamentalism' is hard to discover.

The propagandist stance of Western governments towards Islamism is open to other criticisms. The relations of the great powers to Muslim 'fundamentalism' are much more complex than is ever publicly admitted in the international meetings they call to deter terrorism. For example, the main Muslim ally of the United States in the Middle East is Saudi Arabia, to whose Wahhabi government it is impossible to deny the title of fundamentalist, if this slippery term is going to be used at all.

At times, in spite of the rhetoric used against them, armed fundamentalist groups have been patronized by Western governments. In Afghanistan the US security agencies for years enjoyed a virtually connubial relationship with the *mujahidin*, endowing them with mythical virtues as fighters against atheistic Communism, and supplying them with the weapons and techniques that have since been used in very different fundamentalist quarrels outside as well as inside Afghanistan. As a result, the same Muslim freedom fighters that were once supported have in the eyes of the security agencies become dangerous terrorists. Even so, the agencies still tend to hedge their bets. Their attitude to certain Islamist terrorist groups, like those in Algeria, has been quite ambiguous.

*　　*　　*

The history of holy war in Christianity and Islam, and in the Hebraic and Hellenistic societies that preceded them, can help us to arrive at a better-informed attitude to these difficult religious questions. It does not provide any easy answers to the urgent political questions of our own time. But it does, at the minimum, provide some sort of framework into which we can fit one aspect of the Christian and Islamic – to some extent also of the Hebraic – religions that have so often acted as declared enemies, very occasionally as distrustful friends, and that nevertheless share in some respects a common moral substratum. Acceptance that such a history can be written is a kind of assertion that we possess the values to enable a cross-cultural enterprise of the sort.

It is no longer possible for a person who unpacks his computer components from boxes made up in a variety of Far Eastern locations to think that the modern is fundamentally the Western. The idea that what is modern and progressive in social, political and economic organization is firmly linked to what is Western has been characteristic of thinking in Europe and the Americas for a very long period. But during the past half-century 'Westernization' has become in some senses global, in that the same industrial technologies, the same means of mass and personal communication, the same educational techniques, to a limited extent the same ideological slogans, have become common to the dominant elements in the societies of the greater part of the planet.

It is presumptuous to think that the meaning of these great changes can be interpreted in a short time, or by the efforts of a few persons. We have already learned that communal, cultural and religious conflicts and rivalries may be attenuated, but have by no means been abolished by the world standardization of techniques. It would be surprising if they had been, since techniques are means of achieving ends, and not the ends themselves. To some extent the very purposes of modern society have been exported from the West to other parts of the world. It is not axiomatic that the values and aims of Western society are in some self-evident way different from and exterior to those of other societies.

So much that was Western has become global that some ideas we have inherited from past periods of imperialism impede us from understanding our real situation. Others, though, enable us to understand it. A fear has developed that globalization has already undermined Western financial and political hegemony. It is the same fear of the 'decline of the West' that has been around for the past century, and that links up easily with national-conservative revivals. These fears, which amount to an almost paranoid terror that the decline of a domination like that of the Roman Empire has already occurred, and that the fall of the West may be imminent, are not rational.

In spite of the talk of a new hegemony of international companies, the hold of such companies on the world was already tight before 1914. The international corporations of then were not dissimilar to those of today, save that a few conservative Japanese internationals have been added. The novelty of the type of globalization we experience today is that it is cultural rather than economic. The close association of military power with economic interest that was seen in the 1991 Gulf War resembled the exercise of British power in Egypt and the Middle East during the nineteenth and early twentieth centuries. So far as Britain is concerned, this sort of display of strength flickered out ingloriously in 1956 at Suez, but the same principles are applied by the contemporary United States as were applied by the British in the past. Power-holders have changed, or, at the minimum, their order of precedence has changed, but Western aims and methods have not.

Feelings of insecurity about the continuance of the world power enjoyed by Western states are inevitable. It is, however, difficult to understand why Western fears of external threats should at the end of the twentieth century have centred on Iran and one or two other rogue Islamic nations. The majority of Islamic countries west of the Bay of Bengal have very low development rates and are politically dependent upon the West – a dependence that is even more evident among the minority that enjoys higher development rates than the rest. Fear of militant Islam seems irrational, since Islamic countries have posed no real threat to Western economic interests since the Gulf War. Nor does the overall situation of the Islamic oil producers contain a real threat, since they are tied, whether they like it or not, to Western financial systems and markets.

Holy war, which we think of as obsolete and archaic, is an extreme example of the politicization of cultural and religious conflict. It is no more incompatible with the modern world than other traditional manifestations of conflict like aggressive nationalism, but, like aggressive nationalism (with which it can overlap), it alarms the dominant technological nations by threatening cumulative international disorder. That the dominant nations are not themselves free from aggressive nationalism makes their fears even keener.

The antagonism between the 'extreme' Islamists and the Western nations is not really a conflict between the medieval and the modern; it is, on the contrary, one more phenomenon that can be laid at the door of cultural globalization. The religious enthusiasts who preach the return to Islam, and who sometimes also argue for holy war, profess a strictly traditional approach to their religion; but close examination reveals that their vocabulary and mentality have infinitely more to do with the twentieth century than with the seventh. In particular, the most important areas of Islamist political terminology borrow very heavily indeed from Western sources. And no one can gauge the extent to which modern Islamism is fostered by a feeling of the hopeless exclusion of many large populations from the enjoyment of the technological cornucopia.

In this book I have tried not only to sketch the main phases in the history of holy war, but to investigate some of the ways in which its vocabulary and modes of thought have penetrated into areas that are not strictly religious. Such an investigation is necessarily selective, and it influenced the selection of the main topics. Holy war has been an element in many other religions besides the three interconnected faiths of Near Eastern origin that are discussed in this book, but the field of debate has been deliberately narrowed in order to make it more comprehensible. Even after limiting the discussion in this way, my treatment of holy war in Judaism has been restricted to the period in which it was a formative influence on the other two religions. The historical argument of this book is that holy war is rooted in all three religions, although in both Christianity and Judaism there have been factors that have caused holy war to be eschewed over very long periods.

In Islam holy war was so closely tied in with the early history of the religion that for a long time it was practised, if not everywhere, at least on all the Islamic frontiers. However, from the time of Muhammad onwards the principle of spiritual effort that lay behind Islamic holy war could be invoked under the same name of *jihad* in a totally non-military and moral way.

Other things enabled men to treat holy war as something that could be picked up or put down at will. Piety could make them understand it in a spiritual rather than a physical sense. But worldly factors could also influence decisions about holy war. While in some Islamic areas – particularly the frontiers – military holy war was an integral part of social organization, in others it scarcely played a part. Political convenience and advantage influenced the ways in which it was practised or abandoned, just as they influenced Christian holy war.

In the period of the first Islamic conquests holy war was not just a means of imposing Islamic beliefs upon non-Muslims. The holy wars against Muslims supposed to be heretical, or against societies whose submission to Islam was claimed to be imperfect, in West Africa and elsewhere, were just as important. Conflicting Muslim regimes could always use holy war as a political instrument, as happened with Ottomans and Iranian Safavids, with Fatimids in Egypt and others. Both Muslim and Christian regimes have used or abandoned holy war according to political convenience. In the modern period a domination originally based upon holy war, like the Saudi Arabian state, abandoned it when it became politically necessary to do so.

It has sometimes been supposed that Islamic holy war was a main factor in the resistance of Muslim regimes to European colonialism. There have been places and times where this was so, for example in nineteenth-century Algeria and in early-twentieth-century Libya. In other parts of Africa the holy wars of nineteenth-century Mahdist movements have been important, but in West Africa and the Western Sudan, where holy war had been a very important factor in the relations of Muslim states with one another, it was only a very minor factor in resistance to European power. The most successful Muslim regimes in resisting European intrusion – only partly successful, it is true – were those, like the Moroccan, that relied upon their political skills.

In the recent period holy war has been far more important as a factor in insurgency against Muslim regimes than as a means of directly resisting Western powers. In the many Arab wars against Israel holy war played scarcely any part at all, although it has been important in insurgency in the Israeli-controlled areas on the West Bank, in the Gaza Strip and in the Israeli-controlled 'security' zone in south Lebanon.

Little reflective thought is published in the Western media about the background of the current holy war conflicts, nor about the dramatic way in which they are commonly reported. Suicide bombers are good copy; the problems that create them and the historical origins of their mentality are not. In this respect one small area in the Middle East enjoys an unenviable prominence. Israel and its near neighbours figure largely in the policies of the strongest Western power: headlines about Islamist holy war there are assured. And some Western governments, especially the Anglo-Saxon ones, are content that this is so.

Demonization of the adversary is not the best way of conducting international relations, whether it is done on the basis of the United States being described as 'the great Satan' or of non-Christian states being described by Western governments as 'terrorist'. It is possible, and the course of history related in this book provides plenty of examples, for states to find themselves

in adversarial positions without their being committed to an all-out propaganda war. However, propaganda war is still better than war. It is possible
to conduct a propaganda war without giving up the option of negotiating
with the adversary: this was, for example, a frequent occurrence between
Christian and Muslim in the pre-modern period, and the history of the
Cold War after 1947 is the history, among other things, of a propaganda
war.

It is on the whole damaging to international relations for one side to be
convinced that the other professes an ideology that actually looks forward
to war, even if the threatening ideology sees war as an eventual and not as
an immediate resort. This, again, was the case during the Cold War, as in
earlier periods of history during many times of tension between Christian
states that honoured the crusade, and Muslim states that honoured the
jihad.

It is wrong, I believe, to think that holy war, once accepted in the religious
practice of a society, imposes a permanent and universal duty of military
conflict. The political nature of all holy war imposes limits upon its use,
and has always done so, from the time of the ancient Middle Eastern states
to that of Muhammad and onwards. The crusaders were no exception. The
most typical and permanent factor in the relations between the Frankish
states in the Levant and their Muslim neighbours was the truce. There
were factors that encouraged peaceful relations between Mediterranean
societies, as well as those that discouraged them. Christian or Jewish aliens
living in Muslim societies were protected, first by legal norms written into
the main body of religious law, and then, very often, by specific international
agreements made with the states from which they came. The great cities
of Islam would have died without international trading traffic, and so would
the Islamic civilization that supported them.

While holy war has dominated certain vast and bloody conflicts, and
has also been characteristic of the frontier relations between Islam and
Christianity over quite long periods, it has for the most part not imposed
itself upon the relations between great states as a normal instrument of
policy. At various historical periods from the early Middle Ages onwards,
Abbasid, Mamluk, Ottoman, French, Habsburg and other statesmen in
East and West have accepted the vocabulary of holy war and used it as a
propagandist weapon. But they refrained from following its principles in
their ordinary political behaviour, because the age-old maxims of *raison
d'état* usually prevailed over the imperatives of aggressive religion.

Military holy war is a form of consecrated aggression that cannot be welcomed as a way of regulating relations between human beings. It is not, on the other hand, morally inferior to other ways of waging war, although the religious commitment of holy warriors tends to make them more feared than others. In modern life holy war tends to be regarded as a form of irregular warfare, and it can be argued, as it was successfully during the recent New York trial for terrorism of the Egyptian Sheikh 'Abd al-Rahman, that incitement to wage holy war is equivalent to incitement to wage terrorism, or even to wage urban terrorism. But there is no necessary connection between holy war and irregular warfare. Holy war, as much and as little as other forms of war, accepts certain rules, although to the holy warrior these are usually religious ones.

The only way to deprive holy war of its aura of feared fanaticism is to look at its religious framework and at its political and social history. The circumstances of our own time tend to make people feel that only in the Muslim case can holy war be considered as an element in present conflicts, but a reasoned account of Christian holy war makes it clear that crusading has had a much longer afterlife than is generally thought, and that Christian attitudes of mind that we think of as long-dead may exercise a greater influence upon our present point of view than we imagine.

The twentieth century has not been a time of the triumph of enlightened civilized values, as was hoped when it began, but a period of ferocious conflicts, no less bloody than those of the past. We have learned, as all previous generations have learned, that the modernity of techniques has nothing to do with the morality of the ends that the techniques help to achieve. Religion is often invoked when the justice or injustice of a war is debated, and although Westerners do not normally qualify their wars as holy, they frequently appeal to their clergy to endorse the supposed justice of their cause. When they do so, echoes of the medieval crusading slogans are quite often heard in response.

In order to lessen the fear of the unknown that makes the relations between societies and states more difficult than they would otherwise be, it is important to try to understand the past. Holy war is an area where religion, morality and the search for political advantage all intersect. Its history is complicated and disputed, but I argue that its study is worthwhile.

CHAPTER ONE

Holy Wars of
the Ancient Near East

IF PEOPLE WORSHIP GODS and fight wars, they expect the former to take an interest in the latter. The ancient civilizations of the Near East from Egypt to Assyria all possessed gods of war, and their ruling dynasties all claimed their help and authority in battle. Most of these dynasties were military monarchies that proved themselves on the battlefield; no shame attached to them on account of the enslavement, maiming and massacre that they imposed upon the defeated.

All religions are, ultimately, religions of power, not because they necessarily worship power, but because they attribute it to the forces they propitiate. But the ancient Eastern religions openly proclaimed themselves the agents of power, and the conquered were not accustomed to compose battle hymns: it was common to claim, as the Assyrian ruler Sennacherib did, that the gods of his foes had abandoned them because of their unworthiness. There were degrees of militarism among the great monarchies: possibly the Assyrians were the most ruthlessly militarist, and the Egyptians the least. The gods preceded or stood at the side of the ruler in battle, like Ishtar, lady of war and battle, who 'broke their bow and undid their battle formations'; on another occasion, for a different Assyrian king, 'clothed in fire, bedecked with radiance, she rained fire upon Arabia'. Her equivalent, the Sargonic goddess Inanna, the mistress of storm and flood, was implored to strike down the warriors and to water the earth with their blood, to throw up a heap of enemy bodies on the plain, and to show no mercy.

One of the imagined functions of the war god was to 'go before' the monarch in battle as his vanguard, protecting him from harm and striking his enemies down. In Egypt, as in Assyria, the god went before the victorious king: turning his divine face to the various points of the compass the god Amun-Re 'did wonders' for Amunhotep III, securing for him the submission

I

of Kush, of 'the ends of Asia', of Nubia, of Punt. In the Greek world, too, the goddess Athena 'took her stand' in front of King Menelaus, in order to deflect what would otherwise have been the fatal Trojan arrow.[1] The sun-goddess Arinna went before the Hittite king into battle, holding his hand.

There was no major Middle Eastern culture in which the gods disdained to take part in battle on behalf of their favoured rulers. Often, a culture claimed the exclusive patronage of such a god, as the Babylonians did for Marduk, or the Assyrians for Ashur, and as the Israelites were later to do for Yahweh; but there were important war divinities, such as Ishtar, who were claimed by more than one culture. All the main cultures supposed the relationship between ruler and war god to be co-operative; the ruler, having ascertained through augurs, diviners or dreams that divine favour for his war was obtainable, led his troops into battle, and was sure that the god or gods would help him. This help would be claimed on the monuments and in the hymns that were devised after the war; whether the king had really obtained the victory or not did not matter to the panegyrists, provided that his failures could be concealed or overlooked. In the Empires the warlike favour of the gods was the propaganda of the powerful, as is still visible in the friezes, temples and paintings uncovered by modern archaeologists and viewed by modern tourists.

Most rulers believed that a god, or several gods, gave them help in battle. Their wars were not necessarily fought for the sake of religion, and the combatants on either side might be appealing to the same god or goddess, although a people might feel assured that one particular deity supported and sustained them, and in the case of a nation like the Egyptians the superiority of one pantheon over another was assumed. The rulers might have priestly functions, or might even be thought to be gods. And gods and goddesses could be imported from one culture into another, bringing their battle patronage with them.

The social psychology of such holy wars must have varied greatly between the different cultures that waged them. Rulers, those of our own day included, have seldom attached much value to the lives of their ordinary soldiers beyond their bare military utility. In most ancient cultures, little or no spiritual value was attached to the lives of common people. Their spirits were at some times and in some places deemed useful to serve their masters and mistresses in the afterlife; in many cultures this idea prompted the masters to slaughter the servants so that they could serve them in the tomb. A conviction that they were in some sense fighting for their gods may perhaps have affected the troops of the ancient armies, and they may also have felt that their gods were fighting for them, although outside the Hebrew documents we have no evidence for this. Mercenary or conscripted troops from cultures outside the ruling culture took part in holy wars, and the paid, imported troops perhaps had an ambiguous attitude to the holy wars of their masters. We can think of the Nubian archers whose modelled images survive in the Egyptian tombs, of Uriah the Hittite under King David, of the Turcopole troops of the crusaders.

The holy nature of the ancient ruler, whether he was accounted god, priest, or a man with privileged access to the gods, made his wars holy. But how did his armies understand this? We tend to think that holy wars are normally fought by troops inspired by religious purpose, but what we know about these ancient holy wars warns us against accepting without ado the idea that a holy war is one that is fought entirely for religious ends. Modern ideas about the division between sacred and secular are very recent and very misleading. From the beginning holy war has been full of motives that we would call political.

The post-hostilities commemoration of wars for propagandist purposes in documents and on monuments may also have turned ancient wars that were fought without special religious purpose into holy wars after the fact. We know from the experience of the present century that the way in which the war dead are commemorated in tombs, monuments and ceremonies profoundly affects the way in which we think of the war in which they died; it does not necessarily have much to do with the way in which it was fought.

During the last two centuries of the second millennium BC there was an influx of migrant people (later in Old Testament tradition called Israel and Judah) into the hilly area to the west and north-west of the Dead Sea. After a long effort they managed to annex most of the city-states of Philistine Canaan on the coastal plain. Their tribal god, Yahweh, had strong affinities with 'El, the chief of the Ugaritic gods, patriarch-god of Canaan and of much of the Punic Western world. 'El, besides being a god of creation who kept the cosmos in being, and consequently having great powers over natural forces, was also a war god. Yahweh, like 'El, was called 'the ancient one', and the Old Testament seems sometimes to identify the Hebrew with the Canaanite deity.

As a federation of tribes, the Israelite power was a very modest force in Palestine. A monarchy of Israel and Judah, more powerful than the federa-

3

tion, appeared under a rebellious Israelite general called David in the second half of the tenth century BC, but even so the Israelite monarchy was minor when compared with the dominating powers of the Near East. It was never more than a small buffer state that lay uneasily between the great powers of the Nile and the Tigris-Euphrates. But it claimed the kind of support in war from its god that was normal in Syria-Palestine.

To some extent holy war in the ancient Near East was a matter of propaganda, of the making of rites and monuments that justified and magnified the victorious ruler. But holy war also has roots in the terror and disorder of battle itself. During battle ordinary judgement is suspended, as dust, cloud, and confusion cover men's eyes, and unfamiliar and terrible noises assault their ears. At such times the forces of nature can the more easily assert their sovereignty. Rain, mist, thunder, lightning can settle a battle one way or another, either by their tactical effect or by weakening military morale. Rivers and waters can impede or forbid the movement of troops: how many battles have ended with sad heaps of corpses either lying in the flood or (as in the First World War) sprawled in the mud? In modern times, fog is the commonest metaphor to suggest the confusion of war, and the nineteenth-century German military theorist Clausewitz described the practice of war as being like trying to do in water what one commonly does on land. To peoples who in any case worshipped the gods of nature, battle was a time when the god who gave rain for the crops could also bring thunder, hail or storm for the benefit of one side or the other. To peoples who at other times were trying to spy out the sky and the heavenly bodies, the gods of the heavens could send shooting stars to battle, or make the sky stand still, cause eclipse and unexpected, terrifying darkness.

Yahweh and 'El were both great weather gods, especially able to intervene in battle. 'El's son Ba'l, whom the Israelites after some hesitation rejected, was also a powerful weather and war god, and there are many parallels between his powers and those of Yahweh. Such gods could sow confusion among the enemy by sending thunder, great hailstorms, lightning; they could send showers of stones, cause pillars of fire or smoke, or overwhelm by drowning, as Pharaoh's troops were overwhelmed near the so-called Sea of Reeds during the flight of the oppressed people from Egypt.[2] A rather different version of this divine rescue was offered in the later Hebrew version of what occurred in the return from exile in Egypt: 'he divided the sea and brought them across ... In the daytime he led them with a cloud, and all the night with a light of fire.'[3]

The Psalmist addressed Yahweh as lord of sea and storm: 'the waters saw you and writhed: the deeps shuddered: the clouds streamed water, the heavens roared: your bolts shot back and forth. Your thunder was in the tempest; lightning lightened the world: earth trembled and shook. Your way was through the sea, and your path in the deep waters; your tracks are beyond our understanding.'[4] The same imagery is used in Psalm 18, but with the addition of fire, flame and earthquake. 'The earth quaked and shook; the foundations of the mountains shuddered . . . Smoke rose from his nostrils, and fire from his mouth devoured; coals flamed forth from him . . . From the heavens Yahweh thundered, And 'Elyon gave forth his voice. He shot his arrows and scattered them, lightning-bolts he flashed and put them in panic.' When Joshua defended Gibeon, lethal hailstones rained down upon the enemy from heaven, and the sun and moon stood still.[5]

Yahweh could cause the favoured nation to pass safely across rivers: the parallel to the Exodus sea-crossing was Joshua's crossing of the Jordan. He could also order supernatural beings to transmit or execute his orders; in other Middle Eastern cultures these would have been minor gods, but in the Biblical accounts they are usually called angels. When Joshua opposed Jericho, he encountered a supernatural presence called the captain of Yahweh's army, who granted him powers to demolish the city walls by the sound of his trumpets.

Yahweh was 'strong and mighty, the lord of battle . . . the lord of armies', 'the king of glory before whom the circle of city gate-towers lift up their heads'. He was fearsome: 'the Lord most high is terrible' (some translate: 'Yahweh is awesome Elyon') '. . . he shall subdue the people under us, and the nations under our feet'.[6] 'The Lord shall fight for you.'[7] The Lord God of hosts (*yahwi saba'ot*, or 'the Lord the creator of armies') is the patron-god who goes before the warrior-king as his vanguard. God promised David he would do so before the battle of Rephaim, and would deliver the Philistines 'into his hand'. David after the victory called the place of battle 'Lord of breaking-through'.[8] The tradition that Moses built an altar to mark the holy war with the Amalekites, and called it 'the standard [banner] of Yahweh'[9] suggests an earlier belief that Yahweh 'stood beside' the tribal leader in battle. The ark, the symbol of the divine covenant, was on at least one occasion carried into battle,[10] a tradition that in later times was continued in the Christian kingdom of Ethiopia.

Yahweh sometimes, like other war gods, encouraged his worshippers to fight for themselves. Human initiative is given little credit in Joshua's siege of Jericho (of which the account in the Book of Joshua is unlikely to have much connection with historical fact). Joshua blindly obeyed the orders of the divine messenger-captain in obtaining the collapse of its walls. But when it came to his later attack on the people of Ai, Joshua used his own initiative to execute an orthodox military manoeuvre, the feigned flight and the ambush. God was said to have told Joshua that he had delivered the people of Ai 'into his hand', a holy war formula that was used in all the major religions of the Near East.

However, the accent placed upon God's military intervention in Israelite holy war tradition distinguishes it from most others. Because of the grossly unequal nature of the conflict supposed to have taken place between the Egyptians and the Hebrews during the Exodus of the latter from Egypt, the divine action of Yahweh against the Egyptians is said in the Hebrew scriptures to have occurred in a way that does not place the usual emphasis on synergy, as the co-operation between warlike god and warlike man is sometimes described. The songs of Moses and Miriam speak of a warrior-lord who triumphed gloriously, throwing the horse and his rider (that is, Pharaoh's army) into the sea.[11] The role of the Israelites is subordinated in these victory hymns to the work done by Yahweh, who acted, as it were, alone. This is very different from the propaganda-hymns of the great Eastern monarchies, which place all their emphasis on the conquering monarch and his victorious army.

The action taken by the persecuted had in this case been flight, not assault, and the assistance offered by the god had been to deceive, overthrow and take vengeance upon the cruel pursuers. It is not stated that there was a battle between the Exodus people and the Egyptians: all Joshua says is that the Lord 'put darkness between you and the Egyptians, and brought the sea upon them and covered them'. The conflict between this and a supposedly later version of the event, in which the sea was made dry land for the Israelites to walk upon, does not affect the common principle of the two accounts: that a weak, fleeing people was rescued by divine action, and not by their own military might. On the other hand, although there was no conquering Hebrew army, the language used is the language of holy war: God 'took off the chariot wheels' of the Egyptians, and his waters destroyed them.

Another text (one of the earliest in the Bible, although still not contemporary with the events it describes) that subordinates the role of the earthly warriors to the initiative of the heavenly warrior is the song of Deborah the prophetess,[12] where the role of the Israelite general Barak in his victory over Sisera (probably a Canaanite) in the plain of Jezreel is played down. The victory is ascribed to Yahweh, who 'delivered Sisera into his [Barak's] hand', and completed the divine triumph by willing that the defeated Sisera should seek refuge after the battle with Jael the Kenite woman, whose tribe was supposed to have been neutral in the conflict, but who demonstrated a less than neutral attitude by driving a tent peg through the enemy general's forehead while he slept.

It is unlikely that there were systematic rules for the conduct of holy war among the early Israelites, though there may have been holy war customs, some shared with other nations, some peculiar to Israel and its confederates. It is very hard to say whether these apparent rules for holy wars waged by the Israelites were permanent characteristics of real wars, or belonged only to imagined holy wars that subsequent religious thinkers inserted into the texts of what we call the Old Testament, at the time of the Babylonian Captivity or afterwards. We cannot know with certainty which practices really belonged to the most ancient tradition of Israel, and which were the bloodthirsty reflections of some exiled Israelite priest who inserted them, centuries after the event, into a much later scriptural canon.

Following normal custom, the Israelites consulted diviners or prophetesses before launching the war: the wars of Saul were preceded by some sort of priestly consultation, and so had been the internecine war with the Benjamites.[13] Ritual purification of the troops before engaging in holy war combat was usual. In David's reign even the Hittite mercenary soldier Uriah insisted on observing it, and refused to go to his wife before joining the army.[14] There were Israelite procedures, as there were to be centuries later, in early Islam, for dealing with booty acquired in holy war: this could in the Israelite tradition be consecrated to God, or even destroyed. Under David the booty was part dedicated to the service of God, part distributed to the soldiers.

There were also commands about the treatment of the conquered in holy war. Moses was said to have denounced his warriors for sparing the Midianite women, whom he blamed for spreading idolatry in Israel. He is supposed to have insisted on the massacre of the women and most of the children: only the virgin female children should be left alive (for purposes of concubinage) among the defeated.[15] It would be interesting to know whether this atrocity was actually the work of early Israelites, or whether it was inserted into the tradition by priestly ideologues five hundred or so years later. It is improbable that it concerned a person called Moses, whose historical existence is doubted by many Old Testament scholars. The Israelites are thought to have mingled with the other populations of Canaan after their conquest, which suggests that the murderous fanaticism of the passage is later rather than earlier. Other common practices in the Near East of the time, such as the collection and use as trophies of the genital parts or other organs of the enemy slain, were in use in the holy wars of the Israelites.[16]

In common with most other holy wars of the ancient Near East, Israelite holy war as described in the Old Testament made no distinction between offensive and defensive war.[17] It was used by the Israelites, as it was used by innumerable other ancient governments, to legitimize territorial claims against other tribes and nations, and to avenge treaty-breaking. The beginnings of the Israelite wars of conquest were marked by claims of this sort, such as the war attributed to Moses with the Amalekites, with whom Yahweh swore that he would have war from generation to generation.[18] The action of the god – the same kind of legitimizing idea is in the 'Fear not!' formula so often found in the Old Testament – was to validate what was claimed and done by virtue of his overbearing divine right. ('Fear not!' was commonly Yahweh's oracular reply to the tribe which asked for his authorization to launch holy war.)

The independence – or relative independence – of Israel and Judah after the establishment of David's kingdom was not short; it lasted for approaching four centuries. But from the fourth decade of the eighth century BC the political situation changed radically, and finally to the disadvantage of the Hebrew peoples. Assyrian and subsequently Babylonian domination in the Tigris-Euphrates and also in the Syria-Palestine areas led to a very long period of foreign rule and influence. The Hebrew successor-monarchies to the state of David and Solomon fell into a final decline. There was political vassalage to Assyria first, then, briefly, to Egypt, then, for a longer period, to Babylon. Jerusalem fell to the Babylonians in 587–6 BC. There had been Hebrew migration there at first, and after its fall there was some deportation to Babylon. Finally, the fall of Babylon to Persia in 539 BC brought about two centuries of Persian dominance over the peoples of Israel and Judah.

That the kingdom of Judah ever fought a holy war against the Assyrians is much to be doubted. At the end of the eighth century BC Sennacherib made a major attack on Judah which ended in a siege of Jerusalem that in some way went badly for the Assyrians, although the Assyrian king claimed victory over Judah on his monuments. A divine intervention that destroyed the Assyrian camp by sickness was claimed on the Hebrew side, although this did not stop King Hezekiah from having to pay tribute.[19]

The traits that Yahweh shared with other weather and war gods of the older cosmological myths were not forgotten during the monarchy of David and his successors. In the eighth century BC the prophet Isaiah said of Yahweh: 'Behold, the name of the Lord cometh from far, burning with his anger . . . [he] shall cause his glorious voice to be heard, and shall shew the lighting down of his arm, with the indignation of his anger, and with the flame of a devouring fire, with scattering, and tempest, and hailstones.'[20] Later still, in the sixth century BC, after the fall of Jerusalem and the Babylonian exile of the Israelites, the prophet known to scholars as Deutero-Isaiah said in the same strain of the war-lord of weather that 'the Lord shall go forth as a mighty man, he shall stir up jealousy [zeal] like a man of war: he shall cry, yea, roar . . . I will make waste mountains and hills, and dry up all their herbs; and I will make the rivers islands, and I will dry up the pools.' Yahweh's triumph was not to be a peaceable one: 'I will tread them in mine anger and trample them in my fury; and their blood shall be sprinkled upon my garments . . . For the day of vengeance is in mine heart.'

Sacred texts do not exist outside time and space, although those who are guided by them often suppose them to do so. Enough is known of the history of the biblical texts to say that while some very ancient religious ideas that date from as early as the second millennium BC are present in the Old Testament, and the texts that we possess contain fragments of very ancient religious documents, most of our Old Testament texts were written down in their present form many centuries after the events to which they refer. So although the religious practice of the Near Eastern peoples of the second and third millennia BC dictated some of the vocabulary of Israelite holy war, the way in which Hebrew scribes of the eighth to the fifth centuries BC produced the Old Testament texts to which we now have access was influenced by events much nearer to their own times.

At all periods of human history, those who claim that God fights for them are not making the claim in a remote, dispassionate way, but because they have in mind the real wars or projected wars of their own day, and their own acutely felt needs, whether selfish or altruistic. When Hebrew prophets of the time of the Babylonian captivity of Judah looked back in the sixth century BC to the Mosaic Exodus of seven or eight centuries earlier, they asked God to intervene once more to save them from their current misfortunes as he had saved their predecessors. The prophet Nehemiah assembled the Hebrews who had been repatriated from Babylon

9

to a ruined Jerusalem, and recalled how God had divided the sea for their ancestors and thrown their persecutors, the armies of Pharaoh, into the deeps.

Writing under Persian rule over Palestine, the prophet Joel looked forward to a judgement day of Yahweh. It was to be a time when young and old of both sexes were to dream dreams and see visions. Joel invoked the ancient physical characteristics of holy war: 'I will shew you wonders in the heavens and in the earth, blood, and fire, and pillars of smoke. The sun shall be turned into darkness, and the moon into blood, before the great and terrible day of the Lord come.' So the Gentiles were told to prepare for war, and to expect to receive judgement at Yahweh's hands. Versions of the Book of Deuteronomy that were being written at approximately the same time described a hearing in the divine law court. Yahweh is made to forecast his own final judgement: 'If I whet my glittering sword, and mine hand take hold on judgement; I will render vengeance to mine enemies, and will reward them that hate me. I will make mine arrows drunk with blood, and my sword shall devour flesh; and that with the blood of the slain and of the captives, from the beginning of revenges upon the enemy.'[21]

The main mode of holy war in the ancient Near East may be described as triumphal. The inscriptions of the ancient monarchies, with their endless lists of captives, of the numbers and varieties of the slain, of the kings and princes killed or enslaved, are all in this mode. It was not commonly asserted that armies fought for their gods or their religion; the claim most commonly made was that victory showed that the gods had fought for the victors. This was linked with the widespread idea that the gods judged the nations through trial by battle. When their armies had plainly lost the battle the leaders were silent, or if the issue of war had been ambiguous the records they left were deliberately falsified, as those of Sennacherib were after the failure of his Palestinian campaign at the end of the eighth century B C. But if it could be plausibly maintained that they had been victorious, they claimed divine aid. The stately church services of 'Te deum laudamus' (We praise you, O God!) with which Christian princes for many centuries celebrated victory in their churches have an illustrious pagan ancestry.

Nehemiah and the other learned religious Hebrews of the time of the Captivity lived in a period that for their people was very far from triumphal. Their nation had a proud history, but in the recent past it had experienced only humiliation and defeat. They asserted violently their message of the help promised by Yahweh to Israel and to no one else. Men like Nehemiah and Hosea spoke with authority, and they were centrally important to the preservation and development of Israel's religion. They would have been pleased to know this, but also deeply shocked to know that some of their religious ideas would, centuries later, help to mould the religious language of the two daughter religions, Christianity and Islam. Fragments of their religious terminology have in our own day persisted in cultures in most respects quite alien to theirs, in a world unimaginably different from theirs. When President Sadat of Egypt's assassin spoke of his deed of 6 October 1981, he said 'Pharaoh is dead!', thus uniting by an extraordinary mental leap the millennial tradition of Muslim holy war with the most ancient element of the Hebrew holy war that preceded it.

In spite of the distress of Nehemiah and Hosea, the lot of the Hebrews in Babylon was by no means intolerable. Some prospered there, and one of the problems of religious leaders was to persuade the Hebrew diaspora in Babylon that they had a duty to return to Palestine. For those who did return during the sixth century B C, there was a severe problem to preserve the religion and culture of Israel, as well as to reconstruct the city of Jerusalem and its Temple and to rebuild the economy.

In this drastically changed environment the holy war took on a totally different meaning from what it had had during the time of David and of the successor kingdoms. There was no more question of identifying Israel with the triumphal mode of the holy wars of the great conquering Near Eastern monarchies. From victor, Israel had become victim, and its main holy war myth became that of the victorious victim, the sea event of the first Exodus. Prophets were sometimes opposed (as Jeremiah was) to offering armed resistance to the Mesopotamian rulers who dominated the Israelites. The earlier Israelite holy wars of conquest were not forgotten, and their memory was preserved in the sacred texts that were assembled during this period in approximately the form in which they have come down to us. But Jewish prophecy became concerned less with real hopes of revolt against the overwhelming tyranny of the empire that kept them in thrall than with a sort of seditious dream-world, in which holy wars of fantasy hovered in the background of a symbolically defined polity.

The prophet Ezekiel and his continuators invented the imaginary king Gog and his kingdom of Magog in southern Palestine as part of a kind of ecstatic vision. Its fall, and the simultaneous fall of the unfaithful Israelite dissenters, were predicted. The great Eastern monarchies, which were clearly aimed at in Gog and Magog, had enserfed and transported Israel; both their power and its transience came to preoccupy the Hebrew visionaries, who laid claim to a sort of mystical power to unveil the mysteries of history, which has led them to be termed 'apocalyptic' writers.

The language of holy war pervades Ezekiel's visions: he predicts an invasion of Israel from the north on the part of Gog's armies, and a terrible reply to it in which Yahweh will call for a sword throughout all his mountains, so that every man's sword shall be against his brother. The Israelites will reply with a seven years' war of fire upon the land of Magog 'and among them that dwell carelessly in the isles', until Gog's people are utterly destroyed, and Israel has been 'filled at God's table with horses and chariots, with mighty men, and with all men of war'.[22]

Gog and Magog remained as one of the symbols of the great imperial monarchies until the time of Rome and later. They reappear in the Revelation of John, where their armies take part in the final battle after the unleashing of Satan. Muhammad, to whose ears the story came, imagined the wicked kingdom of Gog and Magog to have been restrained by Alexander the Great, who built a metallic mountain to contain it, that will be removed in the last days.[23]

Ezekiel's is a vision of destruction, but its political side is disguised, because Gog and his land of Magog are not real people or places. Elsewhere Ezekiel predicts the humiliation of Egypt by Babylon in unveiled terms. In Ezekiel's Israel holy war has ceased to be the propagandist instrument of the rulers and generals, and has become the province of religious enthusiasts and of the priestly class.

And in Ezekiel we find one of the main characteristics of all the holy wars of dispossessed minorities, which has persisted until our own day: the fierce denunciation of the apostates, who will be punished by God for their unfaithfulness. His main targets were not the foreign powers that had oppressed Israel, nor even the lesser lands like Edom that had rejoiced in Israel's defeat, but the apostate Hebrews, and particularly those who had lingered on in Judaea, and had failed to support the exiled priests whom he represented. Yahweh is made to refer to a sword sharpened and furbished against the land of Israel, which turns out to be the sword of the Babylonians. But in another sense it is the divine sword: 'I the Lord have drawn forth my sword out of its sheath: it shall not return any more.'[24] The holy wars of the dispossessed and defeated demand the punishment of the unfaithful, the apostates, the hypocrites, the traitors. Jealousy or zeal for Yahweh led inexorably to a call for vengeance upon the unfaithful, who would be annihilated in the coming holy wars; his verdict on them would be proclaimed on a law day, the 'day of Yahweh'.

So long as the deities of holy war were part of a larger divine pantheon, the failure and enslavement of a nation were simply evidence of its inferiority, and perhaps also of the inferiority of its gods. But the idea of Yahweh alone, of a single dominant god and of his people whose identity and purpose depended on him absolutely, no matter what happened, gave Yahweh's wars a nature that was rather different from those of the other war gods, even if the beliefs did not amount to monotheism in the strict sense. The failure and tribulations of the Hebrews were blamed on their unfaithfulness, but the promise made them by Yahweh was to be maintained, whatever the shortcomings of a part of the nation had been.

In these prophetic writings the recipients of Yahweh's favour were defined in a terrifyingly narrow manner. There is no suspicion that those outside the covenant he had made with Israel would benefit from privileges that would make the elect of that nation into something approaching demigods. They were assured of future victory in wars that were not yet predictable, or that could not be named in terms outside the mysterious language of prophecy, but would nevertheless be holy wars of the sort that Israel had fought in the past. Fantasy, politics, piety and war were mingled by the post-Exilic prophets as they were to be mingled in the vocabularies of other holy wars for the succeeding twenty-odd centuries.

CHAPTER TWO

Jewish Sects
in the Hellenistic World

THE END OF PERSIAN DOMINATION in Palestine brought no liberation to the people of Israel. On the contrary, the rule of foreign empires continued, and the ideological pressure upon the Jewish people, who continued to maintain obstinate loyalty to their rites and scriptures, was increased. Under that pressure, new Jewish sects came into existence, some of which reflected the influence of other Middle Eastern or Greek ideas.

When Greek power overran the Near East under Alexander the Great (356–323 BC), the situation of Syria-Palestine was deeply changed culturally, and the Assyrian or Iranian influences in the Fertile Crescent were followed by a rapid but profound Hellenization. From the point of view of power politics, the position of the Jewish population of the area changed only in that it served new masters. These masters were divided among themselves, and the struggle between the Greek ruling dynasty of Egypt (the Ptolemies) and the Greek ruling dynasty based in Mesopotamia (the Seleucids) was principally a struggle to control Syria-Palestine.

The conflict did not end until the final defeat of the Ptolemies in 198 BC. By then the Jews had, at times at least, paid dearly for it. Jewish prophets anticipated resistance to Greek power: Yahweh the lord of armies would 'bend Judah for me . . . and raise up thy sons, O Zion, against thy sons, O Greece!'[1] But Jewish military resistance to Greek power was long in coming. The initial reaction of the Jews to Seleucid victory was one of relief. When the Seleucids finally occupied Palestine in 200 BC the Jewish population were said by the occupiers to have welcomed them.

Israel continued its sad destiny in a Syrian cockpit contested by the great powers of the Near East, and its religious thinkers continued to seek refuge in apocalyptic fantasy. Of their works the most powerful to be written at this time was the Book of Daniel (which may have been due to more than one author), in approximately 167–164 BC. This was during the Seleucid domination of Judaea, which the book regarded, on account of the religious policy of Antiochus IV, as a monstrous rule. In the vision of the imperial dynasties in the Book of Daniel there is something approaching a philosophy of history, since they represent the dynasties that had ruled over the Near East from the eighth century BC until the time the book was written.

The dynasties are expounded in the story of how Daniel (imagined to be in Babylon, although when the book was written the Jews had long since returned from their exile) interpreted the dream of King Nebuchadnezzar, which was of a great image with a golden head, a torso of silver, stomach and thighs of brass, legs of iron, and feet that were part iron and part clay. A huge stone fell upon the image and broke first the feet and then the rest. Then the stone became a great mountain that filled the earth. Daniel told the king that he, Nebuchadnezzar, was represented by the golden head. The kingdoms of Persia and of Alexander the Great and his successors were represented by the rest of the image's body, and the feet of iron and clay were the Seleucid kingdom, strong at the time, but doomed to early dissolution.

The dynasties were to be judged, in particular the Seleucid dynasty, at the court of Yahweh, the ancient of days. 'The son of man' would come to the court 'with the clouds of heaven', to accuse them and to be given judgement against them. The first three dynasties were, in spite of their imperial sway, to be reduced in power and eventually suppressed. By the judgement of the ancient of days the ten-horned beast that had climbed out of the sea, and that was associated with the Seleucid monarchy, was to be immediately destroyed. The eventual beneficiary of the divine judgement was to be the nation of Israel. Israel was to be protected during the subsequent holy war by the archangel Michael, who is described in other texts similar to Daniel as the leader of the heavenly hosts.[2] The war was to cause the wise men in Israel to shine in holiness, and the 'son of man' to rule. The verdict of battle, granted in this way, was an ancient holy war idea, and in describing it Daniel drew not only on Israelite tradition but on other sources from various parts of the contemporary Hellenistic world, and perhaps from the Iranian world also.[3]

The vision of Daniel concerned the last days, and it marks a point where the Hebrew prophets (or rather the religious writers who purported to report their sayings) did not merely unveil the hidden things of the future, but looked forwards to the end of time, to a final consummation of things under a divine judgement. This was an eschatological vision, though not necessarily an other-worldly one, because the authors of Daniel may have envisaged the destruction of the wicked Greek Empire as taking place in this world, and within quite a short time of their writing the book. The war against the evil rulers, however, was to be fought by heavenly, and not human, forces. Daniel perhaps thought it impractical, or at all events premature, to rebel against the hated Antiochus IV (ruled 175–164 BC), the king of a fierce countenance, whose very title (Antiochus Theos Epiphanes, 'Antiochus-God-made-manifest') was a blasphemy.

The vision of Daniel has in later history fascinated people of many religions and cultures. Within half a century of its composition it had become a favourite text of the secluded Jewish sect of Qumran. It left its mark upon the Gospels,[4] and was to be of critical importance to the Christian Revelation of John the Divine. It was also almost certainly known to Muhammad, whom tradition reports as having reproached one of the companions for copying the Book of Daniel. Muhammad's own vision of the last days included the appearance of a beast that would be brought out of the earth to speak to those who lacked faith in his revelations.[5] When Pope Urban II called for the Catholic knights to march to the holy land at the Council of Clermont in 1095, he quoted from the Book of Daniel: God 'changes times and seasons, and removes and sets up kings'. When the later theologians came to try to interpret the Christian occupation of the holy land that began in 1099, they cited the same passage.

Later in the Christian era the Book of Daniel has been drawn on by practically all the visionaries who believed in the power of prophecy, including Dante, who placed the huge, golden-headed image with its terracotta feet on a mountain in Crete, and made the image (the 'old man') turn his back on Damietta, the Egyptian city much contested by the crusaders, and his face towards Rome.[6]

The Book of Daniel was to inspire countless similar reveries at many times down to our own. It was a kind of meditation upon holy war, that purported to unveil secret things, and to predict the execution of divine judgement. How were these divine judgements to be interpreted in the future? If God himself has prepared a bloody judgement, surely man may make war in God's name?

The same generation in Judaea that wrote the Book of Daniel gave a resounding affirmative to this last question. A call for a new holy war of the Israelites had grown out of a new cultural split in the Jewish communities. The gradual Hellenization of the Jews in Syria-Palestine, and also of those in Egypt, had gone a long way by the time the book was written.

The priestly ruling class in Jerusalem had come to depend politically and culturally upon the Greek Seleucid rulers in a way that eventually compromised the integrity of their religious way of life. A political and religious confrontation developed within the Jewish community that was to lead to an attack on foreign oppression.

The Jewish priestly class that controlled the Temple in third-century BC Palestine appears to have accepted or perhaps to have actually requested far-reaching modernizing measures from the Greek government. These measures, which tried to combine the beliefs of Jews and Greeks in a single new religious practice, changed the status of the cult in the Jerusalem Temple, and forbade the practice of important Jewish religious customs in Judaea, including circumcision.[7] Jews were constrained to worship ivy-crowned Dionysus. The god worshipped in the Temple at Jerusalem was no longer simply the Yahweh of the Hebrews. He was now to be styled by the Greek name of Zeus Olympius, or 'supreme god of Heaven', and a new altar was set up above the old altar of burnt offerings in the Temple. This was the 'abomination of desolation' mentioned by the Book of Daniel.

The new Seleucid regime in Palestine was managed from a fortress and administrative centre situated south of the Temple in Jerusalem, styled the Acra, that was to administer a Greek-style civic corporation or polis of the Hellenized Jews. A gymnasium or sports and military training centre was set up in Jerusalem at the same time. The policy was probably regarded by the government as an enlightened one that granted a degree of self-rule to the more civilized elements of the Jewish population.

The Jerusalem priestly class (which had split into contesting factions) and the Greek government were deeply unpopular with the Jewish population of Judaea outside Jerusalem, both for their innovations and for their oppressive taxes. There had also been at least one violent seizure of the treasures of the Jerusalem Temple on the part of the ruler, Antiochus IV. Such seizures were not uncommon, but that did not make them acceptable. When (c.165 BC) a prominent family from the countryside north-west of Jerusalem refused to allow sacrifices to pagan gods in the manner required by the rulers, their revolt quickly gained support in the country districts. The notable who took over the revolt after his father's death and turned it into a serious challenge to the Greek government was Judas Maccabaeus ('the hammer').

Although the aims of the Maccabaean family (later known as Hasmonaeans) were in many ways political and dynastic, their war against the Seleucid rulers and the Hellenized Jewish ruling class in Jerusalem was an authentic holy war. That it was not particularly purist was demonstrated early on, when a group of pietist Jewish rebels was ambushed and massacred on the sabbath because of their refusal to fight on that day, and the Maccabaeans promptly declared their willingness to fight defensive war on the sabbath.

But zeal for the Lord, jealousy for his rights, were the main motives put forward for their actions. The apologist who wrote the first Book of Maccabees quoted the scriptural example of Phinehas, who, when an Israelite coupled with a Midianite woman, took a javelin and ran the guilty pair through;[8] his zeal caused God to lift the plague from Israel. When Mattathias, the father of Judas Maccabaeus, had found an Israelite sacrificing to Greek gods, he had killed him upon the altar. Zeal for the Lord had from the beginning been one of the main constituents of Israelite holy war; it was later to find a parallel in Islam in Muhammad's hatred for *fitna*, aggressive idolatry or persecution, of which he said that war, though evil, was preferable to acceptance of *fitna*; to tolerate it was 'worse than carnage'.[9]

From an early stage the Maccabaean revolt had its martyrs, although they were at the time examples of heroism and not of martyrdom, of which no Jewish doctrine existed at that period. There is mention of two Jewish mothers who had had their babies circumcised in defiance of the new regulations, and who were thrown with the children from the city walls. There is also an account of the torture and execution of those who refused to sacrifice after the Greek manner, or refused to eat pig's flesh.[10] It has been claimed that if the last requirement was really made, it was probably made by Hellenized Jews, as it is unlikely that a Greek would have required such a thing.

Judas Maccabaeus fought a holy war in the Israelite tradition. When his troops prepared for battle against the Greek army they assembled in the ancient cultic centre of Mizpah, fasted and put on sackcloth, and opened the Torah to obtain an oracle that authorized them to fight. According to the partisan account in the first Book of Maccabees he followed the Old Testament custom of holy war, and authorized the fearful to leave the army before battle was joined.

The Maccabaean war was not the amateur work of pious fanatics. It was conducted with all the regard to power politics that could be expected from soldiers who had quite probably been Greek-trained. It was far from despising compromise or manoeuvre; the Hasmonaeans were skilful diplomats as well as good soldiers. Judas Maccabaeus turned to Rome, and made a treaty of alliance with the Roman Senate that was renewed after his death by his brother Jonathan; they did not refuse the help of powerful unbelievers. Eventually, a century after the death of Judas Maccabaeus, his dynasty turned themselves into hereditary high priests, and then (c.139 BC) made a permanent alliance with Rome in order to maintain the counterbalance to the Seleucids. Syria eventually became a Roman province in 64 BC.

But in spite of their self-interested policies, the Maccabaeans' first holy war bore strong similarities to that contemplated by Ezekiel and the other dreamers. Their holy war with the Jewish High Priest Menelaus and his supporters was a civil war among Jews as well as a national rebellion against Greeks. Apostates or supposed apostates were massacred without hesitation,[11] which was one of the most frequent characteristics of holy wars of the weak against the strong, and has remained so down to the present day.

In the short term the Maccabaeans won striking successes. The rebels were able to occupy Jerusalem in 164 BC and to purify the Temple. At the same time freedom of worship was restored by the Seleucids to the Jews in Judaea; some time later an orthodox high priest was installed in Jerusalem. These concessions met the essential demands of the religious groups for the security of orthodox practices, and there are signs that the pietist Jews recognized it, and withdrew their active support from the Maccabaeans. The subsequent history of the Hasmonaeans is a dynastic one, neither particularly national nor particularly religious in character.

The legacy of Judas Maccabaeus was not only to the Jews. The Book of Maccabees was received into the Christian Apocrypha by the early Christian fathers, and its hero became a Christian hero. The author of the apocryphal Fourth Book of Maccabees in the first century AD rewrote the history of the Maccabaean martyrs to illustrate a new Jewish doctrine of martyrdom: that the martyrdom of the just serves to atone for the sins of the people. There were echoes of this doctrine in Christianity, but none in Islam.

For the Christian Middle Ages Judas Maccabaeus was one of the types of the Christian knight who challenges the infidel. Baldwin I, the first King of Jerusalem, was described on his tomb (1118) as a second Judas Maccabaeus. Dante imagined Judas Maccabaeus in Paradise as one of the godly warriors of the faith who rotated round the heavenly cross, spinning like a top – a slightly uncomfortable position to occupy for eternity.[12] But it was a distinguished company: Judas spun alongside the emperor Charlemagne, Godfrey of Lorraine, the first ruler of Christian Jerusalem (1199), and the Frankish paladin against the Moors, Roland. The Book of Maccabees was to become, at the turn of the twelfth century, a main source of inspiration for the crusading policies of Pope Innocent III. The link between Judas Maccabaeus and the Christian crusaders was not negligible, and he anticipated by many centuries their ambiguous position between piety and politics.

The position of educated Jews in the Hellenistic world was in some respects not unlike that of educated Muslims in the Western-dominated nineteenth and twentieth centuries. Though deeply convinced of the superiority of their own religious tradition, they frequently wrote in the language of the dominant culture, and often accepted those parts of its view of the world that were not clearly at odds with their religious convictions.

The Hellenistic Jews were, in nineteenth- and twentieth-century terms, 'modernized'. In some of the Jewish writers there began to appear a sort of implicit internationalism, accepting that their moral doctrine could be applied also to Gentiles, that was conventional in Greek terms but inconceivable for earlier Jewish thought. Much of their thinking was apologetic, in the sense that it sought to present their ideas and their advocacy of the Jewish religion to Gentile audiences. The Jews were very widely spread in the Hellenistic world, and to a limited extent Judaism became, in that environment, a proselytizing religion. The comparisons with modern Islam are obvious, as are also the implications for the early spread of Christianity.

In the heady world of the Jewish sectaries, visions of holy war continued to appear as part of their predictions of divine judgement. That did not mean that the sectaries all believed it was their duty to engage in new Maccabaean wars; such a line of thought was restricted to a few. But the visions recounted in many of the apocalyptic books compiled at this time resemble the vision of Daniel in their insistence that they convey a secret revelation of a coming divine deliverance, perhaps imminent in terms of human time, when God will display his kingdom and justice to men, and execute his judgement. In these days the oppressors and unbelievers will meet with dire punishment, angels will take a prominent part as the agents of the divine will, and the sinful angels will meet with due and terrible judgement. Satan, a malevolent figure who began to appear for the first time in these Jewish visions, had a hand in these events at the edge of time. He entered holy wars, though usually playing only a supporting part. However, he remained on the fringe of holy war long enough to figure in the twentieth century in the rhetoric of Ayatollah Khomeini of Iran, and to become for a time in Iranian Shi'a eyes the personification of American power.

Tantalizing evidence about the sectaries began to emerge from the manuscript discoveries made in the caves at Qumran near the Dead Sea between 1947 and 1956. At Qumran there was a small community of strict, pietist Jewish believers, perhaps Essenes, which came into existence during the second century BC, and was finally obliterated by a murderous Roman attack in 68 AD. The writings of the Qumran sect contain material about holy war that is at the same time precise and profoundly ambiguous. Like the Book of Daniel, the hymns of the sect looked forwards to a terrifying time of judgement, when God's fury is to be poured forth on the dissemblers, and the final doom of his rage is to fall upon all the works of Belial. Belial (Beliar) was not Satan, but a powerful spirit of delusion and deceit whom the Christians were soon to turn into the Antichrist.

The 'War of the sons of light against the sons of darkness', the main Qumran holy war text, appears to give precise instructions for the troops of the holy war to organize themselves on earth, so that they may fight with the divine troops in the long and deadly war against the forces of evil, which after a six-year period of mobilization is to last a further twenty-nine years. This war is not to be a procession of uninterrupted triumphs, but a time of woes for God's people, who will suffer many setbacks and defeats. The theatres of war in the Near East and North Africa are named in terms that look geographically exact, but are largely taken from the Book of Genesis, and are simply symbolic of all oppressive power, like Gog and Magog in the Book of Daniel.

The Qumran rules for the holy army are related to tactical manuals of Greek warfare, and look at first glance like a handbook for freedom fighters, but it is doubtful if they were really intended for practical use. The account of the inscriptions on the trumpets and the standards, and the elaborate description of the pompous costume to be worn by the priests who lead the army, have nothing to do with tactics and everything to do with mystical and cultic expectations, and the references to the numbers of the troops and the precise lengths of each campaign are dictated by numerological mysticism (a feature of all the apocalyptic literature) and not by military needs.

The Qumran sect was perhaps disposed to join with activist groups like the Zealots in resisting Roman rule, but only when the last days came. It seems unlikely that the Qumran pietists wanted as it were to force God's hand, as the Zealots did, by launching immediate revolt. The Qumran War Rule seems to concern mystical and cultic matters rather than practical ones. And it may even be that before the Jewish War broke out in 66 AD the Qumran sectaries shared the pacifism which some contemporary writers attributed to the Essenes. One Qumran text suggests a deep-rooted scepticism among them about all warfare and its motives:

> Do not all peoples hate wrongdoing? Yet, is it not rampant among them all? Are not the praises of truth sung by all nations? Yet, is there a single race or tribe that really adheres to it? What nation likes to be oppressed by a stronger power? Or who wants his property plundered unjustly? Yet, is there a single nation in the world that has not oppressed his neighbour? Or where in the world will you find a people that has not plundered the property of another?[13]

It is hard to think that the authors of that text – which could with advantage be posted in all the halls of the United Nations – were in favour of immediate nationalist guerrilla warfare. It seems more probable that their perspective was other-worldly, and that they looked forward to the eschatological arrival of the last things under the imminent divine judgement. However, the history of the Qumran community was a long one, and there were certainly relations, towards the end of the Jewish revolt, between it and the Zealot defenders of the Palestinian fortress of Masada against the Romans.

From the late first century BC onwards there was strong potential support in Judaea, both among religious enthusiasts and the heavily taxed people, for armed resistance to the rule of Rome and its nominees. The entry of the Roman general Pompey into Jerusalem in 63 BC had marked the beginning of a new period of foreign domination that led to the appearance of new vassal rulers of the country. The Hasmonaeans were eliminated, and an Idumaean family, only questionably Jewish in religion, was placed in power. Its most notable ruler was Herod the Great (37–4 BC).

The most ardent supporters among the Jews of armed resistance on religious grounds came from two overlapping groups. The Zealots were a party of enthusiasts for right religion, whose title meant that they were held to be jealous for God. An early leader, Judas the Galilean, led an unsuccessful rebellion shortly after the death of Herod the Great, but the repression did not suppress the party. Much Zealot support came from religious elite leaders, possibly from certain Pharisees.

The *sicarii* ('stabbers', or more commonly 'robbers') were extremist groups that would in modern parlance be called terrorists; they were termed such by the Roman authorities and by the main Jewish historian, Josephus, for the same political reason that such groups are designated terrorists today. Whether the 'robbers' were absolutely distinct from the Zealots, or whether, as seems more likely, they were simply the military wing of the movement, is uncertain. A political robber of this sort mentioned in the New Testament is Barabbas, who was due to be executed for a murder committed during an earlier rebellion at the time of the trial of Jesus in Jerusalem.[14] As their modern historian has said, the groups all had the same aim: the liberation of the people of God from the Roman yoke, and the purification of the holy land from all transgressors of the law and all traitors.[15]

The Jewish War of 66–74 AD provides as much evidence of the weakness of the Zealots as of their strength. The rapid fall of Jerusalem and of key fortresses like Masada to the rebels, who had hitherto been strongest in Galilee, and the defeat of the first punitive Roman expedition, seemed to point to a powerful and united movement that did not in fact exist. After a very short time the messianic Zealot leader Menahem, son of the original Zealot leader Judas the Galilean and conqueror of Masada, was murdered in Jerusalem, and the rebellion's leaders split into a number of factions. The Zealots never re-established their leadership of the revolt, which in any case had never had much hope of surviving the Roman counterattack for long. The fall of Jerusalem to Titus in 70 AD, and its plunder and destruction, were virtually predetermined. The fall of Masada in 74 and the massacre or suicide of its last defenders meant the extinction of the Zealots as a sect.

The holy war of the Zealots and 'robbers' resembled the holy war of the Maccabaeans in many respects. Like the Maccabaeans, the Zealots carried out summary judgements and summary executions on people who were held either to have violated Jewish law or to have become apostates. The historian Hengel has referred to this as Zealot lynch law. Another common characteristic of the two holy wars was the flight to the desert, which is a natural expedient for a group rebelling against an overwhelmingly powerful adversary in an Eastern country, but one which has precedents in early Jewish religious history. Judas the Galilean retreated to the desert after the first abortive Zealot revolt, and the surviving Zealots also fled to the desert after the failure of the Jewish revolt in 74 AD. Paul was asked in Jerusalem whether he was the Egyptian who had led a force of four thousand terrorists into the wilds.

Some Maccabaean and Zealot characteristics have re-emerged in holy wars of other religions and later times. It is true that the emigration (*hijra*) of Muhammad to Medina was a flight from one town to another, but sacred emigration in the name of holy war has very often, in Muslim history, been interpreted as a flight to desert places. There are today Islamic Jihad rebels who have fled into the Egyptian desert, just as there are other groups of rebel Algerian Islamists in the Sahara, and just as the Afghan *mujahidin* fled into the hills in the 1980s. It is true that the aim of these flights was practical and tactical, but those who made them were strongly comforted by the prophetic example.

Martyrdom was accepted by the Zealots with proud courage. Hundreds if not thousands were crucified by the Romans, before, during and after the Jewish War. The Zealots shared with the Essenes the will to resist torture and to refuse to deny their faith. The shedding of the blood of the martyrs was later regarded by religious Jews as a call to avenge their death, and also as an act that expiated the guilt of the people. Neither Zealots nor Essenes shrank from religious suicide. During the Zealot revolt these ideas were still implicit rather than explicit, and the word 'martyr' does not seem to have been used by exact contemporaries to describe the Zealot witness and sacrifice. There is a parallel here with the first Muslim battle martyrs.

However, the death of Jesus, who must (especially because he was a Galilean) have been believed by many to have been a Zealot, resembled in some respects the deaths of hundreds of Zealot victims of Roman power. He was crucified along with two 'robbers', who may well have been Zealots. At the end of the Jewish War several hundred Zealots who had fled to Egypt were tortured and executed, while refusing to acknowledge the lordship of the Roman Emperor. Many others, including the last survivors of the fortress at Masada, committed religious suicide.

Martyrdom was another attribute of Zealot holy war that reappeared in later holy wars of other cultures. It is sometimes said that Muhammad borrowed the title and concept of martyr (*shahid*) from Christianity, but the idea of witness and confessor is less prominent in his references to martyrdom than that of sacrifice in the holy war.[16] Noticeably, Muhammad asserted that the Gospel and the Torah as well as the Qur'an contained the promises that God had made to those who died in the holy war. He did not make clear in what way the Jewish and Christian scriptures contained such promises, and the Qur'anic passage remains somewhat mysterious.[17]

*   *   *

Although some people of his time presumably thought Jesus to have been a Zealot (and a few modern scholars have also sustained this), this in fact seems most unlikely. It is probable that he on the contrary thought that part of his message was to contradict theirs, and he even perhaps specifically denied that he was a Zealot.[18] His repudiation of violence seems to have resembled that reported of the Essenes. The order he gave during his final confrontation with Jewish priestly power to 'put up your sword' suggests this, and so does the much earlier teaching on loving and praying for enemies.[19] On the other hand, the eschatological prophecy attributed to him quotes the Book of Daniel by name, and resembles many contemporary or near-contemporary writings in its prediction of the days of woe and divine judgement.[20]

After the death of Jesus the Revelation of John was to take up the fragmentary teaching of Jesus on the last things, and to use the Book of Daniel as a starting point for what was to be an immensely influential prophecy. Jesus implied that the end of time would be marked by war; John quite definitely contemplated a final holy war. But it was to be a holy war in which God and his appointed instruments execute judgement alone, without assigning a combatant role to men except in a clearly figurative sense.

The happenings prophesied in Revelation, particularly the overthrow of Rome, were clearly not going to take place without war. The two-edged sword placed in the mouth of the son of man was to be used, and the angels were to be sent out to assemble the kings at the place of Armageddon. There was the customary denunciation of apostates, and the announcement that the son of God shall rule with an iron rod, smashing the nations to pieces like earthenware. The rider of the second horse is given power to take peace from the earth and to make men slaughter one another. The four angels who had earlier been confined at the great river Euphrates were to be released, to kill a third of mankind. The beast that rose from the sea was to be allowed to wage war on God's people and for a time to defeat them. Michael, the leader of the heavenly hosts, was in the end to make victorious war upon the Satanic dragon and the rebellious angels.

The holy war of the Book of Revelation was not an incitement to violence, but a monition that told the Christians (including the specifically named churches of Asia Minor) to expect a proximate final judgement of woes, and holy war conducted by supernatural beings. One of the churches is told, however, that it will in some way be protected from the woes of the last days because of past faithfulness. The language is the language of holy war, but the physical violence that is predicted is not to be the work of men. And this was the attitude to holy war to be taken by the early Christian church, which saw bloodshed as doom, but not as duty. If we can take the Revelation of John as evidence of the attitude of the first Christian generation after its founder, Rome may have been hated by some Christians, but they did not hanker after a new revolt against it. They relied, as the Jewish visionaries two centuries earlier had relied, upon a divine intervention whose holy war would not depend on humans, and would on that account be the more terrifying and irresistible. In this respect the tradition was not that of the Zealots, but of the anti-Hellenistic prophets who had preceded the Zealots.

The Revelation prophecy is not so very far from the prophecy of the coming of the son of man that Matthew stated to have been delivered by Jesus himself. His reply to his disciples who asked him what signs would be given of the divine coming and of the end of the age was no less dramatic and terrifying than that given in more fantastic detail by the Book of Revelation.[21] He made it clear that, as in the Book of Revelation, war was to cause many of the final trials and miseries. There is mention of the inhabitants of Judaea fleeing overnight to the hills to escape the imminent time of distress, and war is also implied by the quotation from Job: 'Wherever the corpse is, there the vultures will gather.'[22] However, the people about whom Jesus expresses concern, in this expected last phase of human history, are not to be actors in the final wars. There is to be war, which may be holy in the sense that it is in some way authorized by God, but God's people are not expected to take an active part in it.

It has been argued that Jesus did not impose a pacifist position upon his disciples, because waiting for the divine judgement and expecting the divine coming were an integral part of his message, and there has to be a temporal gap between the world in which his followers live and the world of the last things. Because we live 'between the times', it has been said that there has always been, and must be until the eschatological hope is fulfilled, a conflict between literal obedience to some of the Gospel's precepts (for example, 'Do not set yourself against the man who wrongs you'[23]) and acceptance of all those ordinances of the state that are not in clear contradiction of the manifest wish of Jesus that his followers should walk in the light.

Some of the precepts of Jesus about not resisting injustice by force seem to have been given in an immediate and urgent way. They would almost certainly have bound Christian soldiers to refuse to commit atrocities. But perhaps their moral effect went further than this. The Christians for a long time thought that the coming of the last things was imminent, and the convenient doctrine that less is expected of the believer during the long interim before the kingdom is manifested was not available to them. One indication that Christians really thought in this manner for a long period is that for a millennium the Christian clergy in both East and West treated bloodshed in war as a sin for which the soldier who killed should do penance, even if it took place under legitimate orders, and even if the blood shed was that of an infidel. Another is that for an even longer period the clergy of both East and West were interdicted from taking part in bloodshed, even in a war that had been authorized by the ruler.

Perhaps the teachings of Jesus implied what would now be called a pacifist position, although the modern term cannot be accurately applied to a world that is morally and culturally so different. At the minimum the position he occupied was a pacific one, since later Christians quite clearly had scruples about the way in which they should condone or take part in warfare. That does not mean that Christ never condemned what he thought to be wrong in a way that the objects of his condemnation found deeply provocative. His career demonstrated in a dramatic manner that he was ready, as the earlier prophets had been, to denounce injustice and impiety from the housetops. He continued to charge those whom he thought to be guilty right up to the very end of his life, when he himself stood arraigned at the prisoner's stand.

But the career of Jesus was also, or at all events was implied by the Gospel writers to have been, a political statement of non-resistance in the face of Roman power. Jesus quite consciously took up this pacific attitude in opposition to the violent resistance to Rome that was being offered by the Zealots. Even if Pilate was deliberately treated by the Gospel writers more kindly than he deserved, as has been suggested, the policy of non-resistance to Rome seems evident in the account of what Jesus said at his trial; it also appears in earlier remarks, like that about rendering Caesar his due.

Jesus himself had dealings with Roman soldiers, without his being said to have blamed them for their profession. Such tolerance would have constituted in the minds of the Zealot freedom fighters a clear case of fraternization with the hostile imperialists. And there is also plenty of evidence that the Christian communities in the later Roman Empire allowed their members to belong to the Roman army.[24] These soldiers must sometimes have been unable to reconcile their religion with the requirements of emperor-worship that their profession made impossible to avoid, and the North African theologian Tertullian said that Christians should avoid enlistment because of this danger. He instanced as implicitly idolatrous the requirement that under certain circumstances a soldier might be required to wear a laurel crown. He also observed that 'Christ in disarming Peter ungirt every soldier.'[25] But although Christian apologists sometimes implied that the Christian function in the pagan Empire was to support society by prayer, and not to wield the sword in the Roman army, they clearly accepted that Christians could perform military duties.

The attitude of Christianity to war was thus from the beginning ambivalent. There is a widespread conviction today that it is an essentially pacific religion, and is to be absolutely distinguished from Islam on this account. It is understandable that people bred in a Christian tradition should often think in this way, but a careful examination of the evidence seems to point in exactly the opposite direction. Abhorrence of bloodshed does not logically lead to the rejection of war, even when that abhorrence is shared by the whole culture, which in the Christian case was not always so.

The factors at work in early Christianity by no means all pointed towards abstention from war. On the one hand, Christianity was born and had to develop in one of the great militarist empires, and if it aspired to conquer the allegiance of the whole population, and not to stay content with the status of a minor Jewish cult, the temptation to adopt a more pragmatic attitude to militarism than can be seen in its founder was very strong. In the Christian Gospels, and in the canonical writings that immediately followed them, the use of military metaphor is notable. The sword is a metaphor that Jesus himself was said to have used on several occasions.

The nature of the religious writings on which the Christians relied took them back to a tradition that not merely condoned war, but called for holy war. From the beginning, Christianity saw itself as the fulfilment of the Jewish law, and not as its contradiction. The Book of Joshua, with its argument for what later was called the justice of the cause for war, was as much a part of the Christian scriptures as any other. Christ had refrained from joining the Zealots, but that did not mean that his followers were barred from accepting the earlier Jewish doctrines of holy war.

That Christianity grew in the Graeco-Roman culture had other consequences. Christianity made great sacrifices, and experienced many martyrdoms, in order to resist the temptation to succumb to Roman power-worship and state-worship. But members of the learned elites, who very early on were to be found in the Christian communities, could bring to the new religion doctrines of natural law and justice that accorded with the Christian preaching of selflessness and reconciliation.

Even before the annexation of Christianity by the Roman state in the early fifth century under the Emperor Constantine, Roman views of justice and good faith in war had already penetrated the upper clergy. St Ambrose, Bishop of Milan (d.397 AD), had been an important imperial official, and he experienced no difficulty in justifying Christian participation in defensive war. Soon after the start of what may be called the Constantinian church, Augustine, Bishop of Hippo (354–430), pronounced what has remained ever since the basic definition of a just war, that is, a war to right a wrong received. Such a war had to be conducted, according to Augustine, in accordance with a code of moderation and of minimum violence that was taken over from Stoic philosophy and late Roman law. Christ's command not to resist the evil man was explained by Augustine as imposing a duty upon a man's moral disposition, but not submitting the Christian to a physical duty of non-resistance. The Jewish tradition of holy war was not forgotten in this cultural synthesis. Joshua's destruction of the city of Ai was accepted by Augustine as the execution of a duty imposed upon him by God.

St Augustine's views on war and natural rights and justice did not immediately become normative for the whole Christian church. They acted, rather, as a powerful long-term influence that took many centuries to be accepted by Western Latin church thinking as a whole. Nor were they accepted or even seriously considered in the Eastern church, whose tradition in the matter, while not entirely dissimilar, because it derived from the same late-classical source, was very different.

However, far from being a pacifist or even a necessarily pacific religion, Christianity was by the beginning of the fifth century well prepared to act as the religion of societies that accepted war as a social duty. At first, the society concerned was the late Roman one, which in the period beginning in the fifth Christian century had to wage war in defence of what we would call Christian civilization. That concept of warfare was to persist in the eastern Roman Empire for the millennium that ended with the fall of Constantinople to the Ottomans in 1453. In the west, after half a century of the Constantinian church (325–375), Christianity became the religion of barbarian societies whose ruling military elites saw warfare as the basic reason for their existence.

It is not therefore surprising that, less than a score of years ago, a distinguished historian of war described Christianity as having been one of the great warrior religions.[26] The same man said on a different occasion that if Christianity was to become a peacemaking religion, which he did not think an impossible or incredible idea, in these matters it would virtually have to make a fresh start.[27] These judgements may be thought exaggerated, or mistaken, but they must act as a corrective to the commonly received notions about the repugnance of Christianity for war.

CHAPTER THREE

Islam and War

IN THE EARLY YEARS of the seventh Christian century, a member of a merchant family of the city of Mecca in South Arabia named Muhammad began to be visited by divine messages. They told him to rise and to warn those around him to change their lives to conform with the revelations being made to him by Allah, or his messenger. Muhammad once described some of his revelations as coming from 'behind a veil':[1] he was thus in the literal sense, as the Greek word means 'unveiling', an apocalyptic visionary.

Mecca was a holy city whose commercial importance depended in some measure upon the gods who were worshipped there. The god who spoke to Muhammad was the one god, Allah, and Muhammad, perhaps after a slight hesitation that is recorded in the so-called 'satanic verses',[2] denounced the worship of all the Meccan idols.

The morality that Muhammad was instructed to preach was severe, but not impossible for an ordinary human being to follow, and always tempered by the assurance of Allah's mercy. His messages spoke constantly of the judgement that is to be visited by Allah upon each man for his life and works, and that may be visited upon whole societies. His message, like that of Jesus and of the Old Testament prophets, was not a revealed code of law, but a statement of a man's position in this world and of his responsibility to God. Muhammad did not repudiate either the Hebrew or the Christian revelations; he also claimed as a predecessor the Patriarch Abraham, the breaker of idols and the worshipper of Allah. But he insisted that his revelation was final in a way that the Hebrew and Christian revelations were not, and he rejected the divinity that was claimed for Jesus. After his death the polemic maintained by Qur'anic commentators with the Jews was much more consistent and sustained than that with the Christians, which suggests that Muhammad and his circle thought the former to have been more important to his doctrine than the latter.

Muhammad's denunciation of infanticide and usury, and his disapproval of the blood feud in its old form, threatened local social organization, and his repudiation of the gods worshipped at the holy shrine in Mecca also threatened the decorum and the commercial prosperity of the city. His unpopularity in Mecca became so sharp that his kinsmen were divided on whether or not they should go on protecting him from his detractors. By 622 of the Christian era his position in his native city had become so difficult that he treated with supporters from the neighbouring oasis of Yathrib (Medina), and fled there with his followers. An oath of protection was given him at the nearby 'Aqaba that carried an implied guarantee to fight in his defence.

The message of Muhammad was unambiguously religious and personal. He called on men to face God's judgement for their works on earth, on a day when all created things would be rocked in a final earthquake, and when men would be known and sentenced to perdition or bliss for their cupidity or their mercy, for their misdeeds such as infanticide or ingratitude to God, or for their acts of generosity and kindness. Muhammad was the honoured messenger who conveyed these tidings, which he had learned from an angelic messenger or in trance, and those who scoffed or derided him, particularly the rich and powerful, would receive a terrible judgement alongside the rest of the wicked. Those who listened to and helped him became a party of God (*hizbullah*), and their struggle with the unbelievers and sceptics in Mecca itself became the subject of further divine revelations.

One of the virtues most required of the helpers of Muhammad, after their submission to Allah, was 'struggle in the way of Allah' (*jihad*). This struggle was a personal and moral one to do God's will, but it was also a struggle with the detractors whose persecution (*fitna*) of hostility and ridicule obstructed the reception of Muhammad's message. At Mecca he told his supporters to 'struggle hard' against the unbelievers, and not to give in.[3] But once the Islamic community had moved to Medina, the struggle acquired a new political dimension, and eventually a military one. Muhammad's position in Medina was anomalous: he had not set up a new tribe, but in many ways the effect was as if he had. His followers were not at first especially warlike, largely because they feared that hostilities with the Meccans might lead – as they eventually did – to Muslims fighting their own kinsfolk.

It was almost inevitable that the move to Medina would lead to fighting with those in Mecca whom Muhammad held responsible for the exile. The custom of the time sanctioned raiding (*ghaziyah*) against people not protected by treaty. Muhammad's followers raided a small caravan belonging to the Meccans, but in doing so they broke religious custom, because the raid took place during the sacred months in which raiding was forbidden. Muhammad at first refused his share of the booty, but he was given a revelation that conferred retrospective authority upon the raid. From that time the *ghazi*, the raider for the cause of Islam, was considered to be carrying out a religious duty, striving with his goods and his person in the cause of Allah.

Muhammad henceforth believed that war could be a sacred duty for the Islamic community. The obligation was in the end linked with his horror of *fitna*, which can be loosely defined as betrayal of the basic social bond by persecution or in some other way – the word is ambiguous, indicating both the temptation to do wrong and succumbing to it. It was revealed to Muhammad that slaughter is an evil thing, but that *fitna* is worse, and that in consequence armed struggle (in the military sense of *jihad*) can be a sacred duty of the Islamic community.

The basic injustice of his party's situation, as Muhammad saw it, was that they had been driven from their homes in Mecca and virtually exiled because they had affirmed the Lord to be Allah. Allah permitted and indeed commanded them, through Muhammad, to fight the oppressors. They were to fight the unbelievers until they submitted, in spite of any reluctance they might have had to do battle. 'Fight in the cause of Allah against those who fight against you, but transgress not ... Once they start fighting, kill them wherever they have driven you out, for *fitna* is worse than killing. When you meet in battle those who have disbelieved, smite their necks, and after the slaughter tighten the bonds, until war lays aside its burdens.'⁴

Muhammad, like the Old Testament prophets and the rest of the ancient Semites long before them, believed that unseen heavenly armies could come to fight on the side of the believers: 'On the day of [the battle of] Badr, it was not you who slew them, but Allah.' Later in his career, after the battle of Hunayn, when the Muslims in spite of their numerical superiority were in danger of being routed, he thought that the armies of Allah had intervened for them.⁵

The military dimension therefore became a moral dimension, although holy war, like all war, remained in the end a practical matter. Muhammad was often unable, in spite of his great powers of persuasion, to convince the whole Muslim community to go to the battlefield. As he saw it he had to deal with feigned or undecided Muslims (whom after the battle of Uhud

he termed *munafiq* – 'hypocrites'[6]), and also with a less guilty category who
were in a sense conforming Muslims, but who 'sat at home' instead of
following the army to the field. These were placed by the Prophet in a
lower moral category than those who truly 'strove in the way of Allah with
their possessions and their lives', and it was implied that if they had been
insincere in protesting their incapacity to fight, hell awaited them.[7] However, when the practical need for a sufficient number of fighters had been
supplied by the Islamic community, Muhammad does not seem to have
insisted further. He allowed some people to pay substitutes to fight for
them in the holy war. And he was not above promising his troops rich war
booty, in order to maintain their loyalty (although the spoils were to be
bestowed by God), as he did at the time of the truce of al-Hudaybiya,
which had disappointed his supporters.[8]

To think that Muhammad's community in Medina was a society organized primarily for warfare would be far from the truth. His moral vision
was so large that the military and political side could not dominate the
whole. But, equally, the early Islamic community could not subsist either
economically or politically unless it defended itself by war. It had to use
any means of defence it could find, and not rely exclusively on the idealism
of the pious. Muhammad made military alliances with non-Muslim tribes,
and used slaves, not all of whom are known to have been Muslims, as
soldiers. Slaves also fought in the first Muslim armies after his death,
in the so-called apostasy war of the *ridda*. The precedent of slave-soldiers
was to be of great importance in subsequent Muslim history. But the
earliest Muslims were a small, in some ways a desperate, group, who faced
extinction if they failed on the battlefield – as they almost did at the battle
of Uhud.

Like any other community, the early Muslims also had to protect themselves against banditry and terrorism. The penalty fixed by Muhammad for
those who spread 'mischief' or vice, which we may understand as banditry,
was crucifixion or mutilation;[9] like some other Qur'anic penalties that strike
modern people as unusual or severe, these were accepted police measures
of the time. But one of Muhammad's main intentions was to discourage
the blood feud, so often the root cause of 'mischief'; the holy war was one
way of doing this.

A modern writer has observed that the Muslim rebellions against Western
political domination in the modern period (and, he might have added,

some of the rebellions against modern Muslim governments) have almost automatically found their prototype in the community of seventh-century Medina.[10] At the time of the later Islamic Empires, when after the triumph of Islam many Qur'anic scholars who lived in an atmosphere of total security from unbelievers disputed the principles of Islamic holy war in a largely academic manner, the agonies of the early Islamic community had become remote. But nineteenth- and twentieth-century Muslim rebels faced many of the problems of early Islam – difficulties of recruitment, tribal conflicts, money shortages, collaboration with the enemy. Some, though by no means all, modern so-called revolutionary fundamentalism has in this way repeated the earliest experience of the religion.

In modern terms the difference between Muhammad and Jesus was the difference between Nelson Mandela and Mahatma Ghandi. Like many of the Old Testament prophets, Muhammad did not seek bloodshed, but did not avoid it when it seemed to him essential if the will of Allah was to be accomplished. He did not want conquest for its own sake, but he adjured his people to fight in the way of Allah to protect the weak and those who could not fight for themselves. 'What keeps you from fighting in the cause of Allah and of the weak among the men, women, and children?' It was obligatory for his community to fight, even though he said that they disliked it.[11]

Many practicalities of war were dealt with in Muhammad's revelations. His own share of the booty was defined, and the taking of prisoners of war was authorized; after the battle they could be released, either as a favour or against payment of ransom. After the unexpected victory over the Meccans at the battle of Badr Muhammad seems to have experienced a scruple of conscience that he ought not to have taken prisoners until he had totally destroyed the enemy. The killing of prisoners was normal in South Arabia, as it had been in early Syria-Palestine. A massacre of the male Jews in Qurayzah after their submission to Muhammad was authorized by the arbitrator whom he appointed.

Very significantly, the first attempts to collect biographical material about Muhammad after his death were called *al-maghazi*, the campaigns of the Prophet. The later annalists attributed twenty-seven major raids to him. These stories fitted into an established pre-Islamic literary genre, that glorified the exploits of the raiders and their families.[12] It may be added that the raid, the *ghazw* (the word came into English after 1830, via the French in the form '*razzia*'), remained in Arabic as the term for a normal feature of desert warfare, with no necessary religious connection.

The question of conquest is at the centre of any modern judgement of Muhammad's message. It is very hard indeed to separate the message from its historical consequences, as historians must try to do, although the case is different for moralists. For six or seven years the main military task of Muhammad's community in Medina was self-defence. But even before his return to Mecca as a victor in 630, Muhammad had become one of the main political leaders of South Arabia, and his troops had made at least one important expedition towards the north, perhaps even over the Byzantine frontier into Syria, although the sources are unclear.

The command to fight the unbelievers in Mecca was clear: 'When the sacred months have ended, slay the polytheists wherever you find them.'[13] Only repentance, acceptance of Islamic prayer and payment of Islamic tax could exempt them from attack. The unbelievers in Mecca were not the only people on whom the Muslims made war during Muhammad's lifetime. Unbelieving tribes, Jews, and the other 'people of the book', the Christians, were also liable to attack if they failed to comply with Muhammad's requirements. The holy war was not to be waged on all who had not accepted Islam, irrespective of their attitudes and policies. The community of Islamic believers had to be supported by all Muslims, and an attack on a part of that community was interpreted as an attack on the whole. But in the case of an attack made by unbelievers with whom another section of the Muslims had a treaty, the obligation of holy war lapsed.[14] From the beginning Muhammad had pursued a sophisticated policy of alliances, and this imposed limits on holy war.

From one point of view Muhammad's doctrine of holy war required the mobilization of the whole population capable of bearing arms. But the practical nature of his injunctions required him to recognize that effective offensive warfare depended in the end upon the cavalry, and the weapons and mounts for a cavalry arm, to which he referred specifically as the assembly of well-readied horses prepared for war,[15] were costly. The payment of a substitute mounted soldier was an acceptable way of executing the moral commitment to holy war.

The final setting up of Muhammad's government in the holy city of Mecca did not eliminate holy war from his programme. On the contrary, one of his first actions there was to confront tribal opposition to Islam in the Hejaz, and to defeat it in a big battle at Hunayn. In 631 Muhammad led his last great military expedition to the very north of the Hejaz on the Syrian-Byzantine border at Tabuk. The preliminary to this campaign seems to have been a revelation that was in effect a declaration of war against the

Christians and the Jews.[16] Strangely, they are described as not believing in Allah or the last day. This may have been a charge of hypocrisy, of the same sort Muhammad had made in reproaching the Christians on earlier occasions. War was to be waged against them – it is notable that the word used for war in this context was not *jihad* – until they paid tribute, and utterly submitted.

Of the believers who were to fight in the cause of Allah in this last great expedition, and were to slay and be slain, Muhammad said that Allah had as it were bought their persons and their goods in return for the promise that they should enter paradise after death.[17] As we have seen, he claimed, rather mysteriously, that the Torah and the Gospel also contain such a promise. This is not exactly a doctrine of war martyrdom, though on one earlier occasion Muhammad had referred to those who died in the holy war as being 'alive, though you know it not'.[18]

Whether Muhammad can be said to have developed a doctrine of war martyrs is not at all certain, but he certainly supplied the elements for one. He used the term martyr (*shahid*) in a manner much closer to the Christian sense of 'confessor' than to that of a soldier dying in battle, and the intimate connection later made between death in holy war and witnessing for God was due not to Muhammad but to the later Islamic compilers of 'traditions' that they handed on as authentic. The Christian doctrine of martyrdom was specific in a way that Muhammad's was not, and was also passive in its acceptance of the violence offered by the unbeliever, in a manner that had nothing in common with the doctrine of Muhammad.

The question of whether seeking martyrdom could be deplored as virtual suicide had been debated by the early Christians. In the same way, it was not always approved in Islam as the best moral course for a man to take, although it was far more often seen in a positive than in a negative light. As was the case with many Islamic doctrines, Islamic martyrdom reflected something of both the Hebraic and the Christian precedents, but carried the stamp of the founder of the religion, of a different revelation, and of different historical circumstances.

Though in 631 Muhammad's army had set off north for Tabuk on a holy war, the expedition seems to have ended as a great military promenade to receive the submissions of the tribes, some of which were on the Christian side of the Syrian border. There was no direct conflict with the Byzantines, whose then recent victories over the Persians had been predicted by Muhammad some years earlier, towards the start of his mission. Supporters who had failed to accompany him on the expedition were let off afterwards with a reprimand and a short social isolation, a final reminder of both the merciful and the practical nature of the Prophet.

After Muhammad's return to Mecca from Tabuk he made a proclamation to his people on the occasion of the pilgrimage to the Ka'bah (the holy stone of Mecca) that may, since he was then nearing the end of his life, be considered the final statement of his message. It is not quite certain which sections of the Qur'an are included in the 'farewell' sermon, but it seems probable that it granted four months' grace to those who rejected Islam, and that at the end of this period unbelievers not protected by treaty were to be slain wherever the Muslims could find them.[19] What geographical area, if any, Muhammad had in mind when he issued this proclamation is unknown. It is indeed rather absurd to think of such a man, in such a time and place, as brooding over some sort of map of Arabia, even a mental one. But when he died in Medina on 8 June 632 AD at the age of sixty-two, or a little older, Muhammad was probably planning a new northern expedition.

Following Muhammad's death there was a very long period of Islamic holy war that extended to much of western Asia, North Africa and parts of Europe. These wars overturned the Persian Empire entirely, and robbed the Roman Byzantine Empire of something like half its lands. Had Muhammad lived we may conjecture that there would have been holy wars of a not dissimilar kind, though their conduct and results might perhaps have been very different.

Muhammad several times asserted that Allah would make the religion of Islam prevail (or conquer, *zahara*) over all other religions.[20] This was a programme of conquest, although it referred to religious and not to secular dominion. The Muslims thus set themselves almost from the outset the task of Islamizing the whole world by force of arms. But religious conquest lay at the heart of the message, and political rule was a secondary, although essential, condition for the triumph of Islam.

The Tabuk expedition showed clearly that Muhammad was well aware of the lands to the north of the Arabian peninsula, but it is very hard to say what kind of ideas of cultural and political space were held in the early Muslim view of the world. It is noticeable, for example, that although Ethiopia was certainly a part of the Meccan perspective, and Muhammad is said to have had Ethiopians in his bodyguard, no major move was made in the early period to conquer the lands lying to the south-west of the Red Sea. That people with a long-lived cavalry tradition and little maritime experience should have held off in this way is easy to explain, but it suggests that early Islamic religious ideology was subject to very practical considerations.

It is hard to call Muhammad's aims 'universal' in a political rather than in a moral sense. Such terminology seems senseless in the context of Muhammad's own life: 'political' and 'universal' are ideas taken from a Graeco-Roman conceptual framework that has no ready application to the life of a South Arabian holy man of the seventh Christian century. It is true, however, that the Islamic Empire that followed Muhammad's death can indeed be described in such terms. After Muhammad the Islamic elites developed with startling speed a capacity to grasp Graeco-Roman ideas, and three-quarters of a century after the Prophet's death the Ummayad caliphs lived in a partially Hellenized cultural world.

As modern Westerners we find it hard to judge equally the ambitions of Muhammad, because we cannot avoid making the assumption that the political and religious realms are separate. The Western order of things that has come into existence since the eighteenth-century Enlightenment has made an essential distinction between church and state. The distinction has not always been clear: it is basic, for example, to the Constitution of the United States, and obvious in those of most republics of the European continent, but blurred in the British monarchical constitution. But it is essential to Western democratic institutions, not least to their principles of religious toleration. A polity in which religion and politics are irretrievably identified is felt, even if obscurely, to threaten the basic principles that govern most Western societies.

Western insistence on the distinction between religion and politics has profoundly influenced Western judgements on holy war. The eleventh-century crusade originated in a period in which the great lines of demarcation between church and state had hardly begun to be drawn. Modern opinion has been able to approve in some respects the idealism of the Christian holy war, often without sympathizing overmuch with the clericalism that lay behind it. Academics who study crusading history may believe themselves to be free of such an outlook, but it is doubtful if this is actually so. The German writer who has most influenced modern academic thought on the subject gave a basic definition of holy war that required its aims to be purely religious, and insisted that such elements as political interests, territorial ambition and national honour should be excluded.[21] It is hard not to feel in this view the echoes of the German *Kulturkampf*, the struggle against clericalism in the young German national state that had taken place in the late nineteenth century; a book published in 1935 may also reflect the new stresses between church and state that were taking place in Germany under Hitler.

But holy war as it had been transmitted in cultural tradition to Muhammad had grown in a Semitic and Hebraic world in which such distinctions played no part. There had been no historical holy war to which they could have been applied at that time. The leaders of ancient holy wars, from the Egyptian Pharaohs to King David to Judas Maccabaeus, had all been motivated by political and territorial ambition, as well as by religion. That Muhammad proved no exception is not surprising. The problem is not to know whether political considerations weighed with him, but the extent to which they did.

Western judgements on the political aspect of Muhammad's career have in the past often questioned his sincerity, a sneer that goes back to the medieval legend of the 'three impostors' (Moses, Christ and Muhammad). There is no proof that Muhammad was ever anyone other than the holy person that his outward conduct proclaimed him to be. Without specifically denying this, it is common to suggest that, although he was a prophet, he was a prophet whose political aims overshadowed all others. Modern historians have talked about the aims of Muhammad as having been state formation and conquest.[22] But it is easy to import into our judgements ideas that have no proper application to earlier times and different cultures. The idea of state formation was entirely foreign to Muhammad, although the idea of conquest was not.

Muhammad had the finest possible political sense and ability, and may very well have foreseen that his work would lead to the creation of a great empire, but his life was directed towards what he understood as the furtherance of Allah's purpose revealed to him, and not primarily towards the achievement of what we would call a worldly kingdom. 'King' and 'kingdom' were indeed terms that were completely alien to and rejected by orthodox Muslims, and that remained so for a very long time after the Prophet's death. On the other hand, Muhammad certainly understood that the triumph of religion meant also the imposition of authority, and the extraction of economic benefit from non-Muslims as a recompense to the Muslims for the conduct of the holy war.

It was also in human terms very far from inevitable that the Muslim conquests, which now seem to have been so unavoidable, should have followed the death of the Prophet in the manner that they did. The American scholar Marshall Hodgson pointed out some years ago that neither the choice of a single new leader of Islam (the first caliph, Abu-Bakr), nor the decision to maintain the Islamic community with the same aims that Muhammad had defined for it, were in any way predetermined. Matters could have gone very differently, and the endemic feuding of Arabian society, which Muhammad had striven to end by his leadership and doctrine, could still have aborted what now appears to us to have been the nascent Empire.

But the tendency of the feuding tribes to pull Islam apart, which first briefly surfaced soon after Muhammad's death in what became known as the wars of the *ridda* (apostasy), was mastered by his successors, though only after the further damaging Islamic civil wars of the late seventh Christian century. Islamic unity was re-imposed, and the holy war remained the main occupation of the Islamic community. What had begun as an amalgam of Arabian tribes became the government of a great empire, and the leadership of a new civilization. The experience of Islamic holy war ceased to be confined to a corner of southern Arabia, and was extended to huge fertile and civilized areas of North Africa and the Near East, including the Indus valley and the Roman or ex-Roman lands from Syria to Morocco. Europe too was Islamicized at its Iberian extremity. The holy war made Islamic civilization into one of the great world civilizations, though from the Muslim point of view this was achieved only at the price of entering into a close relationship with the great cultures of Hellenism and Iran.

In the 'Umayyad palace of Qusayr 'Amra, fifty miles to the east of Amman in Jordan, there is a series of wall paintings that commemorate the victories of Caliph Walid I, and that have been given a date between 711 and 715 AD, some seventy-five years after the death of the Prophet. One wall shows the rulers of the world, among whom Walid felt himself, at the minimum, an equal. Among these are the Byzantine Emperor, the Emperor of Persia, the Visigothic King of Spain and the King of Ethiopia. Other figures may represent the Chinese Emperor or the Hindu King. Muhammad may not have sought a kingdom of this world, but his far from remote successors had found one. The Caliph Walid had succeeded, in his glory, to the powers of a humble and holy man, who during his life rarely ate either bread or meat.

That holy war meant the imposition of Islamic authority, but was not intended to convert all humanity to Islam by force, can be argued from the earlier historical development of the Islamic community. It seems improbable that such a doctrine was widely held at the time of the early caliphate, if only because of the clear implication of Muhammad's doctrines that people should only accept Islam freely in their consciences.[23] Muhammad came to warn, perhaps also to conquer, but not in a spiritual sense to compel.

During the early caliphate the Muslim government was drawing a huge income from unbelievers in the form of taxation that had been approved by Muhammad himself, and the Muslim rulers did not particularly want converts who were not useful soldiers or administrators. The demographic evidence for this period seems to indicate that the Muslim population of the Islamic Empire at the end of the first century after Muhammad's death was only about a tenth of the whole. Conversion did not save the property rights of the converted, which in theory became public Islamic property (*fay*) unless their submission to Islam had been effected under the terms of a treaty. The social inferiority of the first wave of non-Arabian converts, the *mawali*, who in order to convert had to become members of fictitious Arab tribes, shows how ambiguous the attitude to conversion to Islam was at that early time. Two centuries after the death of the Prophet had probably elapsed before Muslims were in a clear majority in the Islamic lands.[24]

By the early eighth century the Islamic Empire already extended from the Atlantic Ocean to the Indus Delta and beyond, and was comparable in size to the greatest empires of the past. It was no longer controlled by a relatively small number of Arabian tribes, and the attitude to conversion changed. When Islam started to be reduced by the legal theorists to a system, some theorists kept to the practice rather than to the purpose of holy war. For example, Malik ibn Anas (died 795 AD) dealt with *jihad* under the headings of the conduct required of the combatant, the division of the spoils, and martyrdom and its rewards. But the influential Muhammad ibn-Idris al-Shafi'i (767–820 AD) named the sending of enough Muslims on campaign to convert the idolaters to Islam as only the second purpose of holy war, the first being to defend Muslim territory. Holy war was regarded as a duty that fell primarily on the able-bodied, male Muslim as an individual (*fard kifaya*); only when the leader of the Islamic community had proclaimed it as a communal obligation did it become a common duty for all (*fard 'ayn*).

There is some doubt whether, in spite of the importance that Muhammad undoubtedly attached to it, holy war was one of the essential 'pillars' of the Islamic faith – a concept that, again, belonged to the later interpreters of Islam. Some Shi'a divines belonging to the sect of that name that emerged in the late seventh century considered holy war a 'pillar', and rather fewer

Sunnis (of the majority sect) did. The Shi'a came out of the first great schism in Islam, which arose from the refusal of the 'Umayyad family to accept the succession of 'Ali, the cousin of Muhammad and the husband of the Prophet's daughter, Fatimah.

Muhammad seems to have thought of piety, and the basic principles of moral action, as not immediately bringing to mind the holy war.[25] Righteousness lay not in formal conformity, but in belief in Allah and the last day, in angels, scripture and the prophets. The pious man gave his wealth to the needy, whether kinsmen or not; he observed proper worship, freed slaves, and paid the poor tax. His word was his bond, and he showed patience in adversity. These things could perhaps only be achieved by inner struggle, or by what later Muslim theologians sometimes called the higher and better holy war (the *jihad al-akbar*), but the metaphor of armed struggle was not necessary to their description, although it could quite legitimately be used.

The idea of struggle in the way of God is thus potentially a general one, that can be seen as having a primarily moral interpretation: it is not necessary to attach it to military action. That Muhammad could have seen it in this light seems probable: 'to strive for the cause of Allah with your wealth and your lives'[26] could be interpreted in a quite general way. At Mecca Muhammad received a revelation that he should 'strive with a great endeavour' to overcome disbelief in his mission, without there being any question of physical combat.[27] Particularly because the last major revelation about holy war occurred at the very end of Muhammad's life, in the 'farewell' sermon for the pilgrimage, many later Muslims were anxious to apply to it the doctrine of *naskh*, the principle of a Qur'anic verse that abrogates all earlier pronouncements in the Qur'an on the same subject. If accepted, this would have made aggressive, physical holy war the sole matter of *jihad*. But this application of the doctrine did not win general acceptance.

In one respect Muhammad's holy war followed a pattern like that of the Jewish Zealots. The struggle of a minority group against a majority seen as oppressors, from the Zealots to the Bolsheviks, has always led to the ferocious denunciation of apostates and dissenters. One of the charges brought by Muhammad against the Meccan unbelievers was that of violating their oaths. There has been however some hesitation in Islam to treat all failure to help fellow-Muslims against unbelievers as apostasy that should be visited with holy war. Apostasy means turning away from or abandoning Islam, and the penalty for such turning away on the part of responsible adult Muslims was generally agreed to be death. Many Muslim rebellions

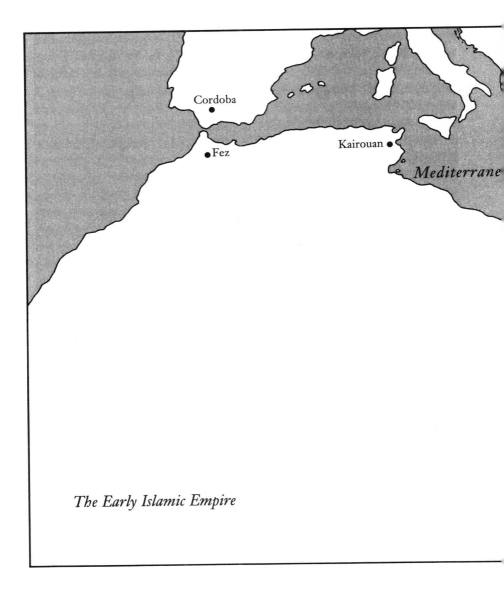

The Early Islamic Empire

against non-Muslims in the modern period have called for the killing of fellow-Muslims who oppose the rebels; the learned men (*'ulama*) have not always assented to this demand. The condemnation of the British writer Salman Rushdie, who made an imprudent use of the matter of the 'satanic verses', has arisen from this body of doctrine, whose legal effects have always been much disputed.

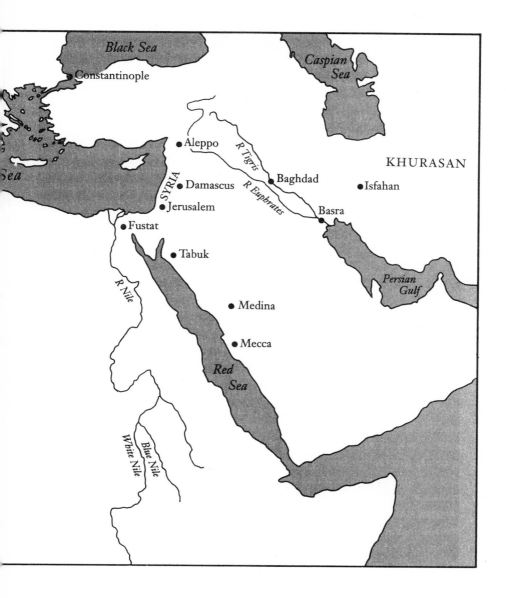

The war of the *ridda* (apostasy) that was fought with backsliding tribes soon after Muhammad's death was by definition a holy war against apostasy. But the opposing candidates for the caliphate in the contest that ended with the murder of 'Ali in 661 AD avoided making such charges against one another, and sought at least to appear to take account of the precept of Muhammad that Muslims in dispute should accept peacemaking.[28] 'Ali's

45

acceptance of arbitration in this quarrel led to the secession of the faction called Khariji, who charged him in effect with apostasy.

Subsequent Muslim rulers were for a long time careful on the whole to avoid throwing apostasy charges at one another when they went to war, although they were not unknown, and were made, for example, during the conflicts between the Sunni believers and the Fatimid caliphate of Cairo during the eleventh Christian century. However, other political errors came subsequently to be visited by holy war. Muhammad himself had condemned banditry and terrorism by depraved persons who 'made mischief' in the land,[29] and in later Islam action on this score was held to be a form of holy war. But rebellion against constituted authority could be viewed as a civil infringement (*bughat*) and not as a religious crime, and the suppression of such rebellion (which quite often amounted simply to a war between two Muslim states) was not holy war.[30]

Muhammad's political and religious doctrines, which had grown out of the problems of a tiny South Arabian religious group that turned itself into a middling-size theocratic government, occasioned a lot of logic-chopping when they had to be followed by big, imperialist Muslim states that disposed of the services of learned religious exegetes. The religious obligation of holy war had accompanied the huge military explosion of the seventh century, and had occasioned the growth of the great Muslim Empires. Once those empires were in place, their rulers could contemplate a much more supple and sophisticated approach to holy war than had been appropriate for the early caliphate.

When the *pax Islamica* extended over three or four continents the practice of permanent and continuous holy war was no longer acceptable to everyone, because it no longer furthered the interests of the huge and increasingly divided Islamic community. By the beginning of the second century of Islam one or two scholars were already saying that holy war was obligatory for Muslims only in order to defend their community against aggression. They no longer wanted it as a doctrine of perpetual attack. It is significant that a *hadith*, or a reported saying of the Prophet, claimed he had said that the holy war would eventually end in all countries except the one in the west called Ifriqiya (North Africa). It is unlikely that Muhammad ever said anything of the kind, but the tradition may point to the people who recorded it as perhaps having thought that the holy war of the whole Islamic community had to come to an end at some point.

One scholar has claimed that permanent Islamic holy war became obsolete, and that it shifted from an idea of eternally active war to one of dormant war, that could be revived by the head of Islam whenever he deemed it necessary.[31] It is very doubtful if this is the best way to describe what happened. It is true that for very long periods Islamic states did not commit all their resources to great holy wars that could be more costly than they could afford, either politically or militarily. The means by which this was achieved was to make truces with the more important unbelieving states. But this did not stop the Islamic powers from countenancing semi-permanent *ghazi* wars carried out by Islamic raiders on their borders with unbelievers.

Medieval Islamic theologians arrived at a doctrine of territorial definition that also, like the idea of Islamic holy war, gave the appearance of a condition of permanent war with unbelievers. The *dar al-Islam* in which Muslim law runs is a domain of peace; the territory controlled by unbelievers is the *dar al-harb*, the abode of war. But this doctrine was itself a territory of legal fictions. From a very early stage indeed there were truces with the unbelieving states: authority for the conclusion of such truces came from Muhammad's own career. There were also, from the time of the early formation of the Islamic domination, trade agreements with peoples outside Islam. There grew up a body of law that protected non-Muslims in Islamic countries, predominantly merchants, who had no permanent residence there.

The relations of Christian states with the Islamic Empires were influenced by factors that antedated the Empires. Even during the lifetime of Muhammad they had been marked by some ambiguity. Christian Arab tribes were to be found in North and South Arabia, and there were some Christians not too far from Mecca. The Ethiopian Christians were still a factor in South Arabian politics, but Christian influence was not so powerful in the Hejaz as that of the Jewish tribes. The main theological polemic of the first generation of Islam was with Judaism, and Christians seem to have incurred less hostility from the Prophet than Jews. Muhammad was willing to reach agreements with Christian tribes that respected their autonomy. He made, for example, a treaty with the Christians of Najran, whose massacre by the Jewish King of Himyar is perhaps remembered in the Qur'an.[32] This treaty was honoured after Muhammad's death, although only for three or four decades, until the Christians of Najran were eventually ordered by the Caliph 'Umar to leave the Arabian peninsula.

However, Muhammad's attitude to the Christians was deeply marked by

his pain that they refused to believe his revelations, although, as he interpreted Christian writings, his own apostolate was foreshadowed there. He
told Muslims not to take Jews or Christians as their helpers, seeing them
as a threat to Muslim obedience, and fearing that they would inflict upon
the believers the mockery that was one of his overriding terrors: 'From
envy they would turn you back to unbelief.'[33] In the last holy war expedition
to Tabuk, shortly before his death, Muhammad had not hesitated to charge
Christians with the total rejection of Allah, in spite of his having acknowledged both implicitly and explicitly the truth of some of their scriptures.

Nevertheless, the 'scriptuary' communities of Christians and Jews were
distinguished by Muslims from those who knew nothing of the commands
of Allah, and both were accorded a special, though still inferior, status in
the new Islamic Empires. Only six years after the death of Muhammad,
the Muslim armies entered Jerusalem, which until then had been part of
the east Roman Empire. The Caliph 'Umar treated Jerusalem with veneration as a holy city; he granted a treaty to the Christians there, like that
already granted to those of Damascus, which guaranteed the persons, property, churches and crosses of the Christians. They were to be taxed, but
not molested for their religion. There was no similar treaty for the Jews,
since Jerusalem had until that point been controlled by a Christian government. But the degree of toleration due to the Jews as a people that had
possessed the scriptures, even if they failed to follow the Qur'an of Muhammad, was extended throughout the lands of the Islamic conquests.

The cultural influence of the ancient Byzantine Empire over the Muslim
Empire that succeeded it in the lands of the Fertile Crescent was decisive.
Not only in Damascus in the early caliphate, but also in Baghdad in the
eighth and ninth centuries, Greek texts were available to Islamic scholars.
There were other important intellectual influences on the Islamic Empires,
such as those from India, but the central importance of Christian channels
made it possible for the British scholar Albert Hourani to say that the early
intellectual development of Islam took place in a Christian environment.[34]

With the Byzantine Empire of Constantinople the early Islamic Empire
developed a special relationship of spoliation and emulation. Many of the
best administrators of the early caliphate were taken from the former Byzantine service, and the structure of the new Empire was very much influenced
by that of the old one. The caliphate proved willing to sign peace treaties
with the Greeks, even when, as occurred in 661 and 678, the treaties
required the Muslims to pay an annual money tribute.

But, having totally subdued the great Persian Empire, the early caliphs put the defeat of the Byzantine Empire at the very top of their objectives. The means chosen was quite new to Arab power: a seaborne invasion of the Byzantine capital. In these attacks the traditional *ghazi* border warfare was abandoned in favour of a huge, imperial-type military and naval enterprise that belonged to the offensive traditions of the great Eastern empires, and not to the raiding operations of the Arabs.

In 669, from 673 to 677, and in the next generation again, from 717 to 718, huge Muslim fleets were despatched to the Straits to blockade Constantinople in preparation for a final assault. On all these occasions the Byzantines resisted skilfully and with eventual success, but in 673–77 and 717–18 the fighting was desperate. 'Greek fire' was an element in Byzantine success, but was far from being the decisive one. On both occasions the Arab investment of the city was in the end broken, and the great Muslim fleets were dispersed by storm or battle.

It is quite probable that the early caliphs, and particularly the 'Umayyads after the accession of Mu'awiyah in 661, saw their empire as the natural successor to East Rome. Their coinage, administrative system and state symbolism resembled the Byzantine ones. The British scholar H.A.R. Gibb thought that the 'Umayyads of this period were grooming themselves to succeed Byzantium.[35]

The Byzantines did not have universally hostile relations with the Islamic caliphate. When the Caliph Walid demolished the Mosque of the Prophet in Medina in order to rebuild it (707–9), the Byzantine emperor sent men, money and materials for its reconstruction. Greek and Coptic architects from Syria and Egypt built the mosque of cut stone with marble and mosaic patterns. The Dome of the Rock at Jerusalem and the 'Umayyad Mosque of al-Walid at Damascus reflect something like a partial cultural fusion between Byzantium and Islam in the field of the arts. The frescoes of the 'Umayyad palace at Qusayr 'Amrar are another aspect of the same phenomenon. The Western architects who work for Islamic employers today in Arabia and the Gulf have their medieval antecedents.

The last siege of Byzantium in 717–18 was a turning point for both empires. Both in Byzantium and in the 'Umayyad court there was an apocalyptic anticipation of the end of worldly history and the onset of a new age. In Byzantium a new imperial leadership emerged under Leo the Isaurian, the 'Arab-minded one', who grew up in Asia Minor in the midst of the frontier wars against the Muslims, and who imposed a new Greek Orthodox puritanism of 'Iconoclasm' that avoided the use of images in the same manner as Islam had done before Byzantine culture had influenced its elites.

On the 'Umayyad side the failure of the siege in 718 led to a turning away from Greek political and cultural models that was in some ways temporary, in others permanent. Although the last great siege of Constantinople had in one respect represented the material climax of Islamic holy war, in another it differed greatly in aims and methods from the holy wars of the preceding century. When the Ottomans eventually took Constantinople in 1453, Byzantium retained only a wisp of its ancient power and greatness, and its empire had virtually ceased to exist. The Ottoman Sultan, Muhammad the Conqueror, was not oppressed by the cultural burden of the Rome he had conquered: he could take what he pleased and reject what he pleased. Had Constantinople fallen to Islam eight and half centuries earlier, within a century of the Prophet Muhammad's death, the case would have been very different.

The Caliph 'Umar II (717–20) brusquely returned to orthodox Islamic practice, and abandoned much of the Hellenized superstructure of 'Umayyad life and government; he paid particular attention to cultural Arabization. Even before the 'Umayyad dynasty ended at the hands of the usurping 'Abbasids in 750, the Islamic polity was already turning away from the Medina–Damascus axis, and facing east.

Like many other things in Islam, the doctrine of holy war began, with the second Islamic century, to reflect the strains between the widely separated regions and cultures that now constituted the Islamic community. On the boundaries of Islam, which encompassed huge disputed zones, there was permanent military confrontation, and service in the holy war was glorified and venerated. In the central areas, where Islam had long ago made its military conquests, people sometimes disparaged the frontier warriors, who were seldom Arabs, and who could even be thought of as mere foreign mercenaries anxious for booty. Islamic culture in the rich and usually peaceful world of the great cities was already very different from the fighting ethos of the frontiers. When there was war in the great Islamic centres of Arabia, Iraq or southern Syria, it was usually between Muslims, and could only very exceptionally be classified as holy war.

A phenomenon peculiar to the frontier wars was the *ribat*. This was a word that in the Qur'an is used to mean assembling cavalry mounts before gathering to meet the enemy, but that in the frontier wars gradually came to have the sense of centres for the reception and logistic support of volunteer troops. These troops were usually termed *ghuzan* or frontier raiders, a term that went back to the earliest days of Islam and to the wars of Muhammad with the unbelievers. In the cities it was possible for learned men to use the same technique of moral equivalence with *ribat* that they used with *jihad*, and to say that scrupulous piety is the true *ribat*. On the frontiers this kind of play on words must have seemed almost frivolous.

The Islamic martyr (*shahid*) was one who died in the fulfilment of his duty in the way of Allah, and the word's use to describe a casualty of battle was perfectly familiar in later Islam: 'The way to Paradise is lit by the flash of the swords!' 'Victory belongs to God: the believer must fight!' On the last day the martyr enters Paradise without examination of his other deeds on earth. Popular custom added to the force of learned tradition. The body of the *shahid* is buried unwashed, in his bloody and sacred wounds. Before he leaves for battle he perfumes himself so that the angels may receive him after his death – the Muslim suicide bombers of today perform the ritual ablutions, and are adorned with henna, kohl and perfume before they leave on their final mission.

However, men could struggle in the way of Allah by other means than in waging war, and many Muslim learned persons used the word martyr (just as they used the word *jihad*) in a purely moral sense. It was claimed, for example, that passionate devotion to holy study which terminated in death could make such a student a 'martyr': perhaps this is an understandable exaggeration for medieval Islamic scholars, who spent laborious lives in the study of the holy texts, to make. The Muslim victims of plague and flood have been accounted martyrs in the same way. It was also said that he who goes morning and evening to the mosque without ulterior motive has the same status as a fighter in the holy war, a *mujahid*. This kind of moral metaphor led some people in the twentieth century to claim the status of *mujahid* for certain distinguished Islamic publicists.

The early Islamic frontiers attracted a big floating population of warriors, many of them recent converts to Islam, and of volunteers of all sorts for the holy war. Among these were scholars who took the precepts of holy war so seriously that they saw the prosecution of war with the unbeliever as their most urgent religious duty. These were scholar-soldiers of a sort that never became familiar in a Christian version in the West, even at the height of the crusading movement. It is not surprising that in this period a saying was attributed to Muhammad that 'the monasticism of Islam is the *jihad*'.

The scholar-warriors moved easily from one end of the Muslim world to another. Asad ibn al-Furat was a native of Khurasan, a well-known theologian who moved to North Africa and became qadi of Kairouan and vizier under the third Aghlabid ruler of Tunisia. In 827 he led the biggest Muslim expedition ever mounted against Byzantine Sicily, which led eventually to the fall of the island, although the conquest took until the end of the tenth century to complete. Asad ibn al-Furat accepted this command at the age of seventy years, and did not live to see even the fall of Palermo in 831, though he died of plague and not of old age. He caused to be executed those members of his army who after the first victories wanted to give up the expedition and return to North Africa with their booty. And he welcomed from all over the Mediterranean volunteer fighters (*mujahidin*) who joined the Aghlabid forces in Sicily, attracted by piety or the desire for loot.

Asad ibn-al Furat went to the holy war as vizier and on the command of the emir. But many Islamic scholar-soldiers went to the frontier wars entirely independently, and there made names as fighters, or became martyrs by their death in battle. Khurasan, the province from which the main military strength of the early 'Abbasid caliphs was drawn, was the area where the *ribat* multiplied most, and where enormous numbers of volunteers for the holy war gathered on the frontiers. The first Muslim treatise on the *jihad* was written by a Khurasanian scholar-ascetic and warrior-theologian, 'Abdullah ben al-Mubarak (died 797 AD).

By the ninth century the Islamic Empires were already beginning to experience problems with the mobilization of manpower, not only for military but for many other purposes. At that time the Turkish tribes constituted the biggest reserve of human resources in central and western Asia. Their conversion, and their employment in the Islamic armies, brought about long-term changes in the way power was distributed under the caliphate. Turkish military slaves were used in the armies of the dynasty, but free Turkish tribes were of great importance in the defence of the Islamic frontiers. From this point onwards the caliphs were expanding a policy of recruitment of Turkish soldiers in central Asia that was to change the shape of Islam, and that was also to make sure that the *ghazi* war continued for another millennium.

By the mid-ninth century there was an immense number of *ribat* in Khurasan and Transoxiana, manned partly by Turkish tribesmen and partly by volunteers for the holy war. By this time *ribat* was not only a military term for logistic support, but often a word for a small fortress. A way of life grew up on the frontiers that was to persist for centuries, based on the conversion of Turkish tribes to Islam, and on their participation in the *ghazi* war of the frontiers. A similar system grew up in North Africa, another area where the *ribat* acquired great military importance: an example was the fortification of the Tunisian port of Monastir.

There were conflicts of interest between the frontier warriors and the classes settled in the heartlands of Islam, who had direct access to power by approaching the caliphs and governors to obtain grants and privileges from them. In the time of the first great conquests of Islam the early caliphs had refused to allow the holy war warriors to expect to benefit directly from the distribution of their conquests; they had been required to allow the caliphs to decide on the distribution of revenues. Two and three centuries later the *ghazi* warriors were again criticizing the way in which permanent grants were being made to a new privileged class, while there was no policy to endow the holy war warriors.

However, it was impossible to stop the frontier warriors from taking substantial shares of booty, and to the recently converted Turkish tribes this became a way of life. In the Central Asian provinces in the ninth and tenth Christian centuries the *ghazi* warriors began to organize themselves into guilds which dominated the societies of those areas, and which could deteriorate into gangs that exploited the neighbourhoods. From such guilds revolts against the caliphal government could arise, and guild leaders occasionally founded small dynasties.

The *ribat* was not only a military centre: it also attracted holy men, and came to have in some places an entirely religious importance. Religious sites connected with a *ribat* that had been a centre of the activity of holy persons became places of pilgrimage. Religious guilds grew up around them, and in their turn conferred power upon their leaders. The frontier settlements came to be centres for Sufis, who were in the first place mystics who speculated on how God created man, and how man could return to God. However, on the frontier Sufism had its practical and military side, and power often devolved upon the local dynasties from whose families the religious leaders had been drawn.

There was also a utilitarian way of looking at the holy war that was bound to be widely followed, no matter what the theorists of holy war declared about its purpose. In the eleventh Christian century, at a time when the caliphal powers had suffered from something approaching total breakdown, the Turkish tribes were in virtually complete control of huge areas of Iran and of Central and Western Asia. One of the junior leaders of the Seljuk Turks, with great lands in south-western Iran, who knew that a band of Oghuz *ghazi* warriors was threatening his domains, told them: 'My territory is not extensive enough to support you or provide for your

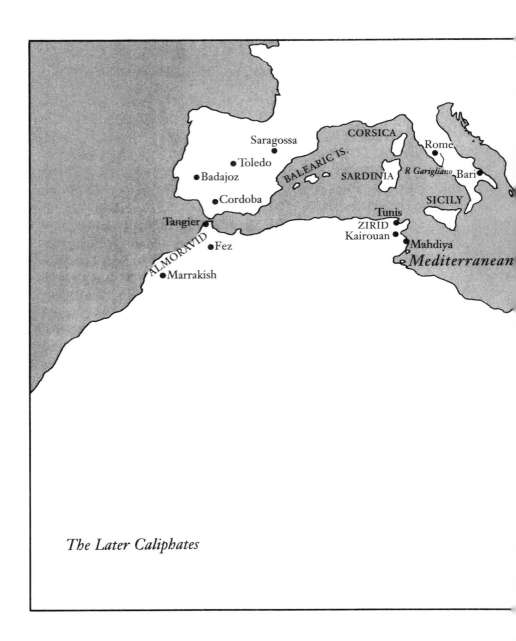

The Later Caliphates

needs. The most sensible thing for you to do is to attack Roum [the Byzantine province of Trebizond], and fight in the way of Allah, and gain booty. I will follow after you, and assist you.'[36]

*   *   *

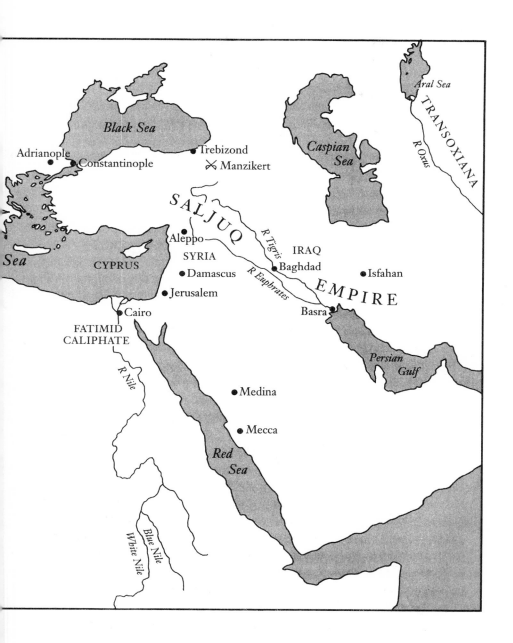

For centuries after the death of Muhammad there was no time, even when the great powers of Byzantium and the caliphate prosecuted no major wars with one another, at which the frontiers of Islam, and huge tracts of the Mediterranean, were not criss-crossed by the belligerent turmoil of the holy war. In Asia Minor on the Byzantine side of the frontier there grew up a Greek class of frontier warriors, the *akritai*, whose lives and military activity were very similar to those of the Muslim *ghazi* warriors. In the later Middle Ages, on both sides of the frontier there gradually appeared a heroic literature based on folk tales of the frontier warriors, Muslim on one side and Christian on the other.

The decay of East Rome in the western and central Mediterranean, which became acute in the eighth and ninth centuries, stimulated the growth of a seaborne holy war. Not only Sicily, but the other Christian islands of Sardinia and Corsica, and great tracts of the Italian and Adriatic coasts, became the targets of armed seaborne raids that were launched from many points of the central and eastern Muslim Mediterranean. The holy war of the Qur'an envisaged cavalry as the main fighting arm, and the experiences of the great caliphs in launching big seaborne invasions had not all been happy. But the occupation of the North African coasts and of numerous Aegean islands, and particularly the temporary occupation of Crete by Spanish emigrant Muslims, brought trained seaborne fighters into the holy war over a huge area of the Mediterranean, from Tangier to the coasts of Asia Minor.

The rise of a new dominion of the Franks in western Europe, and the coronation in Rome in 800 of Charlemagne, their greatest ruler, as Emperor, did little to protect the Western Christians from continued Muslim attack. Even the bishops of Rome, who were the chief bishops of the Frankish Empire, could not be effectively defended. In 846 a fleet of the same size as that despatched against Sicily twenty years earlier was sent from North Africa to attack Rome, the religious capital of the West. Rome was at this time a small provincial city, whose population was tiny and whose defences were pathetically inadequate compared to those of the Eastern capital of Byzantium. A Muslim attack on Rome lacked all the resonance and éclat of the great siege of Byzantium 130 years earlier: the ninth-century clash was only a raid carried out by a minor Muslim dynasty against a Christian bishop. But for all that, it had a certain significance.

A seaborne force of over ten thousand troops, including at least five hundred cavalry, overpowered the pope's coastal defences at Ostia. The Romans had placed a force of Western pilgrims, including a number of Anglo-Saxons, in the way of the invaders: they were swiftly overcome and massacred. The Muslims pressed on down the Via Aurelia and found themselves outside the great Church of St Peter, which at that time lay outside the walls of Rome. The treasures of the church, which we know from papal records to have been beyond description magnificent, were looted, and the tomb and monument under the Confession of St Peter, the greatest and holiest shrine of Western Christendom, were, according to the papal archaeologists who surveyed the site in the late 1940s, deliberately smashed.

The 846 raid on Rome was part of a pattern of Muslim attack that was to harass the Italian coasts for a further century. Bari, on the Adriatic, was occupied, and became for a time a Muslim emirate. The rich monasteries that the Frankish overlords had set up and endowed in central Italy were spoiled and plundered by Muslim troops with the same fury as St Peter's. The monasteries of Subiaco and of Monte Cassino, founded by St Benedict, were sacked. Modern archaeologists found the great decorated doors of the huge monastery of San Vincenzo al Volturno in south Italy, still embedded into the ground where the Muslim troops broke them down and trampled them as they entered to sack the church.

Other Arab bases were set up in central Italy and on the coast of southern Francia: a great Muslim raiding centre was placed at the mouth of the River Garigliano – Pope John X himself, in defiance of all prohibition against priests shedding blood, led the final attack on it in 915. These ninth- and tenth-century raids were important not for their military or political significance, which was minor, but for the way in which they entered the Western Christian tradition. The folk memory of the Sack of Rome of 846, for example, was preserved in the *chansons de gestes* of later generations, and was still alive at the time of the crusades.

The other great scene of conflict between Muslim and Christian in the West, even more important in literary tradition and folk memory, and far more important for its cultural and demographic effects, was the Iberian peninsula. In Spain the holy war was pursued with energy by the 'Umayyad dynasty, some little time after the eastern 'Abbasid caliphate had slid into decline. 'Abd al-Rahman III (ruled 912–61) pressed the Christian rulers of northern Spain hard. Even after the 'Umayyad caliphal dynasty had lost its effective power, the promoted vizier who assumed the title al-Hajib al-Mansur (to the Spaniards 'Almanzor', ruled 981–1002) continued to take the Muslim holy war into the heart of what remained of Christian Spain.

As the 'Abbasid caliphate slid further into decline, and other, competing imamates were set up elsewhere, there was an acute difficulty in finding a convincing way to legitimize the regimes that actually ruled. In the tenth and eleventh Christian centuries the old Islamic Empires fragmented, and new rulers, often called sultans ('the holders of power'), seized various portions of the Islamic territories. Particularly when they had difficulty in getting the caliphs to recognize their rule, the new dynasties found the prosecution of the holy war one of the best means of convincing Muslims that their rule was rightful.

The Hamdanids of Aleppo were led some way in this direction by Sayf al-Dawla (ruled 944–67), who fought the Byzantines in Asia Minor and northern Syria, at first with some success, although this holy war brought about the fall of his capital, Aleppo, to the Greeks. On a far larger scale the Turkish Ghaznavid dynasty in Iran took the holy war on a huge scale into northern India. Mahmud of Ghazna (998–1030) sought out and received the epithet of *ghazi*, and his conquests went as far as Punjab and Sind. It is doubtful whether his wars had a deeply religious tinge in their execution; what mattered to him was the prestige of the holy warrior. And as the various Turkish dynasties gradually took over much of the political leadership of eastern Islam in the eleventh Christian century, they too very frequently sought the label of Islamic legitimacy that the holy war conferred. Similar things were happening in the west of Islam, in North Africa and Spain (Andalus).

Thus by the mid-eleventh Christian century the holy war was an ineradicable characteristic of Islamic life, pursued in varying ways and with varying degrees of insistence and piety over the interminable stretches of the Islamic boundaries, both by land and by sea. There were parts of the Islamic world where it was neglected: the further from the frontiers with unbelievers, the more likely this was to be so. It was often pursued in part for reasons of political convenience, either to give legitimacy to a regime or to bring pressure on a Muslim power to conform with the military policy of another. Or it could on some critical occasions be deliberately eschewed: a historian of the campaign of the Seljuk Sultan, Alp Arslan, against the Byzantine Emperor Romanus, that ended in 1071 with the great Muslim victory of Manzikert which destroyed a great part of Byzantine power in Asia Minor, has emphasized that this was not a holy war, and that there was therefore no religious duty incumbent upon the victor to pursue the Byzantine enemy to destruction.[37] But this takes nothing from the universal way in which the Muslim world recognized the *jihad*.

CHAPTER FOUR

Christianity and War

IN THE MOMENT of the Christian triumph in the fourth-century Roman Empire, Eusebius the Bishop of Caeserea, the friend and confidant of the Emperor Constantine, composed a history of the church. He wrote that other historians had confined themselves to the recording of victories in war and triumph over enemies, of the exploits of commanders and the heroism of their men, stained with the blood of the thousands they had slaughtered for the sake of children and country and possessions. But it was peaceful wars, fought for the very peace of the soul, and men who in such wars had fought manfully for truth rather than for country, for true religion rather than for their dear ones, that Eusebius's history of God's Empire would record for posterity, and not the patriotic wars and warriors of the past.[1]

Eusebius was the prototype of the Christian bishop who fawns upon power, writing at the moment that power had offered itself to his church. His peaceful rhetoric did not lead him to criticize a regime that was militaristic to its army sandals, and he recorded with joy the victories of the armies of Constantine over the heathen co-emperors. He showed no sign of awareness that, by embracing the Empire that had for so long spurned it, the Christian church was bound to connive with imperial aims and methods. In this way the church became a consenting party to war, even if it persisted in its formal rejection of bloodshed. This is not surprising, because an important element in Constantine's move towards Christianity had been its supposed promise of victory in battle.

In 312 AD Constantine was about to fight a final battle, after a long civil war, with his rival Maxentius. Both he and his soldiers saw in the noonday sun (which had hitherto been his protecting deity) something that appeared to resemble the sign of the cross. As he waited just outside Rome in his camp on the Via Flaminia, Constantine dreamed that he should paint on the shields of his soldiers a sign which would bring victory. This sign was not the cross, but the Greek letter *chi*, combined with *rho*, a combination which had not hitherto been used by the Christians, though it could be understood as '*chrestos*' and so '*Christos*'. It was a victory motto of the kind that could equally well have been offered by soothsayers, and if it was a sign of holy battle, it was a sign of a kind that characteristically in the past had been assumed for a pagan holy battle. Constantine had the sign inscribed on his own helmet and on the shields of his inner bodyguard. He won an overwhelming victory on the next day at the battle of the Milvian Bridge, and as uncontested Western Emperor he then proceeded to carry out an increasingly pro-Christian policy.

The *chi-rho* motto seems, then, to have been a hastily adopted magical sign, that Constantine hoped would bring good fortune to his army. Naturally, it was not discussed in this way at the time. Imperial panegyrists talked about Constantine having been helped at the Milvian Bridge by his dead father Constantius (who quite certainly had been no Christian) and an army of heavenly powers. Eusebius suggested that Constantine had entered Rome as a Christian conqueror after the battle of 312, but this also was untrue: on that occasion the Emperor had accepted an old-style Roman pagan triumph, and an old-style triumphal arch, lacking any Christian reference, which still exists. Eusebius nevertheless wrote, using the ancient language of holy war, that at the Milvian Bridge God had 'triumphed gloriously': Maxentius and his army, he said, had been thrown into the sea (or in their case into the Tiber), like the army of Pharaoh.

There were other political motives in Constantine's Christian policy than a dubious victory motto. But the sign carried at the Milvian Bridge was later elaborated into an unambiguously Christian imperial battle standard, a gold cross surrounded by a wreath that enclosed the *chi-rho* sign and supported an embroidered family portrait of Constantine and his sons (the *labarum*). This was carried in 324 at the battle at Adrianople that destroyed the last opposing Augustus, Licinius. One or two modern writers have talked loosely about a crusade, and Eusebius subsequently described Licinius as 'God's enemy', but it is hard to see the campaign of 324 as a holy war, any more than the war of 312 had been.

However, Roman militarism did not triumph over Christian doctrine in every respect. The new Christian Roman establishment was in difficulty when asked to condone the conduct of war, because committing bloodshed was deemed to be a sin, for which penance had to be done. To this extent the church kept faith with its past, and continued to do so for several centuries, although in the era of the crusades the obligation of penance for any military homicide (and not merely that committed in holy war) was to cease. But the Christian church became in the Constantinian era a state church that had to accept burdens of political responsibility. The morality of warfare had been the object of much discussion in pagan terms during the pagan Empire, and after Constantine the debate about just and unjust wars was revived in a new, Christian context.

St Augustine (Bishop of Hippo, 396–430) said that just wars were only so if they sought to right a wrong received, and if the aggressor had failed to restore or make amends. This judgement has been influential down to our own times. But, he added, the war is undoubtedly just that is commanded by God; Augustine particularly cited the divine command to Joshua to destroy the city of Ai. The qualification did not at once open the door to Christian holy war. Augustine's view was that men could not presume to scrutinize the divine providence that permitted war, which may be either a benefit or an evil.[2] The allowance of divinely commanded war meant, however, that Augustine was able to sanction armed action against Christian dissidents, such as the North African Donatists.

Constantine's drift towards Christianity, and his setting up of a new eastern capital at Constantinople, were a recognition of the superior importance of the eastern half of the Roman Empire, the area in which the demographic and economic balance was beginning to tip to the disadvantage of the West. His decisive move towards the adoption of an Eastern sect as the new state religion, although there were precedents in the policies of earlier rulers that pointed in the same direction, threatened the ancient ideology that lay behind the Roman state. But he must have known or guessed that the Christians were too deeply a part of the Romano-Hellenistic world to want to threaten its basis.

Christianity was not the first religion from the Near East to secure official recognition from the Roman state. The syncretism of earlier Roman generations had already accepted many oriental religions, and Romano-Hellenistic intellectuals had already examined and categorized them. Constantine would not have known of the existence of Bishop Eusebius (who has been maliciously described as his minister for propaganda) until a late stage in his reign. But he must in a sense have anticipated the existence of a complacent Christian priesthood when he started to move politically towards Christianity.

With Augustine the Greek and Latin tradition of just war entered the mainstream Latin Christian way of thought. It was deeply different from the Hebrew ideas of holy war. The concept of just war, which had influenced earlier Christian bishops than Augustine, was anchored in Stoic philosophy and in late Roman Law. It allowed that war could be waged to deter or punish wrongdoers, and the Christians of the fourth and fifth centuries argued that the declaration of a just war could set aside the precepts of Jesus about turning the other cheek to the perpetrators of injustice. But Hebrew holy war was still deeply rooted in the Christian scriptures, and its ambiguous legacy was not refused by the Christian theologians, even if for a long time they declined to accept the kind of armed struggle undertaken by the Zealots and rejected by Christ.

Wars with unbelieving peoples were the concern of the Constantinian monarchy from the moment it came into existence. But these were a continuation of the wars with barbarians that the Roman Empire had always waged; such wars were not treated as holy wars. This remained true in the eastern Roman Empire, at least until the late tenth century. In the west the rapid conversion of barbarian peoples to Christianity meant that in so far as there was religious conflict with them, it was concerned with the variety of Christianity that they had adopted. One such schism had been due to the supposedly heretical doctrine of Arius, who had asserted the created nature of the second person of the Trinity, and on this account had been condemned by both the Eastern and Western churches. Wars between Catholics and Arians could thenceforth have a religious tinge. When the first Catholic King of Franks, Clovis, made war against the Arian Goths, according to the Catholic Bishop Gregory of Tours he was led by a divinely summoned pillar of fire to the decisive conflict with the Arians near Poitiers. But no one at this time ever adopted the full Old Testament panoply of holy war, whether they were in conflict with pagans or with Christian dissidents.

The western empire gave place to barbarian kingdoms, but the basic organization of society remained, as it had been, military. The place of Christian bishops in society was subtly changing. Pope Gregory the Great (590–604), who could still fairly be called a Roman bishop, used the old language of the Christian intercessor and negotiator with the barbarians when he spoke of the Pope's role with the savage Lombard tribes in Roman Italy: 'Only the power of God and of the prince of the apostles, transmitted through the medium of his vicar the Roman pontiff, modifies and tempers the ferocity of the neighbouring enemies . . . those whom armed force fails to make humble, bend before pontifical power and persuasion.'[3]

The Germanic tribes of the period before the great migrations that took them within the Roman frontiers had in one sense worshipped war. The representations of animals such as bears and bulls that were carried in front of the barbarian armies were war gods: often the same animals were taken as lineage patrons by the great warrior-nobles. The battle standards borne in front of the barbarian kings as they led the tribes to war had an equally religious meaning. The kings were not strictly priests of the war gods, but their relationship to them was close. The kings were often 'god-born', as, for example, the Anglo-Saxon monarchs were, and so in a sense the heirs of the war gods.

This divine capacity for war clung to the barbarian tribal leaders even after they became Christian kings. Semi-magical powers adhered to the king's mystical body, which was entitled not only to respect but to worship on the part of his kingdom. In this very ancient world, whose continued shadowy existence in the royal lineages was only half-acknowledged in the medieval Christian kingdoms, there were no particular holy wars, but all war was, in a pagan, religious sense, holy. The distant recollection of these traditions tragically reappeared on the surface of European life in the German National Socialist ideology of the present century.

As barbarian tribal leaders turned themselves into Christian kings there were further changes in the Western clerical attitude to war. The relationship between the Christian clergy and the barbarian warriors was close, yet profoundly uneasy. There was a fundamental split between them. The medieval noble devoted his life to aggression and bloodshed: no one can read the history of the Merovingian princes as related by Bishop Gregory of Tours without marvelling at the calm, ironic accounts of royal butchery, theft, betrayal and torture, from a clerical observer who lived in a world as different from the Merovings culturally as it was morally.

Yet the clergy in some respects, and especially through such ceremonies as royal coronations, legitimized the rule of the barbarian kings. Priests and warriors lived apart, but the connivance of one class with the other lay at the foundations of this society. Incorporating the church into the gift-giving society of the barbarian princes made it immensely rich. The great churchmen were the ministers and civil servants of this society; their ceremonies and religious communities immortalized and honoured the great noble lineages.

The barbarian kings, inevitably, became warriors for Christ. Bede recounts how the Anglo-Saxon King Oswald set up a wooden cross (that subsequently worked miracles for believers) before his victory over the pagans at Heavenfield. In the Frankish kingdom the priests blessed the swords of the army in a solemn mass that was celebrated before it left for war. The wars of the barbarian kings, particularly those of the Frankish Charlemagne (King from 768; Western Emperor 800–14), were sometimes wars of conquest aimed at the conversion of the pagans, and forms of prayer were authorized which asked for divine blessing on the army that was to fight the pagan peoples.

Charlemagne said that prayer for the success of the Frankish armies was one of the two main duties of Pope Leo III, whom he protected, and who in due course crowned him emperor. When a pope crowned an emperor, as they did from 800 onwards, he handed him the sword of rule. This symbolism was not empty. The idea of the monarch as defender of the church, bound to use the sword on its behalf, affected not only the kingdom and the empire, but the church, which tacitly acknowledged the legitimacy of such a war.

The cultural and religious colonization that went with the Frankish armies was especially evident in the subjugation of the Saxons. Charle-magne's court historians said the Saxons had previously agreed to accept Christianity, and then broke their word. It is certainly true that after the ferocious Saxon wars of the late eighth century the Saxons were compelled to accept Christianity, and that Charlemagne imposed heavy penalties upon Saxons who subsequently failed to have their infants baptized within the year. Civilization had finally triumphed, as an impeccably liberal historian of the last generation observed.[4]

The barbarian nobles became more and more deeply implicated in the governance of a church that came ever closer to reflecting their interests and prejudices, and the attitude of the Western Latin church to war underwent a long and gradual transformation. The process can be followed in the history of the Roman bishops. Pope Leo IV (847–55), who was elected immediately after the Muslim Sack of Rome in 846, became in effect a military leader, the fortifier of his own church of St Peter and the rebuilder of the walls of Rome, and an organizer if not a leader of armies. He thanked God for sending from his treasure the winds that blew the Neapolitan fleet towards the destruction of the Muslim navy. And in appealing to the emperor for armies to fight the Arab marauders, he promised the Frankish forces that whoever died in this war would not be denied entry into the kingdom of heaven.

So the chief bishop of the Western Christian church at last made the same promise that Muhammad had made to his troops before the campaign of Tabuk. It was not a law-giving promise that was known and acted upon all over the Latin Christian world: papal letters did not at that time command general acceptance as church law in the way that they were to do centuries later. It is rather an indication of the general tendency of ninth-century churchmen to accept their role as propagandists and mobilizers of opinion inside the Frankish Empire, and also of the growing consent given by churchmen to their playing a more active role in a military society.

Yet the popes remained for a time faithful to the precept that a bishop should not take up arms. A generation after Leo IV Pope John VIII (872– 82), a by no means pusillanimous figure, protested against the use of the bishops of south Francia to organize defences against Arab attack. The soldiers of Christ, he wrote to the emperor, were to serve him alone, and to leave the business of war to laymen. Though he passionately appealed to the emperor for Christian troops to fight the Arabs and the Vikings, John was reduced to buying off the Arab raiders – it is interesting that holy war etiquette cannot have stopped them from accepting the bribe. John also made similar promises of heavenly rewards to those who died in battle against the Muslims as had been made earlier by Leo IV. John referred to such war dead as 'martyrs'.

The inexorable pressure of the times was to force the bishops, most of whom came from the great noble families, into assuming the leadership of the armies for which they paid. Pope John X (914–28) accepted the hege- mony of the great Roman family of Theophylact over the papacy, and himself fought at the battle with the Muslims for the control of the mouth of the Garigliano river in 915. In the second half of the tenth century the Emperor Otto the Great forced the German bishops to become a key element in the tight military network of his empire, and their participation in battle became not uncommon. In Rome the family of Theophylact assumed an increasingly direct control over the popes, and the papacy became to some extent feudalized. One of their number, as Pope John XII (955–964), ended by leading armed resistance to the Emperor Otto, whom he had himself crowned a few years earlier. In 963 the German army was opposed outside Rome by John XII clad in full armour, a feudal prince at war.

By the early eleventh century the attitude of the Roman popes to war was no different from that of the other imperial bishops. Hearing a lawsuit in Rome alongside Pope Benedict VIII (1012–24) in the early years of the century, the Emperor Henry II remarked casually to the Pope: 'Lord Pope, give me your troops, so that they can go with mine to take the castles belonging to this monastery.'[5]

This marriage of clerical and royal military power was later to be challenged by churchmen whose consciences were offended by it. The dynasty of popes to which Benedict VIII had belonged was deprived of power in 1046, and replaced by a series of so-called 'Reform' popes whose mission it was to restore ancient church discipline and to take away from impure, self-interested lay hands the holy things that belonged to the church. From the second half of the eleventh century there came into existence a new papal leadership in Rome, with a policy of asserting the independence of spiritual power against the feudal nobles, and of resisting the claims of property right that the nobles were exerting over the church offices 'simoniacally' (from Simon the magician, who was said to have tried to buy supernatural powers from the apostles).

This was only in part a quarrel about the 'investiture' or feudal transfer of church benefices, although the movement in favour of church liberties has found its modern name of Investiture Contest from this disputed practice. In the course of the dispute the ecclesiastical party found itself involved in a church schism that meant civil war in Italy and other parts of the Holy Roman Empire.

But this did not in the least mean that the Reform party wished to relinquish the military power controlled by churchmen. When Pope Leo IX (1049–54) was resisted by the fierce Norman invaders of southern Italy, his biographer says that 'those who did not fear spiritual sanctions he ordered to be smitten by a human sword'.[6] Before the battle of Civitate between Roman and Norman troops in 1053, the Pope promised his men forgiveness for their sins; after their defeat and massacre he prayed over the Roman dead for two days. Shortly before his death he experienced a vision in which the fallen on the papal side at the battle were described as 'martyrs'.

The greatest of the Reform popes, Gregory VII (1073–85) was a formidable organizer of armies, who boasted about the numbers of troops that his partisans in Italy had placed at his disposal. He was to wage a long, bitter civil war for the defence of his bishopric of Rome. He routinely referred to the mounted troops serving him in these wars as 'knights of St Peter', and he also conceived the idea (that never, in the event, materialized in the form he planned) of a new 'militia of St Peter', an army of volunteer knights to be drawn from many countries, which was to serve the policies of the Roman see. One of Gregory's bishop-partisans was among the first to set out rules of behaviour for a new military type called 'the Christian knight', an ideal that Chaucer's 'perfect gentle knight' may have led us to believe as having been typically medieval, but that did not gain much acceptance among the knightly class until the twelfth century.

Feudal practice was integral to Gregory VII's policies, and he used the oath of feudal submission to the holy see, and the consequent obligation of military service, as a normal political device. Both his defenders and his detractors agreed that he expended much money and energy in mobilizing and arming troops, though they disagreed about his motives for doing so. He and his propagandists preserved the idea that there could be a sort of martyrdom for his partisans who died in the wars of the Investiture Contest, and there were also suggestions that the papal dead in these wars could be freed from some of the penalties that otherwise awaited them for their sins. By the time of Gregory VII it is possible to speak of a partially militarized church, that had absorbed feudal military practice into its ordinary way of life, even though it continued to condemn the lawlessness and bloodshed of uncontrolled knightly behaviour.

For example, the Norman invasion of England in 1066 took place with the assent of the popes, and Gregory VII later wished to treat the Anglo-Norman kingdom as a fief of the holy see. Nevertheless, after the campaigns of 1066 the papal legate in England required the Norman knights who had taken part in the campaign, on which the papal banner had been displayed, to do penance for the bloodshed they had committed. To modern readers this may seem to have been a paradox, but it was not one in the eleventh century. The truce of God, which was the imposition of peace oaths upon the warring nobles, and the setting up of a sort of collective security enforcement machinery in which the church participated, had further accustomed people to the idea of a clerical role in war. By the time of Gregory VII God's war, the holy war, was a familiar concept to the bishops, even if many of them rejected it in the form that Gregory pressed upon them.

By the closing decade of the eleventh Christian century the frontier wars between Muslims and Christians had lasted some 450 years: in their more or less traditional form they were at their halfway point. In the eleventh century the course of the frontier wars in the west differed widely from that in the east. In the west the Muslims of the Iberian peninsula, who until the early years of the century had confined the beleaguered Christians to what seemed to be a shrinking mountainous strip in the north, suddenly underwent a political and social collapse.

The great campaigns of the 'Umayyad vizier-turned-ruler Almanzor (Hajib al-Mansur) were continued for a very short time by his son 'Abd al-Malik (1002–8), who had resumed the holy war that had been sustained by his father. But the new dynasty was short-lived, and on the death of 'Abd al-Malik Muslim Spain suddenly and dramatically fell into political chaos, termed by contemporaries the *fitna*, or great rebellion. The feeble representatives of the 'Umayyad dynasty of Cordova could make no impression on the situation, and the Berber and slave leaders of the armies broke up the great Iberian Muslim dominion into a score or so of little principalities. They were known as the *muluk al-tawa'if*, rendered into Spanish as the *reinos de taifas*, the kings of the parties or factions.

The Muslim chaos profited the Christian kings of the north, who were quick to intervene among the Muslim principalities, to exact huge tribute from many of them, and to press their own boundaries inexorably south and west. It was the beginning of the Christian reconquest of the peninsula, that was well under way by the time of the conquest of Toledo by Alfonso VI of León-Castile in 1085. The fall of Toledo provoked, however, a Muslim reaction that held up the enlargement of Christian Iberia for quite a long period. It occasioned the intervention in Spain of the Almoravid (corruption of *Murabitun*, people of the *ribat*) line of Morocco, a holy war dynasty of religious enthusiasts that had originated at a *ribat* in Senegal, and thence had established its chief centre at Marrakech in the south of Morocco. The Almoravids imposed a serious defeat upon Alfonso VI at Zallaqa near Badajoz in 1086, and the Muslim dominion of Andalus was in a score of years reunited under an Almoravid rule that took the holy war seriously once more. Though the check placed on Christian reconquest was only temporary, it was important.

The Christian *reconquista* in Spain had many features of a holy war that involved Christians from outside the peninsula. The bishops and the papal legates gave it their full approval. In 1064 Barbastro, a key Muslim fortress in the Christian conquest of Saragossa, had been attacked by an army of Catalans, Aragonese and knights from many parts of France, including Normandy and Île de France. Pope Alexander II gave the knightly participants an indulgence to excuse some of the penalties due for their sins. This anticipated one feature of the religious privileges later associated with the conquest of the holy land that was launched at the end of the century. The *reconquista* encouraged ambitious or needy French soldiers to try their luck in Spain. But it also meant the diffusion of information about the holy war: another feature of Spanish campaigns of this nature was to familiarize Latin Christians with the idea of a sacred war against the infidel.

All over the western and central Mediterranean the Christians pressed Islam hard during the eleventh century. The Normans of southern Italy were a savage lot, almost as happy in sacking churches as they were in sacking mosques, but they were acute politicians, who from 1059 onwards accepted a feudal relationship with the popes. In that year, besides acquiring most of southern Italy as a papal fief, the Norman leader Robert Guiscard obtained the promise of papal investiture with the island of Sicily when it was taken from the Muslims; the Normans took the island between 1060 and 1091. Their war there had no real holy war characteristics, and they were happy to tolerate Muslim practices and also to use Muslim troops, to the scandal of their papal allies. But the Normans had become acutely conscious of the ways in which the prestige and power of the popes could be used for their advantage if they undertook conquests in the name of Christendom.

In other parts of the western and central Mediterranean the Christians also obtained the upper hand. The attempt by Mujahid al-Amiri to use the Balearic Islands as a Muslim springboard for the conquest of Corsica failed. In 1087 a great coalition of the Italian maritime powers, with papal support, took and sacked Mahdiya in the Zirid kingdom of Tunis, paralyzing for a time one of the great Arab naval centres. The Roman bishop had become a helper to whom the Christians at war with Muslim powers would almost automatically turn.

In the tenth and eleventh Christian centuries the conflict of Muslim and Christian in the east was a seesaw affair. The mid-tenth century saw a great recrudescence of Byzantine power in Asia Minor and the Mediterranean. The Byzantine frontier warriors, the *akritai*, had for centuries maintained a species of holy war against the Muslims: they were in the words of one of the official army manuals 'ready to risk their lives for the holy emperors and the whole Christian folk'.[7] In the tenth century the decline of the 'Abbasid Empire allowed the Byzantines to move from a defensive to an offensive stance, and to mount a very powerful series of attacks in Asia Minor and on the Syrian provinces. Crete, a key island in the naval strategy of the Mediterranean, fell to the Byzantines in 961.

The tenth-century Christian imperial armies started to press forward against 'the Saracens, the blasphemers of Christ the King',[8] with the presumed miraculous help of the Virgin, whose triumph-song (the Magnificat) quoted the holy war verses of Isaiah,[9] and who was thought often to guide the troops in battle. In the second half of the century the Emperor Nicephorus Phocas (963–9) took the war powerfully into Syria, and his successor John Tzimisces (969–76) obtained the temporary submission of southern Syria, including Damascus, as far as the anti-Lebanon range and Mount Hermon (his supposed claim to have seen Jerusalem from afar is very dubious). These were not permanent conquests, but they bespoke a military vigour that persisted in the Empire until the third decade of the following century.

In one sense, holy war had been present in Byzantium at least from the same moment that it entered Islam. The fall of Jerusalem to the Persians in 614 and the Iranian seizure of the wood of the holy cross led to the great Persian war of the Emperor Heraclius (610–41). For a moment it seemed that Rome had finally triumphed in its age-old struggle with Persia. The victorious Byzantine armies in Persia recovered the wood of the cross and returned it to Jerusalem in 630. This was in essence a holy war against the Zoroastrian infidels. As it happened, the opening of this war in 622 coincided almost exactly with the flight of Muhammad from Mecca to Medina, and with the beginning of the holy wars of Islam. Ironically, the Jerusalem that had been thus won back for the Christians was conquered by the Muslims in 635. The great Byzantine victories over Persia turned out to have been a softening-up process that enabled the Muslims in their turn to subdue the millennial Persian Empire less than a generation after the Persian war of Heraclius had seemed to proclaim the triumph of Christianity.

The great Persian war of Heraclius was a holy war in a general sense, and also in that one of its aims was the recovery of the holy relics for Jerusalem. But it did not try to modify the doctrine of the Orthodox Church, which held that killing, even for the faith, was sinful. A later generation of Byzantine rulers, inspired by new wars with infidels in the holy land, thought differently. From the middle of the tenth century, the Byzantine emperors tried to impose something that the Orthodox Church had hitherto resisted, a doctrine of holy war in which killing was not sinful, but meritorious in the sight of God. There was some resistance to this idea on the part of the priests, as being contrary to obstinately defended church tradition.

But in the eleventh century the whole balance of power in Asia Minor and Central Asia began to change, because of the decline of the Byzantine leadership on one side of the frontier, and the triumph of the Turkish warrior dynasties on the other. The key figure in eastern Islam was Tughril Beg, the grandson of the founder of the Seljuk Turkish dynasty. Tughril Beg, having triumphed over the older dynasties of Iran, conquered Baghdad, and was invested by the Abassid Caliph in 1056 with the titles of Sultan, and King of the East and West. Tughril, like many conquerors in the Muslim world before and after him, came to power at the head of plundering nomadic tribes whose indiscipline became an embarrassment when his aim was to rule the settled Muslims. The answer to this problem was to divert the tribes towards the *ghazi* holy war against the Byzantine provinces. From northern Iran the routes ran to Erzerum and Trebizond, and by these mountainous war paths he sent them to fight the Christians.

Tughril Beg's successor, Alp Arslan (1063–72), himself assumed control of the war with the Byzantines, taking it into Byzantine Armenia. The Emperor Romanus Diogenes mistakenly mobilized the main imperial army against him, and encountered him in 1071 near Lake Van in Armenia at the battle of Manzikert, at which the Greek army was destroyed and the Emperor taken prisoner. The establishment of the Seljuk sultanates in Asia Minor at the expense of Byzantium was one result of this great victory. Another was the grave blow it dealt to Byzantine morale, which led to unprecedented appeals to Western Christendom for help. Less than three years after the defeat, Pope Gregory VII asked the German King, the Burgundian Duke and others to succour the Eastern Christians by sending an army to the east after this catastrophe, and even talked of the Pope himself accompanying the military expedition. Nothing came of this, and the Greek Emperor Michael VII, who must have made some diplomatic advance to Gregory, was deposed in 1078. But the incident showed that the Roman bishops were already willing, by 1074, to propose wildcat schemes of military intervention in the east which presupposed a quasi-military role for the Pope.

The revival of Byzantine fortunes was long delayed, and the idea of possible Western military action to assist the Greeks remained in the air for some time. Norman mercenaries were employed by the Greeks in Asia Minor, in spite of their having wrested southern Italy from the Byzantines in the recent past, and of their subsequent landings on the coast of Epirus with the intention to control the Byzantine roads through the Balkans. Alexius Comnenus, who had made himself emperor in Constantinople in 1081, was in the course of time to prove himself the restorer of imperial military power. But he thought the employment of Western mercenaries was one of the obvious ways to help achieve this aim, and a lot of his contact with the Latin West was spent in acquiring trustworthy mercenary troops.

The last great Seljuk ruler, Malikshah, died in 1092. The policy of allowing the Seljuk princes to rule whole provinces meant the fragmentation of the Empire, a process that had been far advanced even before the death of Malikshah. This was not much consolation to the Byzantines, who had lost most of Asia Minor to the Seljuk sultans within ten years of the battle of Manzikert. It was possible to play off one Turkish ruler against another to the temporary advantage of the Greeks, but this did little or nothing to disturb a Turkish hegemony that was rapidly Islamicizing huge areas in Asia Minor which had been under the rule of a Christian Empire since Constantine had built Constantinople over seven centuries earlier. There continued to be huge difficulties, also, on the Danube and Macedonian frontiers: the East Romans faced intractable problems.

Alexius Comnenus was a vigorous and able man, who did a great deal to restore the military muscle of the Empire. He was deeply concerned about the Turkish catastrophe that had removed a great part of the Byzantine heartlands, shattered the elaborate network of southern and eastern frontier defences for ever, and struck deeply at the economic and demographic basis of Eastern Christianity. He knew of the earlier willingness of the Roman bishops to come to terms with the Christian east, and also of their apparent willingness to organize armed assistance to Byzantium.

It is understandable that in these circumstances Alexius Comnenus should have sent ambassadors to a church council called by Pope Urban II in Piacenza in the spring of 1095. It is probable that the Byzantine ambassadors asked for troops to be sent to serve under Alexius, and possible that in asking for this help they mentioned the plight of Eastern Christians under Turkish rule; it is even possible that they referred to the special circumstances of the church of Jerusalem, in order to emphasize the common Christian cause of the Eastern and Western churches.

Jerusalem was a legitimate interest of the Western Christians, because of the large numbers of Western pilgrims who throughout the early Middle Ages had made their pilgrimage there. The Christian pilgrimage to Jerusalem was of economic interest to the Muslim powers, but was also recognized by them as a legitimate spiritual activity of the 'people of the book'. The

legal status of the Christian pilgrims in Muslim countries was that of protected persons who received the *aman* or protection of the Muslims. This
protection was a very wide one, and according to some jurists was not
violated even if the *mustaman*, the protected person, acted as a marauder;
although if he came with the specific intention of acting against Islam the
protection lapsed. There was a striking instance of this principle being put
into action in 1065, when a company of several thousand German pilgrims,
led by their bishops, was involved for several days in a running battle near
Ramleh in Palestine with native Muslims. The quarrel erupted especially
fiercely when an emir tried to secure the person of the Bishop of Bamberg
by tying him up with his turban. The whole incident, which the pilgrims
claimed was occasioned by the theft of their goods, was quietened down
by the sultan's officials, and the pilgrims returned peacefully to Europe.[10]

On the whole the difficulties experienced by Western pilgrims to Jerusalem had been connected with insecure communications by land and sea,
and especially with the very dangerous conditions that had for some time
affected the overland routes to Jerusalem across Asia Minor. Once the
pilgrims reached Syria their position had not on the whole been intolerable,
except for a short period of anti-Christian persecution under the Caliph
al-Hakim (996–1021), a Fatimid (that is a Shi'a) ruler whose dynasty had
ceased to rule in Syria in the mid-eleventh century. The position of Western
pilgrims who had actually reached the holy land, as opposed to those who
sought to travel there, was not especially difficult at the end of the eleventh
century.

The lives of Orthodox Eastern Christians in Asia Minor had certainly
been extremely hard since the disintegration of Byzantine rule after Manzikert. But there seems to be no particular reason to think that those in the
holy land, as distinct from Asia Minor, suffered very severe troubles from
the Muslim rulers during the same period. In the twelfth century, some
time after the establishment of Frankish rule in the holy land, it was suggested that the Patriarch of Jerusalem had appealed to the Western clergy
through Peter the Hermit for help against Muslim persecution, but there
is no conclusive contemporary evidence that this was so.

A church schism took place as a result of the quarrel between Pope Gregory
VII (1073–85) and the Emperor Henry IV (Emperor 1084–1105). The
Roman popes of the Reform obedience stemming from Gregory VII were
still in an ambiguous political position in the last decade of the eleventh

century. Pope Urban II (Odo of Chatillon, 1088–99) was by origin a Burgundian, trained in the great monastery of Cluny, whose cultural outlook belonged to the northern part of the Middle Kingdom and to west Francia, rather than to Italy. The so-called Investiture Contest between the popes and the German kings, that convulsed Germany and Italy for over a generation after 1076, was still unsettled. The 'anti-pope' Clement III, opposed to Urban, was driven from Rome in 1092, but the German king continued to support him, and was excommunicate on that account. The French king had placed himself in an irregular matrimonial situation, unacceptable to the church, with Bertrade de Montfort, and he too was soon to be excommunicated; he could not be of much assistance to Urban II.

When Urban left north Italy for Francia after the Council of Piacenza in 1095 he had already quit his own diocese of Rome, which continued to be racked by violence and civil war. There was need for policies that would unite Western Christendom behind the Roman bishop who claimed spiritual authority over the whole Latin church, but had the most remarkable difficulty in exercising it. Whether Urban's action when he arrived at Clermont in southern Francia was consciously designed to provide such a policy, or whether on his arrival at Clermont his intention went no further than to improvise an appeal to assist the oriental church, on the model of the abortive appeal made by his predecessor Gregory VII eighteen years earlier, can never be known, although the political and psychological origins of the call to send great armed contingents of Western Latins to the east to seek salvation can be guessed at.

The reformers in or near the papal court were not remote holy men, nor were they yet the judges and professional politicians that they were one day to become. They had passed their lives in the hurly-burly of feudal politics and church administration, and wanted to inculcate some spirit of idealism into the turbulent feudal class from which most of them came. It is quite probable that they also, after more than thirty years of violent struggle, in which their authority had been challenged by the German king and by other great princes, wanted a cause that would unite the feudal nobles under their leadership, or in other words under the leadership of the papacy. To what extent this desire occasioned a planned programme, we cannot say with any certainty.

On the last day of the Church Council at Clermont, on 27 November 1095, outside the walls of the town Pope Urban II made a speech that did not form part of the official acts of the Church Council which had just ended. The bishops attending the council came from Francia and the north-west of the Holy Roman Empire, and the gathering was also attended by a large number of lay people whose provenance is unknown, but the majority of whom probably came from central and southern Francia.

The Pope's speech concerned the situation of the Eastern churches, and the persecution visited upon them by Muslim unbelievers. He mentioned that churches and holy places had been desecrated and defiled, and that Antioch (a place that churchmen would have known for its apostolic associations) had fallen to the unbelievers, though he did not explain that most of these misfortunes dated back over twenty years, and were nearer in time to the Byzantine disaster at Manzikert than to the period at which he spoke. He emphasized the uncleanness of the insult offered to holy things, a feeling typical of the Reform environment from which he came.

Urban's appeal was extraordinary in that churchmen in their councils normally addressed and exhorted other clergy; if they spoke of laymen it was usually to deplore some aspect of the policy of princes, or to lament some moral lapse being committed by layfolk. However, the recent great crises of the Investiture Contest had accustomed the popes to making their appeals to a wide European public, and had sharpened their propagandist techniques. Urban's appeal of 1095 was not directed to the churchmen, but to the laymen, and most of all to the class of armed knights (he knew that the great and costly enterprise he wanted had to be financed in some way, and that he and the bishops were in no position to do it). He asked both rich and poor laymen to put aside their quarrels and relent from their lawless persecutions, and to march to the east. His appeal was not only rhetorical: a codicil to the speech confirmed it, and even tried to fix a sketchy timetable so that the expedition could take place in the following year. He attached or allowed to be attached to his appeal a sort of battle cry that fixed itself in the minds and imaginations of thousands of men: 'It is God's will!' ('*Deus le volt*').

Unlike almost all subsequent papal plans for armed expeditions to the east, that of 1095 made no specific mention of the great feudal princes. The reigning King of France had just been excommunicated. There may have been a previous meeting between the Pope and Count Raymond of Toulouse, the biggest feudal magnate of southern France, in which Urban broached the subject of the expedition, but if this had happened Urban did not mention it in his speech. By speaking without distinction of persons, Urban was making a radical and a potentially dangerous venture into the field of popular religion – how radical and how dangerous was to be demonstrated in a very short time by the anti-Semitic massacres it sparked off, and by the mass, unorganized marches like those of the popular preacher Peter the Hermit. Urban followed up the Clermont speech with a preaching tour of France south of the Loire of whose details little is known, but that certainly was directed to harnessing mass enthusiasm for the project he had just launched.

In a vital provision that formed part of the official church acts of the council, in a way that his speech did not, Urban stipulated at Clermont that whoever went to Jerusalem on solely religious grounds, not attracted by honour or money, but only to free God's church, would have his whole pilgrimage accredited to him for forgiveness of sin, and would be free of all further penance. Consciously or not, Pope Urban by this concession invented a social machine of enormous power. He also at the same moment attached the object of the expedition to Jerusalem.

As a British historian of the crusades has remarked, this was a period in which the theology of the Western church was dominated by the idea of merit.[11] Murderers and men whose lives were full of betrayals would undertake not once, but several times if they survived to do it, the most dangerous and arduous pilgrimages to Jerusalem or elsewhere in order to capture some assurance of salvation for their imperilled souls. It was a period in which violence had in many ways invaded the spiritual world, and in which men hoped as it were to storm the kingdom of heaven. With this intention the bloodstained nobles would devote huge amounts of their ill-gotten gains to the setting up of new church foundations, or would suddenly, having passed their lives until that point in violence and extortion, turn aside to finish them in monasteries. To such men Urban II seemed to offer what was, relatively speaking, an easy way out (whatever the dangers of the eastern journey), in which they could continue to lead their ordinary military lives, yet enjoy some assurance of salvation.

At Clermont the Pope said that as a symbol of devotion to their Saviour, the Christians who made the expedition to the east were to wear his cross upon their coats. The words *croisé* and *croisade*, which derive from this cross, were not used by Urban at this time, nor were they to be used by anyone else in French or Latin until the time of the Third Crusade in the late twelfth century. But practically all modern historians have from the eighteenth century (when the English word 'crusade' was invented) accepted an anachronistic term, and have agreed that the 1099 expeditions and the 1095 appeal that launched them may be properly referred to as 'the First Crusade'.

Historians do not, though, agree about the motives or the nature of the appeal made by Urban II at Clermont, and are never likely to do so. The texts that purport to report his speech are very hard to interpret, and were written with somewhat different purposes and emphases. But the problems connected with the interpretation of Urban's appeal are not merely textual: they are much more concerned with the way we look at history, and with the ideas that we bring to it.

The hypothetical causal chains beloved of historians cannot be satisfactorily established for the armed Christian movement to the east that Urban II launched, any more than they can be for the equally abrupt and even more important phenomenon of Muhammad, half a millennium earlier. The see of Rome had seldom shown much affection for the Eastern church since it cast off its allegiance to Byzantium in the eighth century, and it had emphasized its theological rift with the Eastern bishops in a diplomatic rupture that had occurred less than forty years before the Council of Clermont. Why did the Roman bishop suddenly decide that it was time for Western Christians to unite in a venture of armed support for Eastern Christians?

There had in the past, but over a century before Clermont, been spasmodic co-operation against the Muslims, usually of a rather distrustful nature, between Latin and Eastern Emperors. The Western church had played only a very subordinate part in this. There was a significant omission by Urban II in his Clermont speech, which did not mention the leadership exercised over Eastern Christians by the Byzantine Emperor. Yet his predecessor Gregory VII had mentioned 'the Empire of Constantinople' in the appeal for military support issued eleven years earlier, and the presence of the Byzantine imperial ambassadors at Piacenza earlier in the same year must have been fresh in Urban's memory. He knew well that the Byzantine state virtually included the Byzantine church. His decision to skate over this fact in his speech may have been a political one.

The very indefiniteness of Urban's speech showed its genius. He was not elaborating a doctrine of holy war, though in a way his speech presupposed one to exist. He was well acquainted with the wars with the Muslims in Spain, and in documents issued only a year or so later he clearly indicated that he thought of them as a sort of alternative to the eastern journey; but he made no reference to them at Clermont. He was not appealing for the diplomatic or military help of this great prince or that, although he knew well that his idea was so ambitious that without the support of many great nobles it could never come to fruition. Although there had been preliminary diplomatic moves that preceded his speech (and there may have been others of which no record has survived), he made not the slightest reference to them. The pilgrimage to the holy land, familiar to Western Christians for centuries as one of the paths towards salvation, was implicit in all he said, but the word 'pilgrimage' seems not to have been used. As masters and protectors of the Roman pilgrimage the popes had as much experience of popular religious enthusiasm as any churchmen in Europe, and this experience must have guided, or at least strongly influenced, the Clermont appeal.

We are not sure how much direct control Urban wanted to exert over the eastern expedition. We may perhaps call his ideas about the Christian east politically opportunist: he was certainly anxious to regulate some vital aspects of the voyage. At Clermont he appointed a papal legate to accompany the expedition when it took place. He later issued a series of decisions and instructions about its purely ecclesiastical side, such as the nature of participation by churchmen. He also legislated about the security of the goods and possessions of men who were absent on the voyage to the holy land. He tried to act as a co-ordinating authority for the projected expeditions: he sent, for example, legates to Genoa to organize a naval expedition to Syria to support the army that would travel overland when it arrived there. He also set up some kind of timetable for the expeditions.

The legal aspect of the role of papal power in the crusade, that was in later centuries to dominate the role of the papacy in such matters, was not at all prominent in 1095-7. One of the critical issues in the later process of the definition of a crusader, and of his rights and duties, was the nature of his oath to proceed on crusade. There is no indication that Urban thought this problem out; his role was more that of prophet than of judge. There is in his pronouncements and preaching a visionary dimension that cannot be escaped – perhaps a visionary dimension that characterizes all holy war. The visionary who can also – if unkindly – be described as a political opportunist is not unfamiliar in the history of religions: this was, indeed, exactly the charge to be brought against Muhammad by sceptical Western orientalists.

Urban had envisaged only one main expedition to the holy land, and in terms of medieval power politics this is what happened. Nevertheless, the uncontrolled, popular nature of the preaching of the expedition, and the individual character of all medieval pilgrimage, meant that several expeditions set out. The bureaucracy by which the popes were later able to control most popular preaching in Europe did not come into existence until well over a century after Urban II. Peter the Hermit, a rough revivalist outside the official church hierarchy who was by far the most effective preacher of the expedition, found himself at the head of a disorganized volunteer army that left Germany with German, Frankish and Italian contingents in the spring of 1096. After a bloody and disorderly passage through the Balkans, this force was hurried across the Straits by an impatient Byzantine Emperor in early August. By the end of October the Turkish sultanate of Nicaea had reacted in the manner the Greeks had anticipated, and had destroyed and massacred its various contingents. Peter the Hermit had stayed in Constantinople, and so survived to join the main army when it began to arrive at the end of the year.

A second popular expedition started from Germany only weeks after the one led by Peter the Hermit, whose followers were also concerned in the second expedition. This expedition distinguished itself only by sickening massacres and plunder of the Jews in western Germany. Anti-Semitic demonstrations fatally followed most medieval movements that stirred up emotions about the betrayal of Christ in Jerusalem, and looting and murder usually accompanied them. The second popular army was halted and decisively defeated by the Hungarians, who had had quite enough of marauding pilgrims with Peter the Hermit's earlier force, and it penetrated no further.

The expedition of the princes took rather longer to organize than the popular movements. It consisted of four main armies, from west Francia, south Francia, Lorraine and Norman Italy, and all the main contingents had arrived in Constantinople, where they were felt to constitute a serious political problem, but perhaps also a certain military and political opportunity, by the spring of 1097. The leaders came from many of the main feudal families of Francia and the western part of the Holy Roman Empire. Their armies were well equipped with weapons and war equipment, and some of them at least were very well financed. The Byzantine Emperor felt that he had done what he could to contain them politically by taking oaths of allegiance before they crossed to Asia. They were accompanied by a papal legate, Adhemar of Le Puy, who had been appointed at the time of the Council of Clermont.

There are some parallels to be drawn between the earliest development of the Christian crusade and the working out of the meaning of holy war in Islam. How the Christian holy war was to be elaborated after 1095 depended, as some modern historians have insisted, on subsequent events that at the time of the Clermont appeal were unknown. Just as Muhammad's career after the emigration to Medina decided what was to be the nature of *jihad*, only the practice of the Christian holy war could decide what form it was eventually to take. Until the Western Christian armies had made their marches through unknown lands, and fought many battles, the nature of their mission was going to hang in doubt. Similarly, until Muhammad's skirmish of an-Nakhlah and the battle of Badr had been fought, the nature of *jihad* could not certainly be known.

It has been argued that the making of the crusading identity took place after the crusading armies had crossed to Asia Minor in the spring of 1097, and begun combat with the Turkish forces. At the time that they crossed the Byzantine frontiers it was understood by the Greeks that their purpose was to worship at the holy places of Jerusalem, and to liberate the city of Jerusalem from the Muslims. The Byzantines also assumed, mistakenly, that the Western capture of formerly Byzantine places like Antioch would lead to their being returned to Byzantine sovereignty.

But as the Christian armies fought their way across Asia Minor in the severe campaigns of 1097–8 the troops began to acquire their own ideas of their religious mission. These cohered while they were on the march, and in the course of the great sieges in which they took part between the fall of Nicaea in 1097 and the fall of Jerusalem in 1099. One of their first acquisitions was the idea of martyrdom in battle: at Nicaea the fatal casualties 'all alike entered heaven in the robes of martyrdom, calling upon the Lord to avenge the blood shed in his name'.[12]

The question of vengeance is seldom far from any war. It is hard, if we try to use the moral arguments of the just war, to see that the Latin Christians who came to the east in 1097 had any real cause to demand retaliation for wrongs committed against them by the Muslims of Syria and Asia Minor. Of wrongs committed against Eastern Christians they knew very little, and although preachers from Urban II onwards talked of the persecution of Eastern Christians by Muslims, the quarrel did not really belong to the Latin Christians. It is true that they had in a sense been invited to the east by the Byzantine government, but this invitation was rapidly regretted by those who had extended it. Jerusalem, the object of the expedition, had not belonged to East Rome for four and a half centuries. The Byzantines found themselves rather in the position of a modern power that asks for the help of a small expeditionary force and finds itself entertaining troops who intend to wage biological warfare.

The Western expedition was intended neither to ward off Muslim aggression from Eastern Christians nor to spread the Christian faith by missionary work. It had to do with the traditional greed for booty of the whole Western knightly class, but much more with a primitive religious nostalgia and violence that no one can really explain. Once battle had been engaged in the east, there was also a call among the crusaders for vengeance for the fallen.

On 15 July 1099, after unimaginable hardships spread over a period of more than two years, the exhausted Western army, that was too small to surround and systematically besiege the city, took Jerusalem. Only then did they realize what they had achieved. The sheer magnitude of the victory, and its location in the distant and mysterious heart of the Christian religion, convinced the participants that God had indeed fought for them, that it had been Christ who had given them the cities they had taken and the battles they had won. During the Christian defence of Antioch in 1098 the supposed discovery of the Holy Lance had convinced many of the army that there had been divine intervention on their behalf. But the fall of Jerusalem made God's aid in a sense certain. Joshua had smitten the Amalekites with the rod God gave to Moses. It is impossible not to recall the Qur'an: 'On the day of Badr, it was not you who slew them, but Allah.'[13]

The appalling massacre of combatants and non-combatants that took place during the fall of Jerusalem in 1099 was justified at the time as vengeance for the casualties that had been inflicted earlier upon the Western army. A contemporary wrote: 'Who can express the gladness of Christians when those who had once rent Christ asunder in his own members [that is, the crusading troops] now in their own bodies received payment in kind for them?'[14]

Vengeance was soon to become a theme of both the popular and the learned literature of the crusade. The person who was most to be avenged upon the infidels was Christ himself. A parallel can perhaps be found in Islam in the Shi'a laments for the death of Hussein at 'Umayyad hands at the battle of Karbala in 680 AD. The 'Chanson d'Antioche' envisaged Christ upon the cross, saying:

> The people are not yet born
> who will come to avenge me with their steel lances.
> So they will come to avenge the faithless pagans
> who have always refused my commandments . . .
> from over the seas will come a new race
> which will take revenge upon the death of its father.

William, Bishop of Tyre in the late twelfth century, put into the mouth of Godfrey de Bouillon a speech supposed to have been delivered at the siege of Antioch in 1197, in which he expressed his determination to avenge the injury that had (as he saw it) been offered to Christ by the infidel Muslims.

So, in spite of anything said in the Christian gospel, the blood feud, which both Christianity and Islam had sought to moderate and control, came to occupy a central place in the ideology of Christian holy war. The idea of blood feud was adopted by the popes themselves. A century after the First Crusade, Pope Innocent III summoned Christians to go to the crusade to take vengeance upon the injury done to their father, and adjured them to avenge the destruction of their brothers in the holy land by the Muslims.

In the last five years of the eleventh century there was an important, if not a decisive, change in the theology of war in the Latin West. Divine support for the chosen people, mediated through holy war, was one of the main features of the Old Testament. Christians had never, from St Augustine onwards, refused to allow that God may command holy war. They now said, if they followed Pope Urban II, that God might order laymen to make war upon unbelievers. Killing was allowed 'with God's authority'. The acceptance by churchmen of feudal attitudes to war, which for centuries had been intruding upon the traditions that forbade churchmen to be involved in bloodshed, had breached church doctrine at an important point. But the literal fulfilment of the prohibition against clergy shedding blood remained, and Urban II himself forbade churchmen to undertake the 1097 expedition.

However little the lives and rights of Eastern Christians were regarded by the Western invaders when they actually reached the holy land, the circumstances of the first armed expedition theoretically respected their rights of worship. That Jerusalem was a Muslim and a Jewish holy place as well as a Christian one was never remotely considered by the first crusaders or by those who sent them. The Muslims who had 'defiled' the holy places were held to have lost them for ever, and the Jews were not considered; both were excluded from rights in a city that had returned to Christ.

The idea of ownership was inseparable from the new Christian settlement in the holy land. It became a commonplace in crusading propaganda, and also in papal documents concerned with the crusade, to say that the holy land was the property of Christ and of his people – 'the patrimony of the crucified one'. By the time of the Second Crusade in 1147 the holy land could be seen in Europe as a feudal fief that rightly belonged to Christ, and that had been torn from him by the Muslims. A current song ran: 'God has brought before you his suit against the Turks and Saracens, who have done him great despite. They have seized his fiefs, where God was first served and recognized as Lord.' St Bernard in exactly the same vein and at the same time said: 'The earth is shaken because the Lord of heaven is losing his land, the land in which he appeared to men, in which he lived amongst men for more than thirty years . . .'[15]

However paradoxical it may sound, the 1097 expedition had not been clearly defined at the outset as being directed towards the establishment of a permanent Latin Christian presence in the holy land, still less towards the setting up of a Latin colony. It was an army that was also a pilgrimage. There was no obligation upon those who took part to remain in the holy land, any more than there was upon any other pilgrim. Most were expected to return, as a very large number did.

The princes who set out on the expedition, and the church leaders who accompanied them, knew that some permanent settlement to defend the Christian settlement was going to be needed if they succeeded in their aims. That the expedition would create its own political institution of the Kingdom of Jerusalem was not anticipated, and there was some hesitation among the crusaders themselves in 1099 as to what form their regime should take. Godfrey de Bouillon in that year assumed the title of Advocate of the Holy Sepulchre: 'advocate' was a title assigned sometimes in the Holy Roman Empire to the lay protector of a church. In the following year his brother Baldwin of Boulogne succeeded him, not as Advocate, but as King of Jerusalem. The Kingdom of Jerusalem had a nature and prestige that differed in many ways from the Western feudal kingdoms, but it was no more subject to direct clerical control than they were.

What was done between 1095 and 1099 has permanently affected the relationship between Christianity and Islam. The vocabulary used to describe it has changed. It took a century for the more thoughtful and informed Muslims in the Near East to realize that the new Christian presence in the area was due to a Christian equivalent of *jihad*, and the expression 'crusade' was not in use in Europe itself until the same kind of revaluation was taking place in Islam. The term was not generally used in Arabic ('the wars of the bearers of the cross') until the modern period. But all Christian holy war against Islam, and much hostility between Muslim and Christian states that cannot properly be called holy war, has in modern times tended by one side or the other to be talked about in terms of crusade. The charge made against the West that their crusades against Islam have never stopped has been one of the most remarkable assertions of the modern Islamists.

We need to recognize the meaning of the militarization of the Latin church that had taken place over a long period in Western Christianity, and that had enabled Pope Urban II to preach the armed expedition to the holy land in 1095. The prohibition against the Christian clergy taking part in bloodshed was not actually infringed by this expedition, but it was wearing thin, and how thin it had become appeared in the papal authorization given to set up the military religious orders early in the following century. The deep conviction among modern Westerners that the Christian religion is at heart pacific has to be looked at very carefully when we consider the events of 1099 and their consequences. There was a long-term trend at work in the High Middle Ages that has led a modern historian to write that Latin Christendom in the eleventh century was a warrior culture led by a warrior church.[16] Perhaps the Christian church had been slowly drifting towards the conditional approval of holy war ever since the Emperor Constantine received Christianity into the orbit of Roman government in the early fourth century.

CHAPTER FIVE

Muslim and Christian Holy War

THE IDEA OF THE CRUSADE – an armed pilgrimage to the holy places of the holy land, supported by all Latin Christians as a matter of duty – was an absolute novelty in Christian holy war. Attempts by Christian settlements on the Muslim borders to recover what had been Christian land were not new: this had been the situation of the Christians on the northern and western borders of Islamic Spain ever since the first Muslim conquests there. The Kingdom of Jerusalem and the other Latin Christian principates in Syria were unlike the Iberian Christian states, because at irregular intervals a new force of armed pilgrims who had taken the cross in Europe would arrive in Syria (or, in the thirteenth century, in Egypt or another part of the Muslim world) to help their co-religionists defend the holy land.

However, although the resident Franks in Syria have been thought of by modern people as 'crusaders', they did not normally refer to themselves as such. Their interests were predominantly feudal or mercantile, and local. They had not acquired a status equivalent to that of the border or *ghazi* fighters in Islam, and at any time after the 1120s it was unlikely that a high proportion of the Christians in Syria would have taken the crusader's oath. In 1199, when deploring the depopulation of the Christian holy land after the end of the Third Crusade, Pope Innocent III said that 'from those parts nearly all pilgrims have now returned'.[1] At a rather later date, when theologians and canonists set their minds to elaborate a doctrine of crusade, they paid no real attention to the status, rights and duties of the native Franks in the holy land.

Although contact between the Franks in Syria and Europe was continuous, the 'general passage' to the holy land of those who had taken the crusading oath (or what we would customarily term a crusade) was something over which only the most powerful Franks in the holy land had any influence or control. The only numerous category of those subject to life-long crusading vows were the members of the religious military orders, and only a small number of these were permanently resident in the holy land. One of the fathers of modern crusading studies, Paul Riant, wanted a clear distinction made between the history of the Latin states in the east and the history of the crusades, and there are good reasons for this.[2]

But if the Syrian Franks were not, according to the narrower definitions of church law, crusaders, they certainly prosecuted a holy war, and they depended on the European Latins to supply them, to help finance them, and to send new forces to reinforce them. Their settlements have been described by some modern historians as a form of colonialism. There is some difficulty in calling them colonists in the sense in which this word was used in nineteenth- and twentieth-century Europe, because no one European nation corresponded to their origins. Modern French historians have noticed that from the point of view of modern ideas about colonization they lacked a single parent state, a *métropole*: in this respect they differed from the other Latin settlements in the Levant. However, crusading theory was to have some influence on the manner in which Europeans viewed their early modern colonies in the New World and the East, and this is discussed at length below.

The Syrian Franks represented the arbitrary transplant of European culture to a totally foreign environment. Their initial ignorance of Islam and of everything connected with it had been profound: the society from which they came had not in any way prepared them for it. There were, though, incentives to inform themselves. The merchants needed information about the Islamic world, and the Frankish princes, who badly needed political information, soon set up the apparatus to get it. The chronicler Ibn al-Athir records that when the Atabeg Aqsunqur al-Bursuqi was murdered in Mosul in 1126, Bohemund of Antioch received the news before it reached Aqsunqur's son, which shows to what degree the Franks were interested in monitoring Muslim affairs.

The Syrian prince Usama ibn-Munqidh of Shayzar was on extremely friendly terms with a number of Frankish nobles, whose conversation and customs he reported. His testimony is especially valuable because of his longevity: he took part in his first cavalry action against the Franks before 1120, and survived until 1188, a year after Saladin took Jerusalem. He emphasized that the cultivated Franks amongst whom he had friends, whose knowledge of the Arabic tongue and customs could be presumed, were a minority. The first generation of Frankish princes and their entourages spoke no Arabic: Usama remarks of a supposed guarantee of protection given by Tancred, Prince of Antioch early in the century that the Arabs could not be certain that it had been given, 'because these people spoke nothing but Frankish'.[3] However, Tancred's chancery evidently issued letters in Arabic.

The second generation of Franks in the East were often very well acquainted indeed with Muslim ways and with the Arabic tongue. Raymond of Tripoli was Regent for the boy-King Baldwin in the troubled period shortly before the battle of Hattin, at a critical time in the history of the Kingdom of Jerusalem. He had learned Arabic while in captivity after the defeat at Artah in 1164, and was able to conduct his own diplomacy in that language. Reynald of Sidon knew Arabic well enough to take an interest in Islam and its literature. Reynald of Châtillon, whose plundering of pilgrim caravans at the end of 1186 released Saladin from the truce and enabled the campaign that ended only months later with the disaster of Hattin, had spent sixteen years in captivity, and was in some respects the most orientalized of the Frankish princes – although this had not prevented him from looting the Muslim pilgrims of the *hajj*.

The tendency of each of the two cultures to acquire hooking-on points in the other can be read in the history of their peace and truce negotiations. The thoroughness of both Muslim and Christian commitment to the holy war can be seen in the legal conditions under which the two conflicting religious parties in the holy land came to agree, from time to time, upon periods of truce. Neither religion possessed any mechanism that allowed its adherents to make peace with the other once they entered a condition of holy war. This was a less serious restriction than might be thought, because Western medieval diplomacy was in any case more likely to use truce agreements than peace treaties as a means of living peacefully with neighbours.

There were nevertheless one or two Muslim–Christian peace treaties, like the abortive peace with the desperate Fatimid regime made for King Amalric with the caliph in Cairo in 1167. But the Muslims possessed an ancient legal machinery that easily allowed them to grant truces to hostile infidels when to do so was judged beneficial to Islam. The Muslim conception of truce differed widely from that of the Christians. It was a cessation of hostilities (*hudna*) granted by the imam that conceded protection (*aman*) to the recipients for the duration of the truce. The truce with unbelievers could not, even according to the more flexible of the Muslim jurists, exceed a period of something over ten Islamic years; other jurists specified a much shorter period. There was some hesitation among the Islamic lawyers as to whether a truce could be unilaterally denounced at any time if the interests of the Muslims required it: other Muslim laws forbade treaty-breaking, but the *aman* was not so much a treaty as a promise of protection, that could be withdrawn if the protected parties violated their obligations.

So Muslim ideas about international law easily allowed a truce to be conceded, while Christian ones, when the scene of hostilities moved outside Christendom, were less apt to compromise. Twelfth-century Christian lawyers allowed that truces with infidels should be kept, but some later ones wanted to forbid them. There was also a linguistic problem, in that when the two clerks representing the Christian and the Muslim ruler had negotiated the Arabic text of the agreement, the Frankish principals were seldom in a position to check it. The result (a paradoxical one from the Christian point of view) was that throughout the entire medieval period, and indeed well into the early modern period, most truces between Muslims and Christians took the outward form of a concession by the Muslims of protection to the Christians, covered by the truce for the period of its duration. This did not bar the insertion into the truce document of the obligations accepted by either side. Periods of truce were not short in total: it has been calculated that there were eighty years of truce between Muslim and Christian in the holy land between 1192 and 1290.

The negotiation of truces and the acquisition of political information about Muslim powers were necessary to the Franks in Syria. Acquiring serious knowledge about Muslim religion and culture was a different problem, which the Westerners were slow to solve. In Spain, contiguity with Islam had not led to the spread of even a superficial acquaintance with Islamic religion and culture. Muhammad was generally believed to have been a magician who had destroyed the Christian church in the Near East and North Africa by sorcery and cunning, and had clinched his success by authorizing promiscuity.

There were exceptions to the general ignorance about Islam. Something was known of the absolute nature of the prohibition to Christians living under Muslim rule against attacking the fundamentals of the Islamic creed; this was of obvious importance for the protection of Christian minorities in Muslim countries. There were a few scattered references in Latin chronicles to Islamic history, but mainstream Western clerical learning simply ignored it. In the mid-twelfth century the enlightened Abbot of Cluny, Peter the Venerable, sponsored a Latin translation of the Qur'an in the belief that it would lead to reasoned missionary argument. His hope was frustrated: it has been well observed that while in the earlier Middle Ages other (principally Byzantine) Christians engaged in polemic against Islam,

Latin Catholic Christians did not.[4] How little Peter the Venerable's initiative influenced clergy who actually lived in the East can be gathered from the writings of a well-educated clerk of the Kingdom of Jerusalem, born in Jerusalem: William, Bishop of Tyre. In the generation after that of Peter the Venerable, William said of Muhammad, whom he called 'the firstborn of Satan', that he mendaciously claimed to be a prophet sent by the Lord, and caused his errors to be spread not by preaching, but by violence and the sword.[5] There is some indication that William of Tyre was less violent than this in his judgements of Muslim contemporaries, but he cannot be described as tolerant.

Although the learned in the West had gradually increasing access to more accurate information about Islam, the general view that prevailed there and in the crusader states was ignorant and negative. By the late twelfth century not only had the Qur'an been translated, but some of the Muslim philosophers were being translated by Spanish Christians and Jews. This, though, was of no interest to the Christian plantation in the holy land, and was known only to a handful of clerks in Europe. The court of the early Norman kings of Sicily possessed a half-Islamic culture, which failed, however, to penetrate far into the surrounding Western lands until Frederick II of Hohenstaufen, who had been brought up in Sicily, succeeded to the Holy Roman Empire in 1217.

During the thirteenth century there was a beginning of serious missionary interest, and the dawning of the realization among Catholic laity that the Muslims were not necessarily idolatrous monsters. In Spain after the great defeat of the Almohad army in 1212 and the subsequent erosion of the Muslim frontiers, huge numbers of Muslims were either taken prisoner, and most of them enslaved, or were absorbed in other ways into the life of the victorious Christian kingdoms. Many of them were converted to Christianity; some of these converts, who may have expected to retain their possessions by conversion, were of high rank. In Spain and Portugal, in the Balearics, and in Italian cities like Genoa (where the largest slave market of the West was located), acquaintance with Saracens was not an unheard-of thing. Nor was it so in Barcelona, where a large, increasingly rich class of merchants spent their whole careers in trading with the Arab cities of the Maghreb.

Already by the time of the Damietta Crusade of 1217–21 the clerics were beginning to take a serious interest in the possibilities of conversion of the Muslims. St Francis of Assisi, in crossing the army lines at Damietta to seek an audience with the Sultan al-Kamil, was not alone in hoping to turn the enemy into a friend. His German contemporary Oliver of Cologne addressed a letter to al-Kamil asking for his conversion, in which he showed some knowledge of Islam, but justified the Christian attack on Egypt on the grounds of the Muslim refusal to allow proselytism. Later in the century the Dominican preaching order may have set up language centres to train friars in Arabic, first in Tunis on Muslim soil, and then in Spain.

But the still generally low level of knowledge about Islam was made apparent when the French monarchy set itself to discredit the Templar Order. A score of years after the final loss of the holy land in 1291, it was believed by learned French judges that the erring military religious knights, the Templars, who were accused of treason and heresy, had worshipped an image of Muhammad (Bafometz) in their conventicles. The idea that Muhammad should be worshipped was in Islamic terms blasphemous and inconceivable, but the fierce monotheism of Islam was entirely ignored in its vulgar Western image. Both Muslims and Christians tended, in despite of the facts, to view each other as polytheists.

The confusion of the geographical and ethnic information that was available to the Franks is also significant. The Europeans referred to the Muslims as barbarians (as did the Byzantines), Saracens, Turks, Arabs, Persians (especially when referring to the Mesopotamians), Parthians, 'Agulani' and 'Azirniti'. Even highly educated Europeans were extremely vague about Middle Eastern ethnography. The most distinguished Arab geographer of the medieval period, al-Idrisi (died 1166), was a subject of Roger, the Norman King of Sicily, but it is doubtful whether his work was ever known elsewhere in Europe, and still less in the Frankish Palestinian states.

On the Muslim side the level of information about the incoming Franks was initially low, although it subsequently improved. Some medieval Islamic geographers besides al-Idrisi had a good knowledge of Europe. When the Frankish army first reached the holy land, its religious motivation was not at all understood, and the Muslim princes viewed it – not entirely wrongly – as an army of mercenary freebooters that had escaped from the control of the Byzantines. They could scarcely have identified the newcomers as crusaders, since the term had not yet been invented, and was unknown to the incoming Franks themselves. The soldiers of the First Crusade had taken a vow and put on an identifying cross, but this had not yet conferred on them a specific religious identity that distinguished them from all other pilgrims, although it was later to do so. The inhabitants of the Christian Kingdom and of the associated Christian principates in Syria continued to be identified by their race and not by their religion to the very end of their presence in the holy land: they were always known as Franks.

At the end of the eleventh century Muslim Syria was divided between a number of minor princes, most of whom still owed allegiance to the Seljuk sultan and the Baghdad caliphate. But it also straddled the divide between Sunni and Shi'a Islam, in that the boundaries of the lands ruled by the Fatimid Ismai'li caliphate of Cairo reached southern Palestine and northern Sinai. The Fatimids paid the Frankish newcomers only the military and political attention that was necessary to hold the Egyptian lines round the border fortress of 'Asqalan (Askalon). The Sunni princes in Syria, who were more immediately threatened, identified the Franks in the second and third decades of the twelfth century as a formidable military power whose expansionist aims had to be contained.

Although the Kingdom of Jerusalem extended to 'Aqabah at the eastern head of the Red Sea, and important Frankish castles were built in the lower Jordan valley, the Fatimids continued for decades to treat it as being only of slight political weight. At this time the Shi'a Egyptian caliphate was sliding into a weak minority position in the Fertile Crescent, especially because the Isma'ili ('Assassin') groups in Syria withdrew their obedience to the Caliph in Cairo. Half a century elapsed before the final Fatimid decadence allowed a Frankish army to intervene in Egypt, and for a short time to control Cairo (1167–8). But like the attempt made by the Second Crusade in 1148 to get control of the other great Muslim centre, Damascus, the Franks' Egyptian venture failed, as did both their subsequent crusading ventures in Egypt during the following century.

The immediate reaction of Muslim governments to the events of 1099 in Jerusalem had been somewhat passive. But the Christian occupation of Jerusalem, the city of Abraham for whom Muhammad had felt especial veneration, and to which tradition said that he had made his spiritual night journey,[6] could not escape the attention of pious Muslims. By 1105 a preacher in Damascus was urging that the obligation to wage holy war on the Franks had become a collective one (*fard 'ayn*) which weighed upon each individual Muslim. But this injunction went unheard by most of the Muslim world, and was certainly disregarded by the contemporary 'Abbasid caliphs. Holy war does not seem to have been preached for any of the wars with the Franks in the first two decades of the twelfth Christian century. The Seljuk sultan Muhammad Tapar (1105–18) encouraged the subject

Turkish and Kurdish emirs in northern Syria to wage war on the Franks, but he gave these wars no especially religious tinge, and his indifference to the plight of Muslim cities lost to the Franks was notorious.

The first Muslim ruler to appeal to the holy war against the Christian states as an instrument of policy was the Turkish 'Imad al-Din Zangi, the atabeg of Aleppo and Mosul. Zangi called for volunteer warriors in the holy war to support his campaigns to eject the Franks from the critical north Syrian fortress of Edessa (al-Ruha'), an aim which, to the dismay of the Christians, he accomplished in 1144. The conquest of Edessa was only a subordinate part of Zangi's policies, of which the main one was the conquest, never accomplished in his lifetime, of Damascus. But for the first time since the original Frankish irruption of 1097, a Muslim ruler fighting the Christians was widely represented among Sunni Muslims as the saviour of Islam from the aggression of the polytheists.

The holy war was used more consciously and effectively by Zangi's son, Nur al-Din. This may in part have been due to a sort of religious conversion, or at least to a fit of religious shame. Nur al-Din was embarrassed in 1163 by the circumstances of his defeat near Krak des Chevaliers, which was ascribed by the holy men to the presence of music and liquor, forbidden by strict Muslim law, in his camp when the Frankish army surprised him. Be that is it may, it began to be appreciated in Syria that the holy war could be used as a political instrument to help legitimize a new ruling dynasty. The call to holy war sanctified a ruler's policies, and although in fact the political aims of Nur al-Din were only partly concerned with defeating the Franks, the effect of his appeal for holy war was to give his dynasty, founded like many others by a Turkish mercenary soldier, an aura of religious sanctity.

He used it, for example, to justify his intervention in Egyptian affairs, which he claimed to the Caliph was a necessary preliminary to an attack on Jerusalem that would restore the Al-Aqsa mosque (the 'further' mosque supposed to be mentioned in the Qur'an) to Islam. Nur al-Din had a wooden *minbar* (pulpit for the Friday prayer) built in Aleppo, carrying an inscription that anticipated his future conquest of Jerusalem from the Christians. After the conquest of Jerusalem in 1187 Saladin had the *minbar* transferred to the Al-Aqsa mosque, where it remained until it was burned by a religious fanatic in 1969.

There seems no reason to doubt the sincerity of Nur al-Din's devotion to the holy war, which is attested in several inscriptions placed in his buildings. It certainly increased his political clout: one of the minor emirs of northern Mesopotamia, asked by Nur al-Din to send military help against the Franks, wrote that Nur al-Din might charge him with apostasy and take away his power if he refused.

In 1169 the Syrian Sunni dynasty of Nur al-Din finally intervened in Egypt, causing the expulsion of the Franks from the country and the final failure of the Fatimid dynasty in Cairo. There was a vital religious aspect to Nur al-Din's policy, since it entailed the removal from Egypt of the Frankish polytheists and the political elimination of the Shi'a caliphs. The great beneficiary of this policy of holy war was the Kurdish soldier Salah al-Din Yussuf ben Ayyub (Saladin), who was appointed vizier in the stead of his uncle (also an appointee of Nur al-Din) in Egypt in 1169, shortly after the Frankish expulsion. A contemporary writing told the young Saladin: 'As for the *jihad*, you are the nursling of its milk and the child of its bosom. Gird up therefore the shanks of spears to meet it, and plunge on its service into a sea of sword points!'[7]

Saladin was a genuinely religious ruler, whose greatest achievement was probably not to do with his opposition to the Christians in the holy land, but with his proclamation of the 'Abbasid Sunni Caliph of Baghdad in Cairo in 1171, which put an end to the Fatimid caliphate of Egypt and to Shi'a political hegemony (although not political influence) in the west of the Fertile Crescent from that day to this. Saladin also appeared to make a real effort to rule according to Islamic law, to found Sunni religious institutions, especially in Cairo, and to remove non-Islamic taxes. He said: 'Allah has raised us up to remove from among his creatures whatever intrudes upon his worship, and has chosen us to engage in holy war in the way of Allah in the true sense.'[8]

There was a propagandist intention in this, as there was in Saladin's entire prosecution of the holy war, but his indifference to luxury and his religious zeal were sufficiently contrasted with the relaxed morals of the late Fatimid regime to confer great prestige upon him. His attacks against the Kingdom of Jerusalem after 1171 were not continuous – little medieval warfare was. He pursued a two-pronged policy of seeking to subvert Nur al-Din's dominions, and to subdue them after his death, and of prosecuting the holy war against the Franks. The latter policy was often subordinated to the former, especially during his understanding with King Amalric before Nur al-Din's death in 1174. Like all rulers of the era, he made truces to buy time, especially the 1185 four-year truce with the Franks, which Reynald of Châtillon broke, opportunely for Saladin, in 1186.

Saladin's decision to act finally and decisively against the Franks and to recapture Jerusalem may have been taken during his illness in 1186, under the influence of the religious men in his entourage. In the following year he launched a great attack on the faction-ridden Kingdom of Jerusalem, and the campaign ended with the decisive battle of Hattin, with the annihilation of the crusader army and the capture of Jerusalem. The revival of Muslim concern for the fate of Jerusalem had been largely due to Saladin, and its capture crowned his career. However, support for Saladin in Muslim Syria and Mesopotamia was far from universal, and the recapture of Acre in 1191 by the army of the Third Crusade took some of the gloss from his military achievements.

Saladin's intention in Syria and northern Mesopotamia was to succeed as the political heir of Nur al-Din, which meant, in spite of all his protestations of loyalty to the earlier dynasty, thrusting aside Nur al-Din's natural heirs. The religious colour he gave to his policies was used to enable the achievement of his own dynastic ends; this was a charge made against him by Muslim contemporaries, who saw his religious zeal as a pretext to support his usurping the lands of the Zangid rulers whose subordinate he had originally been.

Saladin's declared aim of uniting the whole Muslim world in the holy war against the Franks had only a limited resonance outside Egypt and Syria. He appealed to the Almohad Caliph in the distant west of Iberia and Morocco, Ya'qub al-Mansur, for help for the holy war in Palestine, but got no response, perhaps because not long before he had sent an army against al-Mansur. But the gesture is interesting and important, because it shows that Saladin, after a very long period in which the central area of the Islamic world had in effect left holy war to be the concern of the frontier *ghazi* fighters on the periphery, had restored the idea to mainstream Islam.

Saladin did manage to put some moral pressure on Near Eastern Muslims. For example, after the announcement that the Emperor Frederick I was marching through Asia Minor to join the Syrian Franks in 1190, Saladin wrote to the Caliph to claim that the holy war had now become a personal duty, binding upon all Muslims. The emirs who fell in Saladin's battles with the Franks were routinely referred to by his secretaries as 'martyrs'.

Saladin and the Ayyubi dynasty that he founded in Egypt and Syria brought back holy war in this way into the common language and practice of the central Arab areas. In Egypt the holy war remained for a century and a half after Saladin as one of the touchstones by which rulers were judged, not only for Saladin's own Ayyubi dynasty (which was by no means consistent in its prosecution of the holy war), but also for the Mamluk dynasty of slave-warriors that followed them. But it could not have come into existence save as a political and religious reaction to the Frankish invasion of Syria and Palestine.

Some scholars have belittled the religious results of the setting up of Frankish crusading states, and claimed that the crusades were quite insignificant in the history of Islam.[9] This view seems to disregard the history of the Ayyubi and Mamluk dynasties, and also fails to assess the later attitudes of the Ottoman Empire to its Christian neighbours. Many modern Arab writers have seen the impact of the crusades upon Christian–Muslim relations as negative. A Syrian Christian historian of an earlier generation judged them as having left a 'festering sore that refuses to heal', and as an influence that left Islam 'more militant, less tolerant, and more self-centred'.[10] The crusades have also been judged very negatively by modern Arab intellectuals, who have seen them as precursors of modern colonialism. The poet Mahmoud Darwish has chosen to regard the siege of Beirut in 1982 as a sort of reprise of the siege of Acre of 1189–91.[11]

After Saladin's death in 1193 the pragmatic attitude taken by the Ayyubi rulers – and other contemporary Muslim rulers – to the Franks of the holy land was much criticized in the Muslim world, although people did not go much beyond expressing their pious concern. The historian Ibn al-Athir (who had the Mongol peril in mind as well as that from the Franks) complained that 'among the rulers of Islam we do not see one who desires to wage holy war or to aid religion: each one devotes himself to his pastimes and amusements, and to wronging his flock. I find this more alarming than the enemy!'[12]

It was not until after Saladin's time that Muslims began to appreciate that the religious zeal of the Franks lay behind their military effectiveness. The Catholic military orders, discussed more fully below, began towards the mid-twelfth century to give some idea, especially through the Templars, of the religious element in Frankish commitment. But it took a long time for the religious motivation to be understood. To Saladin's secretary 'Imad al-Din al-Isfahani, the most striking thing about Frankish warfare was its ruthlessness: 'Wanting their fame to be on everyone's lips, both the Frankish soldiers and the rest of them deemed any means of war to be permissible: they took liberties with human souls, and claimed a pious license for what they did. Satan made their deeds seem fair to them.'[13] When 'Imad al-Din recounted the death of the Master of the Temple before Acre in 1189, he mentioned not the Templar's zeal for religion but his chivalrous courage: 'he was not saved from death by his passion for honour'.

In the next generation, in the early thirteenth Christian century, the historian Ibn al-Athir crossed a bridge in appreciating that the wars of the Franks and Arabs in the holy land since the end of the eleventh century could be understood as having been fought on both sides as religious wars. Ibn al-Athir was the first Muslim to see that there was a comparison to be drawn between Christian religious war and *jihad*: he was a reflective historian who did not find the comparison offensive, as perhaps most Muslims before him had. Ibn al-Athir wanted to account for the huge diversion of Christian resources from Europe into the holy land after the disaster that befell them in 1187, and to explain the checks that were administered to Saladin's policies by the Third Crusade. Trying to understand this, he quoted the example of a Muslim who had served with the Franks, and had gone to Rome with them to ask for papal help after the fall of Jerusalem. On the psychological level, he quoted the testimony of a Frankish prisoner who had said that he was the only son of a widowed mother who had sold all her property to equip him for the crusade. In this way the Arab historian said that he could account for the violence of the religious and spiritual impulses that had motivated the Franks.

There are no Christian parallels for the sophisticated attempt at establishing some degree of empathy with the Christian religious war that Ibn al-Athir made. But it is probably much more important that he only made this enquiry into Christian motives at a historical point when the dynamic force of Christian religious war in the holy land was already half-spent, although there were several important crusades still to be undertaken.

Another Arab historian (Abu Shama) claimed to have had a dream, at the time when the Ayyubi Sultan, al-Kamil, was planning in 1227 to hand over Jerusalem to the Emperor Frederick II, in which he saw the second Islamic Caliph, 'Umar, who had ruled Islam in the mid-seventh Christian century, coming to Damascus 'dressed in a Yemeni silk tunic' and promising to lead resistance to Frankish aggression. The Sultan who treated with the Christians to restore Jerusalem to them, 'Umar implied in the dream, would be displaced. Abu Shama also used the Qur'anic term for 'hypocrite' (*munafiq*) to describe the later Sultan al-Salih Isma'il, on account of his disastrous Frankish alliance of 1244. Other religious persons were equally critical of Ayyubi policies that involved compromise with the Franks, but there is no sign that such criticism was taken very seriously by the sultans.

From the second decade of the thirteenth century onwards, the holy war against the Mongols was more important to the Muslims of the Near East than that against the Franks. The mirage of a Mongol conversion to Christianity hovered before the Franks of the Levant until the end of the century, and was also of concern to the Muslims. After the death of the last active Ayyubi sultan in Cairo in 1249, the prestige of victory in the holy war against the Mongols was one of the factors in bringing the Mamluk general Qutuz to power in 1259. Before seizing control in Egypt Qutuz had argued that the nominal sultan, the Ayyubi child and heir, was too young to lead the holy war that had to be fought against the Mongols, and that he had therefore to be supplanted. Ironically, the prowess in the holy war of another Mamluk general, Baybars, the former Mamluk subordinate of Qutuz, and also his murderer, was invoked in the following year to justify the acceptance of Baybars as sultan.

The Mamluk rulers of Egypt were very proud of their zeal for the holy war, and regarded themselves as superior to all their Ayyubi predecessors, with the exceptions of Saladin, the great exponent of holy war, and the Sultan al-Salih, who had set up the slave Mamluk regiments. Baybars, the doughty opponent of the crusading King St Louis of France, was lauded by one of his propagandists as 'one who rose among his companions like the sun among the shining stars. [That he had murdered one of his companions to become sultan was discreetly omitted.] He was like the lion among his cubs in his den, accustomed to fighting the infidel, engaged in the holy war by night and day.'[14] And Baybars was indeed the hunter of the Franks in the east: by his control of the Mongol danger, and by his overrunning Antioch and most of the major Palestinian fortress towns, he made the end of the crusading state all but inevitable.

The significance of victory in the struggle in the late thirteenth century to eliminate the remnants of Frankish power in the holy land was not lost upon Muslim opinion. After the Mamluk Sultan al-Ashraf Khalil had finally taken Acre in 1291 and driven the last Franks from Palestine, a poet wrote in his praise that there was 'no town left to which unbelief could repair, no hope for the Christian religion. Through Ashraf the lord Sultan we are delivered from the trinity, and unity rejoices in the struggle. Praise be to God that the nation of the cross has fallen: through the Turks the religion of the chosen Arabs has been victorious.'[15]

*　　*　　*

The Near East in the Crusading
and Mamluk Periods

From the time of Urban II's crusading speech at Clermont onwards, holy war, wherever it took place, was considered an activity for which men should be promised absolution from the penalties due for their sins. Within two or three years Urban himself was saying that participation in the war against the infidels in Spain conferred absolution of this nature, and before the twelfth century was very old the same argument was being used about the pagans in eastern Europe. At the very moment of the Second Crusade, there was papal approval for another crusade to be launched against the pagan Wends on the eastern marches of Germany. There is some connection here with the debate about forcible conversion to Christianity,

A verse of the Qur'an is revealed to Muhammad during the battle of Uhud, in 625.

Sco in le nef ouert · & estes vous un cheoual blanuch · & ge siet sur as auoun leaux · & uerreis · & il iuge en dreiture · & se combat · ces oilz eurit au sicome

Above The 'Son of Man', holding a sword between his teeth, leads his troops into battle in a fourteenth-century illustration to the Apocalypse.

Opposite Illustration to the Book of Maccabees from the twelfth-century Winchester Bible.

The first crusade of Peter the Hermit, in 1096. Twenty-five thousand men march to Nicaea, where they are massacred by the Turks in a surprise attack (c. 1490).

Christian and Muslim combat, supposed, on the evidence of
the English royal arms on the shield, to represent Richard I
and Saladin.

Godfrey de Bouillon assembles his company of crusaders.
Illustration from *Historia rerum in partibus transmarinis gestarum*,
by William of Tyre.

Left Capital from a lost crusader church in Nazareth, showing the devil as a Saracen warrior.

Below Fourteenth-century fresco depicting the assault of the Saracen king on Christian troops, Chapel of the Corporal, Orvieto Cathedral.

Bottom Eleventh-century combat between Muslim and Christian ships, from 'De Passagiis', in *Venetian Chronologia Magna*.

Ambrogio Lorenzetti (active 1319–47), *Martyrdom of Franciscan Monks
at Ceuta* (Morocco). Church of San Francesco, Siena.

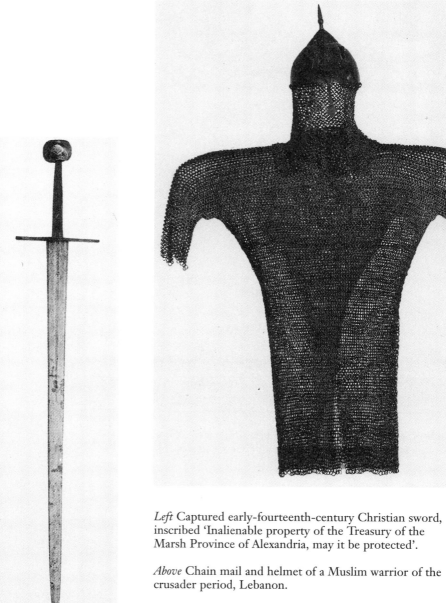

Left Captured early-fourteenth-century Christian sword, inscribed 'Inalienable property of the Treasury of the Marsh Province of Alexandria, may it be protected'.

Above Chain mail and helmet of a Muslim warrior of the crusader period, Lebanon.

which had been widely practised in the early Middle Ages, but which church lawyers and theologians of the later Middle Ages tended to deplore. The arguments about crusade and conversion were not without importance for the future doctrines of Western colonization in the New World.

The course of the struggle between Muslim and Christian states in the Iberian peninsula and North Africa was very different from that in the east. The battle of Zallaqa near Badajoz in 1086 ended with extremely heavy Christian losses; the Almoravids withdrew for a short time, but four years later were able to return to the Iberian peninsula from North Africa with the forces they needed for the conquest. When they came, they had the authority not only of the learned Maghrebi lawyers, but also of some of the best-known Muslim *'ulama* in the East, to deprive the Muslim 'party kings' of their statelets. They also went so far, once their reconquest seriously began, as to obtain approval from the 'Abassid caliph in Baghdad.

By the early years of the twelfth century the Berber Almoravids governed all of Muslim Spain. But though they resisted further Christian pressure, they failed to recapture Toledo, where a hard-line Catholic presence led to the setting up in 1122 of a confraternity of knights who swore never to live at peace with the Muslims. The passionate puritanism of the original Almoravids from the *ribat* did not last long. By the third decade of the twelfth Christian century, like so many other Berber dynasties, they suffered a second phase of regression, and their domination of the sown land and the cities fell into decay. A second wave of Muslim reformism swept the Maghreb and the Muslim part of the peninsula under the leadership of the 'unitarian' sect of Almohads ('*Muwahhids*'), another pietist Berber fraternity: they took Marrakech from the Almoravids in 1147, and in the mid-twelfth century they engulfed southern Spain and Portugal. At this period they ruled virtually the whole of Muslim North Africa outside Egypt.

The Christian *reconquista* profited spasmodically from this ebb and flow of the Islamic Berber tribes. In 1147 there was a rare intersection of the Eastern and Western crusades, when a force of crusaders bound for the East that included a large English contingent disembarked in order to take part in the siege of Lisbon, for the benefit of King Alfonso-Henry of Portugal. But the military importance of the fall of Lisbon was small, and the affair was typical of the piecemeal way in which the reconquest was operating at that time. The last great military effort of Islamic forces in the peninsula came under the Almohad Caliph Ya'qub al-Mansur (1184–99), whose victory over Alfonso VIII of Castile at Alarcos on the Guadiana River in 1195 was the worst defeat suffered by Christian forces for over a century.

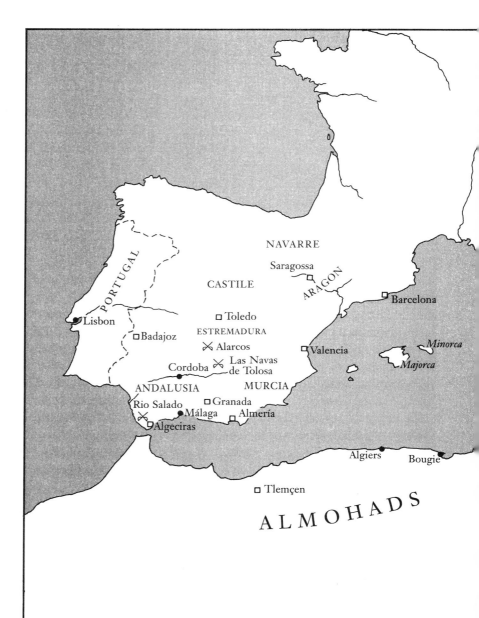

The Western Mediterranean
in the Later Middle Ages

Genoa

● Pisa

CORSICA

Rome

● Naples

SARDINIA

SICILY

Tunis

IFRIQIYA

Mahdiya

Kerkenna

Djerba

HAFSIDS

R Danube

Mediterranean Sea

But the inevitable weakening of the ruling Berber dynasty followed not very long afterwards. Many factors made it difficult to go on fighting the Islamic holy war with the degree of fanaticism and self-sacrifice that marked the first waves. The most important was the settlement in the cities of the ruling dynasties, and the bureaucratization of their governments. The great Islamic philosopher of history Ibn Khaldun took the Almoravid and Almohad governments as main examples for his interpretation of the process by which the Berber fighting dynasties came out of the desert with forces that the urbanized and cultivated Muslim governments were unable to resist, and then subsequently themselves underwent a process of urbanization that undermined the military basis of their power, and led them to the same fate of enfeeblement and decline as had overtaken their predecessors.

A difficulty of these dynasties of religious reformers was the virtual impossibility of avoiding the recruitment of Christian mercenaries, who could supply some military elements hard to find in the Islamic tribes. According to Ibn Khaldun, they were particularly necessary because of the need for a core-force that fought in close formation, a tactic that was not natural to Berber troops. It was not thought advisable to use these mercenaries in the holy war, but in fact they often fought other Christians. Even at its beginnings the Almoravid army had included Sudanese slaves and Spanish Christian prisoners, and shortly afterwards it had recruited Christians, who at first fought only in Morocco. The Almohads had used Turkish *ghazi* troops for the holy war, but they also employed Christians.

The whole history of the Iberian peninsula reflected a tendency for the warring frontier factions of Muslim and Christian to give way to the temptation to bargain with and work for the other side. The classic example of the High Middle Ages was El Cid (Rodrigo Díaz), a Castilian mercenary soldier who fought for both Christian and Muslim rulers (though more frequently for the former) and ended as ruler of a small city-state of Valencia: his career reads more like that of a soldier of the Italian Renaissance than of a medieval baron. El Cid used the Arabic title 'lord, chieftain' (*al sayyid*) from his service in command of Arab troops under the Muslim Hudid dynasty of Saragossa. He was a type many times repeated: Castilian nobles fought on the Muslim side at the bloody battle of Alarcos.

The Almohad dynasty decayed, as had its predecessors. Finally, in 1212, its main army was disastrously defeated at Las Navas de Tolosa, east of Cordova, by a big Christian coalition of Castile, Aragon, Navarre, French crusaders and a detachment from Portugal of the military religious order of Templars. This battle virtually destroyed the Almohads, and pulverized

Muslim civil order in the peninsula. From this point the Muslim holy war in Spain was extremely weak, though never abandoned altogether, and the eventual victory of Christian forces (though it took almost two further centuries) was almost inevitable.

The medieval history of the crusade resembles the history of the Islamic holy war in one important respect, in that after its inception it went through a relatively unstructured period in which its military practice was vigorous and unrestrained, but its institutions and ideas had not been subject to much analysis by theologians and lawyers. In both religions the idea of martyrdom in battle was present by the late eleventh century, although in neither religion was it sharply defined. At a much later stage, as had occurred also with the Muslim learned men who had elaborated the theory of *jihad*, the Latin Catholic lawyers and theologians took cognizance of the crusading institution, and laid down a framework within which they thought the Christian holy war should operate. The concept of holy war was extended and refined, and – as had happened also with *jihad* – circumstances were envisaged in which it could be waged against apostates or dissidents of the same religion.

Like the Islamic holy war, the crusade was in theory an obligation that could be accepted by any believer capable of bearing arms and undertaking the journey, though it lacked the universal nature of the holy war obligation in Islam. And like the Islamic holy war, although universal in theory, the crusade tended to be elitist in practice, because of the highly specialized nature of cavalry warfare and the costliness of the arms and equipment, to which the high costs of the journey to the holy land had to be added. To this extent the crusade also had something in common with the Muslim pilgrimage to Mecca, the *hajj*.

But the crusade has to be distinguished sharply from the Muslim holy war, most of all because of the different natures of the two religions. There was no equivalent in Islam to the predominance of the bishop of the single Western see of Rome, still less to the idea of a single juridical structure in which this bishop should legislate for all believers. The caliphate never played the part in the history of *jihad* that was played by the papacy in the history of the crusade. The Roman see had itself launched the crusading call, which was to be of great importance in its own later history of centralized authority over the Latin church.

At first, the results of the crusade may to some extent have disappointed the popes. The Kingdom of Jerusalem was not a theocratic institution dependent upon the pope, but a Western-type feudal monarchy. The Latin Patriarch of Jerusalem was an influential figure in the kingdom, but not greatly more so than some Western archbishops in Western monarchies.

But within three decades of the First Crusade there were developments in crusading institutions that were integrally linked with papal authority, and with the prestige of Western churchmen who were committed to the support of that authority. Early in the twelfth century a small group of pious and poor soldiers undertook voluntarily the duties of protecting pilgrims on their journeys to and from the Palestinian coast and Jerusalem. King Baldwin gave them quarters in his palace in Jerusalem, on the supposed site of King Solomon's Temple and adjoining the Al-Aqsa Mosque. Their seal showed two knights riding the same horse, as a sign of their poverty, and they voluntarily accepted a celibate and religious way of life.

The 'Templars' led an obscure existence in this calling for some years, but it was evident that they would find no new recruits, nor proper logistic support, unless they were institutionalized along the lines of the monastic religious institutions of Europe. This could only be achieved with the help of the religious authorities and their spokesmen. One of the religious knights went from Palestine to France in 1127 and secured support from the greatest churchman of the age, St Bernard of Clairvaux. It has been argued that the saint gave this support rather unwillingly, believing himself to be ill-fitted for the task. But on the other hand, the idea of a military religious order fitted into his vision of a knighthood cleansed of the bloodshed and ill-doing of feudal greed and conflict, that would serve the new, theocratic world order which he saw as imminent. At a church council attended by St Bernard the body of Templar knights was approved as a corporate organization governed by church law. Eleven years later, in 1139, the pope gave his approval to the arrangement, referring to the Templars who had died in battle in the holy land as having attained eternal life after the sweat of a battle in which they had 'consecrated their hands to God in the blood of the unbelievers'.[16]

Although the church approval of the Templars appears to have gone through without much clerical opposition, it seemed to confuse one of the basic distinctions that governed medieval social life, between the 'religious order' that was forbidden to carry out bloodshed, and the 'military order' to whom this prohibition did not apply. The whole process of church reform during the preceding century had been directed towards stopping men whose hands had been stained with blood from touching holy things. In the Romantic period and later an idealistic glow was cast over medieval chivalry, and the notion of pious knights who fought for the good became platitudinous. No such illusion was present in the minds of twelfth-century churchmen, who knew perfectly well that very large numbers of secular knights were church-robbing brigands who (in Muhammad's term, of which they could not have known) made mischief in the land.

St Bernard, particularly, never referred to secular knighthood except in highly derogatory terms. When commending the new military religious orders he used a paradoxical account of their disreputable origins that to a modern reader seems almost cynical:

> It is really rather convenient that you will find very few men in the vast multitude that throngs to the holy land who have not been unbelieving scoundrels, sacrilegious plunderers, homicides, perjurers, adulterers, whose departure from Europe is a double benefit, seeing that people in Europe are glad to see the back of them, and the people to whose assistance they are going in the holy land are delighted to see them! ... Indeed, the knights of Christ fight the battles of their lord in safety, by no means either fearing to have sinned in slaying the foe, nor fearing the peril of their own deaths, seeing that either dealing out death, or dying, when for Christ's sake, contains nothing criminal but merits rather a glorious reward ... The soldier of Christ kills safely: he dies the more safely. He serves his own interests in dying, and Christ's interests in killing ... He is the instrument of God for the punishment of malefactors and for the defence of the just. Indeed, when he kills a malefactor this is not homicide, but malicide, and he is accounted Christ's legal executioner against evildoers.[17]

In this manner St Bernard justified the setting up of a Christian religious order whose duty was to fight the holy war, thus abandoning the religious conviction of the sinfulness of bloodshed that had endured for a millennium. St Bernard was supremely gifted at sensing the temper and opinions of his times. He had proved to be an organizer and fund-raiser of genius for the Cistercian religious order, and it is not surprising that his propaganda (though after the Church Council of 1128 he took no administrative part in the setting up of the Templars) launched the Templars on a career of peerless feudal respectability. Endowments and estate title deeds poured into their coffers from every land in Christian Europe, and shortly before the departure of the French king on the Second Crusade in 1147, a chapter of 130 white-robed Templars was held in Paris in the presence of the king and the pope. The financial organization needed to transmit funds and supplies from Europe to the new order in the holy land had already by this time enabled the Templar Order to become in effect a bank that served the French monarchy.

After the setting up of the Templar Order in the holy land, a second, parallel military order, the Hospitallers, which had originated among knights who before the First Crusade had served a pilgrim hostel in Jerusalem, was established. The Hospitallers, using similar methods to those the Templars had employed in order to escape from the control of the local episcopal authorities in Jerusalem, obtained papal approval for their order in rather the same manner. Their tradition was more pastoral and charitable than that of the Templars, in that their original employment had been to nurse the sick and indigent, but after a short time they were also employed in Palestine on military duties. By the end of the Third Crusade in the late twelfth century the Hospitallers were as much committed to a military role as the Templars, although their traditional charitable functions were still not abandoned. The military orders, termed 'the new Maccabees' by the popes, were showered with papal privileges and protection, because they were the nearest thing the popes possessed to a direct military presence in the holy land.

The military orders were of great importance to the Frankish establishment in the holy land, because they acted as channels for the funding of castles and other defence measures from their estates and revenues in Europe, and they supplied the only standing army the Franks possessed. The Palestinian feudal lords and the monarchy of the Kingdom of Jerusalem were all subject to the perpetual ebb and flow of feudal quarrels and politics, from which the orders were, at least until their great quarrels in the thirteenth century, more or less exempt. The orders were endowed with enormous ecclesiastical privileges, and they also operated outside the holy land, thus to some extent generalizing the principles of the Christian holy war. The Templars became, for example, of great importance in the Iberian peninsula, particularly in Aragon and Portugal.

There was no real equivalent in the Muslim holy war to the Christian religious orders: the nearest thing was the *ribat*, but the normally decentralized nature of *ghazi* frontier warfare was very far from the papally approved military orders operating under the central control of a master who had a hierarchy of military officials subject to him. Their formidable nature was soon recognized by the Muslims, but their permanent residence in the East meant that some Templars became orientalized, at least to the point of speaking Arabic and accepting Arab friends. The 'Turcopolier', the Templar official who headed the Muslim levies, must have spoken Arabic. The Syrian prince Usama ibn-Munqid tells a story that he was allowed by Templar friends to say his prayers in the al-Aqsa Mosque in Jerusalem (that was directly controlled by the order), and that as he began the Islamic prayers he was roughly interrupted by a Frank. The Templars apologized to the Muslim for the man's rudeness, which they put down to his being a late arrival in the holy land, and ejected him from the mosque.[18]

Throughout the life of the Frankish settlement in the East there was an annual influx of pilgrims who had taken the cross and were expected to play a part in the defence of the holy land, and from whom some slight permanent immigration could be expected. But these modest and usually temporary reinforcements could not solve all the major and urgent problems of defence, nor were the military orders, that had specialized functions in building and manning castles, always able to meet the sometimes desperate military needs. The investments made by the monarchy, the feudal princes and nobles and the military orders in the construction of castles were enormous, and after their construction the expenses of manning them were very heavy for states whose demographic and economic basis was frail. There were occasional dramatic occasions when key strongpoints and lordships were lost, throwing into prominence the precarious nature of the whole Frankish domination. The first of these to make a strong impression on European public opinion was the loss of Edessa (al-Ruha') and all the lands east of the Euphrates to the Atabeg Zangi in 1144.

The Second Crusade, summoned as a result of the loss of Edessa, had few of the popular or tumultuous characteristics of the First. In so far as an appeal to the crowd accompanied it, this was made by St Bernard to the knightly classes. Pope Eugenius III, over whom St Bernard exercised a very strong influence, summoned the nobles and magnates to the crusade in order to defend the land that their fathers had won. The emergency was seen as very largely a matter of feudal right and possession. A contemporary song envisaged a trial by battle between the champions of the lords of heaven and hell:

God has brought before you his suit against the Turks and Saracens
   who have done him great despite. They have seized his fiefs, where
God was first served and recognized as Lord.

God has ordained a tournament between Heaven and Hell, and sends
to all his friends who wish to defend him, that they fail him not.[19]

The Second Crusade of 1147 set most of the pattern for subsequent major
crusades, in that it was led by kings or great magnates, and was organized
through the normal European diplomatic channels, with the papacy as the
prime mover and co-ordinator. In one way it was the first major step towards
the concept of European collective security, and its legacy was remembered
in the seventeenth and eighteenth centuries, when the way began to be
sought for projects of 'perpetual peace'. Like all organizations for military
enforcement of collective ideals, it was very clumsy, and much impeded by
the quarrels and tensions that divided the participating governments. It was
eventually to prove, in spite of the enormous military operation it took to
the East, ineffective. And, like many subsequent crusades, it attracted sharp
criticism from a few churchmen who saw it as a perversion of church ideals
– even, at the most extreme, as a work of Antichrist.

The presence of the two strongest European powers, the kings of France
and Germany, in the Second Crusade was a diplomatic triumph for
St Bernard and the papacy. But the overwhelming preponderance of these
kings over a weak but better advised King of Jerusalem led the expedition
towards the military fiasco occasioned by their insistence upon the attack
on Damascus. The Second Crusade did nothing to help the Franks of
northern Syria, whose plight had occasioned it, and only hindered Frankish
interests in southern Syria.

The Third Crusade, after the battle of Hattin and the loss of Jerusalem
to Saladin in 1187, was a response to a much graver crisis in the affairs of
the Frankish Kingdom. It followed the precedents of forty years earlier in
most respects, and the papacy continued to be the main force in summoning
and co-ordinating the first stages of the enterprise. But there was one major
innovation that was to prove immensely important to the crusade: the kings
were allowed to legislate taxation of income (in England called the 'Saladin
tithe') to help finance it. Within a short time this taxation for crusade was
adopted by the popes and imposed upon the clergy, a development that
had important results for the centralization of the Latin Catholic church.

The earlier departure in 1189 of the German crusade under Frederick
Barbarossa, and the German Emperor's drowning in the River Calycadnus
(Saleph) in Asia Minor before reaching Syria, meant that the overwhelming
Christian military force which Saladin had so much feared was never actually
assembled in the holy land, although what came was daunting enough to

the Muslims. The armies of Richard I of England and Philip Augustus of France arrived to press home the Frankish siege of Acre in 1191. Substantial reinforcements had been reaching the holy land throughout the preceding year, and the Frankish army, under the leadership of the formidable Richard, achieved the fall of Acre, that was to remain Frankish until the final Muslim recapture of the city by the Mamluk sultan al-Ashraf exactly a century later.

With the Third Crusade the pattern for most later crusades (still not referred to as crusades, but as 'general passages' of pilgrims) was now set. Papal summonses and indulgences, papally authorized taxation (instead of the lay taxation of 1185–8) and military participation of the European princes arranged through papal diplomacy were to be constant factors. Church law began to deal in detail with the changes in the law of personal status caused by crusading. Holy war was well on the way to being as institutionalized in the Christian world as it had for long been in Islam.

CHAPTER SIX

Two Societies
Organized for Holy War

IT SEEMS AT FIRST remarkable how long it took Western theologians and church lawyers to recognize the need to confront systematically the problems set them by the crusade and its associated institutions. They probably hesitated because of a distaste for matters that concerned the part played by the church in bloodshed. They were willing to allow, in accordance with the ideas of St Augustine, that the prohibition placed upon bloodshed by divine and human law could be waived if war was waged 'by God's authority'. But the church's responsibility for launching the crusade, and its involvement in the ensuing wars, were hardly ever considered as a subject for debate: when in the thirteenth century they turned to look at crusading matters, church lawyers concentrated on particular points arising from the special privileges and status granted by papal action to crusaders. So far as the church was concerned, what mattered most was the will to contrition shown by an individual Christian's acceptance of penance for sins committed, in making the crusading vow. Once the vow was made, bloodshed committed in its fulfilment was godly, provided the vow was undertaken out of devotion and not to acquire honour or material reward.

The main argument for the propriety of the holy war in the holy land was, in a manner similar to that argued by Zionists nine centuries later, one of divinely authorized property right, which in medieval terms could only be vindicated by men willing to do God's will. St Bernard had written before the Second Crusade:

> The earth is shaken because the Lord of heaven is losing his land, the land in which he appeared to men, in which he lived among men for more than thirty years; the land made glorious by his miracles, holy by his blood; the land in which the flowers of his

resurrection first blossomed. And now, for our sins, the enemy of
the cross has begun to lift his sacrilegious head there, and to devas-
tate with the sword that blessed land, that land of promise. Alas,
if there be none to withstand him, he will invade the very city of
the living god, overturn the arsenal of our redemption, and defile
the holy places that have been adorned by the blood of the immacu-
late lamb. They have cast their greedy eyes especially on the holy
sanctuaries of our Christian religion, and they long particularly to
violate that couch on which, for our sakes, the lord of our life fell
asleep in death ... How great a number of sinners have here
confessed with tears and obtained pardon for their sins since the
time when these holy precincts were cleansed of pagan filth by the
swords of our fathers! The evil one sees this and is enraged, he
gnashes his teeth and withers away in fury.[1]

This was the basis for the idea that the holy land was the patrimony of all
Christians, 'the inheritance of the crucified one' that he had promised them.
There was hesitation to say that war should be waged upon Muslims simply
because they were unbelievers: some thirteenth-century church lawyers
thought that it should not, and that peaceful Muslims and infidels outside
the holy land should be left in peace, provided they neither invaded Christian lands nor interfered with Christian missionary work.

By the thirteenth century the Augustinian theory of the just war was an
important part of scholastic thinking about the crusade, but not a very
important element in the way that people felt about it. It is often claimed
that the theory of just war was an element in the crusade from its earliest
beginnings, but there is no convincing evidence that this was so. St Bernard's
argument about Christian property in the holy land, and the assertion that
Christians had a property right in the Iberian peninsula earlier than that
of the Muslims, were important not only for their publicist effect, but
because they went beyond the simple emotive appeal of *Deus lo volt*, and
began to substitute something like a legal justification for the crusade.
People could logically conclude that the crusade was a just war undertaken
for the recovery of property unrighteously seized; it could in this respect
be called a bastardization of the idea of the just war.

The idea that the crusade was a just war was not unimportant: for
example, the diversion of crusaders from the sea voyage to Jerusalem to
the siege of Lisbon in 1147 was justified by the clergy on such grounds.
But in fact very few people beside the scholastic theorists were much con-

cerned with the idea of just war; it was the insult offered to Christ by the Muslim occupation of the holy places that was in the front of people's minds, together with the means of personal salvation offered by the crusading indulgence. The concept of the just war existed rather uneasily beside that of crusade.

In the closing years of the twelfth century the Third Crusade had marked a changed attitude. It became accepted, by the literate and the noble class at least, that revivals of the emotionalism of the first great armed pilgrimage would never suffice to remove the barrier of Muslim military power that now stood between the Catholic Christians and Jerusalem. Apocalyptic expectation was not dead, as the Children's Crusade of 1212 was to show, and apocalyptic dreams still affected elements in the clergy, and got a ready hearing among laymen. But the trend was towards the mobilization of Christian military resources, and to supplying the diplomatic and financial organization that this needed. The papacy was determined to remain in the forefront of this movement, and the great administrative ability of its leadership made sure that it did so.

Pope Innocent III (1198–1217) has been identified as marking the culmination of a process by which all barriers between religion and war in Latin Catholicism were removed.[2] In this respect, as in many others, this powerful man marked a watershed in the attempt to establish some sort of universal papal order. The call for a crusade in the East that he issued some two years after his election as pope proclaimed a kind of sacred violence that was new in the papal leadership of holy war. Innocent represented Christ himself as calling immediately and urgently for war; the defeat of the Christians in the holy land by the inhuman and barbaric Saracens was portrayed as a re-enactment of the betrayal and captivity of Christ. Pope Innocent said that refusal to serve in the holy war amounted in itself to infidelity to Christ. The parallel with Muslim doctrine is striking.

At the apex of Western Latin Christian society stood the Roman bishop, the pope. At the apex of Muslim society – although in a position that granted honour rather than jurisdiction – stood the caliph. Neither enjoyed uncontested influence over the religious groups that they claimed as subjects. Both had a unique position as to the holy war, of which pope and caliph in one respect could be considered as the two conflicting leaders, although neither could really be said to direct it. But the holy wars of the two religions differed in chronology as in much else: in Islam there had been holy war from the beginning, whereas in Western Christianity an ideology of holy war had grown up some five hundred years later. In Christianity the holy war was closely connected with the office of the main religious leader; in Islam there was a similar historical connection, but one that had with the lapse of time declined. Muslim leaders in the lands of the eastern caliphate at the time of Saladin offered little more than polite compliments to the caliph when *jihad* was discussed. In the same period the popes were almost always consulted about expeditions that were being planned to defend the Western settlement in the holy land.

Moreover, in the West the holy war magnified the role of a particular religious authority. The power and privilege that the Roman bishop enjoyed over other Latin bishops, and the place he occupied in the religious conceptions of Western Christians, had been greatly enhanced by the central role of the papacy from the First Crusade onwards. The papal role depended not only on historic tradition, but on the way in which the popes had authorized and favoured the military orders, and on the part Rome played in co-ordinating the crusading efforts of the Western princes. The Second Crusade (1145–9) had marked the high point of their overt diplomatic and religious influence. Subsequently the great Western monarchies had developed in a way that limited direct papal influence over their policies in the holy land and the Levant. But they accepted the principle of papal intervention and, to a limited extent, of papal leadership, in crusading affairs.

Papal negotiating power in the matter of the crusade was greatly increased by a decision taken by Pope Innocent III in 1199. Having achieved less than he had hoped through preaching of the crusade by papal emissaries, Pope Innocent decided that the sinews for the future war in the East must be strengthened. He therefore, shortly after some of the princes had decided to proceed upon what later became known as the Fourth Crusade, issued orders for a new kind of taxation to be exacted from the churches of Western Christendom. His bull referred to the desolation and depopulation of the Christian holy land, and to the opportunity for a new Western military intervention offered by the current disunity of the Muslim princes. The clerks were told to contribute the fortieth part of their annual revenues towards the expenses of the approaching crusade, after deduction of current debt repayments.

In this way Pope Innocent III – in spite of the promise contained in the same bull that the tax was not to serve as a precedent – made the first step towards setting up a new fiscal machine. The principle of crusade taxation was to prove of great importance both to the crusade and to the papacy.

Once taxation under clerical authority to finance the crusade had been established, there was a powerful inducement to persuade the princes to go to the popes, and to use them as political go-betweens and financiers for crusading policies.

Because of the privileges usually enjoyed by the clergy in West European states, it was normally very hard for princes to draw on the wealth of the church to finance their military adventures. The excuse of a promised crusade now offered the secular rulers, and especially the more cynical ones, new chances to get money out of the church. On the papal side it had in the past been very difficult to find a principle that authorized the Roman bishop to exact taxes from subordinate bishops and their clergy. Still less had there existed any kind of graduated income tax upon the clergy, an absolutely novel idea. Under the influence of new centralizing principles a new holy war order emerged in the West, favourable to papal authority and buttressed by systematic taxation of the faithful. The essentials of this regime changed little between the mid-thirteenth century and the Protestant Revolution of the sixteenth.

The position of the popes drew additional strength from their being recognized as the authority that identified apostates from the faith. This idea had been present in the earlier wars of the eleventh century Reform popes with their anathematized imperialist enemies, before the First Crusade had even been mooted. From the mid-twelfth century onwards clerical approval for holy war against apostasy was often expressed, sometimes in the form of demanding action against those who were said to be impeding the crusade in the holy land from being carried out. This was the origin of the project – not seriously entertained until the very end of the twelfth century – to attack Byzantium, because Byzantine policy was seen by some churchmen (including, at one point, St Bernard) as an obstacle to the proper execution of the war against infidels in the holy land.

In assessing the powers of what came to be called the papal monarchy, we have to be cautious. The pope himself, in a letter written to the Byzantine Emperor early in the twelfth century that was concerned immediately with theological questions, and only by implication with the holy land, put the point realistically:

> We experience great difficulty in this business, because owing to their great diversity, our peoples cannot easily agree on one opinion.[3]

In crusading negotiations, no less than in negotiations about the reunion of the Eastern and Western churches, the pope stood more in the position of the president of an international organization than in that of a religious dictator. This fact was unpalatable to such great ideologues as Pope Innocent III, but it was as true for him as for any other pope, as the history of the Fourth Crusade (1198–1204) abundantly shows. He authorized the crusade, which had originally been intended to proceed to Egypt or the holy land, in such terms as to allow its being turned against the Greek Christian Empire of Byzantium, although the seizure of Constantinople by the Latin crusaders in 1204 took place against his wishes. The fiasco of the Fourth Crusade was typical of the way in which Innocent III and many of his successors would make the most exalted claims for their office, authorize the doing of great deeds, and then have to stand by while things over which they could exercise no control were done in their name.

The princes who left on the Fourth Crusade in 1202 had been unable to do so until they had obtained the promise of shipping to carry them to the East from the maritime republic of Venice. The Venetians, whose treaty with the crusaders had been approved by the pope, managed to deflect the crusading force, first to Zara on the Adriatic coast, and subsequently to a landing in Constantinople, whose purpose was covertly hostile to the Byzantine Emperor. The way was then opened, after the shady replacement of one Greek emperor by another, for the storming and sack in 1204 of the great Eastern Christian capital, and the establishment there of a new Latin Empire. The intended voyage to Egypt and the attack on the main Muslim forces there never took place; the pope had been duped.

The Fourth Crusade was not the last occasion on which a crusade slipped out of papal control. The young German Hohenstaufen Emperor Frederick II, formerly a papal ward, had been obliged by a treaty with Pope Honorius III in 1226 to proceed to the holy land on crusade. In the event the underlying hostility between Frederick and the papal court, which concerned the politics of Italy and had little or nothing to do with the crusade, made its execution virtually impossible. Frederick was placed under excommunication for a delay in the crusade that had been due to his illness. Instead of offering penance and submission, in 1228 he took his army to the East without further ado.

Upon arrival in the holy land (to whose governance he had a dynastic claim) Frederick, instead of launching a general attack upon the Muslims, opened negotiation with the Ayyubid Sultan, al-Kamil. The treaty he made with the Sultan in 1229 seemed to gain for him the holy city of Jerusalem that had been lost in 1187, although its appearance was deceptive. Jerusalem was restored to the Christians, albeit with its walls demolished and therefore in an indefensible condition, and a ten-year truce was concluded. In this way an emperor who was at the time under the ban of the church succeeded in entering the holy city as its ruler, and in crowning himself as king of the Kingdom of Jerusalem. The Christian crusade, once the product of blind religious fury, had become under Frederick a matter of cold, rational power politics, executed by an emperor whose Christian orthodoxy was afterwards to be called in question, and who was accounted as not unfriendly to Islam, in the teeth of clerical opposition.

The crusade that had preceded Frederick II's voyage to the Levant had, however, been the most clerical of all crusades. At Innocent III's great Lateran Council of 1215 churchmen from all over the Latin Catholic world had assembled in Rome, agreed to pay a further swingeing crusading tax, and approved the pope's intention to organize a great expedition to the East. Innocent III died in 1216 before this could take place. An Austro-Hungarian army reached the holy land with other feudal forces in the following year, but the immediate military results were disappointing. The alternative plan, which had been under discussion since the preceding century, of an attack on Egypt, was decided upon, and in 1218 a large Christian force invested Damietta at the mouth of the Nile. When he arrived in Egypt the crusaders accepted the military leadership of one of the papal legates, a Portuguese cardinal called Pelagius.

It might have been possible at that point to have had terms from the Sultan, al-Kamil that, in return for the crusaders' withdrawal from Egypt, restored the holy land west of the Jordan, including Jerusalem, to the Christians. Perhaps affected by the prohibitions in church law against making peace with the infidels, but influenced also by other considerations, Pelagius and the heads of the military religious orders refused to treat. The opportunity for a negotiated peace – that was later to be seized, though on less favourable terms, by the Emperor Frederick II – passed. Damietta fell to the Christians, but they were no better able to hold it against al-Kamil than he against them. Further peace negotiations broke down when they met with the same kind of Christian intransigence that had been shown earlier, and after its defeat on the east bank of the Nile on the road to Cairo the whole crusading force departed ignominiously in 1221.

The Damietta enterprise had not proved to be a good argument for direct clerical leadership of the crusade. But the failure of this particular operation was probably due to the weakness of the strategic concept rather than to the quality or prejudice of the clerical generals. King Louis IX of France experienced a very similar defeat in Egypt in 1245, perhaps through following too closely the precedent of the campaign of 1219–21. Like the earlier expedition, his suffered a decisive defeat at Mansourah en route to Cairo.

The Saracens were by no means the only targets of the holy wars launched by Pope Innocent III. In the conflict with the Hohenstaufen claimant to the empire that took place in the early years of his pontificate, he did not shrink from the holy war. In 1199 he called for a crusade against the German imperial viceroy in Sicily, Markward of Anweiler, claiming that his recalcitrance was impeding the embarkation to the holy land, although Innocent's disapproval seems in fact to have been based on Markward's opposition to other papal policies.

The logical consequence of asking for holy war against apostates was to establish a standard practice by which crusades could be preached against any group of supposed heretics, or even against princes who could be viewed as political enemies of the papacy. Innocent III was a principal agent in authorizing this further extension of the principle of holy war. He proclaimed a crusade against the heretical Cathars ('Albigensians') of southern France, who rejected the Catholic sacraments and priesthood, that was bloodily executed by the feudal nobles of Île de France. Three-quarters of a century earlier St Bernard, who had been in other respects no enemy of the crusade, had refrained from asking for war against the Albigensians, and had contented himself with preaching against them and disputing with them. The Albigensian Crusade authorized in 1207 by Innocent III afterwards served as a pattern for many subsequent crusades against dissidents and supposed heretics: it was in the guise of such a crusade that the Spanish Armada sailed against Protestant England in 1588.

Thus the crusade against heretics became a part of the established spiritual armoury of the church. The great thirteenth-century canon lawyer Henry, Cardinal Bishop of Ostia, wrote that the son of God did not come into the world merely to suffer on the cross, nor to acquire the property of the land of Palestine in which he was to be crucified, but to redeem captives and to lead sinners to penitence. For this reason, he wrote, the crusade against schismatic and heretical Christians was even more important than the crusade against the Saracens.[4] His doctrine marks a turning point in the history of Christian holy war. The Christians had found and accepted their own version of the holy war against apostates that had for centuries existed in Islam, and the holy war against Christian apostasy could now be just as freely invoked as that to free the holy land of Palestine, or to eject the Saracens from formerly Christian lands in the Iberian peninsula.

The new Christian idea of a holy war against apostasy may be compared with the ancient Islamic one. Muhammad waged the holy war in a physical sense to combat unbelief and persecution (*fitna*). But conflict within the Islamic community could be viewed differently. Apostasy by someone who deserted his belief in Islam was met by force on the part of the Islamic community. Immediately after Muhammad's death it became necessary to fight a war to bring back to Islam the Arabian tribes that were starting to drift away from their religious obedience. These wars against apostasy, known as the wars of the *ridda*, were holy wars. In the later history of Islam other holy wars were fought against Muslims judged guilty of apostasy.

Other crusades were in the meantime being pursued against pagans living to the east of the imperial German frontiers. The crusades were no longer restricted to fighting Muslims in Iberia and the holy land: they had given birth to a series of holy wars that were not concerned only with unbelievers dwelling beyond the Christian frontiers, but with an internal struggle against heresy and dissent, that could present itself in any part of Christendom. It is true that the idea of holy war against Christians was not universally accepted throughout the Latin church, and objections were made to it not only by dissidents, but by orthodox believers. These were disregarded by the church authorities, when not actively proscribed.

The popes had fought wars against Christian princes ever since the Roman bishops had become the masters of a substantial territory in central Italy in the early Middle Ages. But though many of these wars had had a religious tinge, none before the thirteenth century could properly be termed a holy war. From the mid-thirteenth century until the end of the Middle Ages, crusades of this nature were preached against Christian princes as a matter of course, and indulgences were granted for them, and subsidies required, in the same manner as for the crusades against Muslims or pagans. It used to be common for historians to discuss these 'political' crusades as though they were in some way morally reprehensible, in a manner that the crusade against Muslims in Iberia and the Levant was not, and sometimes to speak of them as a distortion of the 'original' crusading ideal. It was also usual to deplore the 'political' crusades for their supposed effect of diverting military and financial resources that could have gone towards the prosecution of crusading wars against a common Islamic enemy.

But of late the crusades against supposed heretics and against the political foes of the Roman bishops have come to be viewed differently.[5] There is a widespread opinion among scholars – although there are still plenty who disagree – that the legal and administrative machinery set up by the popes and their lawyers during the thirteenth century enforced a completely different concept of holy war than that of the First and Second Crusades. The new legal measures, whose main purport was systematically diffused throughout Christendom, meant that in the eyes of contemporary Latin Catholics, provided they had been authorized by the popes, there was no substantive difference between crusades against unbelieving Muslims or pagans and those against dissident Christians.

This assessment is convincing, but does not seem to go far enough. Much time and effort has been devoted to demonstrating that the so-called later crusades, even when they took the form of war on dissident Christians, could not be formally distinguished from earlier holy wars in the holy land. It is a conclusion that leads to further, quite radical, deductions about the nature of late medieval Catholic Christendom. From the thirteenth century onwards, the holy war was not in the least restricted to fighting infidels, but could be proclaimed against infidels or Christians, virtually at the discretion of the popes. After the apprenticeship of the first three crusades, Latin Christianity had been fully militarized, and for several centuries holy war was one of the normal ways in which it expressed itself.

The generalization of the principle of holy war had far-reaching effects, as might be expected. One was the adoption of the crusade as a political and military device to protect papal temporal interests in Italy. By this means the high-sounding doctrine of holy war was imported into the petty squabbles of the popes with the Italian princes and city-states. When, in the first half of the thirteenth century, the crusade had been preached against the Emperor Frederick II of Hohenstaufen, the issues had been such as to concern the universal interests of Christendom. But when Pope Boniface VIII came in 1297 to have a crusade preached against the Roman family of Colonna, in effect a part of the quarrel between two Roman baronial families (the Colonna and Boniface's own family, the Caetani), the disparity of means and ends was such as to strike some contemporaries as being morally wrong. Dante wrote of Pope Boniface that he was 'The prince of the new Pharisees, who fought Christian enemies, who were neither Muslims nor Jews, near the Lateran Church in Rome. He did not fight them because they had given aid and comfort to the Saracens in the siege of Acre [the final defeat of the Christians in the holy land, in 1291], and he disregarded in this the high dignity of his holy office.'[6]

Episodes like Boniface's crusade against the Colonna were repeated in the papal state in central Italy for over a century. Petty Italian tyrants of eastern Italy like the Este of Ferrara, or yet more insignificant rulers such as the Ordelaffi family of the tiny city of Forlì, were on account of their rebellion against papal rule visited with the full rigours of the crusade. Clergy were sent out to preach the indulgence for the holy war against them, and the same spiritual favours were conceded to the faithful who gave money to pay the papal troops in Italy as to those who contributed to the crusade against the Muslims or Lithuanians.

Such measures became commonplace. In the mid-fourteenth century a crusade was preached against the 'Great' Company of German and other mercenaries in central Italy on account of their depredations. It might be thought that the popes were intervening to protect the Italian population from a group of lawless bandits, but within a year or two of the crusade being preached against them the very same mercenaries were enthusiastically recruited by the church to serve in the repression of rebels in the papal state. Their clerical recruiting sergeant was the papal representative in Italy who best reflected the spirit of this bellicose spirituality, the Castilian cardinal Gil de Albornoz. Albornoz had as Archbishop of Toledo been present at the decisive crusading battle with the Muslims of Rio Salado in 1340. During his bloodstained rule on behalf of the popes in Italy, he made it clear that anyone who resisted papal policy in any way was to be regarded as a heretic. With such people in control, the routinization of holy war became inevitable.

The common nature of the crusade against infidels outside Christendom and that of the crusade against dissident Christians can be illustrated by the standard way in which they were preached. Whatever the purpose of the crusade, the pope would order chosen bishops to have it preached by secular priests in their dioceses, and might also ask the secular princes to have it announced to their subjects. The preaching of the crusade, and the offer of its accompanying indulgences, were to be made as far as possible in the vernacular. By contributing to the crusading chest people could obtain the benefit of the crusading indulgences, and even commute crusading vows that they had formerly made, for money. The popes made much use of the preaching orders of Franciscans and Dominicans, especially the former, to broadcast and popularize the crusading indulgence.

Such methods were used to proclaim the crusade against Muslims, the pagans of Eastern Europe, Albigensians in France, Hussites in Bohemia, dissident Franciscans, recalcitrant German and Italian rulers, rebels in the papal state, sometimes even against supporters of a rival pope during the long period (1378–1417) in which the papacy itself was contested by rival claimants. In the service of such a crusade English troops went to Flanders under the command of the Bishop of Norwich in 1384 to fight the supporters of the 'Avignonese' pope of the competing papal allegiance. The crusade had become a standard means of defence, used by the papacy for three centuries or so to fight both its internal and its external enemies – or those whom it suspected to be its enemies – and was important to the vast clerical administrative machine of the later Middle Ages. It was responsible for a large proportion of papal taxation of the clergy, and was one of the main excuses for the development of a powerful fiscal engine for the benefit of the popes. When the object of the taxation was the crusade against Muslims, the taxes often ended by being shared between the popes and the secular princes who promised, though they did not always perform, the crusade.

In the meantime, although the theory of Muslim holy war did not change, Islamic rulers blew hot and cold in its execution. An Arabic poem on the fall of Acre to the Mamluk sultan in 1291, which meant the end of Christian lordship in the holy land, states the ethnic identity of the champions of Islam in the Fertile Crescent at this stage of history:

> Because of you [Ashraf] no town is left to which unbelief can repair, no hope for the Christian religion. Through al-Ashraf the lord sultan we are delivered from the trinity, and unity rejoices in the struggle. Praise be to God: the nation of the cross has fallen; through the Turks the religion of the chosen Arabs has triumphed.[7]

The Mamluks, the Turkic rulers of Egypt, came from the class of soldier-slaves. They were typical of their time. Most champions of the Islamic mission in the later Middle Ages were, over a huge geographical area, predominantly Turkish. Only in the Iberian peninsula and the Maghreb were the troops fighting the holy war mostly Arab or Berber. By the time of the fall of Acre in 1291 the Turkic military preponderance had a history some centuries old. As late as the mid-eleventh Christian century a writer on Islamic law could assume that a Turk might well be an unbeliever. But the Turkish tribes were at that time converted to Islam in very large numbers, and they provided a great reservoir of military manpower on which the rulers of Islam were able to draw for a very long period. They needed little stimulus to devote themselves to *ghazi* war, which they very often waged with an eye to booty rather than from religious enthusiasm. Each Turkish ruler pursued his own interests in the *ghazi* war, and co-operation was only spasmodic. In Asia Minor, for example, Danishmend and Seljuk emirs were normally hostile to one another. By the late eleventh Christian century most of Asia Minor had fallen under the control of Turkish rulers, with the exception of the coastal strips.

The Turks of twelfth-century Asia Minor were far from being committed to indiscriminate holy war, and their hostility to the rulers of Syria and northern Mesopotamia often led them to collaborate with the Franks or the Byzantines. When Frederick Barbarossa's army marched across Anatolia in 1190 the main Seljuk rulers did their best to offer him a safe passage, and it was only due to diplomatic and military confusion that hostilities took place. In any case, after an irritated Barbarossa had attacked and taken the Seljuk city of Konya the safe-conduct for the German army was renewed.

The Seljuk rulers of Roum continued to pay little attention in the following century to religious factors in their foreign affairs. The founder of the main thirteenth-century line, Kaykusraw, was the son of a Greek mother, like many of the sultans, and he owed his initial rise to power to Byzantine support. His successor, Kayka'us, was notoriously benevolent to Christians, and it was his alliance that enabled the crusading attack on Damietta in 1218 to be launched. The son and grandson of Kayka'us both in effect headed great coalitions that included Christian Armenian and Georgian princes. It is significant that the biggest internal threat faced by the Seljuks of Roum at this time was from Muslim religious insurgents.

In the period following the great Mongol victory over the Seljuks in 1243, the Seljuk sultans became little more than Mongol officials. There was practically no question of holy war against the Mongols, who now controlled a great part of Asia, and who in a very few years ravaged and conquered Mesopotamia and Iran. The Seljuk state disintegrated, and the Muslims, who continued to be the most numerous people in Asia Minor, passed under the leadership of minor Turcoman beys. During Mongol rule the Turcoman tribes in Asia Minor, most of them originally nomadic, had drifted from east to west, first as refugees fleeing from Mongol armies, and frequently afterwards as groups moved by the Mongol government for military reasons. Religious stirrings went on throughout the Muslim Turco-man world, and when the Mongol grip started to weaken in the late thirteenth century a new generation of small Turcoman *ghazi* states, intent on fighting the holy war against Mongols and Christians, began to emerge.

In the Anatolian and north Iranian world of wandering, displaced Muslim peoples, religious brotherhoods became more and more important as a sort of social cement. From the ninth century onwards there had existed, particularly in the towns, religious brotherhoods that were often at the same time trade guilds of a sort. Holy men would lead and direct such brotherhoods, which sometimes had a *ghazi* or holy war aspect, and which in the later Middle Ages were more and more influenced by Sufi mysticism. In north-west Iran in the fourteenth and fifteenth Christian centuries the word *sufi* had a secondary meaning of a person committed to religious mysticism, but its primary meaning had become that of a fighter in the holy war. It was from the religious *ghazi* groups of this sort that the 'red-cap' armies of the first leaders of the Safavi dynasty that was later to rule Iran were drawn.

The brotherhoods were essentially religious, but from early times they could also have great political influence, often exercised through violence and rioting. Muslim governments, including the Baghdad caliphate itself, were much exercised by the problem of controlling these religious groups, and strove to have them on their side, not always with success. From the beginning such movements were usually called *fitya*, or *futuwwa*, meaning associations of public-spirited young men, but sometimes also, when their motives were suspected or disliked, as *'ayyar*, scoundrels, or in modern parlance terrorists (the learned are somewhat at variance about this, and the *'ayyar* have also been described as having come near to forming a city militia).

Similar violent alliances had, in Christianity, characterized the urban mobs that came out as supporters of the monks and hermits of Byzantine Egypt. And the association of deeply religious, sometimes mystical, Muslim religious groups with sections of the same brotherhood organization that are prone to extreme violence is common in our own times. Like Muslim medieval governments, modern rulers tend when they encounter armed resistance from such people to describe them as terrorists, and to meet their violence with armed violence on the part of the state. But, like the medieval governments, they neglect the religious motive of these groups at their peril. There has also been some secularization of the term: it is significant that *futuwwa* has survived into modern Arabic as a term used to describe acts of heroic desperation of a political sort.

Among the many Turkish *ghazi* tribes in Asia Minor of the late thirteenth Christian century was one headed by 'Osman, with its capital at Bursa. 'Osman formed an alliance with a Sheikh Edebali, the head of one of the religious *ghazi* fraternities, whose daughter he married, and by whom he was girded with a *ghazi* sword. This sword accompanied the first victories of 'Osman, that led in the mid-fourteenth century to the establishment by his successors of a new domination. The rise of the Ottomans to predominance was based on their seizure of the neighbouring Karasi emirate in the north-west of Asia Minor, and on their skilful exploitation of disunity among Christians, that led them across the Dardanelles to set up a powerful new territorial agglomeration in the formerly Byzantine Balkan provinces.

By the end of the ninth decade of the fourteenth century the Ottomans had subjugated or exacted overlordship in a huge area of the Balkans, stretching from Bulgaria and the Dobrudja in the north-east to Bosnia and Serbia in the north-west. There were still many other Turkic *ghazi* states in Asia Minor at this point: it was only at the end of the century that the Ottomans turned against the much older Karamanid emirate, still in occupation of the western half of the Taurus, and required its submission. They alleged that the Karamanids' resistance to Ottoman power was treason against the holy war. The argument of the holy war was used by the Ottomans to legitimize aggression against other Muslim countries for at least a century and a half.

When the Ottomans had recovered from the devastating revival of Mongol power under Timur (Tamerlane) at the beginning of the fifteenth century, they employed similar arguments to those used against the Karamanids against other Muslim powers. After the fall of Constantinople to the Turks in 1453 Mahmud the Conqueror announced, with a curious logic that seemed to value his own pains above those of others, that: 'These tribulations are for God's sake. The sword of Islam is in our hands. If we had not chosen to endure these tribulations we would not be worthy to be called *ghazis*; we would be ashamed to stand in God's presence on the day of resurrection.'[8] At the same time he told the Mamluk sultan of Egypt: 'You have the responsibility to keep the pilgrim routes to Mecca open: we have the duty of providing *ghazis*.'[9] The ideology of the Ottoman state had become that of *ghaziyah*, and was to remain so until well into the eighteenth century. But from 1453 onwards, besides the ancient holy war ideals, there also existed for quite a long period in the Ottoman court a sort of unformulated claim to be the successor empire to Byzantium, a temptation that had not been present in Islam since the 'Umayyads of the eighth Christian century.

Ottoman toleration of Mamluk rule in Egypt came to an end in 1516, when Selim I was planning the final attack on Egypt that terminated the old regime there and placed the country for four centuries under Ottoman hegemony. Selim consulted the learned religious men, who advised him that holy war could be waged against the Mamluks on account of their rebellion: they had made disorder in the land, and on that account could be pursued with holy war as 'rebels'. At the same time and later in his reign, Selim I's wars against the Shi'ite Safavi Shahs of Iran were justified as holy wars waged against infidels. Selim claimed that he intended 'to succour the distressed, to revive the ceremonies of the faith, and to restore the holy law'.[10] The religious men issued a *fatwa*, or formal juridical opinion, saying that the Iranian ruler was an infidel, and should be slain.

The Ottoman power was the feared enemy of Christian Europe from the Danube to the Dardanelles, and the master of many millions of Christian subjects. By the mid-sixteenth century it was the rival, and was to become to a large extent the conqueror, of Frankish and Italian power in the Levant, the ruler of almost all the lands in Europe and Asia that had once been Hellenized. It was also the sovereign of the Fertile Crescent, Egypt, much of Arabia and most of the Barbary states of North Africa, and was for some centuries the only Muslim power west of Iran of which the generality of Europeans were conscious, with the possible exception of Morocco.

The first major confrontation of Frankish crusaders with the Ottomans came at the battle of Nicopolis in 1396. In the preceding quarter of a century Serbs, Bulgarians and Hungarians had all suffered severe defeat at Turkish hands. Hungary, a power with the strongest possible connections with the French court, had succeeded in getting the crusading support of a major West European army. The forces met on the Bulgarian bank of the River Danube, and the over-confident, heavily armed French and Burgundian cavalry were routed. The Ottoman siege of Constantinople, already under way, proceeded, and only the brief revival of Mongol power in the Middle East under Timur, that struck the Ottoman domains in 1402, gave the Byzantines a last, short breathing space.

A second major defeat of a big crusading army by the Ottomans occurred at Varna, the Rumelian port on the Black Sea, in 1444. The expedition had been planned, at the minimum, to take the pressure off the Byzantines besieged in Constantinople, and its failure was one of the factors that made

The Ottoman Empire in the East and the Balkans

Caspian Sea

□ Trebizond

SAFAVIDS

□ Mosul

R Tigris

□ Isfahan

● Aleppo

R Euphrates

● Baghdad

PRUS

● Damascus

□ Shiraz

□ Jerusalem

Persian Gulf

Red Sea

● Mecca

the final reduction of that great city all but inevitable. Byzantine and Latin Greece were equally doomed. After the fall of Constantinople the papacy was made aware once more of the shadowy nature of its leadership of the European powers in crusading ventures. The Italian cleric Aeneas Sylvius Piccolomini, who later became Pope Pius II, lamented Western disunity in a language that recalled Pope Paschal II's letter to the Greeks of three and a half centuries earlier:

> Christendom has no head whom all obey. Neither the supreme pontiff nor the emperor is given his due. There is no reverence, no obedience. Like characters in a fiction, figures in a painting, so do we look upon the pope and the emperor.[11]

As secretary of the Emperor Frederick III Aeneas Sylvius Piccolomini had acquired an intimate knowledge of the problems of Central and Eastern Europe, and of the Ottoman threat. But neither his knowledge, nor his activity as diplomat or pope, helped the crusading plans to great practical effect. The fanatical Franciscan preacher of the holy war John of Capistrano, who successfully led a ragamuffin army to the defence of Belgrade against the main Ottoman army in 1456, had far more success than the learned clerical bureaucrat, even when the bureaucrat became pope.

The Ottoman penetration of Europe in the mid-fourteenth century inaugurated a new period. In Iberia relations between the Christian and Muslim states had seldom been other than hostile, but outside Iberia and the central Mediterranean the two cultures had for centuries stood at a distance from one another. The earlier crusades and the other Latin settlements in the Levant had changed this for a time, apparently at the expense of the Muslims. But when the Ottomans became a European and a Mediterranean power, the defence of Western Christianity against the Turks became, for the first time since the rule of Al-Mansur in Spain at the turn of the tenth century, an urgent defence of the Christian frontiers. The Latin Christian settlement in the holy land was revealed to have been merely an episode, and the idea of its recovery a dream.

The popes remained at the centre of the diplomacy and finance of the crusade, but their leadership did not give them control, even though its connection with crusade taxation gave them a certain limited leverage over the princes. The precarious nature of papal leadership of the crusade was never better illustrated than when a pope tried to take effective military control of the enterprise. This was none other than Pope Pius II, the humanist pope who was the author of a celebrated letter to Mahmud the

Conqueror in which he had pleaded the truth of Christianity and asked – in vain – for the Sultan's conversion. Pius II had conducted a very active diplomacy for the crusade, and had held in northern Italy what he hoped would be a decisive conference of Christian powers to launch a new one. He thought that he enjoyed at least the support of the Venetians, a confidence that turned out to be excessive, if not misplaced. Pius went in person to the papal port of Ancona, on the Adriatic coast of Italy, in 1464. A small papal fleet awaited him, that was supposed to be joined by the Venetian fleet to carry out offensive operations in the east Adriatic and the Balkans. By the time the Venetian fleet arrived Pius was on his deathbed, and it was already clear that the military results of the enterprise were going to be negligible.

Pius II had in one respect sacrificed his own life to the crusade. Yet in another respect his literary career had marked the beginning of the final decay of the old crusading rhetorical lament for the loss of the holy land by the Christians. The fall of Byzantium in 1453 was a political and religious disaster, in that the Eastern church and the Eastern empire fell indefinitely under the sway of Islam. But it was also a cultural disaster, in that the great repository of Hellenic language and culture was threatened by destruction on the part of victorious Islam: the fall of the city, Aeneas Sylvius had written, was 'a second death to Homer and to Plato';[12] the books of the ancient Greeks that had survived in the East might now perish. This pointed towards the replacement of the old commonplace lament for the lost holy land by a new humanistic lament for Greece and its culture.

The Latin Christian settlements in Greece and Morea were swept away in the fifteenth-century Ottoman storm. The many small settlements made by the Italian maritime merchant powers of Venice and Genoa in the Aegean, on the coast of Asia Minor and in the Black Sea had for a time begun to look like Western colonies, but Ottoman power corrected this, and with the exception of two or three *places d'armes* (Crete; Cyprus, that had a long crusading history before the Venetian occupation; Rhodes, that belonged to the military order of Hospitallers) they were relinquished, or returned to being no more than trading posts. The big islands were taken in due course by the Ottomans: Rhodes in 1523, Chios in 1566, Cyprus in 1571, Crete not until 1669.

At the same time, Eastern Christianity entered what was from a political point of view a period of final collapse. That did not mean that in the Ottoman Empire the church was proscribed. It had never been the intention of the Ottomans to impose forced conversion upon the Christian peoples they conquered. There was massive Turkish immigration to the Balkans with the conquests, but that was another story. It was, however, against the economic interests of the conquerors to displace the Christian populations en masse, particularly the skilled, productive workers. The theft of Christian children from their families in order to bring them up as Muslim soldiers cannot be overlooked, but in most respects the treatment of Christians and Jews in the Ottoman Empire was according to Islamic law, and not totally unfavourable, although their subordinate status continued to be integral to the idea of government. The Ottoman policy of maintaining Christian vassal states in the northern and western Balkans in preference to direct Ottoman government also meant that there were large areas where Christians possessed local autonomy.

No Christian effort succeeded either in loosening the Ottoman grip on the Balkans and the lower Danube or in stopping the erosion of the Venetian colonial presence in the Levant. Towards the end of the sixteenth century the West Europeans began to sense weaknesses in the Ottoman carapace, but the Ottoman 'decline' was relative to the failure of the Near Eastern economies to keep pace with the benefits the Western economies gained from expansion in the East Indies and the Americas. In this sense the Venetians were losing ground because they were part of the same economic system as the Ottomans. There were weaknesses in the Ottoman system of government, but not to a point that threatened the cohesion and military power of the empire.

At the other end of Europe from the Ottomans, in the Iberian peninsula, the Muslim dominions had in the later Middle Ages been much reduced by the Spanish reconquest. Without being inexorable or continuous, the hostility to the Muslim states occasionally erupted into holy war. The collapse of the Almohad dynasty after the battle of Las Navas de Tolosa in 1212 meant that there was, after a short time, no Muslim dynasty in Andalus or the Maghreb whose original inspiration had been religious reform or the ideal of Muslim holy war.[13] The Muslim states of Iberia and North Africa were confirmed in taking a pragmatic view of their own existence and ends, a view that found its most trenchant expression in the works of the great Maghrebi historian and statesman Ibn Khaldun. *Jihad* was not abandoned or discredited, but it was no longer one of the main forces in this area of Muslim society.

On the Spanish Christian side, crusade was by no means the only expression of the motives and methods of the reconquest of the Islamic-ruled lands. The thirteenth-century takeover of Muslim Valencia by the Aragonese kingdom was achieved, for example, by the offer of treaties to the Muslim communities that guaranteed the continuance of the Islamic religion and of much of the framework of Islamic economy and society. That did not mean that the absorption of Islamic by Christian Spain was gradual and painless: in most areas the social rupture that accompanied Muslim submission was brutal and rapid, and the conquerors behaved not dissimilarly from the way the Christians of the crusading states in Syria and the holy land had acted to their subject Muslims.

In their relations with the remaining Muslim states in the peninsula, and with Muslims of the Maghreb, the Christians were also extremely pragmatic. The proclamation of crusades on many occasions, and occasional resort to *jihad* on the Muslim side, did not mean that the holy war was the main preoccupation of both societies. Truce, not war, was the normal condition of affairs, as it was in the same period in Christian and Muslim Syria. And the incentives to conclude truces were even stronger in the Iberian peninsula and the Maghreb, because the commercial motive to do so was so powerful.

For much of the later Middle Ages the Catalan merchants in the Kingdom of Aragon struggled savagely to gain commercial and naval predominance in the western and central Mediterranean. Among their main rivals were the Angevin (and therefore also French) rulers of Naples and Sicily, who nourished ambitions to dominate the whole Levant, perhaps by means of a coup against the Greek rulers of Constantinople. By the late thirteenth century this struggle was so fierce that the Aragonese found it advantageous to maintain close relations with the Hafsid dynasty of Tunis, for commercial reasons closely connected with the domination of the seas. The crusade of St Louis of France against Tunis in 1271 was deeply resented in Aragon, where it was seen as a French attempt to support the Mediterranean ambitions of the Angevin rulers of Naples. A decade later the Aragonese were to sponsor a successful coup that threw the Angevins out of Sicily. In such an atmosphere the unity of the Christian Mediterranean behind the crusade was a chimera.

The occasional but often violent pressure of the Iberian Christian powers on the Muslim frontiers continued. In the thirteenth century Christian gains, not only in Valencia but in Murcia, Estremadura and Andalusia, were so great as to give the victors trouble in consolidating and above all in populating the newly acquired lands. In the following century the wars with the Muslims were renewed. There were specifically Iberian Catholic religious military orders that collaborated in the reconquest and stiffened its defences. A Hispano-French crusade that had been planned in 1328 to attack the Nasrid Kingdom of Granada collapsed, and the Castilians had poor luck when they attacked alone. But in 1340 the Castilian-Portuguese army defeated the Nasrid army and its *mujahid* troops from across the Straits at Rio Salado (Tarifa); four years later a crusading army (within whose ranks Chaucer supposed his knight to have fought) took Algeciras.

For much of the remainder of the century the Nasrid kingdom was close to being a vassal state of Castile, to which it gave military support in campaigns against Aragon. *Jihad* was proclaimed once or twice, but the Nasrids found it more effective to exploit Christian disunity than to appeal to Islam. Both Spanish Christians and North African Muslims found the Nasrid Kingdom of Granada to be a convenient buffer state, and for a long time it was in no one's interests to dislodge it.

The unity of Castile and Aragon achieved by the marriage of Ferdinand of Aragon with Isabella of Castile in 1469 sealed the fate of the Kingdom of Granada. The Nasrids did not help themselves by sliding into civil war in the 1480s: a last-minute appeal for aid to the Mamluk sultans in Egypt met with no response, and the end of the Kingdom of Granada came, as is well known, in 1492. But by that time the existence of the last Iberian Muslim state had no more than symbolic importance. Interest had shifted from the Spanish mainland to the Castilian and Portuguese strongpoints seized from the Muslims on the North African and Atlantic coasts. The Mediterranean was gradually to cease to be the major theatre of West European hopes for the triumph of Christian power and religion.

CHAPTER SEVEN

Outside the Holy Wars

For several centuries the Muslim and the Christian holy war were authentic expressions of two great warlike religions. Their believers accepted the holy war as a religious duty, although a voluntary one, that was to be engaged in as a heroic enterprise of salvation. Their rulers embarked on the holy war with more or less frequency, according to religious zeal and political convenience. The holy wars were not all between Muslim and Christian: they could be between Christian and pagan, Muslim and pagan, Christian and Christian, or Muslim and Muslim.

But the holy wars were very far from defining relations between the two religions and the two cultures – three cultures, if we include the Byzantine one. Nor did they comprehend all the types of hostility that could exist between them. Spasmodic holy war could continue on sections of the frontiers of Christendom and Islam for very long periods. It was an essential factor on the big political scene, that no ruler could afford to disregard. But in general the holy war was a phenomenon of enthusiasm and emergency: it did not characterize the everyday lives of the many thousands of traders and venturers, Muslim and Christian, whose meetings and bargaining took place in the ports, the inlets, the markets of the Levant, Anatolia and the Balkans, the Black Sea, Egypt and the Maghreb, the Christian Mediterranean.

To a very great extent, the history of Christian–Muslim relations before the opening of India and the East Indies to Christian trade and colonization in the modern period is the history of the Mediterranean. Long before either Christianity or Islam, profound forces had inspired men to leave their own communities to voyage across the perilous Mediterranean by sea, or to undertake almost equally dangerous trips by land, in order to trade and to exchange. Those forces did not cease to act upon Muslims and Christians. What the great historian of the sixteenth-century Mediterranean, Fernand Braudel, called 'fraternization' was a fact of Mediterranean life:

> Between the two enemy religions, it would be unrealistic to imagine a watertight barrier. Men passed to and fro, indifferent to frontiers, states and creeds. They were more aware of the necessities of shipping and trade, the hazards of war and piracy, the opportunities for complicity or betrayal provided by circumstances.[1]

These 'anonymous carriers' transferred not ideas but things between the cultures – the orange, the lemon, the peach tree, the cactus, the cypress tree, bean varieties, the cotton plant, the compass, the potato, Indian maize, coffee, tobacco. It is a very long list, important to the history of East and West.

Both in Christianity and in Islam, the holy war engendered conflicts of economic interest. Especially in the Turkish-controlled border areas, there was a clash between those who profited from the booty of holy war (*gaza mali*) and those who wanted peaceful trade with the infidels. In both religions there was a clash between those who wanted unrestricted maritime piracy and those who suffered from it. People were not, of course, consistent, and the same folk could trade or loot, according to convenience.

There was also, especially in the Iberian peninsula, the Balkans and the Hellenic-Turkish areas, parts of Syria and other Mediterranean zones, an acceptance of what the Spaniards called *convivencia*, the willingness to accept one another at close quarters. Egypt, where the big Coptic minority had been an established fact ever since the Muslim conquest, was the model for a degree of tolerance, though it was seldom quite free of inter-communal disorders. Even in Asia Minor, the heart of the Turkish holy war, the Christian and Islamic communities were not locked in eternal hostility. In the world of Turkic holy men the religious barriers sometimes proved to be porous. For example, in western Anatolia there was a shrine of a Muslim holy war fighter, Shahid Mustafa at Arapli, that was also a Christian shrine.

There was, of course, a difference in kind between the *dar al-Islam*, that had imposed Islamic rule over Christians and Jews who paid Islamic tax and offered submission, and the relations of Muslims within the Islamic world with Christians who travelled from the *dar al-Harb*, the non-Muslim exterior, to trade. Yet another kind of relationship, much less easy, but sometimes governed by treaty, was that between Muslims and Christians who lived in settlements on the Islamic fringe. There was also a parallel between the relations of Islamic governments with their Christian minorities, and those of the Iberian Christian governments with their Muslim minorities.

Few traders operated alone. The markets of the Christian traders with Muslim lands were either situated on Islamic soil, in trading posts (the *fondaci* of the Italians, *funduq* in Arabic) whose existence and terms of trade had been negotiated with the Muslim government concerned, or in colonies, large or small, that had been seized by Christian powers for their strategic or trading importance. In the colonial possessions, the mother power exercised dominion; in the Islamic countries, the negotiations with the Muslim government that led to the establishment of licensed and protected trading were carried out by the mother power. The licensed trading communities were set up under a *muwa'ada*, an agreement, and were under Islamic protection (*aman*). There were times and places where one Christian power was more important than others. The Venetians, Genoese, Pisans, Aragonese, Portuguese, Castilians, each had their day and their place of dominion, and their histories form a complicated catalogue of shifting power and wealth. No Arab, Berber or Turkish government was indifferent to Western trade.

There were attempts by Christian churchmen to impose upon traders restrictions that derived from the holy war. They permanently prohibited the export to Muslim lands of wood (especially wood for shipbuilding and siege engines, desperately lacking in the eastern Mediterranean), ships, naval stores, war materials and iron, and Christian slaves. In periods when a crusade was being waged or contemplated, many other goods, often all goods, were theoretically placed under a similar embargo. A particularly severe general prohibition of this kind was issued in the third decade of the fourteenth century, but it was broken so often that the papacy ended by simply issuing licenses and absolutions for its breach, and treating them as a convenient form of revenue. In 1327, in spite of the papal trade embargo, there was a large enough number of Christian merchants in the Egyptian port of Alexandria for them to engage in a general fracas with the Muslim populace.

All the trading prohibitions were broken, not only by individual traders but by Christian governments, and sometimes on a huge scale. Muslim fleets were built with wood from Christian lands: the Aragonese government was especially forward in enabling this, and even proved willing to include in treaties with Muslim governments a guarantee that it would not oppose such exports. The Venetians exported wood to the Islamic lands from Carinthia and Friuli. Muslim armies were manned by slaves imported through Christian traders: this was especially true of the Genoese and the Venetians, who exported very large numbers of Circassians, Turks and Tartars from the Black Sea and the Levant to be used in the Mamluk armies. The slave trade was especially important also to the big Christian island of Cyprus, both before and after the Venetian takeover in 1489. The Aragonese kingdom profitably organized quite considerable forces of armed and mounted Christian mercenaries whom they sent to the Maghrebi kingdoms to operate under royal licence. Zeal for the crusade was subordinated to the avarice of governments and the needs of commerce.[2]

The Italian trading powers, some other Christians such as the Provençal merchants, and the rulers of the Iberian kingdoms negotiated the establishment of 'consulates' (these were not diplomatic missions, but organizations of merchants presided over by 'consuls') in most Muslim countries. The agreements covered (in the Aragonese treaties establishing consulates in the Maghreb, for example) the security of persons, freedom of transit, the jurisdiction of consuls over their own nationals, property rights in buildings, churches and cemeteries, the prohibition of piracy, and guarantees for the transport, sale or re-export of goods. The customs rights involved had been, of course, a main subject of negotiation, although in the later Middle Ages most Muslim governments had a fixed customs regime that made them in effect non-negotiable. The jurisdiction of the European consuls over their own people may seem to indicate Muslim weakness, but this was not so in the period when the treaties were negotiated. Much later, in the modern period, similar treaties led to a regime of so-called capitulations that was injurious to the sovereignty of Muslim governments, but the political circumstances were by that time different. Earlier, the exemptions were simply a natural consequence of the religious jurisdiction accorded to *dhimmis*, the 'people of the book', under Muslim rule.

After the end of the Latin Empire of Constantinople in 1261, the nearest approach to a West European colonial empire in the Levant was that of the Venetians. The strongpoints they held, however, and their consulates and trading posts in Muslim lands, did not at all resemble what would now be thought of as a colonial system, although it may have had something in common with the seventeenth-century forts and factories of the English and Dutch traders in the Indies. Essentially the Venetian overseas domination (at all events, in its possessions outside the Adriatic Sea) consisted of a network of naval bases whose function was to give protection and political and diplomatic support to a network of trading posts. Many of these trading posts were located in Islamic countries, and Venetian activity there was determined by the treaties Venice had succeeded in negotiating with the Muslim rulers. There were some areas in the Levant where Venice ruled quite considerable local populations, whom she taxed and exploited as she could.

Venetian diplomatic bargaining with the Muslim rulers of the Levant went back to the early Middle Ages, before the time of the crusades. The same was true of other Italian city-states, and particularly of Pisa, which had a flourishing Middle Eastern trade based on treaties with the Islamic rulers from the eleventh century until Pisan decline began in the late thirteenth. So long as the crusading settlement in the holy land continued, the Italians possessed concessions and privileges there that ranged from autonomous control of certain urban areas to rights that were almost colonial. After the end of the settlement in the holy land in 1291, no Italian city-state was willing to abandon its trading and other remaining positions in the Levant.

The nations trading with Muslim lands relied on long periods of truce for their livelihoods and prosperity. The trading powers, the Venetians above all, were essential carriers for the naval side of any crusade, but they stood to lose heavily from holy war, and were unwilling to take part unless aggression by Muslim powers was already harming them, or there was some substantial political gain to be had. Twelve years after the fall of Acre in 1291 the Venetians negotiated a treaty with the Mamluk government in Egypt for their settlement in Alexandria that conceded all the usual status and privileges, including warehouses in the customs area, security of passage and guarantees that testaments of Venetian subjects who died there would be effective, fresh-water supplies for the settlement, and protection for Venetian ship-owners in case of shipwreck.

Venetian participation in crusading projects was more in the nature of contingency planning than of anticipating an early war. Venice was engaged in 'crusading' negotiations with the French monarchies and the papacy almost continuously at this period, and her trade with Egypt was for a time reduced, but crusading projects had only minor practical results for Venice or for anyone else for most of the fourteenth century.

Venice was irritated by what it claimed was Muslim treaty-breaking on the part of the Turkish emirs of Asia Minor, and took part in so-called crusading warfare in the Aegean in the fourth decade of the fourteenth century because of alleged Turkish bad faith rather than out of crusading

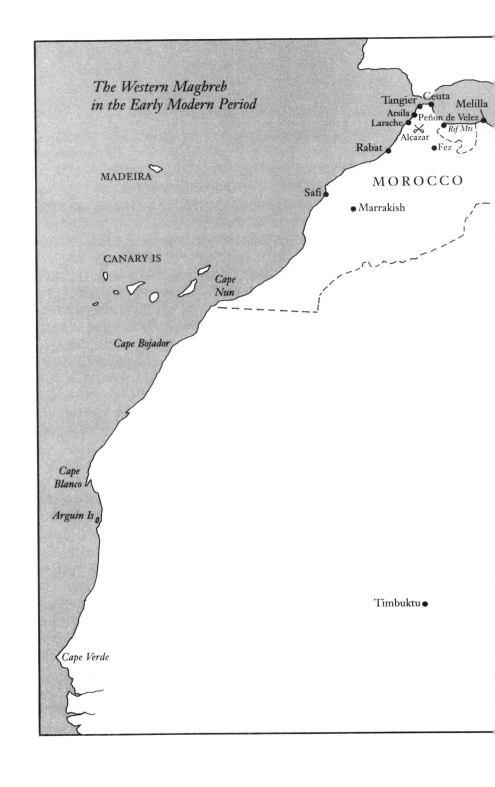

The Western Maghreb
in the Early Modern Period

MADEIRA

Tangier   Ceuta
Arsila   Melilla
Larache   Peñon de Velez
        Alcazar   Rif Mts
Rabat   Fez

MOROCCO

Safi

Marrakish

CANARY IS

Cape
Nun

Cape Bojador

Cape
Blanco

Arguin Is

Timbuktu

Cape Verde

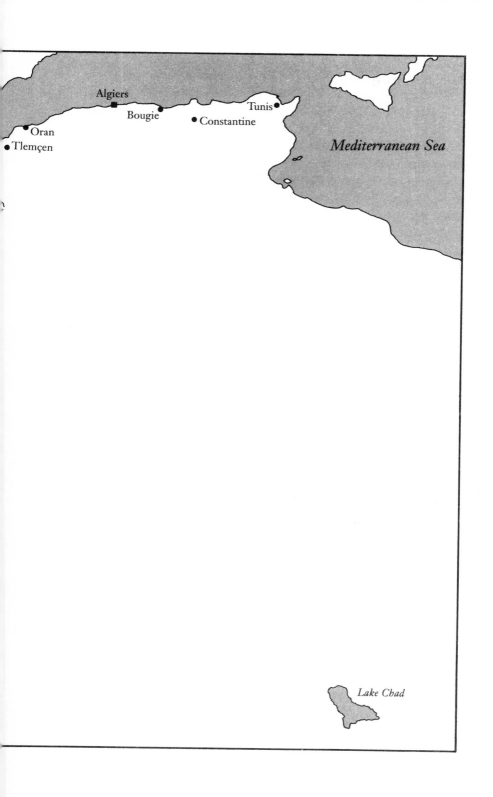

Algiers

Oran
Tlemçen

Bougie

Constantine

Tunis

Mediterranean Sea

Lake Chad

zeal; Venice acquired a passing predominance in Smyrna from this war. In the end not only the Venetians but the popes themselves made peace with the new Turkish emir of Aydin, who replaced the aggressive Umur Pasha. The pope had run out of money for crusading fleets, and a Turkish embassy was ceremonially entertained in the papal city of Avignon in 1349; in fact on this occasion the papal peace with the Turks antedated the Venetian peace by some four years. This was to herald further truces in the Levant subscribed by papal envoys, and a readier willingness on the part of the popes to grant licences to Italian city-states (especially Venice) to trade with the Muslims.

The overriding Venetian concern was the Egyptian trade. Venetian treaties with Egypt had already been renewed in 1344, and there were new agreements in 1355 and in 1361. In fact, until the end of the Middle Ages, although there was an occasional hiatus like that due to the Cypriot raid on Alexandria in 1365, the Venetian presence in Egypt was continually renegotiated. The last Venetian treaty with the Mamluks was made in 1512, only five years before the final collapse of Mamluk rule in Egypt and the victory there of the Ottomans. The florid finances of the Venetian republic owed too much to the Egyptian trade, and on the occasions when there was bitter war between Venice and the Ottomans, the entente between Venice and Mamluk Cairo became even closer. The Venetian implantation of consulates spread over most of the Muslim Mediterranean: her list of treaties with the Hafsid rulers of Tunis, for example, was as continuous as that in Egypt, and she maintained a consulate in Damascus whose history was as continuous as that in Alexandria.

The position of Genoa in the Islamic Mediterranean world was in some respects comparable. The Genoese Levantine colonies were however far less numerous and important, and the most prominent were those in the Crimea, which for a long period depended on the complaisance of the Ottomans in allowing Genoese maritime traffic through the Straits of the Bosphorus. The first Genoese commercial treaty with the Ottomans dated from 1352, but the Ottomans closed down the Genoese settlements in the Crimea in the late fifteenth century. The Genoese settlement of Pera (adjacent to Galata), adjoining Constantinople, was in the late Middle Ages a small quasi-independent walled city, that depended on understandings with both Byzantines and Turks; it did not survive the siege of 1453. The island of Chios in the Aegean was Genoese until the Ottomans took it in 1566.

The Genoese were everywhere in the western Mediterranean, no less than in the east. Like the Venetians, they were very important in Tunis, where they rivalled the Catalans in the strength of their permanent settlement in the Christian quarter. They frequented Tripoli, and established themselves in the Muslim Nasrid Kingdom of Granada before the end of the thirteenth century, enjoying the usual commercial privileges, including a favoured customs rate. Using the older port of Almería and its successor port of Málaga, they imported silk, sugar and fruit from the Nasrid kingdom, and exported in return a variety of goods, including paper, slaves, English cloth and (surprisingly) Spanish olive oil. From the Kingdom of Granada, and also from the Christians of Castile and Aragon, the Genoese also imported gold specie to their homeland. At this period the Genoese established a very strong social and trading presence in both Castile and Aragon.

The Ottoman domination of the Levant and of the whole North African coast was two centuries in building; it cannot be accounted complete until the earlier victories of the reign of Süleyman the Magnificent (1520–66). But by the latter part of the fifteenth century it was already clear that the territorial and colonial aspects of the power of Venice in the east Mediterranean were doomed. Ottoman pressure on Venetian and Frankish Greece was intense from the 1460s onwards. Between 1470 and 1500 the fall of the main Venetian centre of the Greek island of Negroponte (Chalcis in Euboea), and then of the great naval bases of Cotrone and Modone (Kótronas and Methóne, both in the south of the Peloponnese), had reduced Venetian power radically and permanently. Venetian reaction had not always been heroic: in 1470 the Venetian admiral followed the Turkish fleet to the siege of Negroponte and then turned tail without giving battle.

Fernand Braudel has strikingly said of the relationship between the Ottomans and Venice that 'Venice cannot be explained simply by her *Terrafirma* [her mainland Italian possessions] or her empire of shores and islands, although she exploited them with tenacity. She lived in fact off the great Turkish Empire, as the ivy draws its nourishment from the tree to which it clings.'[3] The element of Venetian subordination to the Ottomans cannot be avoided, in spite of the republic's passionate pride. For example, in the fifteenth century the Venetians paid, as the Byzantines had before them, land tax or tribute (*kharaj*) to the Ottomans for some of their most important possessions, such as Albania, and the naval bases of Patras, Lepanto, and Scutari.

Perhaps people would expect the greedy merchants of Venice and Genoa to subordinate holy war to business. But the feudal monarchs were not all so very different from the merchants in preferring gain to glory. In the western Mediterranean the Kings of Aragon had fought the holy war against the Muslims with passion and devotion. One twelfth-century king had gone so far as to attempt to bequeath his kingdom to the military religious Order of Templars. But in the later thirteenth century, after their acquisition of Muslim Valencia, the Aragonese kings pursued a Mediterranean policy that fitted ill with the idea of ceaseless crusade against the infidel.

In 1229–30 the Aragonese had conquered the Muslim island of Majorca, thus opening many maritime possibilities. The Catalans developed aspirations to control the whole western Mediterranean basin. The seagoing merchants of Barcelona were henceforth far more interested in the trade of the Muslim Maghreb and the profits of maritime piracy than they were in backing crusading enterprises against the Muslim Kingdom of Granada, with which they had no common frontier. By mid-century there was an important Catalan consulate in Tunis, and another further west at Bougie. The Christian settlement in Tunis grew until it became a secondary town, almost as large as the Muslim walled city.

More than trade linked the Catalans with Tunis. The Catalan Christian mercenaries serving in the Hafsid army with permission from the Aragonese king, and to the financial benefit of the crown, became quite a considerable factor in Hafsid internal and external politics, and the tribute paid by the Hafsids was important to Aragonese government finances. Piracy by Catalans against Tunisian vessels was quite common, and general hostilities occasionally resulted. But on the whole the relations between the two powers were amicable and on both sides profitable, and controlled by a long series of truces. The crusade of St Louis of France against Tunis in 1270 reinforced instead of weakening the links between Aragon and the Hafsids, who towards the end of the century were in danger of heading a Muslim state that was subordinate to the Christian power of Aragon.

Ifriqiya, the country ruled from Tunis, was not the only Maghrebi objective of Catalan policy. Further west, James the Conqueror of Aragon intervened in the quarrels of other successor states to the dissolved empire of the Almohads; in 1275 he sent a fleet to blockade the Moroccan port of Sabta, for the benefit of the Marinid rulers of Marrakech and Fez. Behind all these manoeuvres lay Aragonese desires to get their hands on the trans-Saharan trade, particularly the traffic in alum and Sudanese gold. In 1291 there was a treaty between Castile and Aragon that came close to establishing zones of influence for each of the two powers in the Muslim Maghreb. The eastern shift in the trans-Saharan route, that in the fourteenth century terminated either in Tunis or in Tilimsan (Tlemçen), favoured the

Aragonese. And the Catalans were not inactive in Egypt: in 1306 the sultan sent the Aragonese king valuable gifts of luxurious Egyptian textiles – perhaps they were in a sense samples.

On this chequerboard of Mediterranean politics the holy war played only a very minor part. Charles-Emmanuel Dufourcq wrote that alongside the warlike trends of the two religions there was another that tended to canalize and limit violence. He even thought he could identify a sort of thirst for peace that seems not to have been inspired even by political calculation.[4] Certainly, there was nothing ideal about this relationship between the two religions: it could permit the peaceful co-existence of Muslims and Christians on the island of Pantelleria, for example, but it did not stop the Aragonese naval and military occupation of many places in the Maghreb, such as the islands of Djerba and Kerkenna; nor did it stop (on those occasions) the inevitable Islamic reaction by the Marinid rulers of Tunis. War and piracy were sporadic all over the Mediterranean, but truces were almost always negotiated to quieten down the hostilities and to renew trade. And the Western Christian merchants often stayed on in the Islamic ports, even when war was raging elsewhere.

The unfavourable balance of trade between East and West had been present since the times of the Roman Empire, which with some temporary success tried to adjust it by theft. In the earlier Middle Ages it had been worsening, partly because the Western products that the East most needed, notably armaments and wood for shipbuilding, were hindered by the ban on the export of war materials. Similar prohibitions also hindered the export of Christian slaves, until the Christian victories in Iberia began to fill the Western markets with Muslim slaves who could be re-exported to the East.

In the thirteenth century technological advances in the Western textile industries gave them a new competitive edge in the Eastern markets, that were no longer indifferent to the offer of high-quality Western goods. The West managed to import gold for its renewed issues of gold currencies, that had recommenced in the fourteenth century, but it was heavily in deficit with the East in terms of silver. The Venetians, especially, exported huge quantities of silver money to the East. The balance between Eastern and Western economies was seldom stable. The ban on exporting wood and metals to Muslim countries was more widely disregarded in the fourteenth century, but Western timber resources were already beginning to run short. In the later Middle Ages the West experienced a big decline in population, which cut production in many areas, and also some export capacity. For example, it drastically reduced the export of European cereals to Muslim countries, that became instead net exporters of cereals to the West.

In the Muslim East there was not only population decline but, in Egypt and Syria at least, industrial decline, sapping the textile and craft industries of Egypt especially. In Iraq the destruction due to the Mongol onslaught had been economically disastrous. And the shortage of Muslim shipping meant that quite a lot of Islamic goods were carried in Western Christian ships, which conferred a valuable competitive advantage.

Some historians, wise after the event, have talked about the West as 'preparing itself for its world role' during the late medieval period.[5] This was not how contemporaries viewed the matter. The fifteenth century listened attentively (if sceptically) to men like the Cretan George of Trebizond, a papal official, who from the fall of Constantinople in 1453 had been convinced that Muhammad the Conqueror was predicted in Christian prophecy to be the destined ruler of the world, and who wrote a tract, *On the Eternal Glory of the Autocrat and his World Empire*, to prove it. Prophecies of a Turkish invasion that would reach at least to the gates of Rome were rife in Renaissance Italy – not surprisingly, since a Turkish base had been set up for a time in Bari on the Adriatic coast, less than three hundred miles from Rome. However, the conversion of the Grand Turk to Christianity was usually the last part of such prophecies.

The alleged Christian domination of the Mediterranean was far from continuous and permanent. Turkish ships may have been inferior in quality to Western ones, but the hugely increased access to Balkan timber in the fifteenth century meant that they could achieve victories through their superior numbers. New military technology that had originated in the West, especially in gunnery, may have been less well managed by the Turkish fleets and armies, but their ordnance was formidable enough. A Turkish pasha is said to have told the Venetian envoy at the time of the collapse of the Venetian bases in the Peloponnese (1500): 'Until now, you have been married to the sea: the future now belongs to us, who are more powerful than you.'[6]

The more extravagant prophecies of Ottoman dominion proved wrong, although Ottoman armies had taken the holy war to the gates of Vienna by 1527. However, 'the Ottoman Empire was one of the largest political structures that the western part of the world had known since the Roman Empire disintegrated',[7] and the historians who have represented it as being in decline from the late sixteenth century at least, unable to master new technologies, ruling an area that was only on the fringe of world economic development because of its remoteness from Atlantic trade, have harped upon its weaknesses without recognizing its strengths. Ottoman rule over such a huge area conferred enormous economic and trading advantages upon the Turkish-controlled world, so that some other historians have referred to a sixteenth-century Ottoman boom.

It has also been usual to underplay the role of the Turks in the early modern period as the dominating power in the Balkans. Sixteenth-century Christian Europeans almost universally feared the Ottoman Empire, respected the discipline and order of its regimen, and competed to get a share in its trade. The reluctant acceptance by Venetian observers of the reality of Ottoman power during the first three-quarters of the sixteenth century has been compared with the acceptance of US power by West Europeans during the half-century following the end of the Second World War.[8]

The Islamic world was by no means in decline at this time. In Iran the Safavids, the inveterate enemies of the Ottomans, who had called for their destruction as Shi'a heretics, ruled over one of the great civilized empires of the world. The Mughal Empire extended from Afghanistan and central Asia almost to the very south of the Indian subcontinent. It was greater even than that of the Ottomans, counting vast numbers of Hindu subjects, and had brought the position of Islam in India far beyond the dominance it had enjoyed in the early Middle Ages. In West and sub-Saharan Africa, in some of the richest and most technically advanced areas of the continent, new Muslim kingdoms had appeared. The rulers of some of these kingdoms justified the legality of their rule through the *jihad* they waged.

The suppliers of gold in Saharan Africa were predominantly Muslim. The medieval kingdom of Mali, the richest gold importer of all the African kingdoms, had been Muslim since the eleventh Christian century, and the sumptuous extravagance of the Meccan pilgrimage of its ruler in 1324 overawed both Egyptians and Arabians. The Sudan, the other gold-supplying area in the continent, was largely Muslim. Not until the gold supplies of the Americas were tapped in the sixteenth century could the Europeans evade this Muslim control of gold specie: the Portuguese attempts in the fifteenth century to get direct access to West African gold had been unsuccessful, in spite of the decline of the kingdom of Mali. In the East Indies, over a huge area of the island chain, Islam was adopted in the fifteenth and sixteenth centuries by many local rulers. Holy war was only a very minor factor in this spread of the religion throughout the world.

The Ottoman Empire was acutely aware of its economic interest in giving truces to its Christian trading partners, whatever the state of war on its borders might be. It sought to encourage competition with its traditional Italian traders, and although the grants of trading rights to the French in Ottoman lands were introduced primarily in order to exploit the political differences between the French monarchy and the Habsburgs, they also had this economic aim. The Ottomans were even willing to grant similar rights to the Protestant English, that for some time the English traders did not really know how to exploit.

As an emblem of the east Mediterranean in the sixteenth century we might take the little Catholic republic of Ragusa (Dubrovnik in present-day Bosnia), on the coast of Dalmatia. Tolerated by the Venetians, but tributary to the Ottomans, and neighbours of the Islamicized Bosnia, having good relations also with the popes and their subjects in eastern Italy, the Ragusans sailed the Mediterranean as precarious neutrals. Their port was precious to the Ottomans as subject to their power and to their customs system, yet was used without hesitation by the Christian merchants of every maritime nation. Ragusa had close relations with the Ottoman hinterland as well as with the seafarers: it was a place where Muslims and Christians could do unhindered business. It was a key location for Eastern and Western trade, and it is no accident that in the making of a great book on the Mediterranean by the French historian Fernand Braudel,[9] the historical archives of Ragusa played a central part.

Muslim and Christian civilizations were not ranged against one another in complementary fortresses from which each looked at the other only as an evil empire, or as the domain of Satan. In spite of the dualist ideology of the land of peace (*dar al-Islam*) and the land of war (*dar al-harb*), and the equivalent lands of the faithful (*partes fidelium*) and the unfaithful (*partes infidelium*), men behaved in a manner that was not strictly consonant with either. Obeisance was made on either side to the dominant orthodoxies, but the two religious territories were both as it were porous. The Mediterranean Sea leaked insidiously into one side and the other.

The factors were not only geographical. The Roman Empire had established itself from Syria to Morocco, and the ground plans of the cities of Aleppo and Damascus have much in common with those of the Graeco-Latin cities of Italy. Mediterranean ports might have a Roman origin, but even where they did not, they often responded in a similar way to the demands of the Mediterranean environment. Patterns not only of settlement but of communal behaviour shared many characteristics in southern Italy and France, eastern Iberia, geographical Syria and North Africa: the cultures of honour and of family solidarity in all these places possessed common factors.

In this century the common social and anthropological characteristics of many parts of the Mediterranean and its inhabitants have been brought to light, both by Braudel and the schools of historians that have succeeded him, and by anthropologists. The overarching theories of the great nineteenth- and early twentieth-century sociologists, especially those of Max Weber (1864–1920), tended to rope off the Western cultural traditions – in Weber's case especially the tradition of the Western city – in a manner that can no longer be accepted as the simple pattern for the history of the process of modernization that Weber conceived. Modern study of Mediterranean cities has represented them as sharing many common characteristics in both the Christian and Muslim zones. Modern study of the anthropology of the Mediterranean peoples also points to many common factors in the two cultures.

In one trade, that the holy wars had done much to augment, Christians and Muslims had dealt with one another almost from the beginning of the Islamic Empires. Throughout the Middle Ages, slaves were one of the main commodities bought and sold in the Mediterranean and East Europe. Almost as soon as Prague became Christian in the tenth century, Muslim slave traders frequented its slave markets. In Iberia and southern France, human goods had always been bought and sold. In the early Middle Ages the south Italian maritime trading states were constantly being reproached by the church for their slaver dealings with the Muslims, that not infrequently led to Christians being sold into Muslim captivity. The vendors were unmoved, and the traffic continued.

The Islamic Empires had from the ninth century onwards been short of manpower, and their demand for slaves was always considerable. In the later Middle Ages the nature of the demand changed somewhat, and in an Islamic world that was increasingly controlled by Turks, the tradition of employing military slaves who could be trained to become part of a military ruling class strengthened the demand for human raw material. The demand was so much the keener because every time a new Mamluk sultan ascended the throne in Egypt he required a new generation of soldier-slaves. There was also a demand for female slaves, either for domestic service or to be treated in a sense as luxury objects; in this respect there was not much difference between Eastern and Western slave markets, in spite of what may be thought of as the demands of the harem. At some points the market wanted one gender, at other points the other.

War prisoners, far from being protected by convention, were subject to the will of the victor. There was some disagreement among Muslim lawyers about whether it was permitted to carry out exemplary punishments (*muthla*: 'atrocities' would usually be a tendentious translation, but not always) in the course of a holy war. It was agreed that women, children beneath the age of puberty, impotent old men and blind or sick persons should not be killed, provided they had not taken part in the fighting. But once the property in them had been established, the fates of prisoners of all sorts and ages, male and female, were at the discretion of whoever had taken them or was assigned them. They could be killed (if male), or kept prisoner until they were ransomed, but if a ransom was not forthcoming, or was thought unlikely, they could be enslaved, as could non-combatants. Christian practice was not dissimilar. When they had become slaves, the lives of former prisoners were still at the discretion of the owner or purchaser, and there were examples at the height of the Saladin holy wars of Christian prisoners being purchased and subsequently executed as a pious act. Fortunately avarice, perhaps allied to human feeling, usually prevailed over fanaticism.

On the Christian side, there was an obligation to avoid the sale of Christian slaves to unbelievers. There was a certain amount of inconsistency in the way 'Christian' was interpreted. It was usually taken to be inapplicable to heretics, so that Bulgarian or Bosnian Cathars could be sold without scruple. But there was some problem in deciding whether or not Eastern Christians were protected: on the whole the church ruled that they should be, but this principle was not always followed, and it is clear from the way that Orthodox slaves sometimes reached the Western slave markets that they had been bought in Crete or Cyprus, occasionally under circumstances that suggest that other Greeks had bought and sold them.

The principle that Christians should manumit their Christian slaves as a pious act was well established, if not always followed. It has been suggested that perhaps as many as a sixth of the slaves purchased in Western markets were manumitted, but sometimes with conditions that obliged them to work as bondmen for a stated period before being fully released. Manumissions were also sometimes given to non-Christian slaves.

All the main Christian trading nations maintained slave markets. There were important markets in Barcelona, Majorca, Valencia, Genoa, Venice and, later, Ragusa, apart from the Christian depots in the Levant like Cyprus and Crete. The holy wars occasionally supplied these markets with huge numbers of souls for sale. At certain moments, like those after great victories in battle, most notably after the battle of Las Navas de Tolosa in 1212, or the fall of Majorca or Minorca to the Christians later in the century, immense numbers of prisoners were enslaved and sold: there is a parallel between these events and the huge influx of Christian prisoners into Muslim hands in the holy land after the battle of Hittin and the fall of Jerusalem.

Most Muslims in the Western slave markets came from Iberia, the Balearic islands or the Maghreb, and comparatively few from the eastern Mediterranean. The number of enslaved Muslims from Iberia who were offered in the markets fell sharply after the end of the thirteenth century, without a corresponding rise in the number of Eastern Muslims on sale. In the later Middle Ages the number of slaves offered who came from the Black Sea (especially at Genoa, which had Black Sea colonies) and the Caucasus rose steeply. Circassians (particularly females), Russians and Tartars were very strongly represented. Balkan slaves were also much sold in Western markets, that often took them from the market at Ragusa. In the fifteenth century female slaves were more expensive in the West, probably because they were used for domestic service, and male slaves more expensive in the East, where there was a strong Muslim demand for military slaves, not yet supplied through the Ottoman levy system. Black slaves, who had mostly been first acquired through Muslim markets in the Maghreb, were a steady, though minority, element.

Re-export characterized all the Western slave markets, but more slaves seem to have reached them through trading in Christian markets in Iberia or the Levant than from traders who had acquired them in Muslim markets. The most important link between the Western and Eastern markets was the export to Muslim markets of slaves acquired in the Levant who were destined for military service in Egypt or elsewhere in the Muslim East. Such slaves were young males, most of whom were sold in the Christian markets in Crete and Cyprus. But the Genoese also traded in the west Mediterranean, for example in the slave market of Almería in the Nasrid Kingdom of Granada. The enslavement of Muslims was technically illegal in Islamic law, but slaves, including Muslim slaves, could be legally imported from Christian lands into Muslim ones, sometimes using the legal fiction that they had been captured in the holy war.

Prisoners of war were not slaves; they only became so when their captors decided it. But the slave markets were concerned in one of the other transcultural operations to which war, including holy war, gave rise. This consisted in the attempts made on either side to ransom or exchange captives, or to buy them as slaves and subsequently to free them. These attempts could be made either as a charitable act or for profit.

The ransoming of captives held in unknown locations in distant lands is a difficult and dangerous business, as we know from the experience of our own day. But it was in the financial interest of the captors to facilitate ransom: selling the captives as slaves on the open market was less profitable than obtaining ransom from their friends and families. Captives without means to pay ransoms faced a bleaker fate than those who could hope for ransom, though in every case the plight of prisoners was sad. For Muslims taken by Christian captors in the course of holy war, the earlier clerical attitude tended to condemn ransom or exchange arrangements as likely to be motivated by avarice rather than by holy zeal. The overwhelming anxiety of Christian authorities was that the Christian prisoners should not, under the pains of an onerous imprisonment, renounce their faith. One obstacle to the exchange of prisoners was the fear that freed Muslims might re-enter the holy war. Another was the vested financial interests of the Christian owners of Muslim prisoners, who saw their captives as an investment that was not to be surrendered without compensation.

However, Muslims were ransomed from Christian captivity, just as Christians were ransomed from Muslims. Exchange was another way of freeing the war captives, although it was more difficult because it was harder for either the captor or the go-between to make a cash profit. In the Iberian case, there was a lively trade in Christian prisoners purchased in Islamic countries by Christian traders and resold to their families. The ransomer (*fakkak*) was an established figure in Islamic lands: he was not necessarily a Christian, and was sometimes a Jew. Much of this trade on either side proceeded from the results of Muslim and Christian piracy against Mediterranean shipping.

On the Christian side and, rather later, on the Muslim side, there were from the thirteenth century onwards pious fraternities devoted to the liberation of prisoners of their own religion. Islamic law contemplated the use of communal religious funds for the liberation of war prisoners. The early thirteenth century saw the growth of at least two Christian fraternities devoted to ransoming and freeing prisoners: the first, that received the patronage of no less a person than Pope Innocent III, was the Order of the Holy Trinity, an order of mendicants who devoted themselves exclusively to the ransom and exchange of prisoners, for which they tried to raise funds, and whose members travelled indefatigably – unarmed and mounted on donkeys – to act as ransomers. The order acquired a hospital in Rome, San Tommaso in Formis on the Coelian hill, where a mosaic was put up that showed Christ tenderly supporting, on one hand, a shackled Christian prisoner, and on the other, a shackled black Moorish prisoner. The implication is that one will be exchanged for the other. But the meaning of the mosaic goes deeper than that, since it is the first known medieval pictorial representation, or at least the first known to the author, of a Christ whose love goes equally to the Christian and to the infidel, in the case of this mosaic to a black infidel.[10]

The Trinitarians were followed in their activities by the Aragonese Order of Merced, whose activities were very similar, although this was initially an order that accepted both lay and clerical brothers. The work of these and other orders that worked to ransom the Christian prisoners taken on the Barbary coasts was difficult and dangerous. The ransomers often had to offer themselves as pledges for the prisoners, and they could easily suffer arduous imprisonment, like that imposed upon the British clergyman Terry Waite in Beirut in more recent years. In the Middle Ages and the early modern period martyrdoms were not uncommon in these circumstances. Some of the problems of the charitable ransomers arose from their having offered to do gratis what others did for profit, which caused them to suffer the hostility of their own co-religionists as well as the religious prejudice of some Muslims.

Medieval Christianity and Islam were both, in theory, unitary societies that offered only a limited tolerance to religious minorities, and were both liable to coerce groups under their control that they saw as an alien presence in the land. For historical reasons the plurality of minorities was far greater in the lands of Islam than in Latin Christendom. In Islam, too, religious minorities were more strongly coloured by ethnic differences than they were in the West. But in spite of their general intolerance, both religions were capable of exhibiting substantial tolerance to minorities that were either so firmly established that uprooting them would threaten the social fabric, like the Copts of Egypt, or so economically useful that successive governments usually (but not always) drew back from severe persecution, as was normally the case with the European Jews, and with the European merchants trading in the Maghreb and the Levant. The educated class of Egyptian Copts perhaps belonged to this class as well as to the preceding one, although their importance was as bureaucrats rather than as traders. There were numerous special cases of this sort, like the Sicilian Muslims in the service of the Norman or the Norman-Hohenstaufen governments, or the Christian troops serving Muslim governments in the Maghreb. For the benefit of such troops and their families, chaplains and churches were introduced on Muslim soil (in Morocco, for example) where none had been before.

The doctrines of Muslim religious law that served to protect Christians and Jews in Islam had no exact equivalent in the West. The treaties with the Spanish rulers that formed the basis of protection for the Muslim communities in Christian Iberia were based in the end upon the convenience of the monarchies, and they were thrust aside when they ceased to be useful. There was a certain basis for the tolerance of Jews in Catholic doctrine, and on the whole the church tended to intervene against the physical maltreatment and despoiling of Jews, but churchmen could also act as persecutors of Jews, and their doctrines (like the Islamic doctrines on the 'people of the book') treated them with a disdain that could become hostility and contempt, and encourage persecution. In both Islam and Christianity the laws on religious apostasy were enforced with a ferocity that made conversion to the dominant religion a very hazardous business – more hazardous, in fact, in Christianity, which possessed an inquisitorial machine of religious control, than in Islam.

The tolerance accorded to Christians and Jews in Islamic lands was based upon practices followed in the original wars of Islamic conquest after the death of Muhammad. The guarantees of Christian lives, property, churches and crosses that was accorded by the Caliph 'Umar in Jerusalem in 638, along with the obligation of the payment of Islamic tax (*jizya*), founded a pattern. No doubt there were good social and political reasons for this tolerance, accorded by a tiny ruling Arab élite to the then religious majority and most important economic group of a huge area.

In every way, Christians lived apart from Muslims in Muslim cities – in the countryside they tended to predominate in certain villages, but they were not differentiated so clearly. Christians and Jews were settled in their own quarters in the cities; in Damascus these quarters remained more or less the same from the Middle Ages until the middle of the present century. They were allowed churches and synagogues, but subject to strict laws that reduced their social importance: Christians, for example, were not in theory allowed bells or bell-towers, nor could they build new churches or alter old ones without permission. Distinguishing clothing was often required of Christians and Jews in Islamic countries, as it was of Muslims and Jews in Christian ones. Sexual connection between members of the dominant religion and members of the other two was severely controlled both in Islam and Christianity, and could be visited with savage penalties. There were distinctions: marriage with Christians or Jews was permitted to male Muslims but forbidden to female Muslims. Marriage with Muslims was forbidden to Christians in Christian countries unless the other party converted.

Not surprisingly, the physical separation imposed upon the religious communities led to a great degree of ignorance within each group about the others, that increased with time. Social and trading elites may have known quite a lot about the other religious communities, but outside the privileged groups ignorance fostered intolerance and sometimes hatred: 'As Islam changed from being the religion of a ruling elite to being the dominant faith of the urban population, it developed its own social institutions, within which Muslims could live without interacting with non-Muslims.'[11] Persecutions of Christians and Jews by Muslim rulers were infrequent, but they did from time to time occur, and they could always be sure of popular support, just as the rather more frequent persecutions of Jews and Muslims could be sure of popular support in Christian countries.

It would be difficult to describe the situation of medieval religious minorities as 'toleration', despite – perhaps because of – the fact that the medieval situation persisted in very many places into relatively modern times. There was then no squeamishness in either Islam or Christianity in proclaiming the absolute dominance of the ruling religion, because in both cases its God-given right to rule was believed in by virtually everyone who professed it.

Talk of 'coexistence' or *convivencia* between the three religions therefore has to take account of these social realities, behind which lay the political realities. If the Muslim inhabitants of the Aragonese, Castilian and Portuguese kingdoms accepted the Christian regime in which they lived and accorded it a degree of loyalty, this was on account of the legal protection that it gave them in many respects, and the overwhelming power that lay behind it. There is much disagreement among scholars about the way in which Christian power was first imposed in the formerly Islamic areas, but it seems likely that in its first manifestations it was catastrophic for the Muslim population at large, and not in the least gentle or gradual, in spite of the fact that many Muslim grandees managed to make their own terms with the new power. There was also a strong religious and colonial dynamic that worked over a very long term against the Muslim minority throughout the peninsula: for example, Portugal began to expel the Muslims before the step was even contemplated in Spain.

With regard to public worship, the rules imposed on Muslim *mudejars* in Christian-ruled Spain were very similar to those imposed on Christians in Islam. The right of worship in a religious building was conceded, but everything to do with the public manifestations of worship was hedged in with restrictions. Minarets were permitted, but the call to prayer could not be proclaimed from them in the normal Muslim way, because Christian clerics found the public invocation of the name of Muhammad offensive: in Aragon only a signal on a horn from the minaret was allowed. Mosques were allowed, but the restrictions on building new ones or altering old ones were tight. The main mosques in principal towns became churches when the areas were conquered by a Christian power: this precedent went back to the case of Toledo in the early stages of the Christian reconquest. Charitable religious foundations (*waqfs*) were sometimes authorized and confirmed in the original agreements, for example for the benefit of Muslim religious schools (*madrasas*). But huge amounts of *waqf* property were confiscated for the benefit of the Christian church, and in practice the decline of religious culture among the *mudejars* was swift.

Muslims followed their religious law in matters of personal status, as Christians and Jews did in Islam. Permits were often available for going on the religious pilgrimage to Mecca, and sometimes also for emigration to the Muslim Maghreb. The wearing of distinctive items of clothing by Muslims was often also required. Retail trade was subject to some restrictions: for example, the shops of Muslim butchers were often forbidden to Christians, because of religious slaughter rules.

The Muslims of Christian Spain tended to suffer from the emotive force of the spasmodic persecutions of Jews, and from the clerical campaigns to convert the Jews, which very often rebounded upon the Muslims. There was also a certain amount of Islamic moral pressure placed upon Muslims resident in Christian Spain to emigrate to an Islamic land. This was due to the tradition of Islamic law, that relied upon Muhammad's injunction to emigrate in the cause of God (*hijra*), and upon his promise that such emigrants would find on earth enough room for refuge and bountiful provision.[12] There was always a trickle of emigration from Christian Iberia to the Maghreb, although Christian rulers placed obstacles in its way if they feared depopulation of the Muslim areas. The religious obligation to emigrate from an impious land remained into modern times as a political factor that sometimes affected Muslims: it was, for example, influential in the nineteenth century upon British India and French Algeria.

Toleration and neighbourliness between the two religious communities in Christian Spain could not be discouraged in all circumstances, because total segregation would be unfavourable to trade and economic prosperity, and to the payment of taxes to the government. The use of churches for Islamic prayer, while not unknown, was severely discouraged. Trading associations between Christians and Muslims were very common indeed, and could not be repressed. Popular religion, also, could bring people together as well as encouraging mutual hostility: Muslims would follow Christian feasts and processions in Spain, just as Christians and Muslims sometimes frequented common shrines to holy men in Asia Minor.

From an early stage, the practical utility of crusading as a means to obtain its declared ends was doubted by some. The sinfulness and avarice often shown by crusaders and settlers in the holy land was deplored, and the question was asked if the many crusading frustrations and failures were not judgements visited by God upon the sins of Christians. Particular groups, like the military religious Order of Templars, or preachers of the crusade whose motives were thought to be grasping and avaricious, were often condemned. People who paid to have crusading vows commuted were criticized, as was the aspect of papal power that facilitated this and profited from it. Some of the crusades against Christians, particularly those waged against the political enemies of the popes, were attacked as being opportunist and unspiritual, and a misuse of monies that should have gone for alms and good causes.

There was also a kind of world-weary, even cynical, attitude to crusading that was prominent at the time of the great thirteenth-century Christian defeats, and that was on occasion shared by men who had actually been crusaders. A troubadour song that may have been written by a returned Templar lamented that:

> Pain and wrath invade my heart so that I almost think of suicide, or of laying down the cross I once assumed in honour of he who was laid upon the cross; for neither the cross nor his name protect us against the accursed Turks. Indeed, it seems clear enough that God is supporting them in our despite . . . Alas! the losses of the kingdom of Syria are so heavy that its power is dispersed for ever!

Then it is really foolish to fight the Turks, now that Jesus Christ no longer opposes them. They have vanquished the Franks and Tartars and Armenians and Persians, and they continue to do so. And daily they impose new defeats on us: for God, who used to watch over us, is now asleep, and Muhammad [Bafometz] puts forth his power to support the Sultan.[13]

The poet went on to say that the Sultan looked forward to replacing all the churches with mosques, and that the pope was only interested in selling indulgences in order to finance his wars in Lombardy; the pope indeed, the poet suggested, wanted to dissuade people from fighting in the East so that they might fight in the wars of Italy.

Such out-and-out defeatism was rare, if only because the number of people who had practical experience of the fighting in the East was very small. But the disillusion it expressed was widespread, and although an appearance of zeal for holy war remained the majority (as well as the ortho-dox) view, there was always doubt about the motives of some of the people who promoted it.

Since the institutions of medieval Christian society were essentially toler-ant of war, if not outright militarist, it was next to impossible for an orthodox Catholic to espouse pacifism, just as it was for an orthodox Muslim. Very occasionally, though, doubts might be expressed about the moral legitimacy of the crusade. A clerk living in Würzburg at the time of the Second Crusade in 1147 was deeply shocked by the massacre of Jews that it occasioned in his own city. Writing the annals of his time, he described the failed military journey to the holy land, in which his own Emperor Conrad had taken part, and the 'vain preaching of the pseudo-prophets, the sons of Baal, the witnesses of Antichrist'[14] who had urged people to go on the crusade, few of whom had not bent their knee before Baal. The crusaders had gone to the places where Christ had trod, bearing the sign of Christ upon them 'in a presumptuous if not in an objectionable manner'. The annalist deplored that so much Christian blood had been shed on this account by the brutish, barbarian Saracens, and that so many Christian prisoners of war had been mutilated and humiliated.

As so often happened with those who condemned the actions of prelates and princes, the Würzburg annalist had based his objections to the actions of constituted authority upon the texts of Revelation, and the apocalyptic vision. Such references recurred throughout the Middle Ages. The greatest apocalyptic writer of all, the south Italian abbot Joachim of Fiore, met King

Richard I of England on his way to the holy land, and promised him final victory there. When this victory failed to occur, Joachim in a conventional way ascribed the setbacks of the crusade to the sins of the crusaders. But he also inserted the war against the Saracens into his vision of the end of time and history. The Saracens were to be defeated once more, but not finally, and in the age that was to precede the age of the holy spirit they were to emerge from their lairs for the last time, on this occasion in alliance with the heretics who opposed the Catholic church, the Patarenes: this would be the alliance of the beast of the sea with the beast of the land.[15] On this last occasion the crusaders would not triumph by force of secular arms, but were to be given a victory and the conversion of the Saracens by means of the operation of the holy spirit. The chapter of Revelation that Joachim cites has the significant passage:

> Hear, you who have ears to hear! Whoever is made prisoner, a prisoner shall he be. Whoever takes the sword to kill, by the sword he is bound to be killed. This is where the fortitude and faithfulness of God's people have their place.[16]

Joachim's doctrines reverberated in both orthodox and unorthodox circles until the time of the Catholic Counter-Reformation and beyond. Numerous writers in the later Middle Ages and the Renaissance periods followed his lead. The thirteenth-century English Franciscan friar and thinker Roger Bacon was not a Joachimite, but he reported a prophecy of a blessed pope who would come to reunite the churches and to bring all the infidels into the one fold under one pastor. Similar prophecies envisaged a time of troubles, including an Eastern Antichrist and a false Messiah, until an angelic pope came who would exterminate Antichrist, destroy the law of Muhammad, and reform the world. In the Renaissance the Turk more and more often became part of the prophetic story, sometimes to suffer submission and conversion, but sometimes to triumph, perhaps to rule as the Good Emperor, before ultimate conversion to the Christian faith as a part of the end of all things. Like the author of the Revelation of John, the Joachimites believed that God himself, not man, would fight and triumph in the holy wars.

The only firm opposition to Christian holy war came from people outside orthodox Catholic obedience. The Cathars, not surprisingly, were opposed to the crusade, since a terrible one had been waged against them. But they, or some elements among them, were also opposed to capital punishment. The Waldensian heretics similarly regarded holy war as wicked, and condemned the preachers of the crusade against Albigensians, Saracens and Slav pagans as being themselves accursed and damned souls. The dissident fourteenth-century English cleric John Wyclif denied that the holy wars of the Hebrews could be claimed by Christians as precedents for holy war: to him the only option available to Christians was to send peaceful missionaries who promised eternal life, and did not threaten to kill. The supposedly orthodox English poet John Gower appeared to reject the crusade: when his Confessor is asked:

> I prei you tell me nay or yee,
> To passe over the grete See
> To werre and sle the Sarazin,
> Is that the law?

he replies that:

> Sone myn,
> To preche and soffre for the feith,
> That have I herd the gospell seith,
> But forto sle, that heire I noght.[17]

Allied to these condemnations was the objection, shared by a number of orthodox clerics, to the forced conversions that took place among the conquered pagans on the East European borders. The good faith of the Teutonic Knights was widely called in question even by orthodox Catholics: they were accused of being far more interested in the subjugation of the Eastern peoples than in their conversion. But late medieval Europe was a dangerous place in which to have independent opinions. Inquisitors, when they interrogated suspected heretics, asked about the legitimacy of crusading, interpreting doubts as a pointer to illegal opinions of other kinds. It would be hard to find a clearer indication of the militarism that suffused orthodox religion at that time.

For well over two hundred years before the sixteenth century religious reformers called Catholic Christendom in doubt, it had been evident that the Christian holy war, while it continued to serve many immediate political ends, had failed to free the holy land from infidel rule, and had singularly failed to improve the lot of Eastern Christians. Western Christian pilgrimage to the holy land continued, but only under the same conditions of Muslim toleration that had obtained before 1095. The only parts of Europe where Islamic rule had been decisively pushed back were the Iberian peninsula and the west Mediterranean islands, where the Christian struggle against the Muslims had long preceded the calling of the Eastern crusade. In East Europe, Greece and the Levant the force of Ottoman power had taken Islam deep into Christian lands that had never known it before, and had totally overturned not only what was left of the ancient Byzantine Empire, but also most of the western, Latin settlements that had been set up in many parts of the area during the Later Middle Ages. Crusading continued partly in order to protect what was left of those settlements and to contain the so-called Barbary states, and partly to try to contain Ottoman expansion in the Balkans and East Europe.

The huge volume of trading and exchange that went on in the Mediterranean and East Europe between Muslims and Christians was evidence of a cohabitation between the two cultures that had begun almost at the same time as the Islamic Empires themselves, and that gave the lie to the sacred hostility both sides professed for one another. That cohabitation continued into the modern period, and in one sense has never ended. But the realities of economic and political power that lay behind it were to be profoundly modified. The Atlantic was, eventually, to be decisive. But not yet.

CHAPTER EIGHT

Holy War, Colonies and Conversion

THE MEDITERRANEAN PORTS, islands and cities sited in Muslim or formerly Muslim lands that were seized by Western Christians, sometimes in the course of crusading ventures, but often outside them, may seem in many respects to have been European colonies. If we look at the whole range of Christian conquests made at the expense of Muslim powers in the Mediterranean area we find several different kinds of settlement, of which some have a colonial look to them, while others do not. There were, until it ended in 1292, the Kingdom of Jerusalem and its associated principalities and successor states. There was a neighbouring 'crusader' kingdom, Cyprus, that became the site of great trading activity and one of the early centres of West European sugar production. These dated from the earlier crusading times. There were the commercial settlements of the Venetians and the Genoese, either those conquered from Muslims or those acquired through the Byzantine Empire or its Latin successor. In the western Mediterranean there were Christian gains like the Aragonese conquests of the islands of Majorca and Minorca, conventionally looked at by historians as part of the Christian Spanish 'reconquest' of Muslim territory on the Iberian mainland, but treated very differently from the peninsular lands.

That there can be a single 'colonial' description which applies to settlements as disparate as the Kingdom of Jerusalem, the Genoese settlement on the Black Sea, the Venetian possessions in the Levant and the places 'reconquered' by the Christian Iberian kingdoms seems highly unlikely. But the mentalities, administrative methods and commercial organizations that developed in these places seized from the 'infidel', and the canon-law principles that the church worked out in connection with the crusade, exercised some sort of influence on all the Latin Catholic peoples. And at the end of the Middle Ages these mentalities and methods influenced the manner in which the Iberian conquerors from across the seas treated their extra-European settlements. This was appreciated by the great German historian Leopold Ranke, who wrote, 170 years ago, that the crusades, and more particularly the Iberian crusades, gave birth to European colonization.[1]

The argument has been made much more specific by later historians,[2] and applied to the colonial methods of the Genoese merchants who traded both in the Levant and in Iberia, and who were concerned from the beginning in the Spanish and Portuguese discoveries overseas. Even before the New World discoveries, their capital had been invested in the early colonies in Madeira and the Canaries. Subsequently the Genoese were very influential in the first Spanish colonial empire: the Genoese origins and connections of Christopher Columbus are unsurprising. To a very limited extent, the Christian trading settlements made in Muslim areas of the later Middle Ages, from the Balearic islands in the west to Caffa in the Crimea in the east, were colonies that foreshadowed in some ways the early colonial regimes of the Americas and the Indies in the sixteenth and seventeenth centuries.

However, one wonders whether the pedigree that these historians offer for modern colonialism is not really rather hazy. If we attribute a pre-colonialist role to the European colonies and trading counters in the Levant and the Maghreb we are using a diffusionist argument. Like all diffusionist arguments, this is useful only if we are careful to separate its various branches, and to identify so far as we can the channels through which such and such an institution or mentality was diffused. We have first to distinguish between institutions and climates of opinion. The influence exercised outside Genoa by the Genoese public and private organizations for the control of overseas colonies is one thing; the influence of the attitudes of Christian colonists in the Levant to infidels and pagans is another. One belongs to the social history of institutions, the other to the social history of the imagination.

During the later Middle Ages and the Renaissance there was a great military, naval and commercial thrust by the Iberian powers to secure strongpoints and trading counters in the Muslim Maghreb and on the Atlantic coasts of North Africa. In this movement, that took many forms of military and commercial penetration and settlement, the privileged motive of the participants was the holy war against Islam. Men took to their ships, though, for many other motives than this: loot, piracy, hope of new lands to conquer and exploit, trade, can all be discerned as objectives of the Portuguese and Spanish African expeditions. These were first to

Muslim lands, and then to places well to the south of those that had been Islamicized.

But the motive that all men – not excluding Christopher Columbus – would willingly acknowledge was the overriding one to fight militant Islam, and even, eventually, to return the Christian military banners to the holy city of Jerusalem. Some of the most visionary and far-reaching motives of the voyages, both of Columbus and of the Portuguese explorers of the same period, were linked with the idea of an eventual joining with the 'Indian Christians' (by whom the Christian Ethiopians were usually meant) in order to discomfort Islam in the East. In a sense the movement to the western Atlantic was to be a prolongation of the Iberian *reconquista*, but one that purported to serve the wider interests of Christendom in its struggle with Islam.

The holy war has its place, therefore, in the spread of colonial ideas and institutions from Europe to the New World. Its main importance lies in the religious ideas, formulated to some extent before the end of the Middle Ages in canon law, that regulated the relations between Catholic Christians and infidels, and that also affected missionary work. The relations between Christians and unbelievers had been fundamental since the earliest times of the Christian religion: we have only to think of the question of pagan–Christian marriage, that had to be faced at the very beginning. But the crusade had revived some questions that had not been posed seriously since the end of the pagan Roman Empire, such as the legitimacy of infidel governments. These questions were to be of central importance to European colonization. The holy war was also of practical importance to the earliest stages of colonization, in that during the Middle Ages the Roman bishops had assumed the leadership of the Catholic world in matters appertaining not only to the crusade, but also to relations with the infidels. This led both the major Iberian powers to solicit, even before the great discoveries at the end of the fifteenth century, papal confirmation of their plans to conquer and subdue various parts of the infidel or pagan world.

There was no straight line that led from holy war to colonialism. By no means all the European settlements in the Levant that are commonly referred to as colonies were fortified and defended places over which some Western Christian government exercised sovereignty. The most important trading posts were those at Tunis and Alexandria, which existed through the concession to Christian traders by the Muslim host government of an *aman* or grant of protection. Such privileges could be and were withdrawn or restored at the will of the host. The Iberian settlements in the New

World were, of course, very different; but Western trading in Asia followed similar methods to those used in the Ottoman Empire, when they were thought expedient, until the American Commodore Perry landed in Japan in 1853. In the mid-seventeenth century the Dutch distinguished the places in the East where they had sovereign territorial rights (which were still at that time very few) from those where they possessed negotiated trading rights on a more or less favoured-nation basis.

It is also worth mentioning that the so-called colonial methods of the Italian Mediterranean traders were not used only by Italians, nor were they applied only in the Mediterranean area. They were, in fact, a basic technique of all late-medieval Western trade. Similar arrangements to those of the merchant powers in the Levant and the Maghreb applied also to the 'nations' of the Genoese and Florentines, and similar non-Italian groups, who traded in the cities of northern Europe. The steelyard of the German Hanseatic League enjoyed similar privileges in medieval London to those that the Italians enjoyed in Tunis and Alexandria; this was often bitterly resented by the English. The Hanseatics sometimes used violence, and were occasionally willing to launch a naval war in order to assert their trading rights in England and in the seas around it. But it would be a very strange sort of history that concluded that the Hanseatic settlement in England was a colony in the same sense that Mexico became a Spanish colony.

There were however many places in the Levant, besides the crusading states of the holy land, that had been occupied by the trading or crusading powers, and that were not merely trading counters but colonies held in some form of sovereignty. The Venetian Empire, particularly, was no illusory dominion, and its rule in Frankish Greece, the Adriatic, the Balkans and the islands of the Levant amounted in the later Middle Ages to a mighty political and naval presence. The Venetians were not frightened of war to protect their interests and conquests, and the use of violence, not only to maintain naval bases and trading counters but also to exact taxes and tribute, was an essential part of their imperial method.

Unlike the Genoese, the Venetians did not allow their citizens to control and govern parts of their colonies in a private capacity. Economic historians have viewed the exercise of Venetian military and naval power as an investment that obtained a substantial economic return. Such methods certainly had echoes in the seventeenth-century colonial empires of the Atlantic powers, at a time when the Venetian Empire of the Levant was already in a state of advanced decay.

No doubt any groups that establish settlements by force in other people's lands have an exploitative attitude towards their unwilling hosts, and this was true of the crusading settlement in the holy land, just as it was true of many aspects of the first conquests of Islam. But this does not establish intimate connections between a bogey called crusading and a bogey called colonialism. There was only a very remote relationship between the crusading states in the holy land, that ended two centuries before Columbus sailed to America, and Iberian colonialism. However, it is much easier to suppose that there were some connections between the practices of the Italian trading colonies in the Levant and those of the first Iberian settlements in Africa and the Americas, although these have proved very hard to pin down.

It is doubtful, therefore, that we can call the settlements of the Italian and Catalan traders in the Levant and the Maghreb a kind of pre-imperialist colonialism: the description is just arguable for the early crusading states in the holy land, but not for their successors after the fall of Acre in 1291.³ However, there are some things about the late-medieval Levantine settlements that seem to anticipate Western advantages which came to be centrally important much later. For example, in the later Middle Ages the Western economies were already showing some signs of a more developed kind of capitalism than could be found in the Muslim states, and they also already possessed marked technological industrial advantages over their Muslim counterparts.

But we must not confound what we now see as the signs of things to come with their realization. The late medieval situation of Levant trade bore little relation to the sharp economic inferiority to the West that was, from the eighteenth century onwards, to be experienced by the Ottoman Empire, nor did it anticipate the marginalized status of the Ottoman economy, that eventually placed the Turkish dominions on the fringes of world economic development. In the later Middle Ages things were very different: the Ottomans still ruled the most powerful single economy, and the European traders lived from them.

In the Iberian peninsula the Christian holy war with the Muslims had preceded the crusades by some centuries. The crusade in the East, because of its profound effects on the general law and practice of the church, on the mentality of believers, and on the chivalric idealism of the ruling groups, changed the way in which the holy war was viewed in the Iberian West. By the end of the Middle Ages the Iberian Christian governments used terminology and administrative methods borrowed from the Levantine crusade, and shared with the other Catholic states a theoretical dependence upon the power and authority of the Roman papacy to back up their holy war ventures and their holy war taxation. There was also the question of mentality and attitude. The way that people think about and behave towards 'infidels' and 'pagans' is influenced by the past experience of their culture, and in this respect the holy war was a powerful cultural influence upon the Iberian generation that made the European discoveries.

It is necessary, though, to distinguish between the main Iberian partici-pants. The kingdoms of Castile and Aragon, particularly after they were linked by the marriage of Ferdinand and Isabella in 1479, represented an already triumphant Christian presence in the peninsula that had for a long time before its final occupation of the area in 1492 treated the one remaining Spanish Muslim kingdom of Granada as a subordinate state. Portugal, on the other hand, was a poor relation of the other Christian powers, and had to do what it could with the talents and resources of its people sailing the seas. Even after the beginnings of the Portuguese trading empire in the early sixteenth century, there remained a big gap between a Spain that could afford to spend huge sums in fortifying and defending unproductive military bases on the North African coast, and a Portugal that could only afford to establish itself abroad where there was a trading benefit that would justify the expense.

The island discoveries and settlements in the Atlantic area, without which the great movement of Europeans down the African coasts and across the ocean could not have happened, took place initially quite outside the context of holy war and reconquest, although the vocabulary of holy war and conversion later came to be applied to some of them. The islands of the Azores, that are near the same degrees of longitude as Portugal itself, appear on fourteenth-century maps without there being any documentary evidence for their 'discovery'. The Canary Islands were known also in the fourteenth century, at the end of which their settlement began. It was initially an exercise in primitive colonization, that started with the occupation of abandoned lands seized from an exterminated population. This was a predatory adventure that had no room, at first, for religious motives. The first settler leader in the Canaries was a French adventurer, who agreed to hold his few acquisitions in feudal tenure from the Castilian crown.

The late-medieval Iberian rulers wished to see themselves as heroic fighters against Islam. After the submission of the greater part of the Iberian Muslims, they were ready to take the war across the Straits of Gibraltar to

the Muslim Maghreb, that had once been Christian, and that could therefore be considered as fit terrain for a new holy and just war to reconquer
formerly Christian soil. In the event, their war of reconquest in the Maghreb
turned out to be a long and exhausting struggle, that after a century and a
half had to be cut down to the defence of a few garrisoned coastal towns
or *presidios*, and that never in the early modern period managed to achieve
even a shadow of its ambitious aims.

It was in one respect a renewal of the same crusading strategy that had
led Louis IX of France to besiege Tunis a century and a half before the
Iberian powers renewed the Christian North African offensive. However,
the later effort in North Africa took place under totally different circumstances. Not only had the crusading states in Syria finally come to an end,
but the whole balance of power – particularly maritime power – in the
eastern Mediterranean had changed. The Christian Byzantine Empire had
ceased to exist in 1453. The Ottoman advance removed most of the biggest
bases of Christian sea power in the Levant, and continued to chop away at
the surviving centres over a long period that extended far into the seventeenth century.

The trading penetration of the Atlantic coast of Africa south of Mauritania by the Portuguese, that gathered force quickly after the mid-fifteenth
century, was in areas which had not been thoroughly Islamicized, although
they often bordered on strongly Islamic zones to the east. The Portuguese
voyagers and traders realized that these peoples were non-Islamic. There
were scattered conversions among them to Christianity, but little or no
attempt at missionary work was made for a long time. The overwhelming
impulse behind the voyages of the Portuguese caravels was the search to
find gold suppliers and slave traders. Colonizing settlements were attempted
in equatorial Africa as far as the islands south of the Gulf of Biafra, but
these and other island settlements in the torrid zone were (unlike the
northerly settlements in the Canaries and the Azores) discouraged by the
hostile environment. There was no way in which such trading ventures and
such colonization could be seen as part of the holy war against Islam, as
were the isolated Christian coastal bastions that were being painfully gained
on the Islamic Mediterranean coasts.

Nevertheless, it was inevitable that Iberian colonization, when it spilled
over from the Islamic Maghreb to other parts of Africa and to the islands,
should still tend to use the language of crusading, and to ask for the exten-

sion of the privileges accorded by the church to crusaders to apply in some measure to the new, non-Islamic lands. The Iberian governments, anxious for their conquests in these new lands to be legitimized, turned to the Roman Popes as the sources of authority over both Catholics and, according to some interpretations of canon law, non-Christians.

When the Portuguese made the important conquest of Ceuta (Sabta) on the African side of the Straits of Gibraltar in 1415, it enabled the Christians to close the straits at will against the Muslim powers. Ceuta was a vital acquisition that was never relinquished: after the Portuguese royal prince, dom Fernando, had been captured in the abortive crusade against Tangier in 1437, the Portuguese allowed him to die in captivity rather than exchange him for Ceuta. It was fully in accordance with the crusading policy of the Roman Popes to issue a series of bulls that confirmed the Portuguese monarchy in the possession of Ceuta, and that set up a Catholic bishop there.

In 1442 Ceuta was still the only Christian-held *place-d'armes* on the African mainland, although considerable colonizing efforts were taking place on the offshore islands, especially Madeira and the Canaries. But just over a decade later things changed rapidly, as the Portuguese caravels began to land further and further south on African soil, and to get closer to people who would sell them gold and slaves. In the mid-1450s, just as Christendom experienced the shock of the fall of Constantinople to the Turks, the Portuguese installed themselves at Arguin near Cape Blanc, on the very southern limit of the coast of Mauritania, and at the limits of Muslim penetration on the Atlantic coast; by 1456 they had landed in Senegambia and were in contact with the Wolofs, who were black pagans.

When in 1455 the Portuguese applied to Pope Nicholas V to legitimize the conquests they were making on the western African coast, he was quite ready to issue privileges that in some ways assimilated the colonial expansion in Africa at the expense of black pagans to the ancient struggle with Turkish and Berber Islam. His bull *Romanus Pontifex*, issued in that year, conceded to Portugal the 'ports, islands and seas' that lay to the south of Capes Non, in the extreme south of Morocco, and Bojador, on the borders of Mauritania, on the twenty-sixth parallel. The bull almost certainly, in so far as it dealt with African discoveries planned or achieved, paraphrased a Portuguese document presented to the Pope. It mentioned the conquest of Madeira and the Azores, and the plan (never to be fulfilled) of a Portuguese conquest of the Canaries. The bull came at a critical point of Portuguese progress in Africa: in the same year as it was issued they reached Buba in

Senegal, and by 1460 they had effected landings right down the south of the coast of Sierra Leone.

The 1455 bull also referred to the Portuguese hope – not in fact to be realized until the very end of the century – to sail around Africa until their naval force could effect a junction with the 'Indians who honour the name of Christ', meaning the Ethiopians. It also mentioned the possible landings in Guinea, and looked forward to the conversion to Christianity of non-Muslim pagans, although the Pope offered no practical support for missionary work, and the religious privileges he granted did not include mention of preaching. By the time the bull was published the seamen in the Portuguese caravels were already working out how to navigate against the Guinea current that impeded their coastal voyages to the Gulf and the Gold Coast; by this point they knew how to take a westerly route that rounded Cape Verde, and then got the help of the equatorial current as it swung east.

Romanus Pontifex set precedents for the Portuguese that were followed later, when the Iberian governments applied for papal legitimization for their conquests in the Americas and other new lands. It also set a precedent by invoking papal authority for the way in which traders and colonists regulated their relations with the indigenous inhabitants. In the context of Muslim North Africa, the issues went back to debates that had occurred a few years earlier, on whether a king who successfully attacked Saracens holding lands that had formerly been in the possession of Christian rulers could lay claim to such lands. The bull stated without qualification that the Portuguese could seize and legitimately possess Saracen lands. But it went on to assign further sovereignties that could only be justified out of the papal 'plenitude of power', since the lands the Portuguese were taking in the non-Muslim parts of Africa could not be said to belong to the Christians by virtue of a holy war. It was implied, though not stated, that they could be claimed by right of conquest in a just war. In effect the doctrines that had originally belonged to the crusade were being applied without too much distinction to a new colonialism.

It is unlikely that the Christian Iberian states saw matters in this light. For half a century and more after they had obtained papal approval for their trading and maritime exploits in Africa, the Portuguese kings treated the attack on the Islamic Maghreb, and the effort to gain toeholds there for Christian forces, as the first call on their resources. In the same year as the publication of the bull the Portuguese seized a strategic fortress in northern Morocco, Alcazar (Qsar al-Seghir). In 1471 a cluster of important places belonging to the Kingdom of Fez, close to Alcazar, also fell to the Portuguese: Tangier, Arsila, Arache (al-'Ar'aish). There was also some success in getting local submission to the Portuguese in Safi, in southern Morocco. In 1485, five years before the submission of the Kingdom of Granada on the other side of the straits, Portugal was still putting all its military effort into the attempt to subdue Morocco. How much advantage was really to be had from these conquests was doubted by some contemporaries. At the end of the century the Portuguese were said to have gained 'more honour than profit' from their efforts against the Maghrebi Muslims.

After the fall of Granada in 1492 the Kingdom of Castile and Aragon took the initiative from the Portuguese in the Mediterranean Maghreb. There is a long list of towns and ports conquered by the Catholic kings in the sixteenth century that sounds impressive, but is less so when it is considered that they were strung out over the enormously long Mediterranean coast of the Maghreb, from Badis (Peñon de Velez) on the coast of northern Morocco in the west to Tripoli in present-day Libya in the distant east. Many of these places were to be lost, though some were recaptured once or twice, sometimes at enormous cost in lives and money. The show-capture of the century was the taking of the port of Tunis, La Goulette or Halq al-Wadi, by no less a person than the Emperor Charles V himself, in 1535, employing a huge crusading fleet of over a hundred ships of war and some three hundred transports, and men and equipment drawn from all over the Habsburg Empire. It was an enormous effort to win a brief advantage. La Goulette and the city of Tunis remained in Spanish hands for only thirty-odd years.

There was never a moment in the early modern period when the Iberian powers could contemplate a systematic conquest of North Africa: such an operation was not only militarily impractical, but was outside the strategic view that had brought the *presidios* into existence. The function of these strongpoints was not commercial, and they bore not the slightest resemblance either to the Italian colonies in the late-medieval Levant, or to the Portuguese forts in Asia and the New World. They were an expensive adjunct to Spanish power in the sea war in the Mediterranean, and a hangover from old conceptions of the crusade, that proved its diminished utility.

The mid-sixteenth century was a bad time for the Iberian presence in the Maghreb. The capture of Agadir on the Atlantic coast in 1541 heralded the disintegration of most of what remained of the Portuguese colonial settlements in Morocco. In 1551 the Portuguese evacuated important places in northern Morocco and on the Atlantic, including Alcazar. The Spanish-held Bougie (Bijaya) was lost in 1555, and in 1558 a Spanish army was totally destroyed in a misguided attempt on Mostaganem, west of Oran. In spite of the successful defence of Malta in 1565 and the great Christian naval victory at Lepanto in 1571, the war on the North African coasts continued to go badly. Tunis was lost back to the Turks in 1574.

The bankruptcy of the traditional, chivalrous crusade finally became evident in 1578. A large but incompetently organized crusading force led by the Portuguese king, Sebastian, was on its way to attempt to regain Alcazar (which gave its name to the battle) when it fought a disastrous battle at a river crossing between Larache and Alcazar that ended with the king's death and defeat. This 'battle of the three kings' also caused the end of Sebastian's dynasty in Portugal, the death of the Moroccan sultan, and the death of the Sa'diyan pretender to Morocco who accompanied the Christian army.

A century before these setbacks in the traditional areas of the crusade, Iberian seamen and traders were already preparing for the transformation of the Western economies and the establishment of the colonial empires. Far from the deadly and useless conflicts of North Africa – which nevertheless had a place in the ideology that the seamen shared – the Portuguese ships plied the Guinea run, and their navigators began to master the sea routes of the south Atlantic. In 1471 the Guinea enterprise reached Prah on the Gold Coast (La Mina), and direct contact with the gold-exporting trade was made at last.

From this point onwards the legitimization of the conquests made in these maritime ventures preoccupied both the main Iberian states. To some extent the problems are easily (though anachronistically) understood in terms of the balance of power and the assignment of spheres of influence. But this does not do justice to the legalistic mentality of the later Middle Ages, nor to its willingness to turn to the church as the supreme arbitrator, judge and leader of the crusade against the infidels.

The first agreement about the partition of the Atlantic colonies between Castile and Portugal came in 1479–80 at the Treaty of Alcaçovas, which recognized Portuguese rights in the Azores and on the west coast of Africa, in Guinea and the Cape Verde Islands, and allowed Castile to continue with the conquest and settlement of the Canary Islands. This agreement, part of which was subsequently in 1481 incorporated into a papal bull that confirmed its operative clauses, formed a model that became of great importance after the Columbus expedition of 1492.

The results of Columbus's voyage became known almost immediately in Lisbon because of his disembarkation on the return trip on Portuguese soil, in the Azores. Fear of Portuguese counter-claims to the New World, based on the Spanish–Portuguese Treaty of Alcaçovas, caused the Catholic kings hurriedly to obtain a bull from the Pope to avert this danger. The Aragonese Pope, Alexander VI, issued in the following year (1493) three bulls, addressed to Ferdinand and Isabella of Castile and Aragon, that cannot be considered an arbitration award, since they were applied for by the Spaniards alone. They resemble, much more than an arbitration, a plan for an international settlement that hopes to obtain the assent of the parties concerned.

The part of the bulls that conceded power, authority and jurisdiction to the Catholic monarchs in the lands discovered in the west resembles the type of land grants made by the popes to princes in Italy. It is also possible that the ancient forged 'Donation' the bulls claimed to have been made by the Emperor Constantine to the popes, with its concession of 'the islands' to the Roman Bishopric, was in the minds of the Pope and his advisers. However, the 1493 grant refers back to the grant made by earlier popes of the African regions of Guinea and Mina de Oro to the Portuguese kings, whose terms are said to apply to the Castilian grant in the New World also. Pope Alexander was trying to demonstrate the cautious even-handedness between the two Iberian monarchies that could be said to have characterized papal policy in these matters.

This was a critical moment in the first modern transformation of the concept of holy war. So far as the Iberian powers were concerned, papal authority in the holy war had in matters of property right always been of a very limited nature, because they would never have dreamed of accepting papal intervention in the way they disposed of lands taken from the Moors in Spain. But when the question of extending the holy war to the lands of the infidel in Africa had arisen, the Iberian powers had been willing to apply for and accept papal concessions or grants. The Portuguese had asked for the papal award of jurisdiction and trade monopoly in their West African conquests. The Castilians had sometimes argued that the North African lands ruled in their own day by the Moors had once been ruled by the Christian Visigothic kings whom they claimed to have succeeded, but this could not be alleged for the Caribbean discoveries.

The bull *Inter Caetera* of Alexander VI laid down a line of maritime demarcation between the seas and regions assigned to Portugal and those assigned to the Catholic Kings. The principle followed was the demarcation

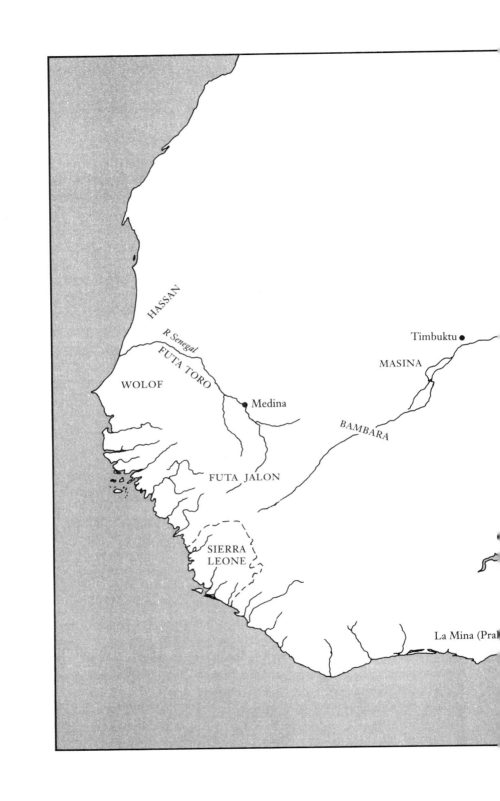

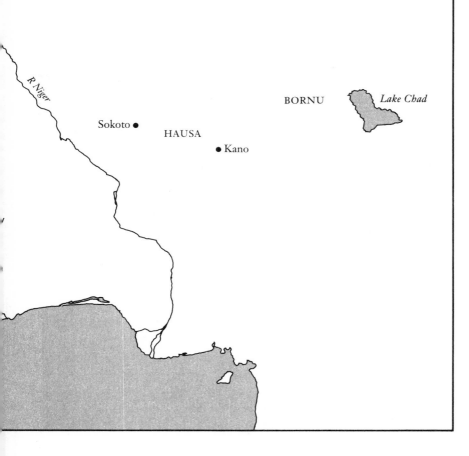

The Western Sudan and West Africa

R Niger

BORNU

Lake Chad

Sokoto ●

HAUSA

● Kano

line established by the Treaty of Alcaçovas thirteen years earlier, that had named the Azores and the Cape Verde islands as the western limits assigned to Portugal. However, the limit chosen in Rome of a hundred leagues to the west of this line proved, when the bull was published, to be too far east for Portugal to accept. The division was subsequently renegotiated, not in Rome, but directly between the two Iberian states, in the Treaty of Tordesillas (1494). The renegotiated line was fixed at 370 leagues (instead of a hundred) west of the Azores. This was a decision of some importance, since Brazil, which was discovered by Portuguese vessels in 1500, would have fallen to Castile under Alexander VI's bull of seven years earlier, but was Portuguese by virtue of the Treaty of Tordesillas. The papal record was obediently corrected by Pope Julius II in 1506, which shows how far from being binding arbitration awards the papal grants had been.

The 1493 grant to Ferdinand and Isabella differs from the papal grants made earlier to the Portuguese kings in the quite different emphasis laid by Alexander VI upon the conversion and evangelization of the pagan inhabitants of the western islands found by Columbus. Earlier papal grants referring to African lands had retained a connection with the holy war in their reference to the possible arrival of the Portuguese explorers in the kingdom of the 'Indians who honour the name of Christ', who could then become allies in the common struggle against Islam.

This same motive of making contact with the Christians accessible from the east coast of Africa had been proclaimed by Columbus himself. Like the Portuguese who made the voyage to the Gulf of Guinea, and talked about their projected voyages to Ethiopia, Columbus had originally hoped to reach the Indies and find gold, which he spoke of as destined to finance the struggle to regain Jerusalem. But he had arrived in regions irrelevant to the Kingdom of Prester John (Ethiopia), regions that he described after his return as being inhabited by peoples who were disposed to receive the Christian gospel. Conquest meant evangelization, and evangelization entailed a duty that lay both on the conquerors and on the church that was behind them.

Conversion had not loomed large in earlier papal grants relating to Africa. The question of the conversion of the pagan inhabitants of the Canary Islands had not presented itself as a major one in the fifteenth century, largely because they had been small in number, and had been practically exterminated by the Christian intruders. The bull for Portuguese colonization in Guinea issued in the middle of the century mentioned the probability of finding 'Gentile or pagan peoples in no way infected by the sect of the abominable Muhammad', whose submission the Portuguese would have to obtain before the Christian gospel could be preached to them. But there had been no suggestion of a clerical effort being mounted for this purpose: the 1455 bull had restricted itself to saying that the costs of setting up churches and providing clergy would fall upon the Portuguese conquerors.

Reticence at this earlier time about missionary work can be explained because the exploring effort was still so new, and because its main aim, as argued by the Portuguese, was not the setting up of African colonies, but the establishment of links with the Christian Kingdom of Ethiopia. Such a link was, in fact, established in the early sixteenth century, as a part of the Portuguese effort to dispute control of the Red Sea and the Indian Ocean with the Muslims. But the hope that it would help launch a new Western crusade to free Jerusalem from Muslim rule proved illusory.

The relationship between holy war and the spreading of the gospel is a long story of Christian inaction, hesitation and uncertainty, that ended when the development of Western colonization of the New World and other parts of the globe brought about a new concept of missionary activity. Forced conversion after battle, as had happened in some of the wars of Charlemagne against the pagan tribes, had not been unknown in the early Middle Ages. But later Christian theologians had a more rational attitude to forced conversion. A conversion not freely made was not a conversion in a real sense, though in the later Middle Ages some theologians did say that 'severities' might be practised on infidels to encourage their reception of the faith. However, even if a conversion was known to have been forced, it was agreed that the convert who subsequently tried to renege on it was subject to the direst penalties.

In the Christian states in the holy land there was throughout the twelfth century very little organized attempt to convert the Muslim subject populations to Christianity. The enterprise was known to be very difficult, and the reward was on the whole negative, since there was a certain moral obligation to free converted Muslims, if their condition was that of slavery. There was a *de facto* toleration of Islam in the Kingdom of Jerusalem: no obstacles were placed in the way of Muslim observance, although mosques were very few. The main preoccupation of the feudal lords was to see that the Muslim peasants fulfilled their obligations of rent and tax.

Clerks in Europe talked about evangelization as an aim of the holy war in Palestine, and an appreciable (though not overwhelming) number of conversions from Islam occurred in the Kingdoms of Jerusalem and Acre. But such conversions seem to have been more of an embarrassment than a cause for rejoicing. To remove obstacles that property-owners might place in the way of conversion, the popes issued laws to guarantee that conversion did not confer freedom upon Muslim slaves. The suspicion that the converts were trying to better their lot, and particularly that they wanted to escape from servile status, made their reception as Christians grudging and unwelcome. Converts were also not unknown among Arab mercenaries serving in the crusader armies, and among hostile Muslims who occasionally converted on the battlefield. In the Iberian peninsula, in the areas recovered for Christianity, conversion of Muslims occurred, though the converts were often mistrusted, increasingly so towards the end of the Middle Ages. The holy war against infidels in Central Europe, in which whole tribes sometimes accepted Christianity in great groups, had a much closer connection with the idea of mission than had the holy war in the holy land.

In the thirteenth century, a time of religious ferment and preaching revival in Europe, more interest was taken in the question of the evangelization of the East than formerly, and one or two high clergy in the holy land itself were fervent supporters of the idea, although they did not get very far with vernacular preaching in Arabic, and the concrete results were sparse. Far more interest was taken, then and later, in the possibilities of converting the Mongols, who until the very end of the century were viewed as probable future allies of the Christians, and who continued for some time afterwards to seem to be open to the persuasion of Christian preachers. The conversion of Muslims in Syria seemed a much more difficult and a much less promising activity than the conversion of the Mongols.

Isolated voices, like that of the English poet John Gower, spoke of the obligation to preach to and convert the Saracens as a binding duty on Christians that in effect excluded the crusade. He reproached those who:

> To slen and feihten ous bidde
> Hem whom thei scholde, as the bok seith,
> Converten unto Cristes feith.
> But hierof have I gret mervaile,
> Hou thei wol bidde me travaile;

A Sarazin if I sle schal,
I sle the Soule forth withal,
And that was nevere Christes lore.[4]

Among the most active of all the groups of preachers was the Franciscans, who were indefatigable preachers of the crusade in all its forms, but who also felt a commitment to spreading the gospel in the East. St Francis himself had set an example in 1218, walking from the crusade army at Damietta to the camp of the Sultan al-Kamil, and engaging in conversation or disputation there. Nothing certain is known about the nature of Francis's approach to the Muslims, but it had indirect results, in that he subsequently encouraged his friars to go to Muslim lands and preach the gospel: the Rule in its final form emphasizes that friars should be equipped for the missionary task, and implies that such journeys to convert the heathen are legitimate and praiseworthy. In the event, Franciscans sometimes goaded Muslim rulers into turning them into martyrs on account of their provocative attacks on Islam, but had scarce success in making converts.

However, the specialized missionary training for the East which would have been needed to achieve Francis of Assisi's goal was never organized in the medieval period. Possibly the Dominicans set up special colleges in Tunis and elsewhere for this purpose in the thirteenth century, but if they were ever established, little came of them. Specialized missionary training for preaching in Arabic-speaking countries was not seriously contemplated until the time of the great Spanish Arabic scholar and contemplative mystic Ramòn Lull, at the end of the thirteenth century. And Lull's Arabic missionary colleges, over which he himself blew hot and cold at various times, were never established on a permanent basis.

No one had a clear answer to the question: does the war against the infidel also entail preaching the gospel to the infidel? Though there were some who were clear about the missionary duties of the church in unbelieving lands, only a very small minority thought that the crusade should be utterly renounced in favour of the pulpit. How, in any case, to get the infidel to listen to the gospel, unless he was under the political control of Christians? There was a parallel dilemma in Islam, and one or two writers on the Islamic holy war said the Qur'an should be recited to the unbelievers before the army attacked, although only if it was certain that the opponents would not cast scorn upon the holy words, which was presumably rather hard to arrange.

A key text on the relations between the church and the infidels outside it came from a thirteenth-century pope who was also a great canon lawyer. Innocent IV (1243–54), in his earlier capacity as the church lawyer Sinibaldo Fieschi, had asserted that by virtue of his being God's representative the pope has jurisdiction over unbelieving peoples, though not in such a manner as to deprive them of the legal rule that they exercise. However, he could intervene where unbelieving sovereigns ruled in a manner that broke the laws God gave for all created things to follow, the 'natural law'. If infidels should offend against the natural law (or, should they be Jews, against Jewish law), the pope, and he alone, has power to correct them, and to use force in order to do so.

The question of the legitimate dominion exercised by non-Christian governments was a complex one. The medieval theological view, that went back to the Christian origins in a pagan Roman commonwealth, had been on the whole willing to recognize the legitimacy that an infidel government might have, and to admit that Christians living under such a government might owe it a duty of obedience. The idea that political legitimacy was founded upon Christian grace was considered a dangerous one, because of the threat it might pose to Christian governments whose moral credentials were impugned, and still more because of the implied threat to clerical property rights.

According to Innocent IV the worship of idols – an important matter in relations with African and, later, American peoples – is against the natural law, and therefore subject to papal intervention even if practised by pagans outside Christendom. Moreover, although no one has the power to compel men to accept the faith, should an infidel ruler refuse to accept Christian preachers of the gospel who have been despatched by the pope, the pope has the power to invoke force to constrain him to admit them. Needless to say, Innocent IV declined to accept the corollary that Christian powers ought to admit Muslim missionaries.

Although this opinion was part of a lawyer's commentary upon church law, and had not the binding force of a papal pronouncement, it was for some centuries to be very influential, and it was of great importance in the sixteenth-century debate about the rights and duties of Christian colonists in the Americas. Innocent IV's opinions on this topic did not directly concern holy war, though they arose in the context of the just war and the holy war. It is true that the influence of theoretical pronouncements of this kind upon events in the later Middle Ages was limited. There was little chance for Innocent IV's views on the relations of Western Christians with infidels to have a notable effect outside the Iberian peninsula, which was the only place in Christendom where papal authority or pronouncements could be applied to large non-Christian populations.

In the sixteenth century the conquest of the Americas led to a flood of passionate debate, in which the Castilian crown itself was closely involved. Its involvement was the more important because of the concession by the papacy to the Castilian monarchy of huge powers to control the new American church. The justification for these powers was the missionary duties that had been imposed upon the Spanish monarchy by the papal bulls of concession issued in the preceding century.

There was a huge gap between the sometimes idealistic orders and instructions issued by the Iberian monarchs in Europe and the brutal realities of colonial conquest. The service paid by the Iberian *conquistadores* to the evangelizing aims of the conquest was often hypocritical. For example, Hernando Cortés, the conqueror of Peru, assured the Aztec ruler Montezuma that the Christian religion taught that 'all men are brothers' shortly before effecting Montezuma's arrest and execution. The failure of the colonists to observe either the spirit or the letter of the laws made for the Americas was readily admitted by people of the time. It was deplored by the Castilian crown itself, part of whose aim in seeking a more comprehensive legal basis for its American administration was to exert more control over its colonists. The *conquistadores* did not see themselves as crusaders, as is sometimes said, because that would have submitted them to rules of canon law about relations with infidels that they found restrictive and unacceptable.

Few people tried to pretend that the situation of the American indigenous peoples justified holy war, although resistance to the entry of either colonists or missionaries was regarded as just grounds for war of the conventional sort. But the vocabulary of holy war occasionally reappeared. In the discussions that preceded the drawing up of one of the first basic directives of colonial administration, the *Requerimiento* of 1514, one of the Castilian crown servants argued that the Indies had been given by the popes to the Castilian crown in the same way that God had granted the promised land to the Hebrews. Moses had sent Joshua to Canaan in fulfilment of this promise, and Joshua had conquered the land and enslaved its idolatrous inhabitants.

There was an echo of this doctrine in the 'Requirement' itself, which guaranteed peaceful possession to those Indians who submitted to Castilian royal power after its terms had been made known to them, but threatened that resistance would be visited with enslavement and spoliation. In practice, the 'Requirement' was used as a bare, formal announcement (incomprehensible to the Indians even if anyone bothered to communicate it to them) that an area was going to be attacked and subdued.

Medieval European culture was not tolerant in the way it described people outside its bounds – few cultures are. Descriptions of infidels as 'barbarians' were not uncommon from the very earliest days of the crusade: Pope Urban II himself in his letter to the Flemings spoke of protecting the Eastern Christians from the 'barbarian rage' of the Muslims. Twelfth-century clerks, not excluding Peter the Venerable who had considerable knowledge of Islam, sometimes also referred to Muslims as barbarians (though 'pagans' was a frequently used alternative, and 'gentiles' another). In the fifteenth century an immensely influential humanist tract on the crusade was written by the Florentine publicist Benedetto Accolti that also referred to the Muslims as barbarians. Sixteenth-century humanists, even the pacific Erasmus, used the same term. Of the equally despised Scythians in the classical period, he said: 'Such was the barbarity and inhumanity of the Scythians that the name became proverbial, just as we call a cruel man "a Turk" and a horrible deed "Turkish".'[5]

The word 'barbarian' was used for so long to describe Muslims that it would be dangerous to give it a terminal date. It was used of the Ottoman Turks by the Austrian Emperor Joseph II in the late eighteenth century, and Gladstone, echoing Erasmus, spoke of the Turks in his 1876 pamphlet on the 'Bulgarian Horrors', or the atrocities committed by the Ottoman Empire in Europe, as 'the one great anti-human species of humanity'. A few years later the great Oriental traveller Charles Doughty (1843–1926) spoke of Muslims as having 'a barbarous fox-like understanding'.[6] The endurance of this usage can seem odd: the great days of the Islamic caliphate were long over by the time of the Florentine Renaissance, and Gladstone and Doughty can be excused, perhaps, for their conviction of European superiority in their day; but in 1099, when the First Crusade was launched, there is no doubt that Western Europe was a primitive backwater when compared with Cairo.

There was, however, no idea in the sixteenth century that Europe had a civilizing mission in respect of the Islamic Ottomans. The Europeans of the Renaissance regarded themselves as manning a rather desperate defence against Turkish power, and when Venetian observers, the great intelligence-gatherers of the period, came to examine and judge the Ottoman Empire, they treated it, as is emphasized in a different context above, with profound respect.

However, when Europeans came into contact with the inhabitants of the Canary Islands, who went naked and used only stone tools, a new variety of cultural relations between 'civilized' and 'primitive' peoples came into being. It did not do much credit to the Europeans, who treated the indigenous inhabitants of the islands with no less than barbaric cruelty, and enslaved the few who survived. A protest was made to Pope Eugenius IV in 1434 by clergy working as missionaries in the islands about the enslavement of their converted Christians. This protest had antecedents in crusader Palestine, but it was the first shot to be fired by churchmen in a long polemic with the overseas colonists on behalf of the Christianized natives. In one form or another the dispute lasted, although it was often diluted more or less by the interests that the missionaries shared with the colonists, as long as European colonization.

It was possible to view the supposedly primitive indigenous inhabitants of the newly found regions either as wild men of the woods, about whom there was a body of medieval tradition, or as innocents reminiscent of the golden age, who were the subject of a different body of humanistic tradition. But a third view was the one that in practical politics prevailed. In the majority view of the colonists, whose own selfish interests influenced their judgement, the indigenous peoples were barbarians likely to relapse into a contemptible way of life if they were not strictly controlled. Such colonists maintained that the indigenous Americans would do better to live as 'enslaved men' under the rule of the conquerors than to continue as 'free beasts'.

Slavery was never accepted by all clerical theorists as the natural lot of colonized peoples that were supposed primitive, although there was a school that gave some credence to the idea. The critical question for the missionaries was whether the colonized peoples could 'live like Christians', which implied their acceptance of the huge paraphernalia of the alien European culture. Of the differing nature of American cultures from one region to another, and of the immense error involved in defining them all as barbarous or primitive, few people had any idea until the early ethnographic enquiries of the American missionaries began to be published in Europe in the late sixteenth century, and even then the impact on European opinion was small.

Islamic culture had in the final analysis grown out of roots that it shared with Christendom: although hated and fought by Western Christians, it spoke a language comprehensible to Western men, and Dante placed

Muhammad in Hell as a heretic, a deviator from a commonly known path. Islam was by the end of the Middle Ages unwillingly admitted to be the religion of a great, powerful civilization, that shared with Christendom the possession of an organized body of belief, and that had eminent theologians and a coherent moral view of the world. All this was alarming to the ordinary Catholic. It was the knowledge, or the suspicion, that it was so that made the Muslim converts to Christianity, and especially the Spanish 'Moriscos', so distrusted.

But the situation of colonized or to-be-colonized infidel idolaters was a different one. There was no equivalent in the New World to the persecution of Christian churches by Muslims, nor were there Christian holy places (such as Jerusalem) to protect in this world of entirely alien religions or superstitions. When Christian holy places began to exist in the New World, their protection still did not fit into the Biblical context of the old holy wars. From the beginning Columbus and his successors emphasized the docility of the American Indians, and their supposed willingness to accept the faith the invaders brought with them. The Indians were credited, often mistakenly, with a sort of cultural and political passivity; so long as this view continued, the concept of holy war was inappropriate to their condition. Culturally, the indigenous populations of the New World were thought of as a blank on which a new identity could be imposed; they were in a sense unworthy of holy war.

Missionary practice in the New World changed radically in the course of the sixteenth century. The conviction of the first Franciscan missionaries, that they had shared with Columbus himself, was reconcilable with a belief that their mission was bound up with the transformation of the holy war and the freeing of Jerusalem. They thought that they went to the infidel lands across the sea on a holy pilgrimage that belonged to the last days of the world and the approaching end of all things. By the end of the century the apocalyptic beliefs of the wandering friars had given place to new generations of missionaries who considered their task to be, besides the bringing of the gospel to the pagan American masses, the socialization of the pagans in a broadly European view of the world. To achieve this the missionaries would reside in the New World in stable, organized centres, into which they would seek to regroup the pagans. The apocalyptic expectation occasionally resurfaced, but only to be rejected by the clerical majority. This was the world of the civilizing mission, in which only scattered and fragmentary memories of the holy war remained.

Only very exceptionally were the Christian missionaries in the New

World armed: both Catholics and Protestants preserved the traditional distinction between the spiritual and the secular realms. This may have obscured the nature of a change in the process of colonization that involved the delegitimization of most heathen governments. Earlier, clerical theorists had been willing to acknowledge that legitimate infidel governments might exist. This concept had affected older Christian settlements in or near Muslim countries, and did not go away; it was to be of central importance in the early development of international law, and was not without importance in the governance of British India. But when Christian governments looked to settlements across the seas in Africa and the Americas a very different doctrine took hold. The idea that there could be such a thing as legitimate heathen dominion was hardly applied at all to the colonization of the New World. Few scruples of this kind troubled the Spanish and Portuguese conquerors, and the Protestants scarcely bothered their heads about them at all.

When Queen Elizabeth I of England authorized Sir Humphrey Gilbert to undertake a colonizing expedition (it would have been nearer the truth to say a pirate expedition) in 1578, she empowered him to 'discover, find, search out and view such remote heathen and barbarous lands, countries and territories as were not actually possessed of any Christian prince or people'.[7] By implication, the only dominion that Gilbert was bound to respect was Christian government. At a time when the Christian doctrine of holy war was entering a stage of final decay, Christianity had come in one respect to resemble Islam more than ever before. In some of its colonial aspects it was becoming, like Islam, a religion of power, in which the sword preceded the word of God.

There had been many precedents for this development, especially in the relations between the church and the pagan peoples of central and northern Europe. It would be wrong, though, to apply it to the whole of what later came to be called 'colonialism': it was never more than very partially true, for example, of British rule in India. But in the Renaissance period the Christian holy war may be said to have died in bringing the new colonial world into existence, having played a not unimportant role in the emergence of what was eventually to become a new world order.

That we can praise or blame the Christian holy war for its influence on colonialism is much to be doubted. Some modern historians have talked about 'filiation' between the Christian settlements in the holy land and the colonies of the times of the Discoveries.[8] But it is a very remote parentage, and there is no obvious way in which the new colonies resembled the Christian states in Syria; still less can it be said that the new colonies were modelled upon the old. The most decisive factor in separating the old from the new is the absence of any substantial, long-term attempt to convert the infidel population of the Syrian Christian states to Christianity, whereas a declared intention of the occupation of the American and sub-Saharan African regions was the conversion of their inhabitants. Even in Muslim and Hindu India, there was an important attempt to encourage conversions to Christianity during the nineteenth century.

The most important relationship between the late medieval Catholic crusade and the settlements made as a result of the Discoveries was unconnected with the imitation of an earlier system by a later one. It was, rather, the process by which, in the late fifteenth and early sixteenth centuries, Spain and Portugal, who began the whole colonizing process, relied upon their crusading past to legalize their occupation of new lands, and also to facilitate the negotiations by which they jointly divided their spheres of influence.

There was also some reliance during the settlement of the new colonial empires on canon-law principles that concerned the legal status of infidels in Christian-controlled countries, reflecting to some extent the situation that had regulated such groups as the Muslims in Christian Spain. But even in this matter the relation with the crusade was rather indirect.

CHAPTER NINE

Decay and Transformation of Holy War

SOME OF THE WARS waged by the European powers with the Ottomans in the sixteenth and seventeenth centuries can properly be called crusades, and the opinion that in the periods commonly called the Renaissance and the Reformation the idea of the crusade became obsolete is mistaken, or at best a simplification. Pope Pius II's pathetic death at Ancona in 1464 is sometimes taken as a symbol of the death of the medieval crusading idea, when it merely pointed to its decline as a common political and military objective of Christendom as a a whole. Popes Alexander VI (1494–1503) and Leo X (1513–21), who represent the Rome of the High Renaissance, were both, in spite of the former's diplomatic links with the Turks, strongly committed to the crusade. That they failed to launch important crusading ventures is not surprising, because they never managed to achieve the harmony of the great powers that the crusade required, but this did not mean that there was total indifference in Catholic Europe.

The accession of Suleyman I in 1520 to an empire that had added Syria and Egypt to its already huge extent meant that the military struggle in Europe was to be taken beyond the Balkans to the Hungarian plains, and beyond them to the historic Austrian heart of Habsburg power. The German Empire could not stay indifferent to the blows delivered to its eastern frontiers by the infidel, even if few German princes were anxious to protect the Habsburg dynasty. It is true that the Mediterranean aspect of Turkish power was distant from German interests: the depredations of the Turkish fleet, the surrender of the Hospitaller island of Rhodes in 1522 and the submission of most of the Barbary coasts to Ottoman lordship were not things that stirred the peoples of western and central Germany to their depths.

But the fall of Belgrade in 1521, the Hungarian defeat at the battle of

Mohacz in 1526, opening the way to the German lands, and the further Turkish advances that led to their investment of Vienna in 1529, could not be shrugged off in Germany, where fear of the Turk became universal. Turkish troops had quickly reached the old Austrian 'marches', the frontier areas of Austria, Styria and Carinthia; attempts to hold them on a new defensive line in Croatia had come to nothing, and at Vienna they were battering on the door of the middle Danube. Even so, the German cities and princes reacted slowly. An army was raised by the German Diet, but it took no part in the defence of Vienna.

So long as the Catholic Habsburg dynasty, that bestrode Europe like a colossus in the sixteenth century, found its most vital interests threatened by the Ottomans and their client states, the crusade could not die. The Habsburgs were locked in conflict with the Ottomans and with one or other of the minor Muslim powers of North Africa for most of the sixteenth century. When the Emperor Charles V met Pope Clement VII at Bologna in 1530, after the end of a great crisis between the two in which Charles's troops had sacked the city of Rome, the papal procession carried three banners: one of the Holy Roman Church; one of the Medici dynasty that had occupied the papacy, with a brief Dutch interlude, since 1513; and a third bearing the sign of the holy cross, that was to be unfurled in the planned war against the Turks. Six years later, a year after his hard-fought and expensive victory at Tunis, the Emperor delivered a bitter speech in the presence of Pope Clement's successor, Paul III, at their summit meeting in Rome. He complained of the bad faith of the French King, whom the Pope favoured, and of the continuation of the dynastic war with France that he did not want. He wished for peace in Christendom, so that he could turn his military attention to the Turkish war.

There were major set-pieces in these great Turkish disputes: Charles V's successful expedition to Tunis in 1535; the failure of the Ottoman siege of Malta (that was held by the Hospitallers, not by the Spaniards) in 1565; the overwhelming Christian victory at the battle of Lepanto in 1571. But none of these marked a definite shift in the balance of power between the two major participants, and the aftermath of Lepanto was exhaustion on both sides, and a running-down of the naval war.

At the end of the fifteenth century the holy war still formed part of the ideologies of the European powers. In 1494 Charles VIII of France set out on his great armed expedition to conquer the Kingdom of Naples that he claimed by hereditary right, declaring that the expedition had the character of a crusade, on the grounds that he was King of Jerusalem by the same right that he was King of Naples, and that his intention was to launch an attack on the infidel once he had regained his kingdom in southern Italy. There is no reason to suppose that Charles's claim, which attempted to link him with the contemporary religious prophecies about the Turkish wars, was fraudulent. That he seriously planned an expedition to the holy land is unlikely; but it is perfectly conceivable that he thought of launching an expedition against the Turks across the Adriatic from Apulia once he controlled southern Italy.

In the event, the French invasion of Italy launched a new period of European history that had serious consequences for the conduct of the Turkish wars. It saw French and Spanish power locked in decades of struggle, principally but by no means entirely in the Italian theatre of war. In the course of these wars France did not hesitate to ally with the Turks against the common Habsburg enemy, so that Francis I of France, whose predecessor Charles VIII had announced the crusade half a century earlier, was in 1543–4 willing to provide the main Turkish battle fleet with a naval base at Toulon. In Germany the religious reformers were to prove, without having wished it, influences that deeply weakened resistance to Turkish power. From the mid-1530s onwards the German Protestant opposition to the Habsburgs was supported closely by France, whose policies were for a very long time pro-Turkish and pro-Protestant.

The gradual trend in Europe towards more pragmatic attitudes to the Turkish war in the east and the war of the Barbary coasts in the west is easy to understand, but it is hard to explain the way in which these alternated with stubborn renewals of the holy war. Fernand Braudel suggested that the ebb and flow of the struggles in the Mediterranean were connected with economic development and depression: that at times of prosperity both Muslims and Christians pursued internal feuds, while in times of depression the crusade and the *jihad* prospered.[1] It is an attractive thesis, but not at all easy to prove.

Outside the main political arena, but often crossing through it, the old commercial ambitions and rivalries of the European trading powers in the Muslim world continued in the same manner as they had done for centuries. Late in the sixteenth century the Protestant English managed to obtain trading privileges from the Ottomans. They came late into a Constantinople where the Venetians had been accepted since the preceding century, and Venice had been a major actor in Middle East trade since the early Middle Ages. The French had obtained trading rights in 1535. The efforts of the

English negotiators were bungling and amateurish compared to those of the experienced Venetians and the sophisticated diplomacy of the French, but in the end, partly by dint of offering the Sultan showy gadgets such as a remarkable clock and an elaborate organ, they got more or less what they wanted.

The arrival of these brash Protestant contenders announced the beginning of the northern trading and shipping challenge to the traditional Christian traders in the Mediterranean and the Middle East area, that the newcomers were shortly to extend to Persia. It was still at this stage a very weak challenge, although Dutch seapower was soon to make it otherwise.

Protestantism opposed the traditional holy war from its beginnings. The German Augustinian friar Martin Luther was above all a man of tender conscience. At the heart of his disquiet was his anxiety and indignation that the church was selling the things of God for money. The sale of indulgences, whether to finance the construction of sacred buildings or the crusading war against the Muslims, was one of the main reasons for his public protest against the churchmen serving the Roman pope in Germany. He did not specifically mention the indulgences issued for the crusade in the theological positions that he attached to the doors of the castle church of Wittenberg in 1517, but his objection to them was implicit, and within two or three years was to become publicly known. Luther's early career as a revolutionary reformer coincided with an acute phase of the Turkish wars. He at first avoided overmuch reference to them, but a religious leader of Luther's sort, whose every move depended upon his sensitivity to German public opinion, could not long remain indifferent to the Turkish threat.

The papacy had reacted to renewed Ottoman aggression in the second decade of the sixteenth century with skilful and energetic, if entirely traditional, diplomacy. The Medici Pope Leo X (1513–21), who was by no means the ineffectual aesthete he is sometimes painted, had used the Ottoman peril as a peg on which to hang a project for the reconciliation of the main Christian powers, and their uniting in a single treaty organization that would relaunch the crusade. To this end he proclaimed a five-year general truce among Christian princes from March 1518, and offered to the European powers the report of one of the countless commissions appointed to plan a united crusading effort against the Turks with whose futile strategies the history of the later Middle Ages is littered. He also, a couple of weeks after Luther had posted his 'Disputation on Indulgences' in Wittenberg on 31 October 1517, issued a new and extensive crusading indulgence to raise money for the Ottoman wars.

Turkish pressure on the German lands of the south-east set Luther a difficult problem. His manner of answering it was slow in taking shape, but was to be the main factor in determining Protestant attitudes to the traditional Christian holy war. At the beginning of his public career as a church reformer he had denounced both the papal leadership of the crusade and the papal taxation on clergy and laity intended to finance it, especially when that taxation took the totally unacceptable form of indulgences. He had said that Turkish aggression was the judgement of God. There were two aspects of the scriptural tradition on which he relied: one, based on Isaiah and other prophets, held that the assaults of tyrants upon God's people were divine punishments for their sinfulness. The other emphasized that divine providence sanctions the rule of tyrants, a rule that itself emanates from God's will: it quoted from Nebuchadnezzar's dream, which said that God rules the kingdom of men, and gives dominion to whom he will.[2] These citations had been used throughout the Middle Ages, and frequently invoked to explain the defeats and failures of the crusades. Luther had by 1521 gone further than most theologians in saying that men should not reject God's judgement by rushing to the borders to fight the Turk, but should accept it.

The urgent action to be taken, Luther had said, was moral reform, not military reorganization; he concurred in this with Erasmus, with whom he frequently disagreed. He had even advised people to refuse payment of the secular tax (the 'common penny') that the German Diet had imposed on the lands of the Empire to raise money for a Turkish war. He wrote that the crusade was to be utterly rejected, not because he approved in any way of the Turks (he had translated into German a thirteenth-century 'refutation' of the Qur'an), but because it was called by the Pope, who was Antichrist, and no better than the Turk himself: 'The spirit of Antichrist is the Pope; his flesh is the Turk.'[3]

Luther's initial approach to the Turkish war was thus pacific, although not pacifist. He could not approve of wars that were waged for worldly reasons, since Christ had taught differently. Nor could he approve of the crusading armies, in which hardly a soldier, he said, was a real Christian. Catholic polemicists attacked him for his attitude to the Turkish threat, and he had to react to their charges. Another side of his teaching about state and church then came to the surface, that balanced those parts of his earlier message that seemed to advise Germans to refuse military service against the Turk.

Luther maintained that the public powers were instituted by God, and that it was a Christian man's duty to obey them, even if the government was one of infidels. But when Turkish pressure on the German east increased, he insisted on the legitimacy of Christian rulers, not on that of the Turks. In 1529, at the time of the Turkish siege of Vienna, he published a pamphlet denying that he had once written against the Turkish war. To obey constituted authority and to fight a just, defensive war against the Turks, he said, was a Christian duty. The crusade, with all its papal paraphernalia, was still denounced as wrong, but the Turkish war proclaimed by German princes was rightful and just. Luther in this way changed the ultimate authority for waging a just war upon the Turks, which he said was no longer that of the Pope, but of the princes.

Within a short time of the end of the Vienna siege Luther published a sermon on the Book of Daniel that seemed to accept the apocalyptic tendency that dated back to Joachim of Fiore at the end of the twelfth century, and that was especially strong in Luther's time. Using the commentaries on Daniel published by his follower Melanchthon, among others, Luther made his own interpretation of Daniel's symbolic account of the decay of the world empires. The fourth great beast of Daniel's vision had sprouted a profusion of horns that lent themselves to almost any prophetic or political interpretation. Luther agreed, comfortingly, with his followers, that the Turkish Empire was signified by the little horn that grew among the others upon the fourth beast, and that it would neither equal the Roman Empire in power nor prevail against the Christians.

Luther on the Prophet Daniel may now seem quaint and credulous. But Luther's main conclusions about the Turkish war and the crusade had been rationally argued, and were far from quaint. In substituting the just defensive war against the Turks for the crusade he was laying down the main Protestant line that was to be followed through the Reformation period, and far beyond it. He argued that men should agree to fight in a just war against impious and aggressive tyrants like the Turk. Plenty of what was said in Europe and North America about the Gulf War of 1991 would fit into the framework of the Lutheran arguments of 1529.

The other great Reformation leader, John Calvin, was more sparing and cautious in his public comments on the Turkish wars than Luther had been, in line with his much cannier and more restrained attitude to politics, and with a tough realism that allowed secular politics very great latitude. In private Calvin was indignant about the French alliance with the Turks in 1544, but his opinions were not made public. Like Luther, he regarded the

Turks as a judgement of God upon the impious Christians. Unlike Luther, and following his own cool rationalism, Calvin doubted greatly the interpretations of the Prophet Daniel that were current in his time, Luther's among them.

Calvinism's respect for the secular power subsequently allowed the Calvinist general François de la Noue to advocate a great alliance of Protestant and Catholic against the Turk in the 1580s, recalling the grand crusading alliances of Christendom so often advocated before the Protestant movement had begun. But Calvin (who died in 1564) had not wished to hear of a crusade, nor did de la Noue use the word. The two major leaders of the Reform had in effect secularized the crusade, and turned the Turkish war into an affair of state.

De la Noue's Protestant argument for what would have been in effect a joint resumption by Protestants and Catholics of the crusading alliances within Christendom was an extreme case, seldom if ever followed by later Protestants. Such ideas never came at all close to fruition. But the elements of continuity between the Turkish wars and the crusades were too obvious for either Catholic or Protestant to overlook. It was allowed by many Protestants that the war with the Turks was a sort of continuation of the earlier crusades, being a struggle between two religions that must end with the victory of one or the other. But though the Turkish war was allowed to be a war of religions, it was not for that reason a religious war.

Whether some or all of the 'wars of religion' between Catholic and Protestant that travailed Europe for most of the century ending in the Peace of Westphalia in 1648 were also religious wars is a question that historians are still discussing. There is no doubt that many of the combatants believed they were fighting for their religion. Some felt that they fought for 'freedom of conscience'. Some Protestant pastors admitted that they had preached war, and claimed that they had 'learned it in the word of God'. Both sides, in the course of those innumerable, often terrible conflicts, felt more often than not that God was with them. Te Deums infinite were sung to celebrate bloody victories; sumptuous churches were built to commemorate them. But this did not make the wars holy in the same sense that holy crusades had been fought two and three centuries earlier.

A perceptive German historian has sought the truth about war aims in the words of the war manifestos of the combatants, where they exist, and has tried to identify religious wars as those in which religion was used to legitimize war, not merely felt as one of its motives.[4] But the question about holy war in the sixteenth and seventeenth centuries has still not been fully resolved. The psychology of the troops who fought the religious wars is mysterious. Unpaid Habsburg troops mutinied when fighting the Dutch Protestant rebels in a war that their government had been careful to avoid describing as a religious war, but returned to their allegiance. Other unpaid Habsburg troops mutinied when fighting the Ottomans in Hungary, and went over to the enemy; the mutiny ended disastrously when they were cut off from their new Ottoman employers by loyal Habsburg troops.

Some Catholic theologians coupled the Turks and the Protestants as equal in infidelity, and as meet to be opposed by crusading force in the same manner. The English Cardinal Allen, exiled by his Protestant government, asserted in 1583 that 'There is no war in the world so just or honourable . . . as that which is waged for religion, we say for the true, ancient, Catholic, Roman religion . . . Whoever seeketh not after the Lord God of Israel, let him be slain.'[5] At the same time the Protestant divines in England took a very similar (though in a confessional sense diametrically opposed) position. Henry Bullinger (1504–75), in a sermon whose reading was made obligatory for Anglican clergy, allowed that the civil power might proclaim holy war of the sort that Moses and Joshua had with God's enemies, against 'arrogant and seditious rebels which trouble commonweals and kingdoms'.[6]

Bullinger's line of reasoning, very far from that of Calvin, became for a time the orthodox Anglican position, supported in dozens of sermons by eminent divines. It announced a position that was eventually, though in a rather different form, to become dominant in most Protestant countries, that assigned the initiative in declaring war to be just or holy to the government. In Anglo-Saxon countries governments have retained this initiative up to the present day. But in the short term government-inspired Protestantism was under strong attack in Elizabethan and Stuart England from the enthusiasm of the sects. Bullinger's attitude, that was acceptable to the reasoning of the 'politiques' who controlled Elizabethan government, was overtaken by a more radical Puritan attitude to holy war, that wished to transfer the authority for its proclamation from the state to the community of the elect.

Only a few European wars against Protestant states or groups were specifically granted crusading status and finance by the popes. The most notable was Spain's war of 1588 against England, partly undertaken in order to place a Catholic candidate on the English throne, in the course of which Philip of Spain despatched his Armada to effect the conquest of England. When the Armada had been dispersed, in part by the English ships, but much more by the weather, Queen Elizabeth I had a victory medal executed which seemed to speak the same holy war language as her opponent. The inscription quoted from the victory song of Moses: 'Thou didst blow with thy wind, the sea covered them; they sank as lead in the mighty waters.' But this was not holy war of the same stamp as had taken place in the Middle Ages.

In Protestant England the holy war was passionately preached by some of the Puritan divines of the early seventeenth century. Decades before the outbreak of the English Civil War they were already making the waging of holy war, in a literal sense, into a religious obligation. The Puritan call to responsible Christian members of society – and particularly Members of Parliament – to become 'men of activity' was linked with a duty to identify the enemies of Christ and to be prepared to wage war on them in the spirit of the Old Testament. The enemies of Christ were named by the preacher William Gouge as 'infidels, idolaters, heretics, worldlings, all sorts of persecutors, yea, and false brethren'.[7] So at the outset of Puritan holy war the apostates, inevitably, were named as deserving especial chastisement. The coming war was to be fought with 'men and women of the world, that do wage war with every Christian'. They were 'men of strife, men of blood, having dragons' hearts, serpents' heads'; the saints must work against them with one hand, while the other holds the sword.

When Puritan theory was applied to politics in the 1640s, and troops were raised to fight in the English Civil War, Puritan preachers used the same arguments. The war to be fought was not merely a just, allowable war, but was commanded by God. William Dewsbury, like many fervent believers who later became Quakers, served in the parliamentary armies, in his case as a trumpeter. The Parliamentary recruiting preachers had intimidated the young Dewsbury into enlisting, quoting the Song of Deborah in which God's angel cursed the people of Meroz, who failed to come to the help of Barak against Canaan: 'They went not forth to help the Lord against the mighty.'[8] But Dewsbury's convictions became very different: 'the word of the Lord' came to him 'to put my carnal sword into the scabbard, and to leave the army'.[9]

Wars against the Turk, on the other hand, continued in many Catholic countries to be termed crusades, proclaimed by the popes in the same manner as before, and fought by Catholic powers in a spirit that was analogous to, though not identical with, the old mentalities. In Spain the crusading indulgence continued to be conceded and collected in the same manner as formerly, and this practice continued until the present century. The wars with the Barbary (or barbarous) powers were conceived in a way little different from their predecessors far into the seventeenth century. The Order of the Knights Hospitaller went on in Malta with its traditional naval crusading functions, that could often be given the alternative title of piracy, almost until Napoleon landed on the island in 1798. At the time of the Turkish siege of Vienna in 1683, and later, the popes were still raising large sums of money and giving diplomatic support for the crusade, in the manner that they had done for centuries.

The English Civil War and the Thirty Years War were the last occasions on which the Hebrew holy war was seriously preached in Europe. By the eighteenth century only small pockets of Christian holy war subsisted in a world in which the leaders of most European states thought that they were behaving rationally, even when this was not so. In 1788 the 'enlightened' Emperor Joseph II said, as he launched a Turkish war, that he intended to avenge mankind upon these barbarians. The wars fought by European against Muslim powers were by that time beginning to be thought of as wars made by more civilized against less civilized societies.

The sixteenth century saw the beginning of the break-up, or at least the transformation, of the orthodox body of opinion about war that had obtained since the canon lawyers had debated it in the thirteenth century. Neither Luther nor Calvin was notable for the originality of his opinions on war, although their condemnation of the crusade was of critical importance. Luther discussed war, as so many moral issues, in predominantly traditional terms. Calvin was reluctant to commit himself on the subject at all. But the great Dutch humanist scholar Desiderius Erasmus (c.1466–1536), who was to some extent an influence upon both Luther (in spite of Luther's hostility to his theology) and Calvin, had things to say about war that were effectively new.

Erasmus was one of the great shaping intellectual forces of his age, and his views influenced, though they failed to dominate, the debate about war in his times and long after. Even at the end of the twentieth century, Erasmian pacifism, with its seditious denial of the military virtues, its sour judgement on the hypocrisy and blindness of the powers-that-be, and its stubborn refusal to admit the inevitability of war, still has much to say to us. He was firm in regarding the Jewish holy wars in the Old Testament as allegories of the struggle between virtue and vice, not as political commands. Of war he memorably said: 'The bishops approve it; the emperor approves it; the princes approve it – but God does not approve it.'[10]

Erasmus, as a publicist who had had a great deal to say about war, must have felt that he had to comment on the Turkish war that was brought so near to his Swiss habitation towards the end of his life. His 'Consultation About Waging War Upon the Turks' was published in 1529, shortly before Luther published on the same topic. The Consultation (meaning an inquiry, a deliberate use of the neutral term) has been described by a sharp reader as 'almost a parody' of the conventional humanistic 'Oration against the Turks'.[11] As he very often did, Erasmus in this little work turned a conventional genre upside down. He allowed, as Luther did at the same time, that a defensive war had to be fought against Turkish aggression, but his criticism of the way in which such a war was commonly discussed ends by being more apparent than his approval for it.

The normal humanistic practice was to expatiate on the wickedness and the anti-Christian deeds of the Turks, and to explain the ease with which war might be organized against them if only the Christian princes would come together to execute this duty. Erasmus was the archetype of what would now be called the 'wet' humanist, though he might be described, paying more respect to history, as the precursor of the eighteenth-century *philosophes*. His 'Consultation' rejects the whole traditional rhetorical treatment of the subject of holy war. He admitted that the 'barbarism' of the Turks had harassed Christianity for many centuries, though he thought this to have been more on account of Christian stupidity than Turkish ability. The Turks were, according to Erasmus, 'effeminately luxurious, to be feared only for their robberies'. He made fun of the armchair strategists who listed the weaponry, manpower and troop movements that were necessary for victory in the Turkish war. He poured equal scorn on the students of the prophecies of the Book of Daniel and the Apocalypse of John, who made unlikely identifications of this monster or that with ancient or modern empires or religions.

To Erasmus it was God's favour that was above all needed for the Christian people: to his pamphlet on the Turkish war was added a commentary on the 29th Psalm (in the Vulgate notation the 28th), in which the pious are exhorted to give glory to God and to recognize his lordship. In Erasmus's view atrocities quite equal to the Turks' were practised by Christians against each other. He dismissed as rubbish the popular idea that an infidel Turk might be killed like a mad dog, adding only too relevantly that if that were so, the same treatment might be applied to the Jews. He said that war martyrdom was an illusion: if Christians died fighting in the Turkish war, they would not on that account be transported straight to paradise.

Erasmus remarked sternly that those who fought the Turks would reach heaven only if their consciences were pure, however they died. He also said that it was in the end far more important to convert the Turks to Christianity than to kill them, and that their conversion was the eventual object of the war that might have to be fought against them. Like some earlier writers, notably the fifteenth-century Rhineland Cardinal Nicholas of Cusa, he could identify strong Christian elements in the Qur'an, and hoped that these might serve as points of contact that would assist Muslim conversions. He said that 'half' (a pardonable exaggeration) of Islamic doctrine was very Christian: the Turks had something of Christianity and something of Judaism in their religion. Erasmus thought they were most like the Christian Arian heretics. Nicholas of Cusa had thought, with more probability, that they most resembled the Nestorians.

In fact, the approval that Erasmus could give to the Turkish war was so grudging, and so hedged about by qualifications, that it was not really an approval at all. The pamphlet is little more than a reluctant admission that the Turkish war is one where a Christian man may take part in a just war decreed by the prince. Erasmus did not specifically argue that the distinction between the just and the unjust war is false, because all war is wrong, but this seems to be implied in his manner of argument.

The insistence of Erasmus that conversion of the infidel Turk was more important than fighting him was taken up by others in his circle. The Spanish humanist Juan Luis Vives, whose perspective also included the American Indian infidels, insisted in the Erasmian spirit that 'Turks are to be loved, because they are men,' and that they, no less than other enemies, should be loved and forgiven. Erasmus was for the rest of the century influential upon those currents of Spanish religion that asked for and to some extent obtained from state authority a more just treatment of the American Indians.

The Erasmian view of war was too radical for the sixteenth century, just as its pacifist message, transmitted by others, has proved too radical for the twentieth. Some of the sixteenth-century sects, notably a large number of the Anabaptists, had what would now be called pacifist views, and refused to fight at the behest of the magistrate, but they were suppressed (not merely on this account) in a barbarous and cruel manner. Erasmus was never wholly trusted by the great churchmen, but in spite of this he was courted by them for his piety and learning. He was never persecuted, because of his great intellectual prestige, just as some great dissidents have survived in modern tyrannies. His attitude to church authority had nuances that were difficult to follow for anyone lacking his great mental agility, and absolutely impossible for pietist pacifists like the Anabaptists to imitate.

Attitudes to the crusade changed as radically among Catholics as among Protestants. It is significant that at the last general council of the church to take place before the outbreak of the Lutheran protest, the Fifth Lateran Council of 1512–17, discussion of the crusade had been endless, and sermons advocating it had dispensed all the medieval commonplaces on the subject that had been a feature of similar councils since the Third Lateran Council in the early thirteenth century. During the Fifth Lateran Council Pope Leo X had sought to launch an ambitious crusading policy that emulated those of his predecessors three centuries earlier.

By contrast, the great reforming church council that codified the ecclesiastical policies of the so-called Counter-Reformation, the Council of Trent (1545–7, 1551–2, 1562–3), devoted no attention to the crusade at all, and issued no decree that concerned it. The crusade was an unpopular topic with the popes and their representatives at the council, because it was essentially of interest to the Habsburg Emperor, whose political influence on the council the popes were usually striving to minimize. Nor was the French monarchy at all anxious to have the matter of the crusade raised at the council, because of the Turkish alliance that the Most Christian King was unable to conceal. At the Peace of Crépy in the autumn of 1544 France had engaged to send troops to the Turkish war beyond the eastern German borders, an engagement she was not called upon to fulfil because the Habsburgs shortly after signed a Turkish truce. But by the time the second series of major sittings of the council started in Trent in 1551 the Turkish war had broken out again with great violence in the Mediterranean, once more with French encouragement.

The fact was that the whole spirituality of the church had moved in a direction that took it away from the traditional crusading ethos. That did not mean that the crusading orders, particularly the Order of the Hospitallers that held the great stronghold of Malta, had lost favour in Rome. Nor did it mean that the popes had ceased to look upon sponsoring the crusade as essential to the holy see. However, the conviction that salvation and eternal life could come almost automatically from personal, physical service in the holy war against infidels had waned among both churchmen and laymen in even the most Catholic countries.

The spirituality of the Counter-Reformation worked in very different ways. Ignatius Loyola, the founder of the Jesuit order in 1540, came from Spain, a country in which the crusade was woven into the psychic fabric of Christian existence. It was not surprising that he pictured a man's life as a holy war in his *Spiritual Exercises*, but his idea of holy war was of a spiritual struggle, not a physical conflict with Saracens. The same alternatives of physical and spiritual struggle had always existed in Islam, although there the option of a physical struggle as a means of salvation was much longer-lived.

In the century of the printing press the level of knowledge available to cultivated Europeans about the Ottoman Empire rose very steeply. The papacy itself was one of the patrons of such information-gathering. For example, the littérateur and papal historiographer Paolo Giovio (1483–1552), the author of one of the best histories of his period from a Roman point of view, included a most detailed account, based on reports supplied by a large number of European observers, of matters concerning the Ottoman Empire. The number of humanists with knowledge of oriental languages was still very small, but before the end of the century one or two printers in Rome had the capacity to print in Arabic. And in Calvinist Geneva a translation of the Qur'an could find (after some opposition had been overcome) a printer.

The French speculative polymath Guillaume Postel (1510–81) prefaced his *Arabic Grammar* with some remarks on the geographical diffusion and power of Islam that were intended to spread appreciation of its world importance. Of the three parts of the world, only one (Europe) approached freedom from Islam. The rest was largely under the sway of Muhammad:

> All Africa, outside the Christian realm of Prester John [Ethiopia]: all Asia, from one extremity to the other, so that when Magellan in his circumnavigation of the globe reached the Moluccas, he found them already Islamicized. And in Europe the Islamic plague has already taken over Greece [meaning Greece and the Balkans].[12]

Postel's intentions were not to clamour for a new crusade: he saw as a far more urgent matter the recovery of Christian unity, to which he summoned the Reformed religions that were guilty of breaking it. Rather he looked forward in the very long term to Islamic conversion.

François de la Noue seemed to show some knowledge of the principles of Islamic holy war when he remarked on the difficulties the Turkish leaders would experience if they tried to halt aggressive action against a Christian state. They would, he said, become discredited with the religious men as well as with the soldiers, because the former were convinced that the sword of Islam had a religious duty to reduce the whole world to subjection.

A change in the approach to the way in which Christians criticized Muslim power came about when material concerning the condition of the Christians under Turkish rule in the European provinces began to be published from the second decade of the sixteenth century onwards. These works were usually written by obscure emigrants from the east or the Balkans, but could be taken up by distinguished humanists like the Spanish friend of Erasmus (who was also the friend of the Englishmen Thomas More and John Colet) Juan Luis Vives. They gave Westerners some idea of the way of life of fellow-Christians under Turkish rule, and emphasized their subject state. There was particular emphasis, usually, on the *devshirme*, that made Christian male children liable to be taken for conversion to Islam and for military life service as Janissaries.

Such pamphlets amounted to a lament for the lot of Christians under Turks, and usually went on to make a call for military action. But occasionally people were more hopeful about the possible conversion of the Ottomans, as for example when they encountered reports of the rebellion of one of the mystical dervish Baqtashi sects, the Qalander-Oghlu, whose membership was connected with the Janissaries, in 1526–7. There was some knowledge in the West of Sufi mysticism and its occasional reluctance to accept the literal meaning of Qur'anic texts, and this encouraged some to speculate that such people might be the more open to Christian missionary work.

Drawing on the increasing volume of literature about Ottoman society, customs, and government, people began to think less about great frontal military assaults on the Turk in the spirit of the medieval crusade, and to contemplate more sophisticated alternatives. René de Lucinges, the ambassador of the Duke of Savoy at the Spanish court, wrote in 1588 that the Turks could be subdued only by using a policy of long-term subversion and destabilization that relied on the discontent in the Empire and particularly on that of the Christians.

The idea of depending upon ideological subversion within the Ottoman Empire did not get far. As had often happened in the earlier Middle Ages, direct contact between Western and oriental Christians often ended in disillusion on either side. A few years before the final fall of Constantinople, the Byzantine Emperor himself had led a deputation to the Council of Florence convened by Pope Eugenius IV in 1439, but the agreements that were reached there between Greeks and Latins were repudiated by the

Greek clergy on the return of the Emperor to Constantinople. In the following century the Lutherans wanted to interest the Orthodox Eastern Christians in their ecclesiastical positions, but the early attempts to make contact only attracted swingeing condemnation from the Greek clergy of most of the key Lutheran doctrines.

However, the trend of all these developments was to make people take account of the real Ottoman Empire, and not to hark back to a mythical crusading past. Propagandists, especially those who wrote in showy Latin, abandoned the rhetorical laments for the loss of the holy land, and the sterile plans to send imaginary armies to recover it. There was a popular literature in Germany of Turkish war atrocities. Such realism, for it is realism when compared with the half-mythical view of the infidel that preceded it, had taken centuries to impose itself on Western consciousness.

A low level of accurate information and political judgement about the Turks had been responsible for such disasters as the battle of Nicopolis in 1396, though in fairness it must be allowed that ill-informed fanaticism had enabled the successful defence of Belgrade in 1456. It would have been possible to look at Turkish aggression in a matter-of-fact way at any time from the mid-fourteenth century onwards, instead of waiting for the fall of Constantinople in 1453. In the sixteenth century the substitution of the common cause against the Turks for the crusade did not mean the abandonment of great projects of war, even in the Franco-Protestant camp that had favoured a Turkish alliance. The former French ambassador in Constantinople, Ogier Ghislain de Busbecq, published a fervent call for war against the Turks, and an admonition that a final reckoning between Western and Ottoman power was inevitable. Plans for a great attack on the Turks by combined forces of Catholics and Protestants were published twenty years later, by the Huguenot de la Noue.

To a considerable extent the concept of Christendom survived the Protestant schisms, though in a very undefined form that resisted being placed in the old categories that had existed under papal leadership. Prayers were said for Catholic Malta in the English churches during the Turkish siege of 1565; bells were rung in Protestant London after the Catholic victory of the battle of Lepanto in 1571. Sir Thomas Roe, James I's ambassador to the Ottoman court, referred to the crusade as 'a good and pious work', and wrote to King James that the latter had given his ambassador 'weighty and vehement command to serve you in taking care of the general estate of Christendom'.[13] The crusades were part of a common cultural patrimony that belonged as much to Protestants as to Catholics. Shakespeare exemplified that patrimony no less than the rest. In *Henry V* the king remarks to his newly affianced Katherine of France:

> Shall not thou and I, between Saint Denis and Saint George, compound a boy, half French, half English, that shall go to Constantinople and take the Turk by the beard? Shall we not?[14]

The part that Catholic Spain played in containing the infidel on the Barbary coasts continued to be acknowledged as late as 1647, when the Anglican divine Thomas Fuller wrote in *The Holy War* that 'all west Christendom oweth her quiet sleep to his [the King of Spain's] constant waking, who with his galleys muzzleth the mouth of Tunis and Algiers.'

English Protestant seamen in the late sixteenth century seem to have had extraordinary knowledge of the detail of the old Catholic canon law about the crusade as it concerned the duties of Christians vis-à-vis the infidels. In 1568 John Hawkins was near Cape Blanc in West Africa when he found three Portuguese fishing vessels deserted and beached. His first thought was to destroy them, 'considering that the country in which we were was of the infidels', and that it was the duty of Christians to prevent possible instruments of war from falling into the hands of the Muslims. This was a remarkable reference to Catholic canon law on the subject; possibly he was anxious to appear to conform to it in case he and his men ended (as many English seamen did) in the hands of the Inquisition. In the event he thought he saw a slightly more profitable option, and he took one ship and left the other two to the Portuguese in the area.[15]

Christendom is the underlying theme of the greatest work of Italian epic poetry of the sixteenth century, the *Orlando Furioso* of Ludovico Ariosto (1474–1533), who wrote most of the poem before the Lutheran schism had become identifiable. *Orlando Furioso* is concerned with the paladins of Charlemagne and their struggle with the Muslims, but the irony and the courtly values of the poem ensure that it is not at all a crusading epic. There is a passage that deplores the divisions of Christendom and the Italian wars that make it impossible to eject the 'unclean dogs' of Turks either from the holy places or from Constantinople and the 'greater part of the world' that they occupy.[16] But the poem treats Agramante, the Muslim king, and his knights as heroic warriors, capable of the same chivalrous acts as the Christians. Ruggiero, the secondary hero of the book, spends most of his career fighting in the infidel army, and is only converted in the final stages by his love for the Christian Bradamante. The heroine Angelica, beloved by the Christian champion Orlando, is another infidel, the daughter of the King of Cathay. The whole poem is suffused with a sceptical irony which ensured that it persisted in European culture, to become dear to the eighteenth century.

Ariosto's poem was the inspiration of the English Elizabethan poet Edmund Spenser (c.1552–99). Protestant culture was, in Spenser as among the Anglican divines, much affected by the supremacy of a state that had from the beginning exercised strong religious control. In *The Faerie Queene* Spenser described the combat between the Red-Cross knight and the Saracen paladin in antithetical terms: 'th'one for wrong, the other strives for right'. But the loyalist tone of the poem, that made the Queen into a mythical poetic presence, went along with the current of Elizabethan England in converting holy war into an aspect of monarchic nationalism.

Half a century after Ariosto, another great Italian epic poet, Torquato Tasso (1544–95), reflected the values of the Counter-Reformation and the Turkish wars of the period, the siege of Malta and the battle of Lepanto. His *La Gerusalemme Liberata* contains both the early modern image of the 'bloody and cruel Turk' and the medieval dream of a holy sepulchre freed from the infidel. Its theme is the First Crusade. Aladino, Tasso's Saracen King of Jerusalem, is a caricatured demon king, assisted by a council of the satanic powers, and entirely alien to Christian chivalry.

Even though the late sixteenth century continued to employ the vocabulary of the crusade, its superior knowledge about the Ottoman world could not but affect the way in which it was written about. Tasso was quite evidently without first-hand knowledge of the Turks, but the great masterpiece of Miguel de Cervantes, *Don Quixote* (1605–15), contains a long 'prisoner's tale' based on the experience of its author in Moorish hands. Cervantes had been present at the battle of Lepanto in 1571, and was subsequently taken prisoner, spending five years in captivity in Algiers. The 'prisoner's tale' is remarkable for its balance and lack of bitterness. It includes the story of the Moorish woman who loves and aids a Christian, and is subsequently converted. This is a feature of most literature of the kind, including Tasso. Cervantes also describes the valiant Christian renegade to Islam, who also appears in Tasso, and who possessed a certain basis in fact. Cervantes never ceased to call for the crusade, and never ceased, either, to call for sympathy and true charity for Christian prisoners. But he also applied his wonderfully humane and ironic understanding of the world to his own captivity and serfdom under Islam.

Both in Ariosto and in Tasso the chivalrous element in the memories of the crusades was strong. This was a factor that especially applied in the Protestant countries which preserved a nostalgic attitude to chivalry. Spenser's *Faerie Queene*, that was close to being a national epic, was just such an idealization. In countries like England, where some of the old medieval knightly orders of chivalry still existed, even though the Catholic order of the Hospitaller Knights had no place in a Protestant country, the attitude to the crusading orders among conservative knightly circles was benign. Protestant antiquaries like Sir George Buc, the Master of the Revels for James I, referred to the defunct military order of the Knights Templar as a pious one that had made war against all infidels, and preserved the holy sepulchre of our Lord from spoil and profanation by 'Turks, Saracens and other barbarous miscreants'.[17]

Some people in the later seventeenth century idealized the medieval knightly religious orders. Bernard Ashmole, the antiquary who is also a notable early figure in the history of science, wrote in 1662 in his book about the Knights of the Garter that the Knights Templar had been 'the principal Columns which supported the Kingdom of Jerusalem for a long time', and that 'their valiant encounters with the infidels, and forwardness to sacrifice their lives for the honour of God and the defence of the holy land ought to be had in everlasting remembrance'.[18] Ashmole pointed towards the crusader-mysticism that characterized some of the eighteenth-century Freemasons, but also towards the romanticism of Sir Walter Scott.

The principle that had always hovered in the background of the crusade had been that of the common action of Christian princes against the infidel. From the First Crusade onwards, the churchmen involved in the crusade had emphasized that war against the infidel required peace among Christians, and that this peace was one of the principal benefits the crusade offered to God's people. In the later Middle Ages the popes had constantly offered their services to Christian governments as mediators, so that when peace had been established the Christian rulers could combine for the crusade. Papal diplomacy of this sort had been especially to the fore in the fourteenth century, during the earlier stages of the Hundred Years War between England and France.

Crusade literature of the later Middle Ages tended to be full of the speculations of projectors, who felt that their visions could in this supremely ideological field secure the favour of princes, and be suddenly translated into a new order of things. The concord of the princes was such an obvious necessary condition for the crusade that it became in itself a theme for intellectual scrutiny. In a sense it had always been implied in the medieval theory of the Holy Roman Empire, but by the time of the loss of the holy land in 1291 this ideal had clearly failed in the context of the crusade, if not outside it as well.

Writers on the crusade were not all visionaries; in fact in the late crusading literature a kind of specious practicality predominates. The crusade could very often be a field for people who saw themselves as political realists, and who could offer plans that were tailored to the interests of the princes who employed them. Inevitably, with the decline of the papacy and empire in the later Middle Ages the power of the national kingdoms impinged much more than formerly upon people's views of the crusade. An example is the work of Pierre Dubois, an official in the French court at the beginning of the fourteenth century.

Dubois wrote a tract on the recovery of the holy land that proposed to transfer the crusade leadership formerly enjoyed by the empire and the papacy to the relatively young French monarchy. In order to facilitate the crusade that he proposed to launch in the East on the huge scale that was common to such theorists, Dubois wanted to organize the princes into a Council of Europe under the presidency of the French king. This, the first international organization ever to be proposed in Europe on lines that are more or less familiar to modern people, was to have the power to discipline recalcitrant members. The political powers of the pope, formerly theoretically decisive in the crusade, were to be drastically curtailed.

In most respects the Dubois proposals were intended to make French power supreme in Europe – not such a premature attempt as it may sound, if we look at the later history of the fourteenth century, in which the brake placed by the English upon the French monarchy in the Hundred Years War was only a temporary check to France as the dominant monarchy of Christendom. Over three centuries later, in the early seventeenth century, a very similar plan for a French-led organization of the European states was produced by the Duc de Sully, the former chief minister of King Henri IV.

Sully's 'Great Plan' involved the humiliation of Spanish and Austrian imperial power, just as Dubois's plan had involved the humiliation of the Holy Roman Empire. In Sully's plan the element of common war against the Turks was much less prominent, and the emphasis was at least as much on Europe as on Christendom. From that point of view it was a more secular, less traditional plan: it aimed to make the European princes more equal (save for the French monarchy) and to rely upon establishing a balance of power in Europe to encourage peaceful solutions of quarrels.

In what seems to have been a late addition to the plan, Sully wanted to force both the Russians and the Turks out of Europe if they refused to accept one of the European forms of Christianity. From a crusading point of view this was in part an attempt to make the Orthodox Church accept Latin dominance, and therefore could be seen as a return to the Fourth Crusade of 1204. From a Turkish point of view it amounted to the customary call for a united Christian front against the infidel, although with the important difference that the political price to be paid by the Turks was to be the evacuation of Muslim-dominated Eastern Europe, not the restoration of the holy places. In any case, the common front against Turks and Russians was not essential to Sully's main plan for 'perpetual peace'; the old crusading ideas were present, but in a different form, and only as a subordinate part of his aims.

In the long interim between Dubois and Sully, the idea of a common council of Christendom that would impose peace upon its members and fight a common war against the Turk had reappeared at various times. One of the most radical-looking of these schemes had been that of the King of Bohemia, George of Podiebrad, who in the mid-fifteenth century had proposed a plan for an alliance of all the main Christian powers, a parliament of princes, a common army, and a kind of international court of justice to settle disputes among them. Influenced by the so-called conciliar movement that had been powerful earlier in the century, the parliament was to meet in Basle, and to vote by 'nations'. In so far as the Turkish war was concerned, one of the main aims of the scheme was to take the crusade out of the hands of the papacy and to give it to the new federation. The balance of power in Europe was to be altered by removing the empire from the Germans and conferring it upon the French.

Like many schemes for international co-operation, Podiebrad's idea had the interests of one state most in mind, his own. His political position as leader of a small country that was committed to a religious settlement that the popes thought heretical, and that was vulnerable to the intervention of the empire, was extremely weak, and he had hoped that this scheme, the brainchild of a French adviser called Marini, might improve it. But it attracted no support from the European princes, not even from France, to whose interests it was intended to appeal.

All these schemes, from Dubois to Sully, had with varying degrees of enthusiasm proposed the war against the infidel as a sort of cement to keep the Christian princes together. The same was true of two late-sixteenth-century Italian writers, the cool Venetian Giovanni Botero and the visionary Tommaso Campanella, both of whom saw the possibilities of a league of the Christian princes, taking place principally in the Catholic traditions of Christendom, and in opposition to the infidel. But an obscure French contemporary of Sully, Emeric Cructé, was the first to envisage an international authority that would transcend religious differences, not only those within Christianity, but also those that separated Christianity and Islam. The organization envisaged by Cructé would be devoted to international peace, and not towards the common military effort against an external enemy.

In 1623 Cructé published a little-noticed but profoundly original book, *Le Nouveau Cynée*. It reflected the realistic views on the Ottoman Empire that had obtained in France for approaching a century. The great French political theorist Jean Bodin had earlier disparaged the German Empire to the advantage of the Ottomans: 'What has Germany to compare with the prince of the Turks? Who better deserves the title of monarch? If imperial authority and true monarchy exist anywhere ... they radiate from the Turk.'[19]

Le Nouveau Cynée criticized all previous attempts to find a means to enforce peace upon Christian princes as having been based on the idea of uniting against a common enemy. To this Cructé proclaimed his opposition, since 'human society is one body'. Peace between states was an end in itself, and although states were clearly unequal in power, they shared a common interest in the maintenance of peace.

Like the earlier projectors, Cructé proposed a council or league of states. In common with many earlier thinkers, he would have given the pope a purely honorary presidency of this league. But, flouting all orthodoxy, he wanted, on the basis of the Ottoman Empire's having replaced the Eastern Empire of Constantinople, to make the Ottoman Sultan the senior figure of the organization, entry to which was to be reserved for Persia, China, Ethiopia and both the western and the eastern Indies. In this new world order there would be religious toleration, at least between states, and liberty of travel and trading. Cructé was in one important respect in advance of his time: it was to be almost a century and a half before 'Europe' and 'Christendom' ceased to be regarded as equivalents.

*   *   *

With Crucé we reach a point where the beginnings of an international idea threw off the constraint that made the search for peace in Christendom only a preliminary for new religious war. But that does not mean that the idea of holy war had been unimportant in the fumbling movement towards some kind of international political instrument to replace the medieval institutions of empire and papacy. In Renaissance internationalism the idea of an eventual war against the infidel had not been an idealistic goal dictated by religious fervour. With the notable exception of Erasmus, people had regarded the notion of uniting against the infidel as a realistic one, that met the political threat of Turkish aggression, and that also linked up with the centuries-old medieval experience of the concord of European princes in prosecuting the crusade. That need not surprise our own generation, which has seen a military alliance created forty-seven years ago to combat a now-extinct ideological enemy turned in the Balkans to the service of the ideals of the United Nations.

In the growth of international ideas, the old order of religious division between Christendom and the rest was slow to change. The initial impulse for change was there: Crucé's concept of an Ottoman Empire received into the comity of nations was by no means out of tune with his times. In the Treaty of Sivra-Torok in 1606 the Holy Roman Empire and the Ottoman Empire for the first time accepted one another as equivalent sovereign states of equal status. The natural law theorists of international relations like Alberico Gentili (1552–1600) and Hugo Grotius (1583–1645) accepted the legal title of the Ottoman Empire to rule in its lands – though Gentili added that 'war with them is almost natural: with the Saracens we have irreconcilable war'.[20] That was not the view of Grotius, the founder of modern international law, but he too regarded the community of Christendom as the necessary international unit.

The strength of political nostalgia for the old order of empire and Christendom was strikingly demonstrated much later in the seventeenth century by one of the most powerful minds of the early modern period, Gottfried Wilhelm von Leibnitz (1646–1716). Early in Leibnitz's career he supplied one of the great models of political despotism of his time, Louis XIV of France, with what he called the *Consilium Aegypticum*, a scheme by which Louis would lead a great Christian alliance to the conquest of Egypt, and would achieve the crusade against Islam as a preliminary to the general peace of Europe. Like most such plans, this had the interests of a particular prince to serve: it was intended to divert Louis from his plans of conquest in the lower Rhineland, an objective in which it conspicuously failed. It is notable that one of the greatest minds of the seventeenth century should apparently have been anxious to revive the medieval crusade of Louis IX of France.

The later schemes of Leibnitz for international government were at bottom very conservative, especially in the ways in which they sought at a very late stage to restore some of the prestige and authority of the moribund Holy Roman Empire. It is true that one of the great aims of Leibnitz's life was the restoration of unity between the Catholic and the Protestant churches, and so in a sense the end of holy war between Christians. But such wars were effectively already over, even if religious persecutions were not: Leibnitz in this sense came too late. However, he did not abandon the idea of war between Christian and infidel. In 1715, at the end of his life, commenting on the proposal of the Abbé Castel de Saint-Pierre to 'achieve perpetual peace in Europe', he wrote to the Abbé that 'helping the emperor to chase the Turk out of Europe would be the best way of solving the [peace] problem.'[21]

It remained true for a long time of internationalist aspirations for an organization for perpetual peace that a hostile attitude towards the Ottoman Empire denoted realism. The Abbé de Saint-Pierre had originally intended, like Crucé, to include the Turkish Empire in his senate of princes that was to be the basis for international peace. So he said in the first edition of his *Projet de paix perpetuelle*, published in 1712, but later editions omitted the idea, because he feared that its inclusion would 'cast an air of impossibility upon the whole project'.[22] He later also argued that the European union should endeavour to obtain in Asia a permanent society like that of Europe, so that the benefits of internationalism might be extended to the infidel, and also serve further to protect European interests.

By the early eighteenth century religious war against the infidel was no longer a factor in the projects for schemes of international peace. It had been replaced by the problem of the Ottoman Empire, which was especially vexing in that geographically this was to some extent a European problem. In the realm of the European imagination the holy war was far from dead. But in politics, even in visionary politics, it was very close to extinction.

CHAPTER TEN

Holy War and
the European Empires

FROM THE MID-SEVENTEENTH to the mid-nineteenth century the Muslim empires underwent a long political and economic transformation that was almost entirely to their detriment. Many of the forces that acted upon them were internal. The idea that Western trade, war and technology were virtually the only agents of change – in the old vocabulary, the only agents of progress – in the pre-industrial world can no longer be maintained. Western arms, commerce and empire were indeed important, but even when, as in British India, they appeared to be in complete control of supposedly archaic societies, their influence was in many respects superficial.

However, the power exercised by the European trading nations was very great. To name only the more important of the late Muslim empires, the Ottoman, the Iranian, the Mughal, perhaps also the Moroccan Sa'dians and the Javanese of Mataram, all these large and powerful units were gradually absorbed into a new world trading system whose pivots were the Atlantic trade and New World silver. For a very long time the economic processes were subterranean, and the extent to which, for example, the Ottoman and Mughal economies were being transformed by Western influences was not apparent. The people who were effecting change on the ground, such as the agents of the English East India Company, were themselves anxious to conceal the sometimes revolutionary consequences of their actions, so that in the second half of the eighteenth century the Company was still pretending to be a merely mercantile organization, when it had already seized an empire.

In the late seventeenth century the military power of the Muslim empires still looked formidable, at least on land. Frontier holy war continued to be the guiding principle of the Ottoman Empire, even though its application was spasmodic and pragmatic. In 1683, at a time when Pope Innocent XI was trying to reactivate the crusading policies of the past and to unite the Catholic princes against the infidel, the Ottoman Grand Vizier, Kara Mustafa, launched a large army against Vienna that brought with it from Damascus the so-called Banner of the Prophet. At the approach of the Ottoman army the Emperor Leopold was obliged to leave his capital in undignified haste. The siege lasted from mid-July until 12 September. Its issue was uncertain almost to the end: only days before the big relief force under King John Sobieski of Poland arrived, there was still a serious possibility that the explosion of a great Turkish mine would lead to the fall of the city.

In the event the Grand Vizier had miscalculated the difficulty of the undertaking, and when he returned to Belgrade, having with difficulty saved the Prophet's flag, the sultan's executioner was waiting for him. His failure pointed to the decay of the Ottoman Empire, not to its resilience. Buda fell to the Austrians in 1686 after a century and a half of Muslim rule; by the Peace of Carlowitz in 1699 Hungary and Transylvania were reclaimed for Christianity and the Empire. In 1718 Belgrade, that had also been continuously Ottoman from the early sixteenth century, was finally lost, and Russia was pressing hard on Turkish control of the northern Black Sea. From this time until it finally ended in 1919, the Ottoman Empire was subject to continuous erosion. But the ideology of holy war remained, both in the Ottoman bureaucracy and in the army, until late in the eighteenth century.

In India Muslim holy war entered the sub-continent within a century of the death of the Prophet, and continued to be a recurrent Indian phenomenon for a millennium or thereabouts. The Mughal Empire, that established itself in the sixteenth century under Mongol-Turkish leadership, and under strong Iranian cultural influence, was only the last in a line of Muslim empires that had ruled from the north almost to the very south of the sub-continent ever since the thirteenth century. Many Muslim invaders had taken part – Iranian, Turkic and Afghan. However, the Mughals, largely by dint of fighting other Muslims such as the Afghans, but also by fighting Hindus, established the largest Muslim political unit ever to have ruled in India, dominating most of the sub-continent, from the north-western passes to the Ganges delta in the east and to the Deccan in the south.

There was some hesitation among the great Mughal rulers about the principle of holy war. Babur, the founder of the dynasty (ruled in India 1526–30), was a Turkish ruler waging orthodox *ghazi* holy war. After his decisive victory over the Rajput Hindus at Kanua in 1527 he assumed the title of *ghazi*. His autobiography records a poem he wrote at the time:

> For love of the faith I became a wanderer in the desert.
> I became the antagonist of pagans and Hindus.
> I strove to make myself a martyr.
> Thanks be to the Almighty who has made me a *ghazi*.[1]

Akbar (ruled 1556–1605) had waged holy war in his campaigns against the Rajput rulers in 1567–9. In the first period of his reign Akbar was observant in Islamic piety, paid homage to the Chishti Muslim saints for whom reverence was traditional in his family, and organized and subsidized the Meccan pilgrimage. But later he developed an eclectic attitude to religion that was more like that of a pre-Islamic Mongol ruler; he reduced the influence of the learned Muslim *'ulama*, and eventually abolished the property tax (the *jizya*) upon non-Muslims and announced his own authority to pronounce upon Islamic doctrine. A personal religious cult of the ruler was cultivated, which declared his mystical religious powers. It was a philosophy of central power, that aimed to create a new class of imperial servants, drawn from all the religious groups. Under such a ruler further holy Islamic wars could not take place, although there were plenty of wars. Similar tendencies to ruler worship, and coolness towards orthodox Islam, continued under Akbar's son Jahangir (ruled 1605–27).

The last great Mughal ruler, Aurangzeb (ruled 1658–1707), adopted a rigidly orthodox Islamic policy, favourable to the *'ulama*, that included the restoration of the poll tax on non-Muslims and was characterized also by a long series of holy wars. Like some of his contemporary equivalents in the Ottoman Empire, but far more energetically, Aurangzeb reverted to the expansion of the frontiers of Islam as the main aim of government. He was rewarded with an apparent extension of imperial power on the borders, but he incurred grave penalties, most of them masked during his lifetime by the fear he inspired. The overloaded central government was subject to great financial strain. Sikhs, Marathas and other powerful groups started to drift out of imperial control within a few years of Aurangzeb's death. The power of the foreign trading companies in Bombay and elsewhere had already in his lifetime caused difficulties that he could not spare the resources to deal with.

Aurangzeb's revival of *jihad* created many problems and solved none, and was the prelude to the collapse of the whole Mughal Empire, that took place within two decades of his death. The Empire continued to exist in theory well into the British period, and supplied the theoretical basis for

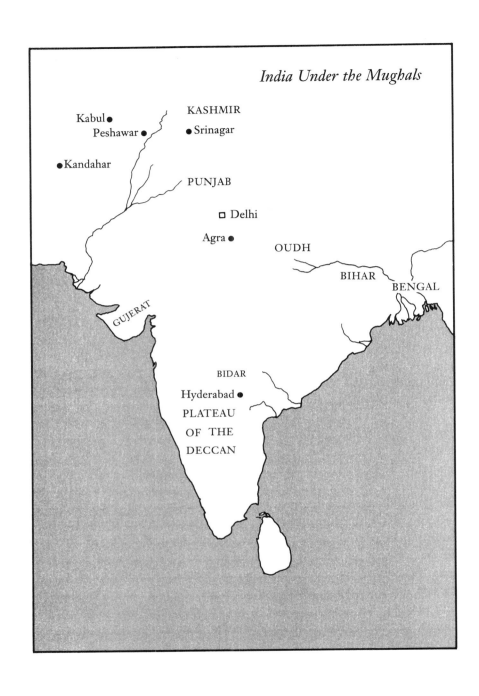

India Under the Mughals

Kabul ●

KASHMIR

Peshawar ●

● Srinagar

● Kandahar

PUNJAB

□ Delhi

Agra ●

OUDH

BIHAR

BENGAL

GUJERAT

BIDAR

Hyderabad ●

PLATEAU

OF THE

DECCAN

early British rule. But by the time of the first sack of Delhi in 1739 by the Iranian Nadir Shah, it had for long been no more than a loose grouping of kingdoms, subject to the covetous attacks of Marathas, Afghans and many others. Outside the Empire the foreign companies, most of all the British, were preparing to tighten the noose.

The empires did not keep the holy war solely for the polytheists: they also practised it, on occasion, against one another. The Turkic Safavi dynasty had based their rise to rule in Iran upon the religious fervour of the 'redcap' Qizilbash tribes who were attached to the Ardabil order of Sufis; in many ways this had not been dissimilar to the patronage given to the early Ottoman dynasty by the *ghazi* religious brotherhoods. Shah Isma'il (as he later became) had in 1500 launched a holy war against Georgia that never reached that country, but that occasioned his seizure of power in Iran. The Ottomans were ferociously jealous of the new Safavi monarchy. Sultan Selim (1465–1520) cited the heretical nature of Shi'a doctrine and reports of Ismai'l's claim to divinity, and denounced the Safavi as apostates. The Ottoman *'ulama* made no difficulty in issuing a *fatwa* that Isma'il should be slain as an apostate; in the same period they also conveniently allowed the campaign to subdue Mamluk Egypt to be a holy war.

In Muslim Africa both north and south of the Sahara the holy war played a very important part in the defence, extension and development of Islam. To some extent this was a holy war against the unbelievers, in the Maghreb often against the Iberian Christians, and in sub-Saharan Africa often against pagans. The greatest dynasties to rule in the Maghreb and Andalucia after the fall of the 'Umayyads, the Almoravids and the Almohads, had both been founded upon holy war, and the prestige that attached to the prosecution of the holy war against Spaniards, Portuguese and other Christians counted for a great deal in the rise and fall of the Maghrebi dynasties. However, in the later Maghreb *raison d'état* often counted for much more than religious fervour. It is noteworthy that at the battle of the Three Kings near Alcazar in 1578, at which the Portuguese under King Sebastian suffered a decisive defeat, the Christian army was accompanied by the deposed Sa'diyan Sultan, Muhammad al-Mutawakkil, and the opposing army was accompanied by Turkish advisers (who were suspected during the battle of having murdered the Moroccan king they came to support).

The brother of the dead king became Sultan (and, as he claimed, caliph) of Morocco as Ahmad al-Mansur ('the victorious'). Ahmad seems to have been more aggressive against other Muslim governments than against Christians, although he pleaded the contrary. The contemporary Songhay government of the Niger and the western Sudan was an Islamic dynasty founded upon its past successful holy wars with the polytheists, and the investment of its sultan as 'caliph'. Ahmad used his supposed commitment to the prosecution of the holy war as an excuse for demanding a salt tax tribute from the Songhay. He sent an army against them, partly composed of European musketeers, that caused the collapse of the Songhay Empire in 1591. But at the same time he maintained a very close understanding with the Protestant English government, a policy he shared with the contemporary Ottomans. These were not policies of unyielding religious fanaticism.

Further south, in the west and central Sudan, from Lake Chad westwards as far as the Atlantic Ocean, holy war served as one of the main instruments of Islamicization. But the manner in which it served to spread the faith became less direct than at the beginning. After the end of the Songhay Empire Islam was no longer spread in the area by the forcible annexation of huge territories by great Muslim military states, as had happened under the Berber and other dynasties earlier in the Christian Middle Ages. The process was rather one of peaceful and piecemeal conversion, followed sometimes, often after a very long interval, by a holy war that tried to transform the partly converted areas into coherent Islamic states.

In certain parts of western Sudan and the southern Saharan savannahs, holy war was never adopted by the learned Muslim class, the *'ulama*, as a way of spreading the faith. The choice depended partly upon the relationship between the learned clerks and the warrior class: where this became close, holy war was a possible outcome, but where the warriors were, like the Touregs of the southern Sahara, disliked and distrusted by the *'ulama*, the clerks eschewed the idea of holy war. Learned opinion could be had that pointed in either direction. An Egyptian theologian of the late fifteenth century thought it more meritorious to keep the peace than to wage holy war;[2] other theologians were very willing to authorize the Muslim of western Sudan to wage *jihad* of the sword.

The clerical Muslim class in western Sudan and the valley of the Senegal river were to some extent wandering mendicants: indeed, one of their warrior-noble opponents taunted them that they were worthless beggars. In some areas like Mauritania they kept their distance from the warriors, but in others, from the later seventeenth century onwards, they found military support to launch holy war against tribes that professed Islam but failed to observe Islamic law. There was a notable holy war of the clerical-led Zawaya group against one of the Senegal kingdoms and the barely Islamicized Wolof south-west of the river, led by a clerk who called himself Nasir al-Din, 'the protector of the faith', and who was defeated and killed in 1671. A century later a further Senegalese holy war on the Wolof kingdom of Kayor also ended in defeat.

But the slow advance of Islam in west Sudan and further south in West Africa was bound to lead to renewed attempts by the *'ulama* to impose full Islamic law on kingdoms that were hanging on to many of their pre-Islamic institutions. In such societies the Qur'anic injunction to 'command good and forbid evil' could have revolutionary results. The dispersal of Islam over huge areas, and the adherence of the Muslim clerks to Sufi orders like the Qadiriya and the Tijaniya that had roots as far away as Egypt and the coastal Maghreb, meant that reform movements that began in places very far from West Africa had local results.

The clerks were ultimately dependent on the goodwill of at least a section of the warriors if they were to wage holy war to command Islamic orthodoxy. But they could also rely on the disquiet of wide social currents, especially because they often preached about the imminent end of human time, and the apocalyptic intervention of a *mahdi*, or rightly-guided leader, who would restore the rule of Islamic justice.

The most radical of the movements was led by Sheikh 'Uthman dan Fodio, also called the Shehu (1754–1817), whose holy war against the Habe kingdoms of the southern Hausaland zone of the western Sudan began in 1804 and was complete by 1812. Such holy war leaders talked of a *hijra* or sacred emigration, and, using the same sacred vocabulary, set up defensive frontier posts called *ribat*. They condemned not only pre-Islamic practices, but oppression and corruption.

The result of the Shehu's holy war was a new empire centred in what is now northern Nigeria, called the Sokoto caliphate. 'Empire' is a large-sounding word to describe a group of emirates south-west of Lake Chad that, though economically prosperous, never possessed a large standing army, nor even managed to rule all its immediate Islamic neighbours. And 'caliph' is equally a large word to describe its rulers. However, its imposition of a new clerical ruling class on a newly orthodox Islamic state changed ideas about Islamic rule in West Africa. Its insistence on literacy in order to enforce Islamic rules meant a multiplication of Qur'anic schools: perhaps it can almost be said to have been a dictatorship of schoolmasters.

The second major holy war of the period was that of Haj 'Umar Tal

(1796–1864), a Muslim teacher belonging to the Tijaniya order that originated in Algeria, whose inspiration came from a senior member of the order who had instructed him in Mecca and had invested him with the same title as that used by the Shehu in Sokoto, 'caliph'. 'Umar Tal's experience of the great Muslim intellectual centres of the East was superior to that of the Shehu, but his holy war was far more conservative, aiming at the expansion of the frontiers of Islamic states rather than at a new and radical social order. The political tradition of the Tijaniya Sufi order, which he followed, had in the Maghreb been favourable to French colonization: its leaders had opposed the *jihad* of 'Abd al-Qadir against the French in Algeria. But after some hesitation 'Umar Tal attacked the French in Senegal.

'Umar Tal's political and military aims were in the area of the upper Niger and the upper Senegal, but chains of French forts already stood in his way when he left his first base in the south-west. It was therefore necessary to fight the French, but the idea of anti-colonialism was not in his mind, and after some military setbacks suffered at European hands on the Senegal river he directed his main attack against the still-pagan area of the Bambara in the mid-Senegal. The attraction of a holy man and the lust for booty had drawn very large armies from the Fulfani Muslims. 'Umar Tal's final campaigns were conducted against another Muslim state, set up earlier in the century after a holy war waged by an earlier *jihad* warrior at Masina. In 1864, two years after the seizure of Masina, he was ejected and killed by the party of the previous reigning dynasty.

A sharp judgement on the whole holy war movement in West Africa was made by the Muslim clerk of an opposing brotherhood, who helped set in motion the decisive revolt against 'Umar Tal in Masina: 'You know the power of *jihad*. But *jihad* leads to kingship, and kingship leads to oppression.'[3]

A notable illustration of the truth of this dictum occurred forty years later, in 1905–6, when there was a rebellion in the territory of the Sokoto caliphate of a large group of disgruntled peasants and fugitive slaves, led by a few radical Muslim *'ulama* unconnected with the ruling clerical aristocracy.[4] The rebellion was Mahdist, based on the expectation of the imminent appearance of the rightly-guided *imam* whose rule would restore Islamic justice and equity. It was immediately directed against the British administration, whose first punitive force it surprised and wiped out. Subsequently the British authorized a big military operation against the rebels, in which their troops required co-operation from the forces of the conservative Sokoto caliphate, that had itself been forcibly reduced to obedience by the

British only three years earlier. At Satiru in March 1906 the rebels were defeated and massacred: two thousand of them were killed, and most of the three thousand women and children were, after some atrocities had been committed against them, enslaved.

In a period like our own in which the earlier modern history of the Third World is seen by many largely as 'resistance to colonialism', it is tempting to see the nineteenth-century holy wars predominantly in those terms. And indeed, a few of the holy wars were in fact defensive wars against foreign, Christian colonization, though more were fought against other Muslims in the interests of reform than against the colonizing powers. There is even an instance of a Senegal Islamic reformer (al-Haj Muhammad al-Ahmin) asking permission from the French in 1885 to launch a holy war.[5] The history of the West African holy wars warns us against interpreting all these wars in a single sense: Islamic reform, tribal and ethnic conflict, the setting up and legitimizing of new dynasties, and resistance to Europeans could all play a part in holy wars, and it is sometimes impossible to disentangle them.

The conflict between the Islamic states of West Africa and the colonizing powers did not become general and direct until the last quarter of the nineteenth century. Much further north, the French occupation of Algeria, that began in 1830, led rapidly to confrontation and to brutal wars. The main Muslim leader there after the elimination of the old Turkish beys of Algiers was 'Abd al-Qadir, the son of the leader of the Sufi Qadiriya brotherhood, the same that had been so important in the contemporary holy wars of West Africa.

'Abd al-Qadir proclaimed and carried out a holy war against the French, justified by the brutality of French expansion from the original base in Algiers and by the absence of any solid legal basis for French rule. Conservative Muslim opinion in North Africa gave him remarkably little aid. The Sharifian government of Morocco, that was equally supported by its Muslim religious role, felt too threatened, not only by France but by Spain, to grant more than hesitant and wavering support. 'Abd al-Qadir's religious status in the Qadiriya brotherhood enabled him to proclaim *jihad*, but he also needed a legal opinion from other learned Muslims that collaboration with the French on the part of Algerian Muslims amounted to apostasy, which could be visited with severe punishment. Probably because a *fatwa* or opinion in this sense might be held to bind their own rulers, and might therefore have disagreeable consequences for themselves, the learned men in Fez and Tunis were unwilling to deliver it. However, 'Abd al-Qadir did obtain a *fatwa* from the Moroccan senior sheikh, 'Ali 'Abd al-Salam al-Tasuli, to the effect that emigration (*hijra*) was obligatory for Muslims who were being persecuted by infidels outside the territory of Islam.

Neither 'Abd al-Qadir nor the remaining Turkish bey of eastern Algeria managed to resist the French armies for long, although 'Abd al-Qadir struggled hard against them. The French commander in eastern Algeria recognized the authority of 'Abd al-Qadir for a time, and in 1837 his government signed a treaty that appeared to confirm this. But 'Abd al-Qadir was too independent in his attitude, the treaty broke down, and a savage colonial war followed. The French general, Bugeaud, adopted a term to describe his own tactics that was not only Arabic but specifically Muslim. This was *razzia*, from the Arabic *ghaziya*, meaning Islamic border warfare. As understood and employed by Bugeaud, such tactics meant systematic massacre and wasting: a notable example was the burning alive of Muslim prisoners who had been penned in caves. The choice of a word taken from the vocabulary of holy war to describe colonial atrocities was ironic.

'Abd al-Qadir had lost the war by 1843. The Moroccans gave him asylum briefly, but had to abandon his defence after the French navy bombarded Tangier. After a further short sojourn in the Rif mountains he found himself in conflict with the French and the Moroccans simultaneously, and had to surrender. Captivity in France and final exile in Syria followed. 'Abd al-Qadir was an able, civilized and humane man, who protected the Christians, Arab and European, in Damascus during the anti-Christian massacres of 1860. But his purely defensive role did not point forward to a purified Islamic state, as the careers of West African reformers like Sheikh Uthman dan Fodio seemed to do.

The religious element in 'Abd al-Qadir's wars with the French was important, but he was a tribal leader before he was a religious reformer. The Saharan rebellion of Bu Ziyan, who installed himself in 1849 in the oasis of Za'atsha claiming to be the Mahdi, the rightly-guided one or the expected deliverer, was essentially a holy war. So was another Saharan rising led by the Sharif of Warqala from 1851 to 1858. The general uprising against the French in Algeria in 1871 was a complex and widespread affair, but one of the events that triggered it was the call to holy war issued by the head of the Rahmaniya religious brotherhood, centred in the Constantine area. There were several other rebellions in Algeria and Morocco that involved the calling of holy war: one of the last was that of a Mauritanian family from the north-western area of the Adrar, led by Ma' al-'Aynan and his son al-Hiba, in 1910–12.

The holy war which attracted most attention in nineteenth-century Britain was that of Muhammad Ahmad, a Sufi religious teacher of the northern Sudan, who in 1881 received a revelation from the Prophet that he was the Mahdi. Apocalyptic traditions had it that the Mahdi would come shortly before the last things were to be accomplished, to restore faith and to cause justice to prevail in Islam.

The initial concerns of Muhammad Ahmad were not with Christian colonialism but with the supposed Muslim infidelity of the Egyptian-Turkish regime in the Sudan. His desire, like that of the West African reformers, was to impose Islamic law and rule. To achieve this he proclaimed holy war against the Egyptian government. There are some indications that he intended to carry the holy war north into Egypt itself.

The Egyptian government of the Sudan was already in severe difficulties when Muhammad Ahmad appeared on the scene, and the British occupation of Egypt in 1882, and the suppression of the Ahmad 'Urabi regime, made its plight even worse. To hold down the immense area of the Sudan, as large as two or three major European countries, was beyond the resources of Egypt at a time when its international position was so critical and its military power exiguous.

Muhammad Ahmad showed great political ability in manipulating and leading the tribes of the Sudan, but his greatest skill was in proclaiming his mission. He emphasized, as another reformer, Said Ahmad, had emphasized in India earlier in the century, that his support came from the pious and the poor, not from the rulers, and he showed great energy in mobilizing the help of Muslim religious leaders far from the Sudan. But it was in the overwhelmingly rural northern Sudan, that was sick at this time both of Egyptian tax-collectors and of British-inspired suppression of the slave trade, that his main power lay.

It was Muhammad Ahmad's initial good fortune that in the critical year of his rebellion, 1882, Egypt virtually lost control of its own destiny to the British. In despair the Egyptian government thought of getting military help from Ottoman Turkey, its nominal suzerains, but the idea was vetoed – not surprisingly – by the British advisers. In 1883 the fortress of El Obeid fell to the rebels, and later in the year an Egyptian relief expedition commanded by the British Colonel William Hicks was brought to a pitched battle: the force was annihilated and Hicks was killed. A solution was thought in England to lie in the appointment of the troublesome but able

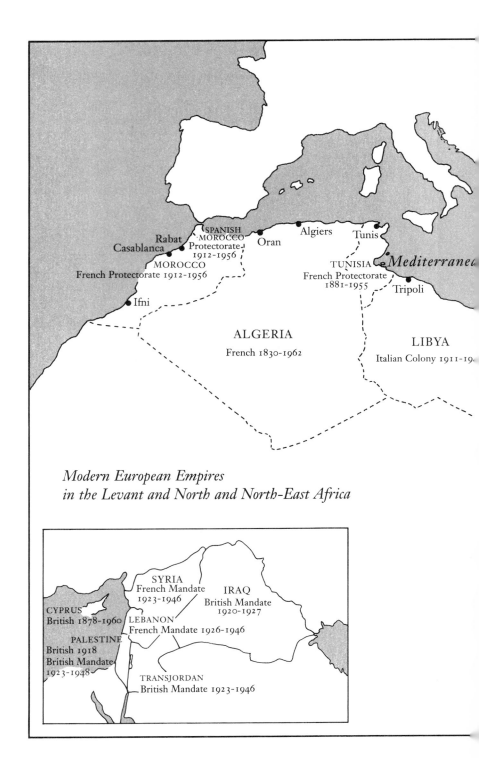

Rabat
Casablanca
SPANISH MOROCCO
Protectorate
1912-1956
Oran
Algiers
Tunis
Mediterranea

MOROCCO
French Protectorate 1912-1956

TUNISIA
French Protectorate
1881-1955

Tripoli

Ifni

ALGERIA
French 1830-1962

LIBYA
Italian Colony 1911-19

*Modern European Empires
in the Levant and North and North-East Africa*

CYPRUS
British 1878-1960

SYRIA
French Mandate
1923-1946

IRAQ
British Mandate
1920-1927

LEBANON
French Mandate 1926-1946

PALESTINE
British 1918
British Mandate
1923-1948

TRANSJORDAN
British Mandate 1923-1946

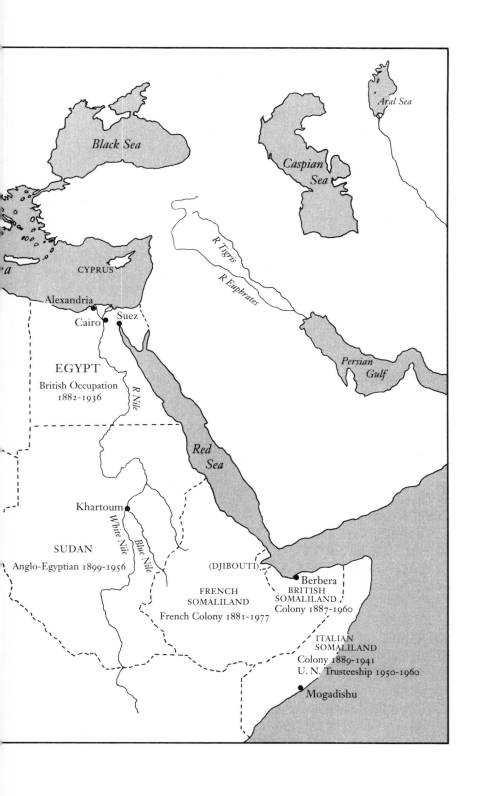

Black Sea

Aral Sea

Caspian
Sea

a

CYPRUS

R Tigris

R Euphrates

Alexandria

Cairo

Suez

Persian
Gulf

EGYPT
British Occupation
1882-1936

R Nile

Red
Sea

Khartoum

White Nile

Blue Nile

SUDAN
Anglo-Egyptian 1899-1956

(DJIBOUTI)

Berbera
BRITISH
SOMALILAND
Colony 1887-1960

FRENCH
SOMALILAND
French Colony 1881-1977

ITALIAN
SOMALILAND
Colony 1889-1941
U. N. Trusteeship 1950-1960

Mogadishu

General Charles George Gordon to the position of Egyptian Governor-General of the Sudan.

Gordon had earlier filled office for the Egyptian government in the southern Sudan with some distinction, but his suitability for settling the affairs of the whole huge area at a desperate moment was very doubtful. Quite apart from what Lord Cromer called his 'flighty' temperament, he had little understanding and less sympathy for Islam, and was not the person to deal with a major Muslim rebellion. His attempt to deal with Muhammad Ahmad by fair words, trivial gifts and the promise of future dignities shows how little he understood of the affair. Above all, he had been sent to execute a policy of withdrawal from the Sudan – a withdrawal wished upon the Egyptians by the British government – and not one of firmness. Gordon imprudently revealed when he arrived in Khartoum as Egyptian Governor-General in 1884 that he came only to withdraw, and that he came without an army. He thus virtually made sure of his own ruin.

The decision taken in London in 1885 to send British forces to relieve Gordon was too late to save him, as is well known. As a result of the fall of Khartoum the Mahdist state in the Sudan became safe, even after the death of the Mahdi in the same year, until the British decided to send a force large enough to suppress it. In Mahdist Sudan the potential of British military power in Africa was not appreciated, and the 'Caliph' Abdallahi, who had succeeded the Mahdi as head of state, hung on to the idea of taking the holy war to Egypt. His army was crushingly defeated by an Anglo-Egyptian force in 1889, and the idea of further holy war was tacitly abandoned. When the British, responding to threats of French and Belgian colonial expansion near the Sudanese borders, finally decided on military intervention in 1896, the Mahdist state was doomed. The end came with Kitchener's expedition of 1898.

The final destruction of Mahdist Sudan after the bloody battle to take its capital, Omdurman, and the establishment of the so-called Anglo-Egyptian Sudan, were quintessentially colonial events. However, it is worth remembering that the original rebellion of the Mahdi had not been directed against colonial rule, but against the Muslim Egyptian government, and, behind them, against its Turkish sovereigns. In using what from a Muslim point of view were Christian mercenaries in the Sudan (that is, Britons functioning as Egyptian governors), the Egyptian government had only been executing policies that had been common in Muslim North Africa for many centuries.

In other parts of North Africa there were holy wars of resistance to European colonization that went on into the early 1920s. A Libyan holy war against the Italians was carried out mainly by a conservative family of religious leaders of a brotherhood, the Sanusi. Ahmad al-Sharif al-Sanusi, who led the initial holy war of 1911, was also the author of tracts about the holy war that denounced the apostasy of those who collaborated with the Italians. Subsequently the Sanusi family were manoeuvred into an ambiguous position vis-à-vis the Italian colonizers. At the same time the British and Italians in Somalia found themselves from the beginning of the century defied by the holy war of Muhammad Abdille Hasan, the so-called 'Mad Mullah' who used the Golis mountains and subsequently Illig as a base. Muhammad Abdille was one of the first of the colonial rebels to be bombed out by air strikes, which destroyed his last refuge in Taleh in 1920.

The first Maghrebi holy war to point forward to later Islamicist positions was that of Muhammad ben Abdul 'Abdul-Karim al-Khattabi, in the Spanish Rif in northern Morocco, from 1920 to 1923. al-Khattabi was one of the first holy war leaders to have received a partly Europeanized education, although he was the son of a member of the Moroccan *'ulama*. Having been employed in the Spanish administration, he led his tribe, the Ait Waryaghar, with other tribes of the Rif, against colonial rule. He was a religious reformer as well as a political rebel. After substantial military success he proclaimed a Rifian republic in 1923, with himself as the first president: the republic came to nothing, but it was one of the first occasions on which practical Islamic political reformers adopted the political language of the West, and spoke of an 'Islamic republic'.

In Africa during the nineteenth century, only in Algeria was the main purpose of Islamic holy war unambiguously that of resistance to European colonial expansion. Elsewhere, although *jihad* was occasionally directed against Europeans, its main intention was to impose Islamic reformism; sometimes, it is true, dynastic or personal ambitions became confused with the main religious purpose. Even in Sudan, the conflict between General Gordon and the Mahdi is not one between a colonial power and the Islamic holy war. The twentieth-century story is substantially different. On the whole, such holy war as took place in Africa in the first half of the century was against the colonial powers. The Rifian republic of 1923 pointed forward to a new development in Islamic holy war, in which its leaders were more deeply marked than hitherto by European culture and vocabulary.

*　　*　　*

One of the key reforming movements to influence the holy war leaders and the reformist Muslim thinkers of the nineteenth century was that of Muhammad ibn 'Abd al-Wahhab (1703–87), a religious leader from Najd in southern Arabia who gave the tribes a restored religious discipline aimed at renewing the primitive purity of Islam. The Wahhabi movement was more radical and more puritanical than most of the Sufi movements that were so influential in Egypt and North Africa. It also aimed to cut out the excrescences of shrines, and the excessive reverence of supposed saints.

Muhammad ibn 'Abd al-Wahhab found an ally in a minor south Arabian tribal leader called Muhammad ibn-Sa'ud. The founding act was a treaty of allegiance (bay'a) between the holy man and the supporting community: the political results were wars of the tribes and rejection of the Ottoman power that was stigmatized as apostate to Islam. The Wahhabi disturbances spread as far afield as Iraq and northern Syria, and Wahhabism came to be feared as a disruptive influence in British India. The Shi'a shrines in north-western Iraq were condemned, attacked, and sometimes destroyed. There was temporary Wahhabi occupation of the holy cities in the Hejaz, and the proclamation of a virtually permanent holy war.

The Wahhabi victories were not permanent or universal in Arabia: Wahhabis never, for example, succeeded in occupying the neighbouring Shi'a state of the Yemen. Early in the nineteenth century their movement subsided into a long obscurity, from which it only awoke early in the present century with the Wahhabi brotherhood of the Ikhwan (1912), which was a critical factor in helping 'Abdul 'Aziz Ibn Sa'ud in the tribal expansion that eventually led to the establishment of the modern kingdom of Saudi Arabia. But it may still be said that the modern kingdom owes its historical legitimacy to the original treaty with Muhammad ibn 'Abd al-Wahhab and the resulting holy wars.

In nineteenth-century India the Islamic holy war was very much less of a threat to British rule than might be supposed. In the gradual process by which the East India Company undermined what was left of the authority of the Mughal Empire until it withered away entirely, the Muslim elites of northern India were very much the losers. But Muslim society in India was already so decentralized and fragmented at the time of the first big intrusions of the Company that it is almost impossible to speak of a general Muslim response to British India until the late nineteenth century, when the British themselves were, in part, the agents that brought into being something that could be called an Indian Muslim consciousness.

The Fara'idi movement, that had been led in the early years of the nineteenth century by Haji Shari'atullah of Faridpur in Bengal, was strongly influenced by Wahhabism, which he had encountered in the holy cities in Arabia. His reform movement in Bengal became associated with the rural discontents of the minor Muslim tenantry: in the words of one British official, it was influential upon 'the most ordinary class of the Muhammadan population'. This strongly popular character stuck also to the nature of a much more powerful movement, also touched by Wahhabism, although not to the extent the British thought, led by a talented soldier-reformer of north-west India, Said Ahmad of Bareilly.

Said Ahmad was a pious and educated man, who early in the nineteenth century was in the military service of one of the petty rulers of the Punjab. Like Haji Shari'atullah, he found his mission in life after spending a year and a half in Arabia, where he came into contact with the Wahhabi reformers. He never became a Wahhabi; he was too much influenced by indigenous Sufi orders. But the propagandist methods and the holy war aims of the Wahhabis he made his own. The British authorities were convinced, wrongly, that his movement was Wahhabi, and it went under this name with them for long after his death. They were acquainted with the Wahhabi movement, since Indian troops had taken part in military action against a Wahhabi tribe in southern Arabia in 1821.

In the early 1820s, having gone to Calcutta and travelled much, especially in Bengal, Said Ahmad organized a new movement (an association or *jama'at*) that drew its strength from grassroots Muslim society and from learned men in many places, all over northern India. It was in effect a reform made at the base of society, that aimed at the eventual establishment of an Islamic state. His missionaries were able to appeal both to an educated Muslim class that was discontented with the loss of the privileged Muslim position to British power, and to the peasant *ryots*.

Strengthened by the contributions and the organization of his adherents, Said Ahmad proclaimed a holy war, not against the British, whom he never specifically attacked, but against the Sikh rulers of the Punjab, with the idea of freeing Muslim Kashmir and the surrounding areas from their rule. Like so many reformers, he made an 'emigration', using the sacred vocabulary to describe his tactics of recruiting troops in other parts of India, and mobilizing them on the North-West Frontier. For a time Said Ahmad and his largely Pathan troops had considerable military success near and in Peshawar, that fell to them in 1831. But his career as *imam* and 'caliph' in Peshawar lasted only a very short time, and in the same year he was defeated and killed.

The *mujahidin* of Said Ahmad remained in being for a long period in the north-west of India, and established a base in Sitana, whose lord had been one of his earliest supporters. There was a long, secret supply-line that went south to a headquarters in Patna, which brought them both finance and volunteers. After a time they became engaged in guerrilla war with the British, who had succeeded the Sikhs as rulers of the Punjab, on the North-West Frontier.

The British acquired further experience of Muslim holy war during the first Afghan War (1839–42), when Dost Muhammad (who for a long period had been virtually a British protégé) proclaimed a holy war, and was for a time joined by the *mujahidin* of Said Ahmad. In the general panic on the British side that followed the Indian Mutiny of 1857 a British expedition under Sir Sydney Cotton was sent against the *mujahidin*, that rooted them out from Sitana for a time; but they soon returned, and further quite large-scale military operations failed to suppress them.

The practical importance of Said Ahmad's holy war was very modest, even if we include in it the continued armed presence of his followers in the north-west until at least the 1860s. There was also a peasant movement in Bengal in the 1820s, led by a Muslim religious revivalist called Titu Mir, that can be compared in some respects with that of Said Ahmad, although its effect was much more local. Such movements were politically not very important. Their significance was much more a symbolic one, of the vitality of Islamic reformist religion in north India.

However, the movement of Said Ahmad did not dictate the main currents of religious life in Muslim India, which for a very long time flowed in a quite different direction. From the 1830s onwards, the British under the influence of the Macaulay reforms had adopted a cultural policy based on English law and language, and had minimized the importance of vernacular Islamic education. The frustration of the Muslim propertied classes in northern India, who found themselves marginalized in the growing new society in which the most Westernized elements, and the most favoured by British rule, were Hindu, found a voice in the second half of the century in the reformist Sayyid Ahmad Khan.

Even though his liberal doctrines in some ways appeared to threaten the main structure of traditional Islamic law, Sayyid Ahmad Khan was convinced that they were true to Islam, and promoted the interests of Muslims. He thought it a duty to provide a reformed, modern educational system that would leave his people at no disadvantage beside those who had been trained by the British, but that would not rob them of their Muslim identity. He

Cosmati mosaic of the vision of John of Matha, founder of the Trinitarian Order.
Church of San Tommaso in Formis, Rome.

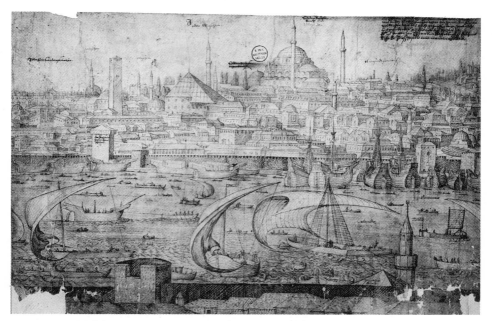

Melchior Loritz, panorama of Constantinople, showing European
trading ships in the harbour.

Conquistadores massacre and enslave the Aztecs, shortly after Cortés had
assured their ruler Montezuma that the Christian religion taught that 'all
men are brothers'. Illustration to Las Casas, *Brief History of
the Destruction of the Indies.*

Nicolas Poussin (1594–1665), *Rinaldo and Armida*, probably painted 1625–30.
Armida is about to murder Rinaldo, but is restrained by the onset of love.

Gianbattista Tiepolo (1696–1770), *Rinaldo and Armida in her Garden*, 1742.
Less sombre than Poussin, though the watching warriors are to be noted.

Frontispiece to the *Description de l'Egypte*, showing Napoleon's troops among
the great Pharaonic monuments.

Eugène Delacroix (1798–1863), *The Abduction of Rebecca*, 1858.
Illustration to Sir Walter Scott's *Ivanhoe* (1819).

Above Delacroix, *Entry of the Crusaders into Constantinople*, 1840.

Opposite Delacroix, *The Massacre of Chios*, 1824.

Above The Algerian holy war leader 'Abd al-Qadir in exile in Damascus in 1864.

Above Hizbullah funeral procession in Beirut, June 1996.

Left Hizbullah women, Beirut, 1996.

was quite clear that holy war should not be waged in or from British India, which he ruled was not *dar al-harb*, enemy territory from which emigration was obligatory. In this he agreed with many much more conservative *'ulama*. However, his attempt to make a new category which gave a 'protected' status to Indian Muslims was much more debatable.

Ahmad Khan's point of view remained very influential far into the twentieth century: A.R. Mallick's *British Policy and the Muslims in Bengal 1757–1856*, published in Dacca in 1961, accounted for the wide support given to Said Ahmad and his successors to their followers being 'ignorant and uninformed',[6] and drawn from the superstitious and backward part of society. The main nineteenth-century problem was seen by the author, even at that late date, as Sayyid Ahmad Khan had seen it much earlier, as the provision of a proper, modernized educational system for the Muslims.

The doctrines of Sayyid Ahmad Khan were roundly condemned by Jamal al-Din al-Afghani (1839–97), the most distinguished Islamic reformer of the last quarter of the nineteenth century. The origins of al-Afghani are somewhat uncertain, but much of his youth was spent in India, and when he was in exile there after 1879 he wrote an influential tract, 'The Refutation of the Materialists', specifically to discredit Ahmad Khan's theories. Al-Afghani was well known in the Ottoman, Arab, Persian and Indo-Muslim worlds; he collaborated closely with the Egyptian Muhammad 'Abdu (1849–1905), with whom he published an Arabic journal in Paris, but this was only a small part of his leadership. He was especially original in identifying European power and influence as potentially hostile to all the peoples of the East, not merely to those who professed Islam, and in recommending that people of diverse religions should act together against European power. The British were the special targets of his dislike, because India, Persia and Afghanistan had loomed so large in his own experience. He was thus an early prophet of the alliance of the peoples of the Third World against Western colonialism, although anti-colonialism was only a part of his message.

Al-Afghani did not preach holy war of the sword, but neither did he condemn it. He held, as it were in reserve, the idea of an eventual holy war against the Western powers, and he seems to have assigned leadership in this future holy war to the Ottoman Empire, where a considerable part of his peripatetic political career was spent. The notion of the sultan-caliph commanding a general holy war against the infidels was far-fetched at the end of the nineteenth century, but not impossible.

Holy war on the Ottoman borders had continued to the end of the eighteenth century; it was also usual for the Ottomans to encourage Muslim peoples outside their frontiers to fight holy war against Christian powers. In the Ottoman Empire itself, by the early nineteenth century the old *ghazi* holy war vocabulary was in decline. One of the last general calls of the Ottoman government to its people to fight the holy war with the Christians was made in 1827–8, against the Russian government with which the Ottomans were about to fight a war that proved disastrous. From the Peace of Adrianople, which followed that war in 1829, Ottoman foreign policy underwent a decisive change. Its aim was henceforth to form a part of the European concert of great powers, and not to treat relations with Christian powers as governed only by truce, that must after a set period be broken for the prosecution of the holy war.

Outside the Ottoman Empire the Muslim peoples were trying with increasing difficulty to defend themselves from Christian expansion. In the Caucasus, where Muslims were subject to intense Russian military pressure from the early nineteenth century onwards, holy war was recurrent. Its best-known manifestation was in Daghestan and Chechnia, where Murid revivalists challenged Russian occupation from 1830. The Murid leader, Shamyl, took up the *ghazi* struggle in 1837. His aims were not narrowly tribal, but were comparable to those of his contemporary, Said Ahmad: as a follower of the Naqshbandiya Sufi order he aimed to found a reformist imamate. When pursued he took refuge in the Ichkeria forests in the south of Chechnia. The climax of his struggle was in 1845–6, but Russian power was too persistent and too ruthless to ward off, and Chechnia was finally reduced to obedience in 1857–9 – although the finality of its reduction is now (in 1996) being called in question, and its new leadership is terming the rebellion a 'holy war'. It is notable that the central Asian khanates, which were absorbed by Russia between the seventh and the ninth decades of the century, produced no equivalent to Shamyl, and that most of them continued to squabble among themselves until the moment of the Russian takeover.

The Qajar government in Iran obtained a *fatwa* from the mullahs at the beginning of the nineteenth century to authorize holy war against Russia. In 1826 the Persian Sultan was faced by an aggressive body of mullahs who demanded the renewal of holy war, and who eventually issued the call to *jihad* against Russia on their own authority, saying that refusal to wage it would be a sign of disbelief in Islam, and would incur the charge of apostasy. The resulting war was a disaster for Persia, and the mullahs failed even to give it the support they had promised.

In 1914 the general Muslim holy war was brought within the bounds of practical politics when the Ottoman government entered the First World War on the side of the Central Powers, and declared a holy war upon Britain, France and Russia. The Ottoman clerics at the same time issued legal opinions to back up the actions of the Sultan, as was normal in Ottoman practice. One of the novelties of Ottoman policy on this occasion was to emphasize that there was an obligation on Muslims from countries subject to the Western Allies not to fight on behalf of their infidel rulers. The Indian, African and Russian Muslims serving in Western armies were particularly the objects of this *fatwa*, that was issued in several languages, although it seems unlikely that it had any great political effect.

The failure of the Ottoman-led holy war to convince other Muslims was demonstrated by one of the best-known episodes in Western–Muslim relations of modern times. The fomenting of rebellion against Ottoman sovereignty in Arabia had been considered in British circles even before the outbreak of the 1914 war. When Turkey entered the war on the side of the Central Powers at the end of 1914, the policy was put into effect almost immediately by Lord Kitchener, who had been the representative of British power in Egypt since 1910. Kitchener made advances to the Sharif Husayn, the Hashemite custodian of Mecca and the other holy places of Islam in the Hejaz, to suggest rebellion against the Turks in exchange for British recognition of Arab claims to independence in a huge area of the Middle East.

The confused way in which British guarantees were given, and the manner in which they were qualified, in 1917, by the Balfour Declaration about Zionist aspirations in Palestine, are well known. So too is the desert war against the Turks in Arabia and southern Syria, led by the British soldier T.E. Lawrence. But in spite of the existence of the Ottoman-proclaimed *jihad*, an important sector of the Arab tribes of western Arabia (but not the Wahhabis of eastern Arabia) proved willing to collaborate with the Christian powers. The idea of promoting the Sharif of Mecca as Caliph of Islam, in opposition to the claims of the Ottoman Sultan, had also been examined by the British, although it never proved to be practical.

When the British established mandates in Iraq and Palestine after the end of the First World War, they met with nationalist opposition in both areas. But the main force of opposition to the colonial power was already controlled by a Westernized class that did not think in terms of holy war. The very first years of the British in Iraq were still marked by a few clerical-led disturbances: the Shi'a *'ulama* of Karbala authorized a holy war in the short-lived rebellion of the summer of 1920. The Palestinian Arab nationalists did not think in such terms: the only *jihad* to be proclaimed in Palestine was the short-lived rebellion in Galilee of the Syrian Sheikh 'Izz al-Din al-Qassam in 1935. This was a small group of zealots led by a single religious *imam*, and British forces had no difficulty in attacking them and killing their leader. However, the incident was one of the things that touched off the 1936 Arab Palestinian revolt.

No Muslim leader called in the nineteenth century for general holy war against something identified recognizably as what would now be called colonialism. There were many calls for the support of other parts of the Muslim world for what would now be called national struggles, such as those issued by 'Abd al-Qadir in Algeria. The idea that leaders like 'Abd al-Qadir were opposing a general movement of European oppression was unfamiliar until the second half of the twentieth century. Jamal al-Din al-Afghani was practically alone in approaching the problem in something like these terms, and in any case he never publicly addressed the issue of *jihad* directly. Al-Afghani's Egyptian follower and associate Muhammad Abdu shunned the whole holy war issue in so far as it concerned the holy war of the sword.

There was some precedent in the Muslim legists for saying that holy war of the sword was obligatory only to the Muslim community living in the *dar al-Islam*, that had to defend itself from attack. Outside the *dar al-Islam* the matter was more debatable. Some zealous writers said that there was then an obligation upon the Muslim to emigrate from the *dar al-harb*. There was a certain elasticity of conscience, afforded by the traditional view that holy war was in the first instance a personal obligation laid upon the individual Muslim, and that it only became binding upon the whole Islamic community when the leader of the community so proclaimed it. Historically, even in undoubtedly Muslim lands that engaged in intermittent holy war with the Christians, like the coastal areas of north-west Morocco, the *'ulama* had in the past very often taken a prudent and diffident line, in which they avoided as far as possible trying to dictate political conduct to the Muslim rulers.[7]

But in nineteenth-century India and Africa doubts persisted, both among Muslims and among the governing Christians. A British orientalizing apologist like W.W. Hunter, writing in India in the last third of the nineteenth century, could ask himself anxiously in his book title: *Our Indian Musulmans:*

Are They in Conscience Bound to Rebel Against the Queen? But most learned Indian Muslims of his time hastened to assure the authorities in their publications that British India was not a 'land of war' in the Islamic sense, and that no obligation either to fight or to emigrate existed. There was a strong prejudice among some Muslim intellectuals of this period against the earlier *mujahidin*. An Indian Muslim historian of the Punjab, writing in English in the 1880s, portrayed Said Ahmad of Bareilly as a self-aggrandizing braggart.[8]

The holy war in the colonized countries could only be a phenomenon of emergency, of revolt. The sheikhs of the Sufi orders, for example in North and West Africa, normally entertained cautious and courteous relations with the European rulers. There was great fear among Christian rulers, particularly among the French, of the influence of the Sufi brotherhoods, but, for example, in Mauritania the Sufi orders and the *'ulama* never authorized holy war. Further south, in Senegal, holy war appeared only very exceptionally, and then usually as an instrument to compel other Muslims to conform to the norms of the Islamic *shari'a* as the combatant party understood them. Although modern writers often describe these holy wars as resistance movements against colonialism, this is using the terminology of a later age to describe something that was at the time seen very differently.

CHAPTER ELEVEN

Modernity and Political Islam

THE FRENCH ORIENTALIST Jacques Berque once wrote that 'Moderniz-ation, for a people, does not just mean compliance with new requirements: it means reviving in oneself the battle between the old and the new.'[1] The kind of sensitivity to be found in Berque, who was born in Algeria, has during the present century been rare among Westerners, orientalists or not. The manner in which most Western people have assumed that modernization is 'becoming like us', and the equally unimaginative and mechanical way in which most Western sociologists have conceived a sup-posed 'process' of modernization, have for long distorted the common view held in the West of the twentieth-century transformation of non-Western cultures.

The first generation of Muslims to be conscious of the general principles that were held by Western thinkers to govern material and moral progress was that of Jamal al-Din al-Afghani and the Egyptian Muhammad Abdu. In a way their position in respect of European culture was not unlike that of the Renaissance Europeans who looked at the rediscovered heritage of classical civilization and determined to find a way of 'imitation' that did not mean slavish reproduction of the model. Perhaps, although the grasp of men like al-Afghani and Abdu on Islamic religion was as firm as that of Renaissance men on the heritage of the classics, their grasp on Western science, political thought and culture was general, indeed sometimes rather tenuous. *Taqlid*, or slavishly following the older Islamic authorities, was the one thing they were determined to avoid. Their attitude to European thought was more ambiguous. But the resulting cultural clash, although its religious resonance tended to drown the other parts, was in some respects not unlike the much earlier European clash between the Ancients and the Moderns.

It would be a mistake to think of the *salafiyya* reformers such as Afghani and Abdu as without experience of Western methods in the contexts of their own society, even at the end of the nineteenth century. Al-Afghani himself was first introduced into Ottoman governing circles by a modernizing pasha, and a cruder version of his main thesis, that it was necessary to absorb Western scientific and technical progress while reviving and supporting Islam, was conventional in the Ottoman society of his day. Ottoman elites were being trained in the Western positive sciences. Education in subjects such as geography, physics, chemistry and biology tended towards a schematic mastery of general principles rather than an ability in practical or laboratory work.

Al-Afghani, who placed the internal revival of Islam infinitely above the following of Western models, was aware of the perils of slavish Westernization ('Frankification', *tafarnuj*), and was very critical not only of the Westernizers in British India, but of some of the Ottoman modernizers. Several of the grand viziers of the reform (*tanzimat*) period were Freemasons, an affiliation that would in theory have filled al-Afghani with horror (although his first protector, Ali Pasha, was a Freemason). Al-Afghani's fears were to be amply fulfilled. The very theoretical approach to Western ideas that was standard in the Ottoman educational system led, eventually, to attempts to speculate about social and political matters, using concepts such as 'civilization' (a Western concept that al-Afghani himself used liberally) and 'nationality' that had never before been current in societies of Islamic culture.[2] An over-schematic approach, and the free use of a Western political and social vocabulary, were in the present century to become important not only in Turkish secularism, but also in later Islamist mentality.

At that early stage of Islamic reformism, Western civilization was considered in an essentially positive way. The Egyptian reformer and nationalist Ahmad Lutfi al-Sayyid in the early twentieth century condemned British rule in Egypt, but also wrote: 'The dominant civilization of today is European, and the only possible foundation for our progress ... is the transmission of the principles of that civilization.'[3]

Holy war of the sword did not figure overmuch in the way that the Westernized Arab or Arabo-Ottoman intellectuals of the first decades of the century thought about public affairs. But holy war in the moral sense was not forgotten. The Druze nobleman and publicist Shakib Arslan (1869–1946), the author of *Why are the Muslims Backward While Others are More Advanced?* who was involved in many Islamic and Arab nationalist matters in the period following the First World War, talked about the *jihad* ethic as a political dynamic for Muslims, but only in a general, moral way. Islam and the modern world were to become compatible because the *jihad* ethic was to impose a collective responsibility on Muslims to make them so. Arslan's admirers talked of him as having been a *mujahid*, a fighter in the holy war, but only in the general sense of 'refuting every injustice, resisting all oppression'.

From the 1930s onwards a new variety of religious revivalist began to appear, in a sense continuators of the work of men like Jamal al-Din al-Afghani and Muhammad Abdu, but very different both from the old *'ulama* and from the notables-turned-reformers who had been a typical product of the last period of the Ottoman Empire. The two main common characteristics of Hasan al-Banna (1906–49), the Egyptian founder of the Muslim Brotherhood, and Mawlana Abu'l-A'la Mawdudi (1903–79), the founder of the Pakistani Jama'at-i Islami, were their modern cultural formation and their will to found a modern political party. The context of their parties was religious: they intended to found holy communities, not to start new parliamentary groups, though under certain circumstances their parties could became parliamentary.

What distinguished both men, as it had distinguished earlier reformers, was a determination to find equivalents in Islamic vocabulary to Western cultural and political vocabulary as it most affected Muslim communities. Both saw Western culture and policy as threatening to Islam. Both were bitterly hostile to the political conduct of the Western countries in the Islamic world, and their colonial or semi-colonial dominance of Egypt and India. Both were connected with the earlier movement to restore the doctrine of the 'pious ancestors' known as the *salafiyya*, but both also intended to preserve and if necessary re-interpret the constructive parts of modern Western culture and civilization, including its science and technology. Hasan al-Banna's creed, to which the early Muslim Brothers were required to subscribe, included a clause to the effect that the believer accepted that 'the backwardness of Muslims' arose from their neglect of religion. The appreciation of Western scientific culture in Mawdudi and al-Banna was very general: they borrowed from Western essays in popular science of various kinds, as did their followers – the propensity to quote extensively from Western popular science is heavily marked in Sayyid Qutb, who is discussed below.

Jihad was the topic of the first published work of Mawdudi, whose influence on Islamic reformist movements was in the end to go far beyond the

Indian sub-continent. Not that he called for *jihad* of the sword in India as a main part of his basic message: such a call would have been politically very dangerous, although he did in fact call for a *jihad* during the last few days of the India–Pakistan war of 1965. However, his attitude to Islamic holy war was original, and destined to be very influential. He rejected both what he said was the Western idea of Muslim *jihad* as a call to arms, and the Muslim reformist idea (held, for example, by al-Afghani's associate Muhammad Abdu) that *jihad* of the sword was a philosophy of defensive war.

For Mawdudi, as for many Islamic reformers ever since al-Afghani, the philosophy of holy war was essentially the activist principle used in order to achieve a desired moral and political result. *Jihad* was a way in which the holy Islamic community (*umma*), that was both a religious entity and a sort of territorial (though non-national) unit, would resist the fragmentation threatened by the decay of its social bonds (*fitna*), and would also achieve certain goals that he defined in a new way compared to earlier religious reformers.

Mawdudi saw Islam as a 'revolutionary ideology'. Like al-Banna, he combined an Islamic religious vocabulary with translations or sometimes straight borrowings from Western languages. Where, half a century earlier, al-Afghani had on the whole reserved Western borrowings like 'naturism' (the contemporary term for materialism) to describe the philosophies of liberal Muslim adversaries, or Western concepts thought hostile to Islam like communism and nihilism, Mawdudi used the original Western terms to import a variety of ideas that he redefined in a novel Islamic context.

Al-Afghani had made an important exception to his avoidance of the use of loan words in that he adopted the concept of 'civilization', and propagated the idea of an Islamic civilization that could expect a great future as well as a great past. This concept was to prove important to twentieth-century Islamists. The Arabic word normally used (*khadira*) was one that described a region, with towns and villages and a settled population; it was therefore not unlike the Latin word in its derivation, although it had resonances concerning the tension between the desert and the farmed that were different from the Western equivalent. At the end of the century it could be used in Islamist countries as a political slogan: the 1996 Sudanese elections for the re-election of President 'Umar al-Bashir saw hoardings announcing 'Bashir the leader of the civilization project'.

But Mawdudi's use of Western vocabulary and concepts went far beyond any such usage in the recent Islamic past, and it can only be interpreted as

235

embracing modernity – a concept that he himself used quite freely. With Mawdudi and al-Banna arrived the idea that Islam was itself an 'ideology' or a 'system', words that already possessed a long Western intellectual history, but had no real Islamic counterparts. Ideologically Islam was to these reformist thinkers a 'complete and perfect system', a concept that was distinguished from that of an Islamic state. The Islamic system was conceived as being opposed to evil and oppressive Western systems, that it intended to replace by its own programme of social and moral reform.

Both Mawdudi and al-Banna thought that their religious philosophies could be given an active political form through a political party. It was an important part of their philosophies to assert, as is perfectly reasonable, that there is no distinction between politics and faith in Islam. However, even the way they treated this delicate area was new. They used concepts that cannot be found in the earlier Islamic political thinkers, such as *hakimiyya*, sovereignty, or the rule of God on earth. Following the general lines laid down by Al-Afghani, that Islam is a religion of political action, both Mawdudi and al-Banna founded political parties, the Jama'at-i Islami in pre-partition India, and subsequently in Pakistan, and the Muslim Brotherhood in Egypt, which are discussed in the following chapter.

From the end of the First World War to the end of the Nasserist period of Arab nationalism in the late 1960s, the holy war was only a minor background motif in the Islamic world. It did not really have a place in the main orchestration of the conflicts between national forces and Western interests. Particularly in the French-educated parts of the Arab world, but also in Iran and in the Indian sub-continent, Marxism was from the 1920s onwards an immensely powerful influence on the elites. After 1950 the practical importance of the Soviet Union and China in liberationist politics also counted for much. The Western liberal of an older generation who travels in the Arab world is still occasionally asked, in a touchingly nostalgic way, whether he retains no feeling for Marxism from his earlier days.

The Third World seemed during the Nasserist era to be on the way to acquiring a common voice. It has now become very hard to recover the feeling of the period between the Bandung Conference of 1955 and the Arab–Israeli Six-Day War of 1967. The 'non-aligned' bloc of nations, that existed both within and without the politics of the United Nations, appeared to have become a worldwide anti-colonialist force that benefited from the support – however self-interested and arbitrary – of one of the two superpowers. The concession of sovereignty to new nations in the formerly colonialized areas, especially in Africa, was proceeding at what seemed to be a dizzy rate. New theorists of development and dependence in the Third World, and others offering 'world systems' of social and economic analysis, appeared to have charted maps that would assist the progressive forces in the world to make their way, and to help one another. There was no room in these doctrines for religious enthusiasm, although some of the religious enthusiasts thought that they could learn from them.

In the Muslim countries of the 1950s and sixties the holy war seemed archaic, and irrelevant to the main play of political forces. It had no practical role in the conflicts with Israel, and it did not seem as though the religious groups were ever going to play an important role in events. Though occasionally courted by those in power, they were more frequently victimized and persecuted. To many Western observers of the Arab world at the height of its dominance by Jamal 'Abd al-Nasser, it seemed as though the real struggle for the control of the progressive forces of Islamic society was going to be between nationalists and Marxists. Nasser liked to play with the idea of the Islamic dimension of Arabdom even while he brutally repressed the Muslim Brotherhood.

In Iraq and Syria the 1950s theorists of the nascent Ba'th party held that Arabdom contained Islam, rather than the contrary, as was held by the Islamists. Most of the leadership of the Palestine Liberation Organization has until now been overwhelmingly secular, and it is at the moment meeting the desperate resistance of the religious groups. Outside the Arab world the religious revivalists in Turkey, Iran and Pakistan were for a very long time only on the fringe of active nationalist politics. There was a brief participation by religious and mullah elements in the movement that supported Mosaddegh's brief period of power in Iran in 1951–3, but until the 1979 revolution the Iranian national and left-wing parties were more important elements in the opposition to the regime than the mullahs.

In most parts of the Islamic world nationalism seemed totally to have ousted the language and mentality of pan-Islam and Islamicism. In Algeria, where resistance to French domination had for over a century had an Islamic character, the bloody rebellion that broke out in 1954, and that ended in independence in 1962, was overwhelmingly secular in leadership and ideology, and predominantly French in culture. Many of the leaders came from the trades-union movement; others could be described as intellectuals who had had the misfortune to translate their lessons on the French Revolution into Arabic. Their diplomacy as a rebel government embraced pan-Arabism, but it also meant heavy reliance on the Soviet Union and China.

There was never any question on the Algerian side of describing the war as a *jihad*. The 'North African Star' Islamic religious party of Messali al-Hajj was in the course of the rebellion repudiated and proscribed by the FLN secular nationalist leadership. There was an 'oriental' Arab wing of the FLN movement, but it was weak: many of the exiled FLN (especially Ferhat Abbas, who was at one time their main leader, and whose Arabic was particularly poor) spent an unhappy time in Cairo because they could not understand Egyptian Arabic.

When Algerian independence had been attained, it was inevitable that the country's leaders should tend to see themselves as destined to take a major part in the Third World struggles against colonialism. The main leaders – Ahmad Ben Bella, Ferhat Abbas, Krim Belkassem – all used this rhetoric, sometimes in the course of visits to Peking: 'From the edge of Asia to the heart of Africa the universal liberation movement has become a decisive force, capable of ending the dreams of the West to master the earth.' Algeria's concept of herself in the post-independence period was as the spearhead of movements against colonialism in Africa, and as having a kind of parallel mission to that of Cuba in the struggle against colonialism and economic enserfment. It was the idiom of the times: very similar language (although without making a parallel claim for Morocco) was being used by Mehdi Ben-Barka, sometimes styled the Hamlet of the Moroccan nationalist movement.

In those early days neither the long-term results of the close economic relationship with France nor the outcome of the struggle for power in the FLN were predicted. But these two factors were in the long term to disable Algeria from performing any such function as Ben Bella and the rest dreamed of in the first heady days of independence. One might say that in Algeria the secular *jihad* first succeeded, and then failed. In these terms it was a close contemporary parallel to the secular *jihad* of Jamal 'Abd al-Nasser.

The Islamist movements are often described as a Third World phenomenon, and this is true in that the majority of their supporters live in what can loosely be described as Third World countries. However, there are limitations upon this general statement. There are many areas where Islamist movements are strong, such as the Arabian Peninsula and the Gulf,

Turkey, Iran and parts of Western Europe, that cannot be described as Third World. The idea that Islamism is a movement of the dispossessed poor may look credible in Bangladesh or the Gaza Strip, in Algeria, Upper Egypt and the underprivileged areas of Cairo, or parts of south Beirut, but it is not at all credible in the other countries that have just been mentioned. The social make-up of some of the Islamist groups does not suggest that the movements are fuelled only by the discontents of the poor: most Islamist leadership comes from other social levels, in disadvantaged areas as well as more affluent ones.

The Iranian religious theorist Ali Shariati (1933–77), while he was living and studying in Paris translated some of Frantz Fanon's radical works on the plight of the Third World peoples and the moral responsibilities of the ex-colonial powers. He wrote to Fanon to challenge his claim that the peoples of the Third World had to give up their religions in order to fight imperialism. On the contrary, Shariati said, they could not regain their cultural identities unless that identity depended upon popular religious traditions.[4] This was a defence against progressive Third World ideology that obscured the nature of the mullah tradition from which Shariati came, since his Islamism was only very loosely connected with popular religion, and depended upon a learned re-interpretation of Qur'an and *sunna*. However, Shariati was not in the ordinary usage of the word a 'fundamentalist'.

In many ways the Islamist trends before the triumph of Nasserism in Egypt had treated the holy war in the same somewhat ambiguous way that it had been treated since the 'modernists' of the late nineteenth century. The Egyptian reformer and Muslim Brother Sayyid Qutb (1906–66) through his writings had a very different attitude to *jihad* that was deeply influential, although his maximum influence occurred only after his execution in prison. Qutb maintained fiercely that the Islamic movement in history had not been defensive, as the 'treacherous' Western orientalists maintained. *Jihad* is obligatory upon the Muslim: not only to fight in defence of the homeland of Islam, but to take the initiative to free human beings throughout the earth from servitude to anyone other than God. But *jihad* is not primarily the imposition of Islam through the sword: it is striving to make the Islamic 'system' dominant in the world.

Qutb's position about holy war is linked with his equally fierce denunciation of 'ignorance' (*jahiliyya*), by which he meant first the ignorant condition of the Meccans before Muhammad came, and second the abusive, stiff-necked ignorance of modern Christians and Jews, and also of the secularized governments of Muslim countries that claimed to be Islamic although they were not. He said that *jahiliyya* was the worship of some people by others. Some people, he wrote (meaning in the first instance the Nasserist government of Egypt), become dominant and make laws for others, regardless of whether these laws are against God's injunctions and without caring about the use or misuse of their authority: 'Islam is people's worshipping God alone . . . and freeing themselves from servitude to God's servants . . . Islam is not "Islamic democracy" nor "Islamic socialism".'

Qutb maintained that between those who obey Islam and those who are 'ignorant' there has to be a 'rupture', a break (*'uzla*). That break can involve the waging of holy war against those who assert the sovereignty of man over man instead of accepting the sovereignty of God. Like Mawdudi, he assigned the task of leading this movement to a small 'revolutionary vanguard'. Under this leadership non-Islamic sovereignty had to be overthrown: in the first instance this meant the overthrow of the false governments that only pretended to observe Islam. The target was the Nasserist government, which accepted the challenge in a terrible manner by authorizing the execution of the challenger.

Qutb's denunciation of whole states and societies, whose individual members had submitted to Islam by pronouncing the formula of submission (the *shahada*) and said the prescribed prayers, as no better than pre-Islamic polytheists, was radical in the extreme, and was destined to have sharp effects upon radical Islamists who came after him. His position – although this would be very sharply denied by most Islamists, and it is perhaps foolish to compare a twentieth-century intellectual with seventh-century tribesmen – seems to have had something in common with that of the Khariji rebels who refused to accept either the Caliph 'Ali or his 'Umayyad rivals in the first Islamic century.[5] Qutb dissented here from the founder of the Muslim Brotherhood, Hasan al-Banna, who was unwilling to use the charge of religious unbelief against those who did not deny the existence of God. After Qutb's death new Islamist groups came into existence in Egypt, one of which, the Takfir wa Hijra, used the word that contained the charge of unbelief (*takfir*) as a part of their title.

The quality that is ascribed to the Islamic community by al-Afghani, by Mawdudi and by Qutb is activism. God will not change what is in a people until they first change what is in their hearts.[6] All three repudiated the passive resignation that was attributed to Islam by so many Westerners, and substituted for it a doctrine of relentless activism. That activity was not specified by any of them as having to be politically violent, although we now know that the vehemence of the language that Qutb used about the *jahiliyya* could under certain circumstances be used to justify violence.

The *jahiliyya* societies, even though most of their individual members had pronounced submission to Islam, were, according to Qutb, to suffer 'judgement in accordance with the law of ignorance',[7] and to be deposed from the leadership of men, which could mean their destruction by divine decree. In other words, the Egypt in which the Muslim Brothers lived was condemned by God, and its government was de-legitimized. The abolition of oppressive political systems and the preaching of Islam were assigned by Qutb to a body of men whom he called the 'vanguard' of dedicated fighters. This was an elitist type of revolutionary action typical of the Muslim Brotherhood in the form that Hasan al-Banna had already organized it. The vanguard, according to Qutb, had to be ready to embrace martyrdom, and executions of Muslim Brothers had already taken place when Qutb wrote: he may already have been anticipating his own.

There is paradox in the life and ideas of Sayyid Qutb. Far from being an agitator who preached only violence, he was much more an intellectual and a teacher, intoxicated with the beauty and subtlety of the language of the Qur'an. Like Mawdudi, he wrote lengthy commentaries on its text. He also, following in the tradition of al-Afghani, preached the unity and the virtues of the ancient Islamic civilization, that was not to be identified with Arabdom, and was 'never a nationality, always a community of belief'. He contrasted Islamic civilization with modern Western civilization, based on greed, and with Communist civilization, based on hatred and envy. The racial inclusiveness of Islam is contrasted with the racial discrimination of Western societies, and also with what – following a visit to the United States that profoundly shocked him – he regarded as their moral decadence. Islamic civilization was superior in every way to Western civilization, that it is destined to supplant.

The crusades were the first occasion on which Westerners had successfully assaulted Islamic civilization, and Qutb, following texts from modern Muslim India, picked up the idea of their being carried over in some manner into the modern period. He was moderate about this, but definite: 'The spirit of the crusades, though perhaps in a milder form, still hangs over Europe, and that civilization in its dealings with the Islamic world occupies a position which bears clear traces of the early crusading spirit.'[8] It was unfortunate that Qutb picked up from the Indian author Muhammad Asad a statement that has turned into what might be called one of the modern fundamentalist myths. The British General Allenby was said to have remarked, when he entered Jerusalem in triumph at the head of a British army on 11 December 1917, that 'Only now have the crusades come to an end.'[9]

Asad and Qutb were almost comically wrong about Allenby, who had many Muslim troops in his army, and who quite certainly made no such remark. But the matter may well be described as tragicomedy. In fact the entry of Allenby into Jerusalem had been very carefully stage-managed in advance by no less a group of directors than the British Cabinet, and he had received their instructions a fortnight before his entry into the holy city. British policy had had two main aims: the first was to make it publicly clear that Allenby's entry on foot was totally different from the pompous and absurd entry that the German Emperor Wilhelm II had made twenty years earlier, also by the Jaffa Gate, but on horseback and dressed like a medieval crusader, a Teutonic knight. Secondly, Allenby's entry was supposed to demonstrate goodwill towards Islam, by its modesty and also by his placing the Mosque of Omar under an Indian Muslim guard. It is true that British deference to Muslim sensibilities was inspired by political calculation, but the deference was nonetheless real.

There is a curious but equally tragicomic pendant to this story. In Asad's book there is a reference to the medieval Christian expression 'Mahound' as a derogatory name for the Prophet. Asad had ridiculously translated 'Mahound' as 'my dog': as the medieval word was French, this seems, at the minimum, unlikely. But unhappily the British novelist Salman Rushdie came upon 'Mahound' many years later and used it for the Prophet Muhammad in his novel *The Satanic Verses*, a usage that Islamists regarded as having compounded his offence. It could be pleaded that Sir Walter Scott used the same term.

Qutb's own story was a tragic one. It is sad that this sensitive, religious man should have been treated as a seditious plotter, and ironic that his works, which are full of aesthetic considerations and fine shades of meaning, should after his death have been widely used as primers for a rather over-simplified version of Islamism. But his doctrines were scarcely compatible with a Western liberal approach to politics, and it is unlikely that he would have been satisfied, as the Muslim Brethren leaders al-Banna and Hudaibi would probably have been, with an Egypt that had been given genuine democratic reforms.[10]

The decisive impulse to modern radical Islamism came from the Iranian revolution of 1979. It arose from the Shi'a branch of Islam, that has a different religious tradition, and a different tradition about the relations between government and religion, from the Sunni world. In particular, the disappearance or 'occultation' of the Twelfth Shi'a Imam in the ninth Christian century has led to a curious provisionality or uncertainty about the nature of some Shi'a religious duties. It has been argued that the frequently confrontational nature of Shi'a attitudes is linked with the earliest history of the doctrine, that was connected with the supporters of 'Ali (the last of the 'rightly-guided' caliphs) against the victorious 'Umayyad Mu'awiya in the seventh Christian century. 'Ali's son Husayn was killed by the 'Umayyads at the battle of Karbala in 680, and his death was seen by the Shi'a as a martyrdom suffered at the hands of a victorious and worldly orthodoxy. This martyrdom has been celebrated ever since in the Shi'a obedience as a suffering endured for righteousness under persecution.

There have been divergences within the Shi'a world, and one worth mentioning in the context of modern reformism is that of the Isma'ilis, the sect whose best-known manifestation in the West was that of the so-called Assassins, whose military power was important in crusader Syria. Al-Afghani singled out the Isma'ilis for particular disapproval, since he had decided that they were to blame for the victories of the Christian crusaders. His reasons were of a moral and religious order, but he may also have had in mind the military support that the Assassins had sometimes been willing to give to the crusaders. However, the Isma'ilis were not approved in modern Persia by mainstream Shi'ism, that had itself been a minority religion on Persian soil until the Safavid regime in the sixteenth Christian century. It is also just possible, if al-Afghani really was born a Persian Shi'a, as some people have claimed, that he was anxious to exonerate himself in Sunni eyes from being linked with a Shi'a heresy like Isma'ilism, and that his holding the Isma'ilis responsible for the moral decay of medieval Islam had some link with this.

There is no clear sharing of a common ancestry (apart from the common allegiance to Islam) among the Shi'a and Sunni Islamic reformist writers of the period following the Second World War. The doctrine of Ayatollah Ruhollah Khomeini (1902–89), that overwhelmingly shaped Iran after the 1979 revolution, was quite different not only from the ideas of radical lay Shi'a Iranian intellectuals like Shariati, but from the ideas of most of the other Shi'a ayatollahs, Khomeini's peers. And except in a few vital matters, like the concept of Islamic revolution itself, the proposal of a 'republic' and the idea of an Islamic 'system', Khomeini's doctrine was conceived and expressed mostly in the traditional language of the learned Shi'a mullahs.

In so far as he was a modernist – which he undoubtedly was – Khomeini refused to acknowledge it.

Khomeini's key doctrine was that of governance by the learned in the law, or the supremacy of the learned jurist, the *vilayat-i-faqih*. Implacably opposed to kingship in Islam (though this was merely a facet of his disapproval of the Pahlavi dynasty and of Muhammad Reza Shah), Khomeini maintained that the *'ulama* were the authority to which the Islamic community should turn not only for guidance but for government. One of the governing mullahs could even be singled out to enjoy powers analogous to those of the early caliphs: it was this mullah who would qualify for rule because of his title as 'learned jurist'.

This central idea was an astonishing innovation in terms of traditional Islamic political thought, and it enjoyed very little support from the other senior mullahs. It had no well-known equivalent in Sunni Islamism. Khomeini may perhaps have arrived at the idea through interpreting the prominent role that the mullahs had played in Persian political life in the late nineteenth and early twentieth centuries. But the victory of the *vilayat-i-faqih* doctrine after the 1979 revolution was the personal victory of Khomeini. It has been well observed that where it has succeeded, religious revivalism has taken the political process unawares;[11] as a result, the Iranian revolution was able to impose a solution of a type that nobody could have predicted.

Khomeini was modern in that almost from the beginning of his public opposition to the government he proclaimed his ideas to be 'revolutionary', although he did not use that expression to mean a violent political revolution against the Shah until a very late stage. He was modern in thinking that 'the people' would impose an Islamic republic, and in the way that he selected his political targets. From the time of his first violent confrontations with the Iranian regime in the early 1960s, he singled out the United States and Israel as the particular objects of his dislike.

The reasons for Khomeini's anti-Americanism are not hard to find in terms of Iranian politics. The Shah's dependence on American power had been acute from the time of his restoration and the simultaneous fall of the Mossadegh regime in 1953. In the early 1960s Iranian dependence on America had not yet been obscured by the growth of Pahlavi triumphalism. Some Americans in Iran, especially those from US security services, behaved with a public arrogance that was practically unconcealed. The situation was made evident by the passage of a law that in effect revived the humiliating regime of nineteenth-century Western 'capitulations' with Muslim powers, the 1964 'Status of Forces Law', that conceded judicial immunity to American military staff in Iran. Khomeini's resistance to this law, which he said acknowledged that Iran was an American colony, led to his first exile.

The explanation for the singling out of Israel as another target for Khomeini's denunciation may be less obvious. On the one hand, the domination of Jerusalem and its Islamic shrines by a new Jewish power was unacceptable – even if this domination was incomplete before 1967. But by 1963 Khomeini was denouncing the evil interference of Israel in Iran. In exile in the following decade he associated himself with the Palestinian resistance to Israel, and issued religious decrees telling Muslims to oppose the Jewish state. 'Imperialism' became another of his main bogies.

The tone of this Islamic theologian was by the 1970s beginning to sound remarkably like that of the other prophets of Third World resistance to capitalist imperialism, even though he was careful to keep the main body of his pronouncements inside the normal Islamic discourse.

The collapse of the Pahlavi regime in Iran began seriously in the autumn of 1978. From his exile in Paris Khomeini was able to influence the course of events in his home country to a degree totally unexpected by outside observers. When he returned to Iran on 1 February 1979, a fortnight after the flight of the Shah, he already held the political initiative to the extent that he could nominate a government opposed to that left in power by Muhammad Reza, and in a few days cause it to prevail. The Islamic constitution passed in November of that year named Khomeini as the *faqih*, the principal learned jurist, but it was far from giving absolute power to the mullahs without setting up any countervailing secular authorities.

Formally, clerical power is exercised in Iran in a revisionary way through the Council of Guardians, which is empowered to enforce Islamic principles upon government. For a considerable time after 1979 the revolutionary situation did indeed make the mullahs the *de facto* rulers of the country, and as long as he lived Khomeini was its undisputed leader. The war with Iraq (1980–8) gave his regime a more nationalist cast than it might otherwise have had, and also, while it lasted, consolidated its revolutionary powers. But Western and Islamic political ideas were confused with one another from the outset; for example, the very notion of 'revolution', that was so important to the regime, is an openly Western one.

Khomeini was a propagandist of genius, and when the opportunity offered, on a world scale. Nothing showed this more strikingly than his handling of the Salman Rushdie affair, that until he took it up was not an affair. In 1989, the year of his death, the modern-minded mullahs brought to Khomeini's attention the Pakistan-born British novelist's *The Satanic Verses*, a fantasy that uses a well-known episode in the life of Muhammad in which the Prophet seems to have hesitated, or to have made some short-lived reservation, in his denunciation of the idols that were worshipped in the sacred compound in Mecca. Rushdie also wrote about the role of poets during the life of the Prophet. Fear and dislike of poetical satire can be found in the Qur'an itself, and Muhammad is known to have acted fiercely against some poets. Rushdie spoke of this fear in his book, in which he used elements of the sacred story in a modern novel of magic and myth.

Both the Iranian revolution and its subsequent repercussions on the Islamic world owed much to modern electronic communications. Just as Nasserist Arabism of the fifties and sixties had been enabled by the transistor radio, so many of the triumphs of Khomeini were enabled by the television set and the video-cassette. But the videos were intended to reach Muslims already disposed to hear their message. In reacting to Rushdie's book, which had not been intended as an irreligious statement of disbelief, Khomeini's genius was quick to grasp the opportunity to denounce what he saw as Western-inspired blasphemy in a manner that actually reached those he thought responsible for it.

Khomeini's *fatwa* against Rushdie, calling for the author's death, was publicized throughout the globe by the electronic media. The worldwide appetite for news meant that Western media that were on the whole hostile to Khomeini served as his messengers; it was the same mechanism that transmitted the messages of acts of terrorism. But the extremely modern nature of Khomeini's tactics went unnoticed in the West, where all that was immediately understood was the supposedly medieval nature of his verdict. The effect of Khomeini's denunciation was especially sharp upon Muslims living in Western countries, a category to which Rushdie himself belonged. Through the opportunity offered him by the case of a sceptical, imaginative and Westernized Muslim, a Shi'a cleric was enabled to address a huge Sunni constituency.

A remarkable feature of the revolutionary regime in Iran, after the Iraqi invasion of the south-west of the country in 1980 had caused what turned out to be a bloody eight-year war, was the caution with which the Iranian clerical rulers approached the matter of holy war. In spite of the secular nature of Saddam Hussein's Iraqi regime, no *jihad* was unambiguously pronounced against it. Among the mullahs opinion about the holy war was divided. There was divergence between those 'ulama who thought that *jihad* was permissible during the continued absence of the twelfth Imam, and those of another opinion, to whom Khomeini appears to have belonged. Ayatollah Morteza Motahari, a member of the original Revolutionary Council, said: 'The most excellent *jihad* is to speak of justice before the ruler,' a principle not widely followed in Iran after 1979.

On the other hand, martyrdom was seen as something that could be embraced outside the context of holy war. Ali Shariati had also maintained this view. Khomeini, who rightly (from a factual point of view) treated the Iraq war as a defensive war, and who appears not to have spoken of it as a holy war, nevertheless told his soldiers that 'killing or being killed will lead to your salvation'.

The social composition of the Islamist groups and parties in different parts of the Islamic world is so infinitely various that anyone who undertakes a 'sociology of fundamentalism' is doomed to failure. On the other hand, there are some relevant social factors that are Third World rather than specifically Islamic, and these are well worth examining.

The overwhelmingly important phenomenon is that of urbanization. For a generation more than half the populations of most Islamic countries have lived in cities, and this has had drastic effects on education, housing, social services, and deterioration of contact with rural and tribal origins. However, the idea that most Islamist groups consist of deprived 'peasants' who have been disorientated by their transfer from a rural to an urban environment is little short of grotesque. It is true that there are some areas, like the Gaza Strip or the peripheral slums of Cairo (such as Imbaba and 'Ain Shams), south Beirut or the Palestinian camps in Lebanon, where social deprivation is extreme. But these are urban or quasi-urban extremes, not the norm – and even in these most deprived areas there may be important social services.

Entry into the leadership and directing hierarchy of all Islamist parties is educationally selective, in that their doctrines require a basic acquaintance with the holy texts. Conservative educationalists complain about the poor Arabic and defective Qur'anic scholarship of modern Islamists (though some of the leaders are extremely learned *'ulama*), but university, polytechnic and traditional school students supply the most important basic recruiting ground for the majority of the pietist movements: this is true in Afghanistan to such an extent that the latest important Islamist party to enter the political arena is called the Student Party. Educational selectivity is also evident in

Pakistan, where less than a third of the nation is literate, but the Jama'at-i Islami is essentially an Urdu-speaking party, not equipped to communicate effectively with the underclasses, that speak various non-Urdu vernaculars. Similar problems seem not to obtain in the Berber-speaking areas of Algeria, where the religious parties are more firmly entrenched.

Exceptions abound, but it is likely that the majority of Islamist activists will have received a modern-type schooling. Leaders, where they are not senior *'ulama*, are likely to have had advanced Western education, and ex-students of Harvard, the Sorbonne and MIT are not unknown among them. Two leaders of Palestinian 'Jihad' parties in recent years have been medical doctors: another 'Jihad' leader and theorist, the Egyptian Muhammad 'Abd al-Salam Faraj, was an electrical engineer.

The situation in Iran, where the revolution was to some extent a mass-movement of the mullahs, is somewhat different, but although the mullah class was assigned a privileged position after the revolution, the uprisings were actually made by a lay majority whose leadership was on the whole Western-educated to a high level. And at the top of the Iranian clerical hierarchy, many of the mullahs are insatiable readers in Western languages; the same can be said of the Lebanese Shi'a group Hizbullah.

Political Islamism has a long history in Egypt, where the mainstream Islamicist group, the Muslim Brotherhood, is well-established, middle class, professional. The Muslim Brotherhood controls or strongly influences most of the professional syndicates in Egypt – lawyers, engineers, dentists, doctors – and in 1994 the government introduced special legislation affecting elections in these syndicates to make exercise of Muslim Brotherhood control more difficult (the Brotherhood is still oppositional enough in 1996 to attract widespread arrests from the government). Muslim Brotherhood presence in the mosques and in meetings is usually emphasized by the wearing of conservative dark suits. Something like 40 per cent of the membership of the syndicates is below the age of thirty-five, and critics have said that the young Muslim Brothers are merely 'candidates for sheikhdom'. There is a not dissimilar social basis to the metropolitan elements of the Islamist Welfare Party in Turkey. On the other hand, both in Egypt and Turkey, a social analysis of the parties with a broader base that went outside the capitals would place more emphasis on conservative and rural elements.

In the more recent and more radical Egyptian organizations, there is a considerable difference in social make-up. Al-jama'at al-islamiya and Al-jihad al-islamiya have social bases more akin to activist parties in other Third World countries: university and secondary school students, unemployed university graduates or holders of technical certificates, and literate artisans and small businessmen. Membership is much younger than that of the Muslim Brothers: active leaders are often in their early twenties. They are usually educated, motivated young men from rural or small-town lower-middle-class backgrounds, often living away from their families in large cities. About half the radical party members come from Upper Egypt, which still does not argue for an entirely rural base, since there is, for example, a university in Assyut which is an important centre for Islamism.

The complexity of the social bases of Islamist parties is especially clear in Algeria, where deprived urban groups seem to be the main source of Islamist support just as they are in Egypt: unemployed ex-students from high schools and technical schools supply the majority of militants, and the outlying areas of Algiers are as important as those of Cairo. But in the movement that led to the construction of large numbers of unauthorized mosques, that became the Islamist organizational centres, the old class of landowners, hostile to the corrupt government bureaucracy, was important. Regional factors also play a big part: Kabyl regionalism split the FLN, the old resistance movement to the French, and the importance of Berber areas in the new Islamist groups is not accidental. All this led various Algerian Islamist leaders to look for very diverse patrons abroad: some got funding from Saudi Arabia, others went to Afghanistan for activist and guerrilla training.

Almost all Islamists adopt a position of strong hostility to what they term cultural Westernization. But at the same time they accept modern science and technology on the basis – which few of them seem to have discussed seriously – that they are culturally neutral, and capable of being incorporated into an Islamic culture. Since a very large number of Islamist leaders and militants have had, unlike their theorists, some sort of scientific training, this is not surprising.

It can be argued that much popular Islamism is a manifestation of a phenomenon that the British author C.P. Snow defined almost forty years ago as that of the 'two cultures'. As in the West, the problem is double, and comprehends both people trained in the arts who have only a sketchy knowledge of the sciences, and the reverse. On the one hand, the older theorists of radical Islamism received an on the whole literary formation in Western culture, and a theological and literary one in Arabic, Persian, or Urdu. Their knowledge of Western science, necessary when they came to talk of 'civilization', was largely derived from popularizers like Julian Huxley, or from far more obscure and popularized sources. Qutb, for example, in his theological works quoted liberally from an American industrial chemist called Abraham Cressy Morrison (b.1864), who had been employed in the food industry and had contributed to a dispute about the chemistry of baking powder.

The scientifically trained Islamists of the generation after Qutb could suffer from the reverse problem from his, in that their knowledge of the humane subjects sometimes tends to be superficial. This can make topics that require a comparative approach, like the theory of human rights, unnecessarily difficult to discuss with people who are not at all stupid, and are by no means indifferent to moral issues.

Like spiritual leaders all over the world, the Islamists have to face the problem of consumerist materialism imposed through the world markets that are relentlessly thrust upon everyone, including the excluded poor, by the electronic media. They have replied by offering a severe puritanism, and the comradeship of religious affinity, giving people bonds that may replace or supplement traditional social linkages that have decayed because of various sorts of physical and social displacement. Within the often elaborate hierarchies of their religious associations they can offer something in the way of dignified function to people with little hope of advancement, or even of employment, in the predominantly clientelist societies in which they live.

To a very small number of people in a small number of Islamist groups there is the possibility of militancy in the literal sense of military or guerrilla revolt, though in practice this obtains only in zones of extreme political crisis like Algeria, south Lebanon and Afghanistan, or the troubled parts of the Palestine National Authority and the Israeli West Bank. In some of these factors, including the possibility of holy war, the Islamist associations are replacing the functions of the old religious brotherhoods, although it has to be remembered that these are far from obsolete. There are, for example, several million Sufis in the Egyptian brotherhoods, and the Naqshbandiyya Sufi order is still one of the most influential bodies in the Islamic world, present and powerful from central Asia to Western Europe.

Consumerism is not incompatible with Islamic puritanism: in fact there is something in the manner in which such puritanism concentrates almost exclusively upon the family unit that favours it. Wahhabi Saudi Arabia and the Islamic Gulf states equal the United States in their social acceptance of consumerism, and in Egypt there is a fear that Wahhabism, rather than

Islamism, will be the ideological victor, bringing unlimited consumerism with it. This has a parallel in the fears of some Western Europeans about their cultural future in the face of what they think of as transatlantic pressures.

Some Islamists offer material assistance to people who are socially deprived. In the past two decades whole clusters of social services have grown up around the mosque and the Islamic association in many countries. Clinics, libraries, crèches, sports and youth facilities can be of great importance to the communities in which the Islamist groups operate. In areas like the Gaza Strip, some Algerian cities and the zones devastated by the 1992 Egyptian earthquake the Islamists were practically the only organizations able to act in this way on the ground. Not surprisingly, their social welfare arms have not been welcomed by the clumsy and often corrupt national bureaucracies. In Turkey, too, the Islamists sponsor their own social services, and also act politically to improve government ones, although in the provinces there have been complaints that mosque-building enjoys priority over the provision of social facilities.

Not only are the populations of the Islamic countries very largely urbanized: in common with much of the Third World they are also very young, with an age ratio that is hard to imagine for a citizen of the ageing populations of the West. This has had very negative effects indeed on youth unemployment, that is extremely high: such situations are notoriously socially explosive. In such circumstances Islamism is not offered as an elitist product to be consumed by a small number of intellectuals, but as having immediate appeal to a mass audience. The way it is diffused is very different from the way in which Nasserism was diffused: its penetration is deeper because of the part played by the local mosque. This is nevertheless quite like the situation that obtained popular support for Arab nationalism in the fifties and sixties, exacerbated now in many countries by the very disappointing results of industrialization.

The educational standards in the lower levels of leadership in the Islamist parties can be very modest indeed, although a thick line has to be drawn between countries with low resources in terms of educated population like Algeria and (to a lesser extent) Egypt, and Turkey or the Gulf states. And the top leadership of some Islamist groups that sponsor violent policies, like Hizbullah in the Lebanon, or Hamas in the Palestine National Authority and the West Bank, contains highly educated people, both in a traditional Islamic and in a Western sense.

The refusal of some Islamists to reject all modernism is prominent in the question of women. In Iran, despite many restrictions that attract attention in the West, women have the vote, enter employment and education in a more or less Western manner, and drive cars. Sa'udi Wahhabism denies women the vote and the automobile, and has a more restrictive policy in other matters. In Saudi Arabia the call for a more liberal policy towards women now comes from the Islamists. In Afghanistan and Iran women have also borne arms in war. However, to be judges and to be given political leadership is denied to women even in Iran.

In Algeria and the Sudan the Islamist attitudes to women are a great deal more restrictive. There is a political point here: the ruling regimes in Algeria, Tunisia and Egypt have all applied Western codes to the personal status of women that the Islamists in those countries denounce. The supposedly shameless behaviour of Westernized Muslim women in matters of dress and social conduct is one of the targets of a lower-middle-class Islamist membership that has espoused puritanism, and that wants strict female dress and public behaviour codes to symbolize its devotion and correctness.

Perhaps one of the most significant words of the Islamist vocabulary is *hijra*, whose primary meaning is sacred emigration based upon the emigration of Muhammad from Mecca to Medina. This sacred emigration has very often in the past been tactical and military; there have been many modern examples, from the nineteenth-century holy wars to the Afghan wars of the 1980s, the flights of the modern Egyptian Islamist extremists to the caves of the desert, and the cover from government attack provided by the sugarcane areas near Assyut. The Egyptian Takfir wa Hijra group, that have probably engaged in armed activity, incorporated the sacred word into their title, that means, loosely translated, 'denunciation of disbelief and sacred emigration'. It may well be that the ancestry of such modern flights is not properly Islamic, but has also to do with the nineteenth-century Russian nihilist flights of the revolutionary intelligentsia to the countryside, and with the post-1967 country hideouts of the Italian Red Brigades.

But sacred flight is not only military. *Hijra* means withdrawal, even rejection. The whole life of the Islamicist activist is in a sense one of attempted withdrawal from the alien Western culture. In this withdrawal the activist is quite likely to divert himself with television, provided that the programme (or, more likely, the video-cassette) is of an approved sort. But the principle of rejection of an alien culture that has been imposed through a sort of imperialist violation is found throughout the Third World, and is in no way confined to the Islamic countries. It can obtain even for some members of Muslim communities permanently settled in Western countries, though in these cases the issues are substantially different.

It is impossible to say how purely or authentically Islamic the principle of withdrawal from Western culture is. A kind of inner emigration from the unacceptable aspects of Western industrial culture, and an assertion of traditional values that are supposedly derived from the Middle Ages, though usually invented as an idealized norm, has been one of the main intellectual and social trends in the West over the past century and a half. It was important in Russia from the time of Tolstoy and the *narodniks* at the end of the last century, and Europe and North America were full of movements, some Marxist or quasi-Marxist, others not, that exemplified the same romantic trend. The Islamists of today may be closer to the environmental rejectionists than either supposes.

CHAPTER TWELVE

Faith, Government and Dissent

THE END OF the First World War also saw the end of the last of the old Muslim empires. The Ottoman Empire proper collapsed in 1919, and the Turkish Republic was set up in 1922. The Qajar dynasty in Iran, which like that of the Ottomans was overtaken by revolution after popular refusal to accept a Western-imposed settlement in 1919, was replaced in 1925 by the new dynasty of the former commoner, Riza Khan Pahlavi. Of the older Muslim dynasties a very few survivors, like Morocco, limped along under virtually colonial control. The Wahhabi emirate of 'Abd al-'Aziz Ibn Sa'ud in Arabia, who was recognized by the British and others as King of the Hejaz by 1927, and the Zaidi imamate of the Yemen, were under British influence rather than British control. There was a brief Anglo–Afghan war in 1919, but after this Afghanistan escaped to a degree from both British and Russian direct influence for quite a long period. In Malaysia and Indonesia there was direct colonial rule, British or Dutch, and such sultans as survived had only the shadows of privilege; the same was true in the wreckage of Muslim India.

By 1919 the question of 'modernization' was nearly a century and a half old in the Ottoman Empire, and the policy of a modernization programme (*tanzimat*) had been in operation for almost half that period. This experience decided the innovations that accompanied the new Turkish Republic. Comparable, but rather less radical changes occurred in the post-Qajar Iranian state. In other areas of the Islamic world various parts of society were at different stages in appreciating the enormous problems that had been set them by the technological and industrial transformation exported by the West, by the forcible annexation of their economies to the world markets, and by the challenge of alien cultures and governmental systems.

European-influenced constitutions began to be granted in the Islamic world as part of the nineteenth-century quest for reform in the Ottoman Empire: a constitution was accepted in the beylick of Tunisia in 1860, the first Ottoman constitution was given in 1876 and the second in 1908, and a constitution was granted by the Qajar dynasty in Persia in 1906. These were only interim modernizations. Most countries with Muslim majorities that are sovereign states at the present time were set up in something resembling their present form between 1919 and 1965. The form of government they adopted at the outset was in very many cases determined or influenced, more or less, by the previously dominant European power. But in what is perhaps the most important example of all, the new Turkish regime in 1924 gave itself what was then by far the most secularized (and therefore 'Westernized') constitution in the Islamic world, after a nationalist struggle that had been based on a war against some of the main Western states.

Some Muslim states resisted European influence upon their political structures, notably Saudi Arabia and the emirates of the Gulf. However, in conservative Muslim states the Christian powers dominated where they did not influence: an example is French pressure upon Moroccan administration and government. Pakistan was not given a constitution by the British, but British constitutional and legal practice were extremely important there in 1947 and later. None of this was peculiar to the Islamic world. The Muslim states whose forms changed or were made anew during the present century were examples of a political process that operated throughout the world in the colonial and ex-colonial spheres, and that affected societies and governments belonging to many religions and cultures.

In the realm of ideology and politics many Muslim states experienced drastic change in the second half of the twentieth century. Political transformations of every kind have taken place. There were also in the Arab world, especially in the Nasserist period, attempts at merging states into larger pan-Arab units. That most of these attempts failed, down to the more recent Yemen merger, does not mean that they were unimportant.

Numerous changes in the forms of government in the Muslim states have not meant equally drastic changes in the forms of sovereignty. The sultanate or its modern derivative has persisted in a small number of conservative countries, but in most, even those that call themselves Islamic, sovereignty has been formulated and exercised according to Western rather than Islamic political traditions. Only in Libya has the form of sovereignty arguably been modified, and then in a modern and not in a conservative Islamic sense. That 'national assemblies' in Muslim states seldom conform closely to Western democratic ideas does not alter the fact that the idea of a national assembly is relatively new in Islamic political tradition. New, but not so new. Both in Iran and Egypt, and much more in Ottoman Turkey, the attractions of Western constitutionalism were experienced from the latter half of the nineteenth century.

In almost every case the tradition to have prevailed in the Islamic world, as in the modern post-colonial world generally, has been that of the territorial sovereign state. The sovereign state has in most cases been combined with the idea of the national state, a combination that points to an underlying ideology of government which is pre-eminently Western. The Pakistani President Ayub Khan, speaking in Cairo in Nasser's presence in the autumn of 1960, said: 'Whether we like it or not, and certainly we should not like it, religion today is not the motive power that it used to be. It is national territorialism which is the motive power.' Ayub Khan was no more of a friend to Islamist parties than his host, but he spoke with the voice of sovereign national power, and this power has not receded in the Islamic world since his day.

The failure of Egypt's Nasser and Libya's Mu'ammar Qadafi in their attempts to merge their countries with other Arab states, and the obstinate persistence of newly national governmental units that were once maintained to be 'artificial', like Iraq and Jordan, are evidence that the territorial national state is a mould that the Islamic countries are going to find extremely difficult to break. The lesson of the twenty-year period that ended in the Arab–Israeli war of 1967 was that pan-Arabism, viewed as a struggle for the political amalgamation or merger of Arab states, was as much a failure as the old pan-Islamism had been in the twenty years that followed the abolition of the caliphate in 1924.

The mechanism of modern government gives a considerable degree of control over religion to any regime in the Muslim world in which religious freedoms have no entrenched legal protection. Such controls may affect religious minorities considered heretical, like the Bahai in Iran. They may also affect the Muslim majority. This is not new in Islamic history: the sultans have always exerted a considerable degree of control over religious institutions, notably over charitable institutions (*waqfs*) and the positions and pronouncements of the learned clergy, the *'ulama*. The Ottoman Empire exercised a tight rather than a loose control over the *'ulama*, and, rather than play a merely supervisory role, ran a policy that tended to make the religious class into state servants and propagandists. The present Saudi government exercises an iron control over religion in the Kingdom, not only through supervision of the *'ulama*, but by means of a religious police that surveys the ordinary citizen, and acts harshly against him when he goes against official religious policy. This rule owes more to control techniques borrowed from modern Western governments than to traditional Islam.

The abolition of the caliphate after the Ottoman Empire was finally abandoned in 1922 was a break in Islamic tradition that should not be underestimated. That the Ottoman Sultan's claim to the caliphate had had only a very modest practical influence during the preceding two or three centuries made no difference to the negative effect of its loss upon Muslim political thought. It was also felt as an emotional loss, especially in Muslim India. The Atatürk revolution in Turkey, in which the entire Islamic religious hierarchy was abolished, enforced a secularization that has still not found any real equivalent in other Islamic countries, and that is being implicitly challenged in Turkey itself by the religious parliamentary party – though, now that it is in office, it has so far not mounted a constitutional challenge.

In Turkey the religious law of Islam ceased in 1926 to be the law of the land. This was a revolutionary change, but a less drastic one than it may sound, since the precedents for Ottoman secular legislation (*qanun*) were ancient, and the importation of much European civil, criminal and commercial law had taken place in the mid-nineteenth century. The Atatürk legal changes thus only took to their logical conclusion trends that were quite old in the Ottoman state. However, in the 1920s reforms of the law of personal status were made, under the strong influence of Western legal concepts and systems, that were unacceptable to the former *'ulama*. Strong action was taken against the religious brotherhoods and their possessions, and the system of religious education was shut down (though it was in effect partially reopened after the Second World War). Secularism and religious equality were again proclaimed in the 1961 constitution, and no notable relevant change was made in the constitution of 1982, in spite of the growth during this period of a strong Islamic party.

Most modern governments of Muslim countries have also interfered radically in religious matters in the direction of Western-type modernization of the law. Commercial law and the law of personal status were their most important targets. In Egypt and in parts of the Maghreb, as also in Turkey, the importation of sections of Western legal systems dates back to the nineteenth century. The legal reforms of the Bourguiba regime in Tunisia after 1957, some of the now bitterly contested changes made in

Algeria after 1962, and those of the Qadafi regime in Libya, that were adopted in the teeth of opposition from the *'ulama*, are examples.

In Pakistan, that came into existence terming itself an Islamic republic, the question of legal reform has had a rather turbulent history. More moderate and piecemeal legal reform and modernization have occurred elsewhere. But the so-called Islamic fundamentalist legal changes that have been imposed by some countries professing Islamist principles are examples of the same state supremacy in religious matters that has enabled modernizing legal changes to take place in other Muslim countries. In the Sudan, for example, the appearance is of a reactionary religious fanaticism that forces the adoption of a medieval code. But the reality is an oppressive and incompetent government, unable to settle its southern civil war, that shores up its threatened authority by measures that give it greater social control within the country, and a specious international Islamist prestige without.

The country by which modern revolutionary Islamic religious and legal reform tends to be judged is Shi'a Iran. To be 'revolutionary' was the claim that Khomeini made for the movement at the time of the seizure of power, although there are many elements in the regime that are socially and religiously conservative, apart from its declared anti-Marxism. The referendum that led to the creation of an Islamic republic in 1979 was followed by arrangements that kept surprisingly closely to the constitution of 1906 (this is less surprising when it is considered that the 1906 constitution had been supported at the time by the clerical party). The Khomeini regime also added quasi-democratic arrangements, adopting a universal franchise and an executive that is in some respects independent. This independence was qualified, however, by the adoption of the principle of rule by a person wise in Islamic law (*vilayat-i faqih*, the leadership of the jurisprudent), and by the introduction of the clerical Council of Guardians. What was created in Iran was a sort of pluralist rule between lay and clergy. However, after the Islamic state had been set up the intervention in the application of religious law was drastic, as an attempt – only partly successful – was made to have the whole legal system of the country Islamicized.

Holy war in a partly or fully modernized Islamic state is not an impossible option. The examples that can be given show, it is true, substantial confusion among the Muslim learned class upon the subject, but that is far from new in Islamic history. Holy war of the sword in Islam is primarily a military and political option for the community, a collective duty (*fard 'ayn*, an

eminent duty) and not an individual one (*fard kifaya*, a sufficiently per-
formed duty). The responsibility for making the duty collective rests upon
the leader of the community, and this leadership does not belong automatically to a collectivity that could be defined as 'the state', but rather to
religious leadership defined as the *imam*. On the other hand, under normal
circumstances the clerical class, the *'ulama*, have been willing to accept the
initiative of the sultan in proclaiming holy war – a situation that normally
applies also to the proclamation of a 'just' war in Christian countries. Where
the clerical class takes this initiative in matters concerning holy war without
the consent of the governors, be they Muslim or non-Muslim, sanctions
against them may result.

The Iraqi war of 1980–8 was fought to resist the aggression of a neighbouring state with a Sunni leadership, that was denounced by the Iranian
clergy as apostate from Islam. That some of the most important holy places
and teaching centres of the Iranian Shi'a are located within the boundaries
of Iraq, and that there is a very large Shi'a minority in Iraq, gave a dimension
almost of internal dissension to the war: Ayatollah Khomeini himself had
spent many years teaching in the Shi'a centre of Najaf in Iraq. But, as has
been emphasized above, the Iranian clergy was extremely cautious in apply-
ing the doctrine of *jihad* to the Iraqi war, and adopted a kind of compromise,
in which those who fell in the war were considered to have been martyrs,
but the war itself was not unambiguously said to be a *jihad*.

The history of the Islamic republic of Iran may be contrasted with that
of the Islamic state of Pakistan, which has never seriously contemplated,
either in the East Pakistan War of 1971 or in the numerous conflicts over
Kashmir, the declaration of a national holy war. Holy war with Hindu-
majority India would expose the huge Muslim minority in India to unthink-
able dangers that would make the terrible events of 1947 appear trivial. It
may be added that the 1971 breakaway of Bangladesh showed the inability
of the common religion of Islam in Pakistan to keep the two halves of the
country united when the regional and social pressures reached a certain
point.

The only modern Islamic state to have a history of waging genuine holy
war in this century is the Wahhabi state of Saudi Arabia. The tribal Ikhwan
(i.e. (Muslim) Brotherhood) were a main factor in the rise of the Kingdom
of Abd 'al-Aziz Ibn Sa'ud, and holy war was one of their main occupations
for many decades. However, Ibn Sa'ud's suppression of the north-eastern
tribes in 1929, to deflect them from holy frontier warfare in areas that were
now protected by the British, put a stop to this phase in Saudi history, and

the Ikhwan were dissolved. The help and theological agreement of the *'ulama* were vital at this time to Ibn Sa'ud's action against the tribes, and the maintenance of a close relationship with the *'ulama* has remained one of the main principles of Saudi government.

The history of the Saudi attitude to holy war in more recent history is ambiguous. On several occasions the Saudi regime called for a *jihad* against Israel, but the call seems to have been issued in the sense of launching a political and economic struggle, without matters ever approaching linked military hostilities. Early in 1981, following a long period of frustration about Israeli settlements on the West Bank, the Saudis led the conference of Islamic countries (including Jordan), that was in session at Taif in Saudi Arabia, to call for such a *jihad*, whose main purpose was to enforce the existing boycott of Western firms that traded with Israel. The boycott was strengthened, and was only called off after the Oslo Palestinian accords of 1993.

The Gulf War of 1991, following Iraq's invasion of Kuwait, revealed a large degree of confusion throughout the Arab world, far from unprecedented if we look at earlier Islamic history, about the religious position of the participants.[1] Saudi Arabia's King Fahd obtained several declarations from the Saudi *'ulama*, at least one of which declared that the war against Iraq was a *jihad fi-sabil allah*, a holy war in the way of God. A status of martyrdom was therefore claimed for the Saudi war dead.

The Saudi move was naturally countered by Iraqi propaganda depicting Saddam Hussein as the champion of Islam against American imperialism. In 1991 Saddam Hussein obtained declarations from the Iraqi Sunni and Shi'a *'ulama* that conflicted directly with the Saudi *fatwa*, in stating that Iraq was waging a holy war against Kuwait, Saudi Arabia, Egypt and their Christian allies. This position was approved by some Islamist groups whose leaders were in exile, like the Tunisian Rashid al-Ghanoushi, and by at least one of the leading Palestinian *'ulama*, Musa al-'Alami. Outside the Arab world, Saddam Hussein was backed by the Pakistani Islamist party, the Jama'at-i Islami.

In general, Arab declarations about holy war tended to follow the policies of the governments or political parties concerned. The Egyptian *'ulama* approved a statement about the validity of holy war against Iraq on the same lines as the Saudi one. The Sudanese Islamist leader Hasan al-Turabi made a declaration promising holy war in support of Saddam Hussein, although the Sudanese government made no move in the matter. There was some confusion among Algerian Islamists over which side to support in the Gulf War, perhaps because they were receiving financial help from elements in Saudi Arabia. However, some Islamic Salvation Front (FIS) leaders supported Iraq, although this support made no reference to holy war, and it is significant that Abbas Madani of the FIS called for the overthrow of regimes, like that of Kuwait, that clung to colonialist-drawn borders. The Iranian clergy, quite understandably, since it involved former bitter enemies – Muslim and Christian – of the Iranian regime who now fought one another, on the whole avoided making declarations about the religious status of the war

There were elements of propagandist theatre and also of *Realpolitik* about the holy war conflicts of the Gulf War that recall much earlier episodes in Islamic history: Ottoman policies had often involved this sort of posturing, as far back as the sixteenth-century conflicts with the Iranian Safavis. It is much to be doubted whether many of the Muslim combatants took more notice of such things than Christian combatants did of the kind of statements that Western clergy made to them.

When the hesitations, inconsistencies and conflicts that attend the application of the doctrine of holy war of the sword to modern political reality are borne in mind, it can be seen that the modern groups and parties that profess the cluster of doctrines loosely called Islamism are not the components of a single holy war weapon directed against 'the West'. Some Islamist ideologues like Hasan al-Turabi in the Sudan occasionally imply them to be so, as do analysts and journalists in the West, but the proposition engenders more heat than light. In spite of their drawing upon common sources of doctrine and inspiration, both ancient and modern, and in spite also of a degree of interchange of counsel and help between them, or some of them, the individual Islamist groups only make sense in the context of the societies and nations from which they came.

The Muslim Brotherhood was founded in Egypt by Hasan al-Banna in 1928; the Jama'at-i Islami were founded in India by Mawlana Mawdudi in 1941. As a political party the Muslim Brothers have spread very widely beyond the boundaries of Egypt, partly because, unlike the Jama'at-i Islami, they did not have the disadvantage of their activity being mostly in a language (Urdu) not widely spoken outside the Indian subcontinent, partly because they could in a sense ride upon the sentiments of pan-Arabism, even while they opposed it. But the histories of both parties within their native lands are instructive about the directions of modern Islamism, its attitude to holy war, and its relations with the modern territorial state.

There is no special emphasis on *jihad* in the main founding documents of the Muslim Brotherhood. Hasan al-Banna spoke of the charge that might be brought against them, of being revolutionaries, and said that the reply was: 'We are voices for right and for peace ... If you rise against us or stand in the path of our message, then we are permitted by God to defend ourselves against your injustice.' This is an implicitly conservative reply. Like the Jama'at-i Islami, the Muslim Brotherhood wanted both moral renovation and political action. Like the Jama'a, and like the late-nineteenth-century Islamic Benevolent Society, in which Muhammad Abdu had a hand, they offered a modern alternative to the Sufi brotherhoods, that many thought superstitious and lacking in relevance to modern life.

In encouraging a youth movement, and at one stage the wearing of a uniform, the early Muslim Brotherhood may have been influenced by contemporary European fascist movements: but these were superficial matters. Student organizations were and remained important, and the development of social services was critical. There was a hierarchy of branches and cells that, while less effective than that of the radical Islamists of the 1970s and eighties, was the first extension into the Muslim world of European populist party organization. There were explicitly modern parts of the Brotherhood's doctrine. For example, they held that women should be educated and should be allowed into the workplace, provided that what were supposed to be traditional gender distinctions were maintained in the schools and at work.

From the beginning there was an obligation upon members to work for their living, and to contribute to the welfare of those who could not work. This meant a duty to finance the social services – schools, clinics, clubs – that were the foundation of the Brotherhood's popular base. This was to lead to the development of new doctrines of Islamist economic theory. By the end of the Second World War the Brotherhood owned a complex of business enterprises that gave it substantial economic power. The propagandist side of the movement (*da'wa*) could be translated as missionary activity, but this underplays the influence of European examples. The 1930s were, after all, the peak point of the early development of European techniques of propaganda. The Brotherhood exerted considerable influence on Egyptian public opinion until Nasser came to power in Egypt in 1952 and deployed more modern propagandist methods. After this, they had to wait until the Mubarak government relaxed its controls in the 1980s before they could revive something of their old public leverage.

The most problematic part of the Brothers' activity was their relations with government. They did not aim to replace civil government, but to influence it. In this they were extremely successful until the decay of the Egyptian constitutional system after the Second World War. But they were unable to maintain their ambiguous position, in spite of sharing the anti-British nationalism of other parties. After the Wafd constitutional party began to act against them in 1946 they drifted into conspiratorial activity; a minister was murdered, and Hasan al-Banna himself was killed. The ambiguity became even more acute after the revolution of the Free Officers in 1952. The Brotherhood, and especially an able leader called 'Abd al-Qadir 'Auda, were closely associated with the earliest leader of the Free Officers, Muhammad Naguib. In 1954, after the fall of Naguib at the hands of Nasser, and a further murder of a minister, the Brotherhood was proscribed. Its secretary and others, including 'Auda, were executed, and its leader, the 'Supreme Guide', sentenced to life imprisonment.

By the time of the Nasserist proscription in Egypt the Muslim Brotherhood was already important in several other Arab countries. The Syrian branch was founded in Damascus in the 1930s, and attracted members of the traditional *'ulama* families, as well as small traders and some other sectors that represented, after the Ba'th party victory in the sixties, Sunni elements that were opposed to the Alawi rule of Hafiz al-Asad. There was a big repression of the Syrian Muslim Brotherhood after 1979, ending in big military actions at Hama and Aleppo in 1982 and the bloody obliteration of a large part of the Syrian movement.

The Muslim Brotherhood were present in Jordan from the early fifties, and were consequently already established on the West Bank at the time of the Israeli occupation of 1967. In Jordan they were for a long time uneasily tolerated, but they began to take part in constitutional politics in the 1980s, and have become a parliamentary party in the nineties.

The most ambiguous of all the roles played by the Muslim Brotherhood has been in the Gaza Strip. Present, but dormant, when the Israelis occupied the Strip in 1967, at the time of the outbreak of the Intifada resistance to Israel in 1987 they were being encouraged by the Israeli government as a counterweight to the PLO, and financed partly by Brotherhood funds emanating from the Gulf. However, in 1988 the Gaza Muslim Brotherhood gave birth to the Islamist resistance group Hamas, an organization quite distinct from the Brotherhood, but that was formed from it through an initiative that included members of the Gaza *'ulama*. From the beginning Hamas had an important military wing, and the Egyptian Muslim Brotherhood took part in the negotiations with Yasser Arafat that led to a period of co-ordination between Hamas and the PLO.

In the Sudan the Muslim Brotherhood became politically influential when the long-established ruler Jafar Muhammad Nimeiri turned to Islamism to shore up his regime in 1983. The Muslim Brotherhood leader in the Sudan, Hasan al-Turabi, first held office under Nimeiri (who at the end dismissed him and renounced the Brotherhood), and then returned to power with the new military regime of Omar al-Bashir in 1989. Al-Turabi did not carry the whole Sudanese Brotherhood leadership with him on the second occasion, but under Bashir his political influence enormously increased, and he became something like the unofficial associate leader of the regime, or if not that, unquestionably its propaganda chief.

Al-Turabi's organization is not termed the Brotherhood, but the National Islamic Front, and the insertion of the word 'national' is deeply significant. He has heavily emphasized his own version of internationalist Islamism through a series of conferences to which he has invited delegations from all over the Muslim world. But it has been clear that this activity has been intended to benefit specifically Sudanese interests. Al-Turabi is remarkable for the supple way in which he has expressed the Islamist philosophy of the regime, especially to Westerners, and his public emphasis upon the military *jihad* has been small. But it seems probable that *jihad* has been invoked on the governmental side in the civil war in southern Sudan, whether through or without the initiative of al-Turabi is not clear.

In the Gulf the Brotherhood acquired influential and wealthy supporters. The financing given by Gulf Brotherhood members, particularly to social welfare, has been important in Egypt at many times, and in the Israeli-occupied areas after 1967. There has also been extensive financing from Saudi Arabia of Muslim Brotherhood organizations as far afield as Algeria, although Saudi support is denied to the present Sudanese regime.

In its native Egypt the Muslim Brotherhood has had, after the Nasserist proscriptions of the 1950s and sixties, a career almost as chequered as its earlier one. President Sadat decided to reinstate the Brotherhood in Egyptian life in the early 1970s, and it was allowed to rebuild its propaganda and social welfare organizations, and the investments and financial basis that underpinned them. The secret Islamist organization that murdered Sadat in 1981, al-Jama'at al-Islamiyya, was not a Brotherhood one, but was an independent breakaway group of radicals who were dissatisfied with the conservatism of the Brotherhood and the elderly nature of its leadership.

For some time after coming to power, President Mubarak continued cautiously to tolerate, occasionally to encourage, the Muslim Brotherhood as a legal organization. In 1987 the Brotherhood formed a coalition with the Socialist Labour Party and the Liberal Party, and won a substantial number of parliamentary seats. But the deteriorating climate of Egyptian political life in the following period, and the growing violence of the insurrectionary Islamist parties, made it very difficult for the Brotherhood to take much part in a political process that was every year becoming less democratic. The government passed laws to try to stop the growing takeover of the Egyptian professional associations by the Brotherhood.

The government frowned on the Brotherhood, but made spasmodic efforts to treat with it, especially in a dialogue with opposition notables that it conducted in the autumn of 1994. In November 1995, having entered a large number of candidates for the parliamentary elections, the Brotherhood failed to win a single seat in an election that was notorious for fraud and violence. At the same time a considerable number of Muslim Brotherhood leaders, including some who were widely respected in the Egyptian community for their ability and rectitude, were sentenced to long terms of imprisonment for alleged illegal activities. This repression appeared to be ending two decades of government toleration of the Brotherhood, although the situation is unlikely to be made clear in the near future. The Brotherhood refused to give up the game of constitutional politics, and in the new year of 1996 some of them participated with other opposition groups (that included Nasserists and Leftists) in the foundation of a new 'Centre' (*Wast*) party and a new newspaper called 'The Constitution' (*al-Dustur*), a title worthy of a nineteenth-century opposition group.

The history of the Muslim Brotherhood shows that an Islamist doctrine of this sort can lead some people – as it led Sayyid Qutb – to a philosophy that idealizes *jihad*, and that can end in an ideology of violence. When a young Egyptian researcher interviewed a senior member of the Brotherhood in the early 1980s, he told her that the imprisonment and tortures inflicted on many Muslim Brothers during the Nasserist repression had affected them in two different ways. One group accepted that what had happened had been the result of their own moral failures as good Muslims, and had resolved to do better in the spreading of the faith, in *da'wa*. Others felt that those who could inflict such tortures on fellow-Muslims were unbelievers, fit to be charged with and punished for their apostasy.[2]

This was only one of the paths that could lead to political violence. But even after this disaster and persecution, the main organization could still take a pragmatic approach. The later history of the Muslim Brotherhood shows that such a party can perfectly well participate in liberal constitutional politics. A similar story seems to have emerged in Jordan.

The history of Mawlana Abu'l-A'la Mawdudi's Jama'at-i Islami party in Pakistan has some points of contact with that of the Muslim Brotherhood. It too experienced tension between its mission as a religious revivalist movement to recreate the inner life of Muslims and its mission as a political force that had to make all the compromises necessary to survive in political life. Mawdudi survived for a longer period at its helm than al-Banna had done in the Brotherhood, and perhaps as a consequence he ended by adopting a more pragmatic approach than had al-Banna, though no more pragmatic than some of al-Banna's successors. The Jama'at-i Islami was to outlive other contemporary Islamic parties, like the Khaksar (Tahrik-i Khaksar) party.

The first big crisis of the Jama'at-i Islami was a sedition crisis not entirely unlike that of the Muslim Brotherhood after 1946, though the charge of abetting violence was much weaker against Mawdudi than that against Hasan al-Banna. In 1953 Mawdudi was sentenced to death for the part he was supposed to have played in riots against the supposedly heretical Ahmadi sect. This appears to have been an unfair charge, in that he had opposed the participation of his party in sectarian violence of the sort sponsored by another radical Islamic party, the Ahrar (Majlis-i Ahrar-i Islam) party. In the event, the capital sentence against Mawdudi was not carried out and he was released after two years in prison. Gradually, as he became a more experienced politician, Mawdudi's policies became more realistic; he also gave his party a patriotic face during the 1965 and 1971 wars against India.

Under the military authoritarian General Zia ul-Haq, who came to power in 1977 after overthrowing Zulfikar 'Ali Bhutto, the Jama'at-i Islami co-operated with government in a way that recalls the behaviour of the Muslim Brotherhood under Sadat, although the Jama'a distanced themselves from Zia during the last phase of his regime. Since the return of a constitutional regime under Benazir Bhutto in 1988, the Jama'a has pursued more populist, but still constitutional policies. There is no evidence that it has ever plotted a political takeover in Pakistan, nor done anything to build up the kind of conspiratorial organization that would be necessary.

The history of the modern clandestine Islamist groups in Egypt begins under Nasser. But the Nasserist crackdown on the Muslim Brotherhood was so effective that the movement cannot be said to have begun until after the 1967 Arab–Israeli war. The effects of that war are hard to exaggerate. In a few days the whole structure of Nasserist Arabism seemed to collapse, not only in Egypt, but all over the Arab world. There was a violent return of the overwhelming sentiment of *maghlub*, of having suffered defeat at the hands of imperialism, and of having recovered the will to reject Western domination, that had characterized the Islamic world during the first half of the twentieth century. Moreover, the part played by Israel was no longer resented only in the Arab world: anti-Israeli and anti-American feeling came also to characterize the Iranian Shi'a religious activist movements.

The 1978 Camp David agreements between President Sadat of Egypt and Menachem Begin, the Prime Minister of Israel, were seen in the West as the foundation for a future Middle East peace, and they did in fact prove to be the basis for the 1993 Oslo agreements. But they were not so regarded in the Arab world. When the assassin of President Sadat, the army lieutenant Khalid al-Islambuli, came to explain his actions in 1981, he said that he had acted as he did because the *shari'a* (Islamic law) was not applied, because of the peace treaty with the Jews, and because of the arrest of Muslim *'ulama* without justification.

Khalid al-Islambuli was one of those who felt that they had to 'rise up in anger for the sake of God', and to accept martyrdom in this cause if necessary. He belonged to the *jihad* organization connected with Muhammad 'Abd al-Salam Faraj (eventually tried alongside al-Islambuli for the assassination), the author of an influential book called 'The Absent [or unexecuted] Duty' (*al-farida al-ghaiba*), a title that referred to the alleged neglect by Muslims to carry out the full obligations imposed by the duty of *jihad*.

Like all the radical Islamists (including Sayyid Qutb), Faraj thought that an impious ruler who seemed externally to be a practising Muslim could be stigmatized as an unbeliever, and he relied on the writings of a medieval theologian who had thus denounced the Islamicized Mongol rulers during the thirteenth century to assert that this was so. As far as the obligations in an Egyptian context were concerned, the main issue was whether it was correct to describe President Sadat as an infidel or a heretic (*kafar*). That this was accepted by the conspirators is evident, because al-Islambuli said at the trial that he would not have attacked Sadat unless Faraj, who was more learned in Islamic law (*fiqh*) than he, had decided that it was so.

The issue of whether a theological point could be decided without the help of learned *'ulama* was taken seriously by the conspirators, in spite of the absence of a defined priesthood in Islam. It is an issue that has recurred in the later history of Islamist groups. There was a doubt, left undecided at the Sadat murder trial, whether the learned sheikh 'Umar 'Abd al-Rahman, since condemned and imprisoned for involvement in terrorism in the United States, might have given the conspirators a theological opinion about President Sadat's status. 'Abd al-Rahman had before the assassination been pressed urgently by the insurrectionary Islamists to assume their leadership, but he had been prudent in prevaricating about this, perhaps citing his blindness as a reason.

The *jihad* organization that murdered Sadat was the immediate successor to earlier groups with the same purpose, one of which had sprung up in ignorance of the existence of the others. One important group of the sort, al-Jama'at al-Islamiyya, survived it. These groups were highly organized, with a central council and directors in charge of each regional governorate to whom local 'emirs' answered. There was a doctrine current in the movement that it was directed towards an eventual 'popular revolution', a modern and non-Islamic idea that has some point of contact with the ideas of the contemporary Iranian revolution and the Afghan *mujahidin*, although at this early stage there is no evidence of Egyptian contact with either.

The appearance of the violent revolutionary religious groups corresponded with the growth of structural weaknesses in Egyptian society, that cannot merely be ascribed to its growing urbanization, although that was one of the main factors. Under Sadat the policy of economic 'openness' (*infitah*) – a policy pursued in many Arab states – had shifted the balance between public and private elements in the economy to the advantage of the latter, besides re-admitting foreign capital. Problems arose from inflation, and from the attempts to control it, that usually bore down hard on the lower middle classes.

The Egyptian legal system works badly, not so much because it is largely Westernized as because of inefficiency and of a degree of clientelism. The clientele systems that emanated from government have changed, to the advantage of some groups and the disadvantage of others. The traditional social checks and balances in the countryside, and especially the older mediation practices, have decayed. Old tensions, such as those that collected around the Christian Copts, were resharpened: during the Sadat murder trial one of the defendants referred to the Copts as a 'Crusader conspiracy'. The social control once exercised through the *'ulama* has also decayed: one of the victims of extremist assassination in the early eighties was a Grand Mufti.

There had been no real representation granted to Egyptians under the

Nasserist one-party regime, and although its successors very hesitantly moved in the direction of a parliamentary system, and authorized the appearance or reappearance of some parties, they did not succeed in producing a system that gave genuine representation. The practice of Egyptian government was – and is – to consult with the various sects and groups that make up Egyptian society in an informal and occasional manner, in a sort of consultation with the notables that recalls the old Ottoman practices. Because this does not work very well, the state security system operates with a violence equal to that of the conspiratorial groups. Although Egyptian society as a whole continues to be civilized and peaceful, it has become vulnerable to extremist disruption.

The growth of the Egyptian radical Islamist groups occurred at a time of extreme tension in the Islamic world. In the same years as the Iranian revolution there was a violent occupation of the holiest places of Mecca by an armed Islamist group that denounced the corruption of Saudi society. The bloody operation to evict them from the Prophet's Mosque was authorized by the Saudi *'ulama*, who, however, hesitated before agreeing to bloodshed in such a holy place. And 1979 also saw the Russian-sponsored coup in Afghanistan, that gave rise to a decade of Soviet occupation and to an even longer period of civil war, dominated on one side by the Islamist groups.

In 1982 the Israeli invasion of Lebanon, only a few months after Sadat's murder in the preceding year, led to further crises of consciousness in the Islamic world. The military elimination of the PLO in Lebanon was in one sense the final defeat of the old, secular Arab nationalism, that had never recovered from the debacle of the 1967 war with Israel. It also led to the spectacular appearance on the scene of the Lebanese Shi'a community, that had in the past seemed a poor and neglected minority, but that after 1982 gained substantial political advantages. The Israeli invasion of Lebanon also gave Iranian Islamism the chance to exert strong direct influence in the otherwise overwhelmingly Sunni area of geographical Syria.

Since 1982 radical Islamism has advanced by leaps and bounds in various parts of the Arab and Middle Eastern world. Outside Iran, some of its most important aspects could be seen in Afghanistan. The structure and composition of the Islamist parties in Afghanistan was unremarkable: like the rest, their militants tended to be drawn from the lower strata of the more modernized social sectors, and tended to use a modernized, Europeanized vocabulary to describe their aims and methods. They also referred to their leadership as 'intellectuals', a usage that is in Islamist terms Iranian rather than Arab. Their Western historian Oliver Roy has singled out the Afghan Islamists as examples of what he has called the 'lumpenization' of the Islamist intellectuals: he sees them as autodidacts with only the roughest grasp of the religious and ideological material on which their lives and their parties' policies are based.[3] In this they may be said to resemble the rank and file of many modern fundamentalist groups belonging to other religions. But they were important not only in the Afghan context, but in the training they gave to non-Afghan Islamists.

The Afghan experience was especially important, for example, to the Egyptian clandestine Islamist party al-Jama'a al-Islamiyya. One of the al-Jama'a leaders was Ahmed Hasan 'Abdul-Jalil, known as al-Ustaz ('the professor'), who had spent six years in Afghanistan as a *mujahid*. 'Abdul-Jalil was said by the Egyptian security forces to have headed the military wing of al-Jama'a from the spring of 1994. It was claimed that he was killed in the Nubian desert, near Aswan, in November of that year.

Since the mid-1980s al-Jama'at al-Islamiyya has been the principal adversary of the Egyptian government in a covert struggle that has mostly taken place in Upper Egypt. Its head appears to be Amin Muhammad Rabie al-Zawahry (b.1956), a medical doctor who was a member of the *jihad* party at the time of the 1981 plot against Sadat, and who is said to live in exile in Switzerland. Over the past two years there have been pitched battles with the Egyptian security forces in Minya, Asyut, Qena and Sohaj provinces, with up to a score of dead on either side. The rebels have hidden either in the desert or in sugarcane fields, and have launched attacks on foreign visitors in other areas, intended to cripple the Egyptian tourist industry. It is probable that the Jama'a were responsible for the attempt on President Mubarak's life in Addis Ababa in June 1995.

The Lebanese 'party of God', the Hizbullah, although far from immune from local criticism, is accepted by the government and by most parties – save for the most radical Christian Maronites – as serving the cause of national resistance to the Israeli presence in South Lebanon. Hizbullah is not at all a clandestine party, as it is recognized by no fewer than three national governments, including the one on whose soil it operates. Growing out of the Lebanese civil war and the 1982 Israeli invasion, it had from the beginning a close, though not always amicable, relationship with the new Lebanese Shi'a party, Amal. Because of the Syrian quasi-protectorate in the Lebanon and the Syrian patronage exercised over the Lebanese Shi'a factions, it has also had a close relationship with a second national government, the Syrian, besides a less distinct, although probably a closer one with the Iranians. There were some elements in Hizbullah that, because of the multiconfessional Lebanese constitution which excludes a single Islamic form of government, refused to recognize Lebanon as a country, but they appear to have been overborne by a more pragmatic policy.

Although the party was encouraged and financed by the Iranians, the aims and concerns of Hizbullah have been predominantly Lebanese. Members of the group regard as their most important acts the 1983 suicide bombing attacks on American and French troops in their respective embassies, which cost almost three hundred American and sixty French lives, and that Hizbullah believes, with some reason, to have caused the withdrawal of US and French forces from the Lebanon.

Hizbullah is a small, elitist party. Its leaders have always been men of intellectual distinction: in particular Sheikh Muhammad Husein Fadlallah (b.1934 in Najaf, Iraq, where he was theologically trained) is a man with all the suppleness and subtlety of the Shi'a intellectual mullahs. Fadlallah did not go along theologically with some of the main political doctrines of Ayatollah Khomeini, although his tactics accepted the Khomeini line. But, subtle or not, the Hizbullah leadership has always preached the doctrine of martyrdom in the cause of God, and the military consequences of this continue to make themselves felt.

The radical Islamist movement in Algeria has mobilized mass opinion and organized widespread violence on a scale that in recent history is surpassed only by the Iranian revolution. However, in spite of a decade and a half of violence, and in spite of their having come quite near to a constitutional takeover of power in 1991, the Algerian Islamists have still not overcome the authority of the hostile Algerian state. Whether a revolutionary or a negotiated solution will occur in Algeria, or whether widespread armed conflict will continue for a long period, cannot yet be said.

The political activity that preceded Algerian revolutionary Islamism was very restrained compared with the parallel, and far less effective, movements in Tunisia and Morocco. As in Egypt, the Algerian movement grew to a large extent out of the proliferation of 'private' mosques. From the beginning it was treated by its followers as a holy war. Though it had no lack of learned theorists once it had been fairly launched, its early and critical stage as an armed insurrection was due not to an Islamist theorist but to an employee of the national electricity company called Mustafa Bouyali (1940–87), a former FLN militant who in 1982 plotted to kidnap the Algerian Prime Minister, Ben Ahmed Abdelghani. Bouyali was killed by Algerian security forces in 1987.

As in Iran, one of the factors that provoked Algerian popular revolt in the autumn of 1988 was an economic crisis. Unlike Egypt, the Algerian government had persisted with a state-controlled economy far into the 1980s. The country's oil revenues had enabled it to keep up to some extent with economic pressures, and to maintain a certain level of social services, until near the end of the decade. Although the youth unemployment in Algeria was similar to that in Egypt, other social factors were very different. There may, however, be some suspicion in Algeria, where the population is overwhelmingly young, of a literal war of the generations that could be compared with that of Egypt.

Early in 1989 the Algerian government abandoned the formerly one-party system and took the risky course of liberalization, to be achieved through a new constitution that was issued in February of that year. Although religious political parties were still formally forbidden, the Islamic Salvation Front (FIS) was launched in September under the leadership of two religious teachers representing different tendencies in the movement, 'Ali Benhaj (b.1956) and Abbas Madani (b.1931). At the outset its formation was not opposed by the government.

What followed does not give much comfort to people who wish for the peaceful liberalization of one-party regimes, although it does not leave them entirely without hope. At the very end of 1990, although the two main leaders of the FIS had been arrested and imprisoned some six months earlier, the Algerian people went to the polls, and in the first round of what had been intended as a two-round election gave the FIS a national vote roughly double that obtained by the FLN, leaving the strong probability of an absolute FIS majority after the second round of voting. There was, however, no second round. The FLN leadership, until then divided and demoralized, reacted to its electoral defeat by using its continued control of the state apparatus. In the new year of 1991 a coup d'état installed an emergency FLN government, and an armed repression of the FIS was resumed that continues today.

The bloody civil war that followed the 1991 crisis has taken tens of thousands of lives, and continues without the main combatants having managed to reach a compromise. A promising initiative in early 1995 seemed to have won wide support, only to be renounced by the military wing of the FIS as well as by the government. Various talks with the detained FIS leaders have broken down. A variety of new groups, some armed, have come into existence on the Islamist side. The most important has been the Armed Islamic Group (GIA), a descendant of earlier activist groups that has denounced the various attempts at negotiation, although there seemed to be a flash of hope from them in the spring of 1995.

The multi-party presidential election in Algeria at the end of 1995, although boycotted by the FIS and FLN, may have loosened up Algerian politics to the point where compromises are at last possible. Although the sitting incumbent, President Liamine Zeroual, was returned, the participation of the Algerian people seemed to be genuine. An Islamist candidate, Sheikh Mahfoud Nahnah, 'moderate' in the sense that he is connected with the Egyptian Muslim Brotherhood, obtained a quarter of the votes cast.

The nearest parallel in the Islamic world to the Algerian situation, in which Islamist parties seem to be caught up in a cycle of violence from which there is no obvious escape, is an area physically tiny compared with Algeria, but at the centre of world attention, the territories of the Palestine National Authority and the Israeli West Bank.

Hamas, the 'Islamic Resistance Movement', was in its earliest Muslim Brotherhood stages tolerated by the Israeli authorities in the Gaza Strip as a counterweight to the Palestine Liberation Organization. It was liberally subsidized by local and Gulf-state sympathizers, by no means all Palestinians, to set up a network of social services – prayer halls, clinics, libraries, clubs – that gave it a secure foothold in a very deprived area. Its intellectual base was in the mosques and upper educational establishments of the Gaza Strip, and from the beginning it had close support and leadership from the *'ulama*, notably from Sheikh Ahmad Yassin, who has been imprisoned since 1989.

In 1988 Hamas produced a 'Covenant of the Islamic Resistance Movement in Palestine' that in some respects contradicts the Covenant of the PLO, and that has made it difficult for all Hamas members to accept the Palestinian peace process since the Oslo accords of 1993. Hamas is located in the areas that economically and physically bear the worst consequences of Israeli security measures. It enjoys the support of a network of local community and mosque loyalties that are reinforced by its still considerable powers to offer social welfare. It is not invulnerable to pressures that can be imposed by the Palestinian Authority, but its voice will not be easy to silence, although that now seems to be the objective of Arafat's government, the PNA. The belief of its members in the morality of offensive *jihad* and Islamic martyrdom has been only too sadly demonstrated.

A second activist party in the same geographical areas as Hamas, that has also claimed responsibility for terrorist attacks, is the Islamic Jihad Party, led originally by Fathi Shqaqi. Shqaqi was born in Gaza in 1951, and was a medical student in Egypt in 1975–81, a period when he joined the Muslim Brotherhood. He practised briefly as a doctor in Jerusalem. He has said that he started the group in Egypt with Palestinian students he recruited there, and then set it up in Gaza and the occupied territories, originally as the 'Palestinian Islamic Vanguard'. Describing his outlook at that time he told an interviewer: 'As Palestinian students we would discuss Islam and Palestine, but the nationalists forgot Islam, and the traditionalists forgot Palestine.'⁴ Shqaqi, who was a partisan of collaboration with the Islamist government of Iran, and claimed to have met Ayatollah Khomeini on more than one occasion, was assassinated in Malta in October 1995. His successor as leader of the group was Ramadan 'Abdullah Chellah.

To go from the small, desperate world of the deprived Palestinian communities of the West Bank and the PNA to that of the Turkish Islamists is to pass from the prison cells to the light and air of a country that, although not without its ethnic and cultural problems, was still a European power early in the present century. Turkey has its Islamist party, but a narrative that passes from Palestine to Turkey must emphasize the enormous national and cultural differences that can exist between parties that describe themselves as Islamist.

Although the Turkish constitution formally forbids the use of religion for political purposes, there has been an intermittent political presence by an Islamic party operating under various names since 1969. Having failed to get representation in the 1987 parliament as the Welfare Party (*Refah*), it became the largest group in the 1995 parliament. It has formed a coalition with the Motherland Party and entered government, and is now an important force in Turkish politics.

The Welfare Party is not a revolutionary party, and although its language in some ways resembles that used by some Arab Islamist parties, there is no reason to suppose it other than constitutionalist. There is some comparison with the situation of Pakistan in its earlier years, in that the Turkish military on the whole represent a threat to Islamism, as the Pakistani military did in the first years of the republic. Turkish Islamist intellectuals use a very different language to that of Arab Islamists, and the intellectual debate in Turkey is very frequently couched in Western terms, in spite of the theoretical hostility of Turkish Islamists to Western influences. Electorally the Refah party depends on conservative social forces; its political programme was very like that of the conservative Motherland Party. However, the Refah also benefit from a Kurdish vote.

That is not to say that there is no Islamist extremism in Turkey. In July 1993 a meeting of secularist Turkish intellectuals (including a well-known poet from the unpopular Alawi sect) took place in a hotel in Sivas in Anatolia. The building was set alight, leading to the deaths of over sixty persons, including the Turkish publisher of *The Satanic Verses*. There have also been assassinations by very small Islamist groups, that in one instance turned out to have been Kurdish Islamists connected with Iran.

The Turkish and Pakistani examples in particular show that there is no fatal connection between Islamism and extremism, still less between Islamism and terrorism. Under certain social and political circumstances Islamism can lead to terrorism; under others it shows itself as capable as any other strongly held belief of living peaceably in a constitutional system. But there must be a working constitutional system for it to inhabit. In too many places either no such system exists, or it exists only on paper. Perhaps the most interesting example of all is the Pakistani one, where a party set up and launched by the Islamist ideologue Mawlana Mawdudi, whose works have been quoted and cited in many other parts of the Islamic world to justify extremist politics, can in a national context usually pursue a cautious, pragmatic and constitutionalist line. However, the Jama'at-i Islami took part in street demonstrations in Karachi shortly before the fall of the Bhutto government in 1996, and there were unconfirmed reports that some of its members were being sent to camps in Afghanistan for military training.

CHAPTER THIRTEEN

Western Dreams, Memories and Fears

THE EIGHTEENTH-CENTURY ENLIGHTENMENT was, in one respect, an attempt by Western Christians to rethink the history of their religion. The crusades were bound to come off badly in this process, not least because, from a military and political point of view, they had failed. Militant Islam in some ways remained a problem to the statesmen of eighteenth-century Europe, but their Turkish and Barbary Coast policies had little to do with the unfocused aggression of traditional crusading categories. At the end of the eighteenth century the British in India began to regard knowledge of Islam as a tool of colonial policy, and so announced the beginnings of what has come to be known in our own times as 'orientalism'. But before things could turn in this direction, the great anti-clerical debates of the French *Encyclopédistes* and their immediate successors entailed the formation of judgements on the crusades as an aspect of medieval Catholicism.

The judgements were quite incidental to the main eighteenth-century debate about the secular and the sacred, because the crusades were a striking illustration of the possible political and social consequences of clerical power, but did not in themselves enter into its formulation or formation. Eighteenth-century rationalism treated the crusades in an essentially ironic way. The irony was imposed partly because the *philosophes* often paid lip-service to religious orthodoxy, and partly because of the manner in which they treated all history, which to them was the working out in human affairs of the consequences of unchanging human passions and dispositions.

Seen by the *philosophes* as barbaric, the crusades had nevertheless been the vehicle for the importation of a wider culture and of more civilized manners from the Muslim East into Europe. The bigoted Turks had been responsible, through their capture of Constantinople in 1453, for the migration of the knowledge of most of what remained of the ancient

Graeco-Roman learning from Byzantium to Europe. In both cases, fanaticism had been the unwitting reason for European advances in polite learning and customs.

Leaders of Enlightenment opinion, when they pronounced on the crusades, did not stray far from the judgements already passed by the Reformed churches. Rousseau wrote firmly that the crusades were essentially a pagan phenomenon: all holy war was impossible to Christians, there was no such thing as 'Christian troops', and the crusading forces were simply 'the priest's soldiers – citizens of the church, who fought for their spiritual country, that had in some mysterious way been turned into a temporal country'.[1] The ironic mode dominates in this passage also: Rousseau saw the crusades as an example of the trickery that had turned civic duty to the service of priestly interest.

In the mouths of the *philosophes* the expression 'crusader' was not used eulogistically, although in common speech it has continued to be so used down to the present day, as a glance at British newspaper headlines will confirm. I recently heard the ironic use from a Christian Maronite leader in the Lebanon, who deplored the militarism that some Maronite 'crusader' clerics had displayed during the Lebanese civil war.

Voltaire's opinions on the holy wars are not hard to imagine. He treated the wars of the biblical Joshua as examples of primitive religious hypocrisy and aggression, quoting the German Hebraist Fabricius: 'What would you say if a Norwegian came into Germany with a few hundred compatriots and said to the Germans – "Four hundred years ago one of our people, a potter's son, travelled near Vienna. So Austria belongs to us, and we are going to massacre its inhabitants in the Lord's name!"?' However, Joshua, Voltaire mockingly added, lived in a different age, and could not be judged by eighteenth-century morality. Therefore 'One must humble oneself here before the dispositions of divine Providence, who punished the sins of the Canaanite kings by the sword of Joshua.'[2] It is not surprising, he continued, that the neighbouring peoples of Palestine failed to notice that the Jews were the sacred instruments of divine vengeance, besides being the means of the future salvation of the human race, and instead considered them to be abominable brigands. These are examples of the Voltairean technique of indirect and rather snide attacks upon clericalism.

When Voltaire came to the First Crusade, he took a line that has reappeared in enlightened historians ever since, from Gibbon in his own century to Steven Runciman in ours. The complaints of the returning pilgrims (particularly those of Peter the Hermit) about their treatment by the

Muslims in Palestine had no foundation: Christian and Muslim pilgrims visited their holy places in Jerusalem, and were the main support of the local economy. They paid minor dues to the local emir and the keepers of the shrines, and that was all there was to the matter.

As to the motives of the crusade, Voltaire was as trenchant as might be expected. He ascribed the migratory crusading movement to religion, avarice and vexation of spirit (*inquiétude*). Like his successors of like mind, he singled out the civilized chronicle of the daughter of the Byzantine Emperor of Constantinople, Anna Comnena, as the preferable literary source for the judgement of the leaders of the First Crusade. He complained that most historians (meaning the clericalist historians) of the crusade had depicted Anna's father Alexis Comnenus as treacherous, because of his treatment of the Frankish leaders. Whereas, Voltaire wrote, 'any disinterested person would have called him wise and magnificent';[3] and the Emperor Alexis had been firm with the crusaders because he did not wish to become the slave of a dangerous, armed multitude.

The entry under 'Crusades' in the 1779 *Encyclopédie* of Diderot and d'Alembert took the expected Voltairean line. The pilgrims returning to Europe from Palestine had complained about the misfortunes and the servitude under the Turks experienced by their brothers in the Eastern churches. They were for a long time rightly disregarded: it was not easy to convince the peoples and the rulers in the West that intervention in this distant country was in their true interests. But a historical point arrived at which giddiness of judgement (*le vertige*) was transferred from the hot head of a pilgrim (Peter the Hermit) to the head of the ambitious and scheming (*politique*) Pope Urban II. In this way the inhabitants of one part of the world were led to travel to the unhappy little country of Palestine, in order to cut the throats of the inhabitants and to get control of a bit of rock (the Temple Mount in Jerusalem) that was not worth a drop of bloodshed. All this in spite of the fact that the Christians could have worshipped the holy places in the spirit, from either far or near, and that the physical possession of these places was unnecessary to the honour of their religion.

The *Encyclopédie* put the occurrence of the First Crusade at that particular historical point (a question that has bothered historians ever since) down to the self-interest of the popes and some of the European sovereigns, Christian hatred of Muslims, the ignorance of the laity, the authority of the clergy and the cupidity of the monastic orders. Guilty laymen charged with crimes thought that by going on crusade they could purge their offences by washing themselves in infidel blood. Finally, the article singled out the 'disorderly' passion of the knightly classes for war, and the political need for a foreign diversion that would suspend for a time the long-standing internal broils of that period.

These judgements tended to treat eleventh-century rulers as though they belonged to the eighteenth, and, also in the manner of their time, to deplore the unruly conduct of the feudal nobles. Their anti-clericalism is often crude, but their point of view is not negligible, even if they do not make much attempt at historical sympathy. For example, the eighteenth-century doctrine of countervailing passions, of compensating for the evil effects of one passion by utilizing another, might have led the *Encyclopédistes* to sympathize with St Bernard, who maintained that the taste for robberies and murders common to the knightly class was being sensibly diverted to the pious activities of the crusade.

The Enlightenment witnessed one basic change in the attitude of cultivated Europeans to Islam. People who could accept the idea of dispassionate enquiry into social and religious matters abandoned the notion of Islam as a religion diabolically different from and opposed to Christianity. The first elements of what in the twentieth century has been called 'sympathy for alien concepts' were beginning to appear in the way people regarded other cultures and civilizations. That did not mean the abolition of religious prejudice, far from it. But it meant that the historian Edward Gibbon (1737–94) could treat Muhammad as a religious teacher to be compared with Jewish and Christian religious teachers, and the Islamic Empire as one to be compared with the Roman Empire.

In one way the Islamic Empires presented Gibbon with a difficult problem, since their occurrence testified to the growth of a dominion as powerful, or at least as formidable in dimensions, as that of Rome. Gibbon had less trouble in conceding to the Arabs a literary and scientific culture far superior to that of contemporary Frankish Europe. He complained – it was a complaint to be endlessly repeated down to our own times – that 'oriental despotism' had prevented the Arabs from asserting the principles of civil and religious freedom that they could have found in the Greek and Latin texts in their possession. But the implication that a new civilization had grown so quickly from the operations of a bigoted religion must have been a worrying one to a writer who had been concerned to illustrate the Christian Middle Ages as having been the 'triumph of barbarism and religion'.

One way of dealing with this problem was to represent Islam as having been less bigoted than it was commonly said to have been. There was some assistance in taking this line from earlier writers like the English translator of the Qur'an George Sale (c.1697–1736), who had emphasized the qualities of integrity, intelligence and good sense that were to be found in Muhammad, and who had also made comparisons between Christian, Jewish and Muslim doctrines of holy war that were to the advantage of Islam and to the disadvantage of Christianity:

> The Jews, indeed, had a divine commission, extensive and explicit enough, to attack, subdue and destroy the enemies of their religion; and Mohammed pretended to have received one in favour of himself and his Moslems, in terms equally plain and full; and therefore it is no wonder that they should act consistently with their avowed principles; but that Christians should teach and practise a doctrine so opposite to the temper and whole tenor of the Gospel, seems very strange; and yet the latter have carried matters further, and shown a more violent spirit of intolerance, than either of the former.[4]

This swingeing denunciation of Christian bigotry would not have been unacceptable to Gibbon.

Like Voltaire and the *Encyclopédistes*, Gibbon disapproved of holy war. In a not unfriendly examination of the life of Muhammad, he made a distinction, the same that many have made since his time, between the Muhammad who preached unavailingly at Mecca and the Muhammad who led armies from Medina.

> In the free society of the Arabs, the duties of subject and citizen imposed a feeble restraint; and Mahomet, in the exercise of a peaceful and benevolent mission, had been despoiled and banished by the injustice of his countrymen. The choice of an independent people [at Medina] had exalted the fugitive of Mecca to the rank of a sovereign; and he was invested with the just prerogative of forming alliances and of waging offensive or defensive war. The imperfection of human rights was supplied and armed by the plenitude of divine power; the prophet of Medina assumed, in his new revelations, a fiercer and more sanguinary tone, which proves that his former moderation was the effect of weakness: the means of persuasion had been tried, the season of forbearance was elapsed, and he was now commanded to propagate his religion by the sword,

to destroy the monuments of idolatry, and, without regarding the sanctity of days and months, to pursue the unbelieving nations of the earth. The same bloody precepts, so repeatedly inculcated in the Koran, are ascribed by the author to the Pentateuch and the Gospel.[5]

Gibbon declined to accept the notion that Muhammad took the idea of holy war to any degree from the Gospel, no matter the 'intolerant zeal of princes and bishops, who have disgraced the name of his [Christ's] disciples'. But 'the military laws of the Hebrews are still more rigid than those of the Arabian legislator'. Like his enlightened predecessors, Gibbon cited Deuteronomy and Joshua with distaste and repulsion. He considered the comparison between the Jewish scriptures and those of Muhammad to be in the latter's favour.

> The fair option of friendship, or submission, or battle, was proposed to the enemies of Mahomet. If they professed the creed of Islam, they were to be admitted to all the temporal and spiritual benefits of his primitive disciples, and marched under the same banner to extend the religion which they had embraced. The clemency of the prophet was decided by his interest, yet he seldom trampled on a prostrate enemy; and he seems to promise that, on the payment of a tribute, the least guilty of his unbelieving subjects might be indulged in their worship, or at least in their imperfect faith.

So Gibbon noticed, and approved, the institution of a tolerated and protected status in the Islamic state for the *dhimmis*, the Christians and Jews who had submitted and agreed to pay the Muslims a capitation tax. It may be assumed that he knew that this was not merely an institution of the Prophet's day, but the normal guarantee of a protected status for Jews and Christians in the contemporary Ottoman Empire.

Gibbon was not the first modern historian to approach the topic of holy wars, which, as he said, have been 'waged in every climate of the globe, from Egypt to Livonia, and from Peru to Hindostan', and that 'require the support of some more general and flexible tenet' than mere religious mystery and miracle. He noted three general characteristics in the arguments of the Christians of the time in favour of the crusades: they 'seemed to insist on the right of natural and religious defence, their peculiar title to the Holy Land, and the impiety of their pagan and Mahometan foes'.

Gibbon was inclined to sympathize with the decision to launch the First Crusade, as the prosecution of a just war. But he had doubts about what was termed by later just war theorists the question of proportion.

> The right of a just defence may fairly include our civil and spiritual allies [meaning the Eastern Orthodox Church]: it depends on the existence of danger; and that danger must be estimated by the twofold consideration of the malice and power of our enemies. A pernicious tenet has been imputed to the Mahometans, the duty of *extirpating* all other religions by the sword. This charge of ignorance and bigotry is refuted by the Koran, by the history of the Musulman conquerors, and by their public and legal toleration of the Christian worship. But it cannot be denied that the Oriental churches are [the use of the present tense is noteworthy] depressed under their iron yoke; that, in peace and war, they assert a divine and indefeasible aim of universal empire; and that, in their orthodox creed, the unbelieving nations are continually threatened with the loss of religion or liberty.[6]

Gibbon thought that a just war waged in favour of the oriental Christians was reasonable, not least because of the vital interest the Latins had in supporting Constantinople against Islam as the most important barrier of the West. So he believed there was a political interest as well as a religious argument for intervening against the Muslim power, although he wished that this could have been accomplished by offering the Greeks a 'moderate succour' of the kind that Alexis Comnenus had sent to ask for from the Papal Council of Piacenza, thus avoiding the despatch of 'innumerable hosts' to 'remote operations' that 'overwhelmed Asia and depopulated Europe'. It may be that the problems of Christians in the contemporary Ottoman Empire were not entirely absent from Gibbon's mind when he wrote this, even if he believed in the 'fading confidence' of the modern Turks.

Gibbon felt he could justify the offer of help to the Eastern Christians by those of the West, but he found it impossible on the grounds of a just war to agree with the conquest of Palestine, that 'could add nothing to the strength or safety of the Latins; and fanaticism alone could pretend to justify the conquest of that distant and narrow province'. Yet he noticed the medieval doctrine that grace is 'the sole fountain of dominion as well as of mercy'. He noticed, too, that the barbarians of Germany had seized the western provinces of the Roman Empire at the same time that the barbarians of Arabia had seized many of the eastern ones. The Christian Franks regarded their conquests from Rome as having been legitimated by the passage of time, but, in common with the Byzantine Christians, they held that the Muslim conquests had not been legitimated by the same right of prescription, and so could be rightly recovered. It is doubtful if Gibbon's argument, that he took from the clerical church historian Fleury, does justice here to the medieval argument that Palestine was 'the patrimony of the crucified one' – no doubt because it was an argument that he ascribed to 'fanaticism'.

It would be wrong to suppose that the anti-clericalism of the Enlightenment destroyed the common ideas of what we may think of as the glamour and romance of the crusades. These persisted in many ways. One of the most striking was their revival in Freemasonry, a movement that may at first glance appear to have been one of the most typical products of eighteenth-century theism and rationalism, that supplied a means to crusading chivalry to secure a sort of spurious modern afterlife.

It is easy to forget that the fashion for the gothic and the bizarre was just as notable a feature of the eighteenth century as was the scepticism of the Enlightenment. Far from being cool and enlightened doubters, many eighteenth-century people were credulous in the extreme, as David Hume never tired of remarking. This was a society in which astrologers were said to have been as common as bakers. Moreover, at this time chivalrous rank was being dispensed by the eighteenth-century monarchs, those 'fountains of honour', to large numbers of prospering freemen who either bought the rank from the crown or received it (as is still said in Britain) for 'political services'. Since demand exceeded supply, the idea of a back way to some sort of chivalrous status was very attractive.

Such a route was offered by some of the Masonic lodges. The fashion for a new Freemason chivalry arose from the activity of Scottish Freemasons in France during the fourth and fifth decades of the century. These mission-aries, headed by a Jacobite Mason with literary connections called the Chevalier Ramsay, succeeded in convincing some of the French noble lodges that 'our ancestors, the Crusaders, who had come from all parts of Christendom to the Holy Land, wanted to group persons from every nation in a single, spiritual confraternity'.[7] According to them, the headquarters of this medieval movement had been in England and Scotland, where the crusading Knights of St John of Jerusalem had formed a connection with the Masonic lodges.

The Knights of St John proved to be a not very happy relationship for the Freemasons, since they were still very much in existence in Malta and elsewhere, treasuring their chivalrous and noble status, and no doubt not at all anxious to be connected with a movement that was widely held to be anti-Catholic (although it counted large numbers of priests in its ranks), and that seemed to be unavoidably descended from humble stoneworkers.

However, there was a second military order of knights, the Knights Templar, who had been conveniently dealt with as heretics by the French and papal authorities at the beginning of the fourteenth century, and whose order had been dissolved in disgrace in 1312. There were no existing Templars to complain when in the mid-eighteenth century the Masonic lodges began to pretend that a hidden, occult wisdom had passed down a chain of medieval Templar knights, and that these had at the time of their disgrace and dissolution passed the vital secrets on to a fresh line of secret Templars, who took refuge in medieval Scotland.

From these flimsy beginnings the Freemasons invented a new chivalry of Masonic Templar knights, who wore 'crusader' garb, bore chivalrous titles and acted out complex rites with theosophical meanings. The new chivalrous orders were patronized in France, and later in England, but were most powerful in Germany, where they were spread in some instances by colourful charlatans whose main object was profit. They were taken up by many of the German princes, and became the object of strange debates. On one extraordinary occasion, two rival groups of Masonic Templar knights actually confronted one another in full medieval war-gear in a Thuringian castle, and threatened battle, although none actually took place. The Templar knights were supposed to have obtained some political importance, although it is doubtful that they really possessed any.

There is a certain religious and social interest to these Masonic Templars, who have survived into our own day. But in their eighteenth-century context they testify to the hold that the crusades continued to exercise over men's imaginations, and to the failure of the *philosophes* to convince people that the crusades had been an empty manifestation of medieval religious fanaticism. At the time of the French Revolution the Masonic Templars were subjected to a further transformation, when part of the clerical party convinced itself that the modern Templars were part of a centuries-old conspiracy, one medieval manifestation of which had been the Isma'ili organization of Assassins. They claimed that the neo-Templars had organized the French Revolution in order to avenge the persecution of the medieval Templars by the Capetian monarchy.

A last attempt at giving the phantasmal Masonic crusader knights a place in modern political life was made by the British Freemason Admiral Sir William Sydney Smith (1764–1840), who after the peace of 1815 tried to launch a scheme by which a new order of Freemason-inspired crusader knights would replace the historic Order of St John of Jerusalem in Malta, that since the Napoleonic War had been British-controlled, and that would assume the duty of suppressing the Barbary pirates and the slavers in the Mediterranean. Nothing came of this initiative, and the suppression of the pirates was left as a duty that could be taken up by the French government as an excuse for the occupation of Algiers.

The crusades were far too deeply etched upon the myths and memories of early modern culture to be expunged by a little historical scepticism. In most European literatures they had left a notable mark. In the works of the Italian poets Ariosto and Tasso, they were part of a patrimony that was European and not merely Italian. When the romantic conservative writer François René de Chateaubriand (1768–1848) visited Jerusalem in 1806, he cited Tasso's *Gerusalemme Liberata* at every turn of the road.

Through the influence of these Italian writers a notable body of art grew up that adopted the crusades as a permanent artistic theme. Tasso's stories, that were once required reading for educated Europeans, are now forgotten outside Italy. So today we need a learned note to remind us that Poussin's rather grim picture *Rinaldo and Armida* (in the Dulwich Gallery), and Tiepolo's charming but powerful treatment of the same subject (now in Chicago), show the attempted seduction of a crusading hero by a beautiful Saracen spy. There is a gap of a century between the two pictures, and the comparison shows how far the romanticization of the crusades had gone by the mid-eighteenth century. The neo-Gothic wave, and the Romantic wave after it, only confirmed the crusades as an era for romantic and nostalgic dreams. Such dreams could be restrained and disciplined in their artistic expression, as was the play *Nathan the Wise* (1779) by the German dramatist and critic Gotthold Ephraim Lessing, that was set in crusading Jerusalem, and that treated crusaders, Saracens and Jews in an equally balanced way.

The period between the French Revolution and the Napoleonic defeat in 1815 saw the greatest wars that Europe had known for many centuries.

After Waterloo the medieval idea of battle as a kind of judgement of God became widespread in Europe. William Wordsworth, in his 1815 'Ode', came very near to accepting a modernized doctrine of holy war:

> Nor will the God of peace and love
> Such martial service disapprove.
> He guides the pestilence – the cloud
> Of locusts travels on his breath . . .
>
> But thy most dreaded instrument
> In working out a pure intent,
> Is Man – arrayed for mutual slaughter,
> – Yea, carnage is thy daughter!

Not surprisingly, Wordsworth subsequently felt theological doubts about the stanza just quoted, and expunged it from later editions. But in the year of Waterloo, it did not seem excessive. In the following year Wordsworth celebrated the anniversary of the raising of the siege of Vienna in 1683 by the Polish King John Sobieski in terms of extravagant rejoicing, if in rather flat and conventional phraseology.

> Chant the Deliverer's praise in every tongue!
> The Cross shall spread, the Crescent hath waxed dim;
> He conquering, as in joyful Heaven is sung,
> HE CONQUERING THROUGH GOD,
> AND GOD BY HIM.

The otiose capitalization announced a Wordsworth whose poetry was already beginning to suffer from a sort of premature senility. But the sentiments were not unacceptable in his time.

The European image of the Islamic East had been brusquely changed by the irruption of Western power when Napoleon invaded Ottoman Egypt in 1798. This was only one of the military ventures that were bringing European armies into the heart of the Islamic lands: British power in Muslim India was already half a century old. But the symbolic importance of Napoleon's rule in Egypt was much greater, and although it only lasted two or three years, its resonance in France was equal to that of the conquest of India in Britain. As in many other things, Napoleon was repeating the exploits of the medieval French kings in a modern way: it was hard for a Frenchman to think of Napoleon in Egypt without recalling the crusade of St Louis in Egypt.

Western iconographies of the East at once reflected the new political realities. Brief as French rule in Egypt was, it had time to set up new systems of academic enquiry. The frontispiece to the great *Description de l'Egypte* (that was published only after Napoleon's death) showed the immense Pharaonic monuments with French troops and their arms and followers everywhere around them, and Arabs grouped as mere adjuncts to the picture, looking rather like the fever-stricken Italian peasants whom the Italian engraver Piranesi showed beside his Roman ruins.

Chateaubriand travelled in Palestine and Egypt in 1806, and set a new pattern for travel accounts of oriental lands – which he called barbaric and anarchic – that was consciously reactionary. He denounced the *philosophes* of the preceding century for their 'ignorance and injustice' in having represented the crusades in such a poor light. Far from being acts of folly, as the eighteenth century had termed them, the crusades were rightful reprisals for the earlier Muslim aggressions in Christian Europe. They were concerned not merely with freeing the Holy Sepulchre from Muslim rule, but with the main issue of political power. Chateaubriand continued in words that had no obvious application to 1099, but that he must have thought applicable to 1806. Should Islam prevail, that was the enemy of civilization, hospitable to despotism and slavery? Or the Christian faith, that had revived antique wisdom in the modern world, and that had abolished slavery? Should Islam conquer, that stood for persecution and conquest, or the Gospel that preaches toleration and peace?[8]

These were the words of a writer who was a notable government propagandist both under Napoleon and under the subsequent Restoration. It is true that Napoleon had talked a great deal about toleration and peace when he had established himself in Egypt, but his practice of these virtues had not been notable while his armies were effecting the conquest.

The principles that Chateaubriand had laid down began to be put into practice by other, lesser, French propagandists. The royalist journalist Joseph Michaud (1767–1839) published a 'History of the Crusades' in 1808 that was intended to correct the rationalist bias of earlier histories, and to push the view of the crusades in the direction indicated by Chateaubriand. The book was a great publishing success, but it suffered from the method by which Michaud wrote it. He was a compiler rather than a historian, and his greatest achievement was a huge, collectively written 'Universal Biography'. He employed a plagiaristic, scissors-and-paste method of writing history, borrowing a largely Voltairean phraseology from the writers he copied. This, according to his biographer and main collaborator Poujoulat, contradicted the book's originally conservative intention, and was criticized by some clerical and royalist readers.[9]

Michaud had the happy idea of securing royal finance to enable him to make a an elaborate tourist trip in the Middle East in 1830–1, to collect material for a revised and ideologically purified edition. The resulting book, *Correspondance d'Orient 1830–1*, published two years after his death in 1839, was a great success. It came out at a critical point of the occupation of Algeria under the July Monarchy that had come to power in 1830, and at a time when Louis Philippe's government had also begun to take a lively interest in Egypt and Syria.

Predictably, Michaud's account of his trip to Jerusalem sounded the crusading trumpets. He deplored the condition of neglect and isolation in which modern Christendom had left Jerusalem (the tone is not far from Chateaubriand's account of his own visit in 1806). The eighteenth-century *philosophes* had made people forget the roads of Sion. Great learned works were written on Pharaonic Egypt, but not a line on Jerusalem, formerly thought to be the earth's centre, but that had been shunned, and left, as it were, in an obscure corner of the world. In a passage that echoed Edgar Quinet, whose *La Génie des religions* was published in 1832, Michaud called for a new 'crusade of philosophy and knowledge' that would link East and West for ever together.

Michaud especially regretted that when Napoleon's army had marched from Egypt to the siege of Acre in 1799, and a French force as large as that of the old French crusaders had entered Palestine, the name of Jerusalem had not even been mentioned.[10] When French diplomacy was busying itself with the affairs of Muhammad Ali's rule in Egypt, and had opposed the action taken by the other European powers to force his deputy Ibrahim to evacuate Syria – that included Palestine – these matters had become topical.

Other, more distinguished writers than Michaud published travel books on the East that had the same romantic-conservative tendency, and contained the same endorsement of the crusades. Alphonse de Lamartine (1790–1869), a poet and politician whose career was a sort of rerun of that of Chateaubriand, told his readers how he had seen the ruins of Chateau Pélerin near Mount Carmel, large as a village, where six hundred years earlier St Louis and the Templar Grand Master had held the infant Count d'Alençon at the font.

The treatment of the crusading theme was not dissimilar in German-speaking lands. The Austrian orientalist Joseph von Hammer-Purgstall

(1774–1856), who was one of the advisers to Metternich's Austrian chancery on Ottoman affairs, had a sort of double personality. As a bureaucrat, and also as the austere historian of the wars and governments of the Ottoman Turks, he was a man of practical advice and a dry-as-dust compiler of chronicles. But he was also a wildly romantic visionary, who thought that the medieval Templars had been double agents for the Shi'a Isma'ili sect, and the inheritors of a seditious doctrine that had come down from the very early Christian heretics, and had been instrumental in engineering the French Revolution. His opinion on holy war as practised by the Muslims of his times was trenchant: he quoted with approval the opinion of the contemporary English adventurer Stamford Raffles: 'The Arab Sheikhs and Seyyads, whatever doctrines they failed to inculcate, did not neglect the propagation of one, the merit of plundering and massacring the infidels; an abominable one, which has tended more than all the rest of the Alcoran, to the propagation of this robber-religion.'[11]

Romantic treatment of the crusades was one of the standard literary themes in French, English and German literature in the early nineteenth century. Sir Walter Scott published *Ivanhoe* in 1819, and *The Talisman* in 1825. In his introduction to the latter he modestly disclaimed special knowledge of the East, and observed that by the time he wrote it 'the Eastern themes had been already so successfully handled by those who were acknowledged to be masters of their craft' that he had been diffident about attempting it. In this new crusading literature eighteenth-century scepticism about the motives and methods of the crusaders had been miraculously sponged away.

The dignity and moral authenticity of the crusading idea was resoundingly confirmed by Scott and the other romantics in a manner that now, almost two centuries later, appears to be culturally irreversible. Crusading behaviour that in another context would have been stigmatized – particularly by the Protestants – as religious fanaticism was condoned. The connection between the crusading movement and the practice of granting papal indulgences, that had seemed so important to the reformers of three centuries earlier, was forgotten. It was to be discussed by the technical historians later in the nineteenth century, but by that time there was a strong trend towards taking such discussions out of the orbit of religious controversy.

By the early nineteenth century the religious strictures passed upon crusading by the sixteenth-century reformers had been reversed in the Protestant countries, and the later strictures of the *philosophes* much modified in the Catholic ones. This occurred partly because of the neo-Gothic revival and the nostalgia for chivalry, partly because the new colonial policies of the great powers in the Islamic countries had emphasized the oriental picturesque in an unreflective way. The Orient was treated as a sort of touristic spectacle that illustrated, as Scott remarked, 'the ancient doctrines, history and manners of the Eastern countries, in which we are probably to look for the cradle of mankind'. In such a literary ambience, unforgettably analyzed by Edward Said in his *Orientalism* (1978), Scott's sentimental treatment of Saladin and the crusading heroes swept all the holy war issues under an ample oriental carpet.

However, in the visual arts the greatest of all romantic treatments of the crusades preserved, interestingly, the moral reservations of the *philosophes* about the motives of the crusaders. *The Capture of Constantinople* of Delacroix (1798–1863) showed the taking of the city by the Fourth Crusade in 1204, in a way that made it clear that the centre of civilization was being sacked and looted by the barbarians. Delacroix had an awareness of the fragility of civilized life that was emphasized by the late Kenneth Clark, who shared it. Another of his greatest paintings, *The Massacre of Scios*, showed the maltreatment of the Greeks of his own time by the Ottoman Turk rulers.

As the colonial idea took hold in nineteenth-century Europe, people began to wonder whether the medieval settlements in the holy land could not be looked upon as precursors of modern colonialism. The idea was especially attractive in France, where in mid-century crusading studies could get the political support necessary to sponsor new editions of the main historical sources for the crusading texts, including translations of sections of selected Arabic and Armenian sources. These have been the basic editions on which scholars have worked on crusading history ever since, although some have been superseded.

In the mid-nineteenth century historical scholars began to accept the doctrine that all sources must be studied in critical editions in their original languages. German scholars began to turn their attention to the crusading sources, and Heinrich von Sybel (1817–95), one of the best-known medievalists of his generation, made his name with a study of the sources for the First Crusade which showed that Peter the Hermit, who had been universally thought until then to have travelled to Jerusalem before 1095, and to have started the agitation for an armed pilgrimage to the holy land on his return to Europe, was very unlikely to have done so. But, very surprisingly, the doctrine that the sources must be read in the original tongue was never, and still never has been, generally applied in the learned world to the Arabic and other oriental sources for the history of the crusades. This does not mean that all crusading historians have been ignorant of oriental languages; there have been immensely distinguished exceptions. But, at all events until very recently indeed, they have remained in a minority.

The only plausible explanation for the nineteenth-century ring-fencing of crusading history in this manner is that it was thought of as resembling a branch of colonial history, that concerned the history of the colonizing nations and not that of the colonized. Academic habits played a part in this. Once the practice had been established, and crusading history was habitually studied outside the 'Oriental Studies' faculties in European and North American universities, the ideological reasons why this was so were never re-examined.

That this was never seriously criticized requires explanation. Even from the point of view of orthodox historical treatment of texts, it must always have seemed odd. The anomalous practice of 'doing history in translation' is usually reserved in modern universities for students of limited abilities; that it should be allowed to distinguished professors reflects deep-seated attitudes that concern the relationships between cultures. In effect it is a case in which the now almost archaic genre of books with titles such as 'A History of the British Empire', 'Histoire de la Colonisation Française', and so forth, written entirely from the point of the view of the ruling power, has been translated into a religious category, and preserved into the second half of the twentieth century.

That many nineteenth-century historians associated crusading history with colonial history is undoubted. The most explicit was the writer and oriental traveller Emmanuel Rey, who in 1883, at the height of the colonial frenzy, entitled his work on crusading history 'The Frankish Colonies in Syria in the Twelfth and Thirteenth Centuries'. Rey claimed that the political organization brought by the Franks to Syria was the result of a consciously premeditated movement by colonizers who had come to the East with that intent, and that the crusade had not been the spontaneous religious event that it was often claimed to be.[12]

The great German historian Leopold von Ranke (1795–1886), who in 1824 in his first book, on the history of the Latin and Teutonic peoples, had identified the crusading spirit as the impulse behind colonization, was equally explicit at the end of his life, in the early 1880s, when in his *Weltgeschichte* ('World History') he referred to the need after the military disasters in Palestine of 1187 to bring reinforcements to defend 'such a formerly flourishing colony' from extinction.[13] In exactly the same period another, younger German historian, Bernhard Kugler (1837–98), remarked on the Islamization of previously Hellenized lands by the Turks, and added that 'only from 1683 [the Siege of Vienna] has the fear [of Turkish aggression] abated itself; only very recently has Western cultural superiority asserted itself.'[14]

The influence of French policies in the Near East over French crusading historians is also clear. Nineteenth-century French writers suggested, for example, that Charlemagne had at the beginning of the ninth century established a so-called protectorate over the Latin churches located in Jerusalem. There had, indeed, been diplomatic contact between Charlemagne and the Caliph Harun al-Rashid, who may even have sent the Western ruler a banner and the keys of the churches in Jerusalem. But this was one of many cases in which the Muslim concept of protection (*aman*) was misunderstood by nineteenth- and twentieth-century Americans and Europeans as a grant of sovereign rights.[15]

In the twentieth century the idea of the crusading states in the holy land being a form of medieval colonization, anticipating and equivalent to the nineteenth- and twentieth-century colonial forms, has been revived. This position was notably taken, though in a spirit that was uncritical of colonialism, by the Israeli historian Joshua Prawer, who in 1972 entitled the English version of his book *The Latin Kingdom of Jerusalem: European Colonisation in the Middle Ages*. This is a debatable idea, as I have argued above. But it has also been taken up by the distinguished French historian Michel Balard in a series of books and articles. The political implications of this view are that the European presence in the Near East has a history of systematic exploitation and domination that can be traced from the Middle Ages to the present day.

Thus crusading history has not been politically neutral. In the nineteenth century the issues that concerned it were not primarily colonial, but rather confessional. The deep rift running through the writing of nineteenth-century history was between Catholic and Protestant, although some great figures like the Anglo-German Lord Acton managed to span the divide. When Paul Riant, one of the founding fathers of modern crusading studies, founded the *Archives de l'Orient Latin* in 1881, he was consciously launching an institution that hoped to provide a Catholic counterbalance to the German Protestant expertise in the evaluation of the historical sources.

But the debates about crusading history did not divide the Catholics from the Protestants and the freethinkers in the same way as some other issues did in the period of the greatest nineteenth-century tension between them. The concept of Christendom still unites the West in the same manner that it to some extent united it ideologically against the Ottomans in the seventeenth century, and this seems to have been just as true in the more recent period as it was a century ago.

While it would be an exaggeration to describe the emphasis of crusading history in the past century as partisan, the decision by most writers engaged in it to take a Western point of view has had its effect. The late Kenneth Setton, one of the main inspirations and editors of the Wisconsin History of the Crusades, was a man of almost religious devotion to the principle of historical detachment; yet even he could write of the late fifteenth century that 'the Christians of Greece and the Balkans were entering the long night of Turkish domination', or, of Florentine collaboration with the Turks in the same period, that 'The historian of Italy may find it sad to note that through the years when Venice fought, however unwillingly, for the Christian cause in Greece and the Aegean, the Florentines had been receiving such favours from the Porte as to make them "the sultan's most faithful and obedient sons".'[16]

In their treatment of the later crusades, Western historians have tended to fasten upon the question of whether the supposedly declining enthusiasm for the crusades in the later Middle Ages was as important in the weak resistance offered by the Christians to the Ottomans as has commonly been represented. There is inevitably a note of moral judgement in this enquiry, as is evident in the citation from Kenneth Setton above. It is a matter that might be described, in Muslim terms, as one of 'the unfulfilled duty'. The waging of holy war is in the last analysis a religious duty, and tepidity in supporting the holy war can only be a religious failing. It is extremely hard for the historian of the crusade to avoid this moral dilemma, because as soon as war with the Ottomans is removed from its crusading context and placed in a national or a purely governmental one, it ceases to concern the crusading historian directly. The matter would be different if the historian was concerned with the general question of the relations between Christian and Muslim states.

In popular memory the crusade has in Christian countries kept all its over-tones of right and justice. The *Song of Roland* said before the First Crusade ever left for Palestine that 'pagans are wrong and Christians are right'. Spenser said under Queen Elizabeth I that in the combat between the

Saracen and the Red Cross knight, 'th'one for wrong, the other strives for right'. Not much has changed since then.

It might be said that in Muslim countries *jihad* has kept its moral meaning in the same way. But the parallel is not exact. *Jihad* has a moral meaning that is quite independent of holy war of the sword, and crusade has not. I remember my surprise on finding Christian Lebanese males who were called Jihad. But the persistence of crusade as a eulogistic term, in societies whose Christian leaders have all long ago theoretically distanced the faith from holy war, shows how enormously powerful cultural constructs can be when they are rooted in profound human dispositions.

In times of war the term crusade has relentlessly reappeared during the course of the present, bloody century. The newspaper proprietor, financier and convicted swindler Horatio Bottomley (1860–1933) said at a mass meeting in 1915: 'This is not a war in the ordinary sense but a holy crusade against the devilries of militarism that have been the canker of Germany for forty years.'[17] Even more provocatively, the Bishop of London, A.F. Winnington-Ingram (1858–1946), delivered a sermon that said: 'Kill Germans! I look upon it as a war for purity, I look upon everyone who dies in it as a martyr.'[18] Not all bishops were so bloodthirsty, nor even all newspaper proprietors. After the war, many war memorials in Great Britain represented a crusading figure as the symbol of those who had died for high ideals.

The symbolism of the crusade has remained. The Stalingrad sword presented to Stalin (that pattern of Christian knighthood) by Churchill at the Teheran Conference in 1943 was also called the Crusader sword. A British Second World War tank was called the Crusader. Fifty years after its end, that struggle was being generally termed, as it was often termed at the time, a crusade to liberate Europe from tyranny. A book on the Gulf War by the American journalist Rick Atkinson, published in 1993, was entitled *Crusade*: its title blithely ignored the presence of something like an equal number of Muslim states to Christian in the coalition against Iraq.

Newspapers, rather than the electronic media, have been the most jealous custodians of the crusading metaphor. The London *Daily Express* has for half a century printed the device of an armed crusader on its front page. Dictionaries record 'crusade' as having a possible meaning of 'vigorous and dedicated action in favour of a cause'. The cliché is as acceptable as any other, but in newspaper parlance '*jihad*' has acquired a close association with terrorism.

*   *   *

In the nineteenth century the European fear of Muslim holy war was not all in the realm of cliché, but was connected with genuine concerns in colonial policy. France, in particular, had to deal with a long series of holy wars in North Africa, and as late as the wars in the Moroccan Rif in the third and fourth decades of the twentieth century, her policy registered a genuine fear. However, towards the end of the nineteenth century some Islamic specialists began to advise the French colonial authorities that the various Islamic brotherhoods were by no means devoted to the inevitable preaching of holy war, and that judicious patronage of their leadership could pay political dividends. It was unfortunate for the main proponent of this policy, a certain Xavier Coppolani, that in 1905 he was ambushed and murdered in Mauritania.

In India the threat of Muslim holy war exercised the British colonial authorities throughout the nineteenth century, though by its end the liberal doctrines of Sayyid Ahmad Khan, that discouraged the whole idea, had become important among Indian Muslims. Mirza Ghulam Ahmad (1839–1908), the founder of the north Indian Ahmadi sect, maintained that *jihad* of the sword discredited Islam: holy war in his view was entirely a defensive duty, and 'there is no sword except arguments and proofs'[19] in Islam. However, the disorderly followers of the tradition of Said Ahmad of Bareilly were spasmodically active on the north-west frontier almost to the end of the century, and the Afghan wars had exposed the British, in the same area, to the continued force of the doctrine of holy war. Hunter's question: 'Our Indian Musulmans: are they in conscience bound to rebel against the Queen?' continued occasionally to be posed until the time of the Queen's death in 1901.

The colonial traditions managed to ignore the fact that most of the nineteenth-century Muslim holy wars against colonial powers could have been classified by an impartial observer as just wars waged against foreign aggressors. They were not viewed so in the West at the time, other than by a few eccentrics like the English Wilfrid Scawen Blunt (1840–1922). The Mahdist movement of Muhammad Ahmad in the Sudan convinced the main body of British opinion of Muslim fanaticism, in spite of its having been clear that poor Gordon had been just as much of a fanatic as his Mahdi opponent. In the twentieth century, as often occurs, determined political opposition was sometimes thought the same thing as insanity, and the bitter resistance to British policy in Somaliland was attributed to the 'Mad Mullah'.

The idea of an Islamic threat could take a literary form. In 1916, when

Turkish adherence to the Central Powers was two years old, sober British diplomacy was planning to launch a Hashemite opposition to the Ottoman claim to exercise the caliphate; within a further year it was also planning to set up an intrusive Jewish homeland in the heart of the Muslim world. The novelist John Buchan, in the preface to his 1916 novel *Greenmantle*, remarked: 'Let no man or woman call its events improbable. The war has driven that word from our vocabulary.' *Greenmantle* has as its theme the idea of a new Mahdi appearing in the Ottoman world, who (though himself innocent of political ambition) would be used by German policy to further the interests of the Central Powers. 'You never know what will start off a Jehad.' 'A seer has arisen from the blood of the Prophet, and will restore the Khalifate to its old glories and Islam to its old purity.' Whether Buchan knew that he was attributing the Islamic political designs of his own country to Germany cannot be known; it seems unlikely, but is not impossible.

In the interwar period, and still more definitely after the end of the Second World War, the fears of Islamic activism retreated, and were replaced by fears of Arab nationalism. Sir Ronald Storrs (1881–1955), once the first British Military Governor of Jerusalem, and the quintessential old Middle Eastern hand, wrote in 1942 that: 'For practical purposes Theocracy has been displaced [in the Arab world] as in Europe by Ethnocracy: pan-Islam by National Independence, so that it is no longer true to repeat *La wataniya fil Islam*, "There is no nationality in Islam." '[20]

CHAPTER FOURTEEN

Assumed Identities

THE RECEPTION OF holy war in medieval Christianity after a millennium of eschewing it, and its subsequent abandonment by Christians after a further half-millennium, seem to point towards the possibility that a tradition of holy war may suffer a final disruption. A similar disruption seems to have occurred in Judaism after the destruction of the Temple in 60 AD. That does not mean, of course, that the peoples who profess Christianity or Judaism are more pacific than others; the record down to the present time does not suggest that this is so, although Judaism was a pacific religion over a very long period. Nor does it mean that holy war was without effect on some of the ways in which early modern Christians conceived their relationship with non-Christian peoples.

Nevertheless, only a tiny number of Christians think of the people of God as subject to the duty of waging holy war, and when some modern Islamists assert that the policies of Christian states are still today dictated by the religious zeal of the crusades, modern Americans and Europeans are troubled by the charge; they may even be disturbed by their countries being described as Christian.

To wage holy war is to assume an identity, to become a *mujahid* or some other kind of holy warrior. Because of the secularist hiatus in Christian tradition, that has sometimes enabled believing Christians since 1789 to persuade themselves that their religion is in its essence pacific, it has become very rare for modern Christians to assume a crusading identity in the sense of a willingness to take weapons and to fight the holy war of the sword in God's name. Though rare, it is still not inconceivable. I remember, as a journalist covering the Algerian war in the late 1950s, being told by a group of French generals that they saw themselves as waging the crusade. And during the Lebanese civil war of 1975–90 some of the Lebanese Catholic Maronites saw themselves, similarly, as crusaders.

The general unwillingness of modern Christians to consider participation in holy war seems to apply to most modern so-called Christian fundamental-ists, who usually refrain from thinking that man must co-operate in the execution of God's judgement. Anticipation of Armageddon among funda-mentalists can, however, entail an anticipation of the final holy war, that takes place at the end of all things, an eschatological waiting time like that described earlier in this book.

But rejection of holy war does not mean that many Americans and Euro-peans of any persuasion are unwilling to 'fight for the right': pacifism remains, in the late-twentieth-century West, very much a minority option. And a war thought just may still be described as a 'crusade'. In Western cultural tradition the positive associations of the word are still intact, and the suggestion that crusading was an occupation for religious fanatics may be unpalatable to some people. Sir Walter Scott and his imitators have done their protective work, and Richard the Lionheart and Saladin are romantic figures, to be absolutely distinguished from the murderous Assassins of their own time and the holy war 'terrorists' of ours.

The crusading identity is thus rejected by almost all modern Christians, and the Maccabaean identity by almost all modern Jews. But the *mujahid* identity, understood as one who wages physical holy war, is not rejected by all modern Muslims, even if the spiritual understanding of the word is more prevalent by far in modern Islam than the temporal.

The willingness to adopt a *mujahid* identity in parts of modern Islam induces a very large number of Westerners to think of such an identity as archaic, and of the religious attitudes that inspire it as 'medieval'. Such people confirm the widespread acceptance of the idea – not just a popular one, but one shared by many orientalist scholars – that Islam is a permanent bundle of beliefs and practices that are accepted in all parts of the world, and that its main characteristics have persisted from the earliest times of the religion until the present. Islam thus comprehends not only the religion itself, but the societies that profess it, at all stages of their history. This type of religion and culture is generally distinguished by those who think in this way from religions and beliefs that have shown 'development' and 'progress'.

A large number of scholars concerned with Islamic religion and with the politics of Islamic countries, though, do not think in this manner, and even amongst those that do, nuances and distinctions exist that can make the description I have just given sound like a caricature. The charge that some orientalist scholars are 'essentialists' in the way they define Islam can become a polemic device that is just as rough-and-ready as other polemical tactics of the kind. But even when account is taken of these qualifications, the fact remains that in the main currents of educated opinion in Western countries the waging of holy war is connected with the backward areas of the world. The waging of war, on other hand, is not; although war itself is generally deplored, getting ready to wage it is one of the main occupations of some of the most advanced countries.

If 'backward' countries means 'Third World' countries, then the association of holy war with areas that have an unsatisfactory degree of economic development is undeniable. Is Islam, then, principally the religion of backward societies and underdeveloped economies? Many people, even those who regard holy war as a medieval phenomenon, would be unhappy with this inference, although others would not.

Holy war, and the terrorism that is sometimes associated with it, removes the restraints that multiculturalism, or the version of it that often gets acceptance in the West, usually imposes on how minority religions are publicly described. There are obvious ways in which holy war (like any other war) can threaten citizens of Western countries, and the threat should not be minimized. However, *jihad* has not been waged by a Muslim state against a Western one since the end of the First World War.

Holy war is also an implied threat to the secularism of Western institutions that is interpreted as a kind of challenge across cultures. The commonest way to respond to this challenge is to accuse the holy warriors of cultural retardation, of medievalism. But holy war, that may be only a minor annoyance to a citizen of an American or European country, can be a mortal threat to a citizen of the country where it is preached. Secularists in the countries affected by holy war are challenged in a direct way. Those secularists can be democrat minorities, as in Iran or the Sudan. But they can also be embattled authoritarians, and in Egypt, for example, *mujahidin* are more likely to be the victims of authoritarianism than they are to be its friends. In Saudi Arabia an authoritarian government professes fundamentalism but represses Islamist holy warriors – a phenomenon that goes back to the origins of the political system of the Saudi Kingdom in the late 1920s.

During the nineteenth century not only Europeans but a number of oriental Muslims accepted the Western ideas of progress in a manner that caused them to consider their own Islamic societies as 'backward'. This did not mean that there was no appreciation in the West of the attempts being made by oriental societies to change their structures. The German Leopold von Ranke wrote in 1828 of the Ottoman Turkish Sultan Selim III (ruled from 1789 until his murder in 1806) that he had been a reforming enlightened despot of the same stamp as his European near-contemporaries the Emperor Joseph II and Pope Clement XIV.[1] But the historian of the crusades Joseph Michaud wrote three or four years after Ranke of the Egyptian students sent by the Khedive Muhammad 'Ali to Europe for training:

> I have read that in the remote regions of the skies there are stars that our astronomers have not yet discovered: the light emanating from these stars has been on its way to the earth since the time of the Creation, but it has not reached us. I am really sometimes tempted to think that the same will be true for the illumination (*les lumières*) emanating from our Europe – not only in the case of Egypt, but for many other oriental countries.[2]

Michaud had a sharper idea of the prejudices of normal Europeans than Ranke, and his view was the prevailing one, not only during his own century, but far into the twentieth. The question of religion goes to the heart of the prejudice about the application of ideas of progress and modernization to the Islamic countries. Paying little attention to the parallel conflicts in Europe and the Americas between conservative religious opinion and rationalist currents of thought, Europeans tended to fasten onto the intensely traditionalist nature of Islamic thought, and to be deeply sceptical about the capacity of Islam, that they treated as a coherent and changeless unit, to produce people who would respond to the challenges of what they thought of as modernity. Lord Cromer, effectively the British ruler of Egypt at the end of the nineteenth century, knew Muhammad 'Abdu, the main Egyptian disciple of Jamal al-Din al-Afghani, well, and was his protector, but he still quoted with approval the dictum of a British orientalist that an upper-class Muslim of his day must be 'either a fanatic or a concealed infidel'.[3]

A century after Cromer, the prejudice about Muslim 'fanaticism' is still there, moderated in some respects by the need to consider the large Muslim minorities in some European countries, just as the old prejudice was moderated in some respects by the need to be mindful of the huge Muslim populations of British India and colonial Africa. The growth of economic power of some Middle Eastern and African states, based essentially upon oil revenues, has had only a modest effect in increasing the esteem in which they are held in the West, and in enforcing respect for Islam.

The question of holy war is central to Western opinion of Islamic religion, countries and institutions, because it is so closely linked with the imputation of fanaticism that has been imposed upon Islam by modern Americans and Europeans. From the nineteenth to the mid-twentieth century the phenomenon of Muslim holy war was generally thought of as a colonial one, and as on the whole a minor matter. This view persisted into the 1970s, because holy war had not been a characteristic of the Nasserist Arab nationalism that dominated Middle Eastern politics in the fifties and sixties.

By this time many of the nineteenth-century views about the relation between Western modernization and the rest of the world had been systematized by sociologists into a body of doctrine that was of great importance for that relationship. Societies were evaluated by indices of modernity, development or modernization. Traditionalism was reckoned as a powerful negative element, and the whole paradigm of traditionalism and modernity that the sociologists derived from their great precursor Max Weber (1864–1920) depended on this polarity. Quite apart from its obvious inconveniences for colonial policy, and its subsequent inconvenience for Israeli policy, holy war, that was thought to mobilize traditional social forces, was regarded as an obvious indicator of social backwardness when it reappeared in some Islamic countries.

From the time of the Arab–Israeli war of 1973 the Islamic *jihad* (that was hardly noticed in the West at that moment, although the Egyptian President Anwar Sadat proclaimed the attack upon Israel to be a holy war) began to impinge upon Western political consciousness. The critical moment was the Khomeini revolution in Iran in 1979 and the seizure of hostages at the American Embassy in Teheran. This was not in fact an act of holy war, since no *jihad* upon the United States had been proclaimed at that moment by Khomeini and the religious radicals, nor would one be in the future. Nor did denunciations of the United States as 'the great Satan' amount to a declaration of holy war, although they were sometimes treated as though they did. But the fact that the most powerful nation in the world could be held to ransom by an Islamist government that proclaimed its adherence to the doctrine of holy war meant that the deed was thought of in the context of the doctrine.

The second stage in popular Western ideas about Islamic holy war was the development of the conviction that there was an intimate connection between *jihad* and acts of terrorism directed against the West. One organization that received the attention of the Western media was Hizbullah ('the party of God'), the military Lebanese Shi'a group led by learned *'ulama* which enjoyed, at some times, Iranian support, that appeared after the Israeli invasion of Lebanon in 1982. Another was Hamas (an Arabic acronym for 'Islamic Resistance Movement'), organized in Gaza and the West Bank in the *intifada* period of resistance to Israeli rule in 1988, made up mainly of elements of the older Muslim Brotherhood. There were, of course, many other groups, located in many countries, that used military or terrorist tactics that were inspired entirely or in part by doctrines of holy war, but these were the two that made most impression on the West.

There has been some understandable confusion in Europe and North America about Islamic 'terrorist' movements connected with holy war, whose actions are represented as having been always mainly directed against 'the West'. The main grounds for the conviction that Hizbullah's actions were directed against the West was its part in the seizure of a number of Western hostages in Beirut during the 1980s, a sad and lamentable affair, but one that has been recurrent in Islamic–Christian–Judaic relations for many centuries. Hizbullah's bombing of the US Embassy in Beirut in 1983, killing twenty-three Americans, is unlikely to be forgotten or forgiven, nor is their attack on the US Marine base in the same city, also in 1983, which cost 242 lives. Hizbullah has not been known for acts of terrorism committed in the West since the end of the Lebanese civil war. Nor has Hamas, although its political director, Musa Abu Marzuq, was arrested in New York in July 1995, probably at the instance of the Israeli government.

One of the mastering, almost obsessive, fears about the revival of Islamic holy war is that of an 'Islamic International' that exports holy war from one part of the globe to another, and that finances and supports it outside the countries that inspire it. In practical terms the accusation of favouring Islamist terrorism can be brought against four countries, of which the most obvious is post-1979 Iran, whose whole foreign policy has to some degree been connected with the diffusion of the ideology of Islamic holy war.

The export, not of Islamist terrorism, but of Islamism and its social support mechanisms, and also, very occasionally, of terrorism, is bound up with one of the main economic and political anomalies of the Middle East and North Africa: the existence of huge oil revenues that accrue to states that, with the exception of Iran, have a less advanced history of political and social development than many of those over which they exert influence and leverage. In the context of Islamism, this influence extends not only all over the Middle East and into Asia, but also to the Muslim communities resident in Western countries.

It is a particularly formidable kind of influence, since the oil-producing countries, and especially Saudi Arabia, also exert leverage on Western Christian governments and governing classes. This was especially apparent in Britain during the al-Masari affair in 1995–6, when Saudi pressure almost succeeded in obtaining the expulsion from Britain of a fugitive Islamist Saudi dissident. There are aspects of this relationship between Eastern producers and Western traders that recall the relationship between the Venetians and the Ottomans at the end of the Middle Ages.

Saudi Arabia is the richest and most powerful of all the conservative Islamic countries, and one that could in the literal sense of the term be described as 'fundamentalist'. Saudi Arabia has once or twice called for holy war against Israel, and, at the time of the Gulf War, against Iraq. That financial support has come from Saudi Arabia and several of the Gulf states for the Muslim Brotherhood and its offshoots in many parts of the Islamic world, especially Palestine, Egypt and Algeria, is beyond doubt. Most of this support has gone towards the provision of social services, which has always been an important part of the activities of the Brotherhood. But it would be very surprising if some had not gone towards military purposes, especially in the case of Palestinian Hamas and the Algerian FIS.

In exactly the same period that the impression of a close connection between extreme Islamic religious piety and anti-Western terrorism began to prevail, a bitter holy war was fought in Afghanistan against a Russian-protected government, and subsequently against a Russian army, in which the fighters, the *mujahidin*, received very substantial, though theoretically covert, support from the United States. The holy war fighters became – for a time – a byword in North America for heroic resistance to tyranny. Military help was channelled through Pakistan, that also may be presumed to have given its own. In Pakistan the holy war of the Afghan *mujahidin* was recognized as such. At the same time the Shi'a Afghan guerrillas, though neglected by the Pakistanis and Americans, who supported Sunni groups, were receiving support from Khomeini's Iran.

The backing given by the US and its allies to the Afghan rebels was not officially denied. In March 1986 a Hizb-i Islami representative was officially received by the British Prime Minister, Margaret Thatcher, in London; he was described in *The Times* as being 'like a leader of the French [1940–5] resistance'. In June of the same year the Jama'at-i Islami leader was received and praised by President Reagan in Washington. The costs to the US at the height of the war, when the Afghan rebels were facing regular Russian forces, were officially given as $600 million annually, and possibly the real figure was much higher. Other subsidies came from Pakistan, Saudi Arabia, and Egypt. These figures make the support that Iran has given to holy war fighters in various areas – and the much-contested US subsidies to the Contras in Nicaragua – appear modest.

To the embarrassment of some of their former patrons and backers, the Afghan Islamist parties conspicuously failed to solve their own differences, and waged a bloody civil war long after the Soviet withdrawal. The Hizb-i Islami leader, Gulbuddin Hikmatyar, turned out to be just as ruthless and authoritarian as those he supplanted.

Nor was this the only embarrassment. The Afghan rebels acted as a catalyst for Islamist radicals in other parts of the Muslim world. US support for the Afghans must have been given without thought for the consequences it would have for the many Muslims who entered the country from other parts of the Islamic world to fight as *mujahidin*. It is curious – to say the least – that the United States in this way enabled Afghanistan to become the largest and most effective training ground for what has subsequently been described in the US and elsewhere as international fundamentalist terrorism. Trained to some extent by Pakistani and American mentors, the Afghan activists mastered the use not only of many modern weapons, but also of techniques of modern propaganda and communications, that they adapted especially for the sort of guerrilla warfare in which Islamists were to be involved in many other countries. Volunteers who had fought in the Afghan war returned to Egypt, Palestine and Algeria, and applied there the techniques that they had learned.

From a mixture of conviction and calculation, Iran since 1979 has embarked on a policy of supporting Islamist movements throughout the Middle East and parts of Africa, that certainly has included a great deal of covert action. The hidden Iranian hand has been detected by its critics in dozens of places, from south-east Turkey to Algeria, and at one point even in the holy city of Mecca itself. Only in one area has the Iranian support of local Islamist forces met with substantial success, in that of the Lebanese Shi'a group that gave birth to the Hizbullah party. At some stages of the Lebanese civil war small forces of Iranian troops were involved. But there is no doubt that the rise and continuance of Hizbullah depended first of all upon purely Lebanese factors, and secondly upon the interests of other players in the Lebanese field, notably the Syrians.

The role of Iran in the financing of radical Islamist propaganda is just as important as that played by the Saudis; in fact it seems that, especially in Europe, fundamentalist journals and 'Institutes' have often received Saudi and Iranian support simultaneously. This may have been true of the Islamic Institute located in London and run by the late Kalim Siddiqui. The journals are not always extraneous to holy war, since they have, for example, been redistributed in the Gaza Strip. The financing of propaganda (or missionary work, *da'wa*) is a far-flung operation, extending from Germany to Algeria and the Gulf.

The Sudan, that officially became an 'Islamic state' in 1990, is not in a financial condition to contribute money to great international enterprises, but its ideological leader, Hasan al-Turabi, has organized several 'Popular Arabic and Islamic Conferences' that have been attended by a large number of Islamists from all over the Middle East and North Africa. The Sudan has been held responsible by the United Nations for harbouring the men responsible for the attempt made on the Egyptian President Hosni Mubarak's life in Addis Adaba in 1995, and Western security services have claimed that the Sudanese government has set up training camps outside Khartoum for Islamist terrorists from various countries who have operated throughout the region, but above all in the neighbouring state of Egypt.

The collective representations that a society makes of itself and of other societies change in the course of history. There has never been a single Islam, save in the brief period in which the Prophet Muhammad and his helpers transformed their own pre-existing society. The origins of Christianity are rather more obscure, and its development as a religion was more tortuous. But the succession of historic images that Christians have held of themselves and of others is analogous in its malleability to those successively held by Muslims. 'Christendom', for example, although now a concept several centuries old, and still in general use, is not a term that could be applied to the Christian religion in its earlier stages.

This historical view has specific applications. We live in a society that is rightly (as we are bound to see it) conscious of the way in which historic prejudice is enshrined in the way in which we use language. The history of anti-Semitism in Christian countries, for example, shows how hostile representations of a religious minority can become as it were fossilized and enshrined in a society. Such hostile descriptions have continued to be applied, in the Jewish case, in a grotesquely consistent way, and for many centuries. They can affect people of every level of intelligence, who are sometimes quite unaware that they are using language, or even composing music, in a loaded manner. For example, the passages of Bach's *St Matthew*

Passion that describe the part assigned to the Jews in the trial of Christ powerfully transmit traditional hostile images of this sort.

The psychological process that for centuries supported anti-Semitism has some analogies with the growth of anti-Islamism. The tendency in Europe and North America at the present time is to construct powerful 'cultural' images to do with other groups of nations, that are represented as active principles in social and political life, but that have no substance beyond the imaginations of their begetters. Anyone who has read this far will realize how protean both Christian and Islamic holy war have been in the course of their histories: how different, for example, *jihad* has been in the Mediterranean, in Najd, in the western Sudan, in Algeria, at various times and in various places.

Many people regard 'the West' as a unitary principle, and not a heterogeneous collection of countries whose number and identities are by no means easy to define. The physical boundaries of their mythical West are also uncertain in the extreme. Conservative seekers after the Great Tradition of Western culture hypostasize a civilization that is in some respects a metaphysical entity. But metaphysical entities can be politically convenient: in moments of crisis like the Gulf War of 1991 the West can be identified with miraculous ease in the governments of a few powerful countries, that can, amazingly, be relied upon to know and defend its true interests. All this is in the romantic-conservative tradition of nineteenth-century politics, that has been powerfully resurrected, in Anglo-Saxon countries particularly, in the past few years.

As a complement to the reassertion of the Great Tradition of the West there has been at the same time a revival of the idea of complementary cultural unities in other parts of the world, that to Westerners are supposed to represent the alien other, or rather the alien others. A few American and British liberals have denounced the misleading usages of what they have termed 'orientalism', but the impact of their criticism has been limited. 'Islam' and 'Islamic culture' have been painted by polemicists as substantial cultural giants that stride out of the ideological mist with aggressive intent. Such threatening monsters are assumed to be followed by attendant terrorists, although the hostile aspect of the menacing religion can be softened by 'Islamic moderates' whose interests happen to coincide with those of the West.

The American academic Samuel Huntington has even given birth to a prophecy, not unlike those of the late Middle Ages, in which the next historical period is predicted as one in which the religious giants will engage

in worldwide conflict, and in which the 'Confucian-Islamic' states will challenge 'the West'.[4] This sort of oracular mish-mash obtains a respectful
hearing in the US, though it would be fair to say that it has also been
challenged there. It is clearly directed towards the exercise of influence over
US State Department policy, but it is to be hoped that the policy-makers are
harder-headed than this sort of adviser appears to be.

It is hard to neglect the Islamist analogies to Samuel Huntington's argument, that I have just cited, and he does indeed quote one Islamist analysis,
by a Pakistani writer, to support it. The rhetoric of many Islamist pietists,
in particular that of the Egyptian Sayyid Qutb, looks like a mirror-image
of the American's jeremiad, although it was written thirty years earlier.
Qutb asserted Islam to be the only true civilization, and denounced so-called
Western civilization as a Jewish-imperialist trick intended to mislead
and betray Muslims. But to a large extent the Islamist writers, in their
search for Islamic authenticity, were drawing upon the same 'Western'
romantic-conservative tradition as the American prophets of cultural conflict draw upon now. So the similarity of the tunes that each plays is not
surprising.

The question of Islamist terrorism raises the matter of human rights in two
ways. On the one hand, Islamist terrorists very frequently violate human
rights. Statistically, few citizens of European or North American countries
suffer violations of their human rights due to the action of Islamist terrorists,
although if the sufferings of Israeli citizens are added to the others the total
becomes larger. Morally, the numbers do not matter: all violations of human
rights are without qualification to be condemned, whatever government or
organization executes them. Nothing will excuse the reckless murder of
innocent civilians, however noble the cause is alleged to be, and whatever
provocation may be alleged to have been given.

However, in the statistics of suffering by far the most numerous victims
of Islamist terrorism are the citizens of their own countries. This is most
flagrantly true in Algeria, where a war of terror has been going on for at
least five years, not dissimilar in its nature to the war of independence with
France in the 1950s, and deeply tragic in its essence, as that war also was.
It is also true in Egypt, where in parts of the country there is a condition
not far removed from a popular uprising, with all the bloodshed that attends
such events. Victims have also been common in the Palestine National
Authority, West-Bank Israel and Israeli-occupied south Lebanon, all areas

where Muslims suspected of collaboration with Israelis have been very harshly dealt with.

The question of human rights recurs in the manner in which supposedly militant Islamists are dealt with by governments, Muslim and others. The record of Egypt, Israel, Saudi Arabia, Syria, Tunisia, Algeria, Iraq, Afghanistan and Iran in dealing with dissidents, to name only the most obvious transgressors, is poor, to say the least. In most cases, although Israel can be considered at least a partial exception, the victims of brutality and oppression are citizens of the country concerned. It is to be regretted that at the meeting of heads and important members of governments at Sharm al-Sheikh in 1996 to discuss terrorism, at the instance of the Egyptian government, no reference to human rights was made.

It is usual at this point to discuss the difficulties that Islamists and Islamic fundamentalist countries and groups have with the Western legal background of human rights, but this is a debate that gets nowhere except to supply ammunition for the irredeemable cultural diversity argument, and is not directly relevant to the practice of modern holy war. Most modern Islamic holy war is conducted by irregulars or guerrillas, and is to do with rebellion, not with wars between sovereign states. So far as the latter are concerned, it has been rightly said that although 'jihad may be proclaimed in a variety of military or political contexts by contemporary leaders, conducting holy war is obviously incompatible with the modern scheme of relations between nation-states'.[5] So far as irregular war goes, there is a body of Islamic law that concerns it,[6] but there is no way of telling to what extent this is applied in the struggles that take place today.

The history of holy war does not show that men are condemned ceaselessly to kill each other out of piety. One of the most striking things about the history of the peoples and groups committed to a doctrine of holy war is that periods of armistice or truce have vastly predominated over periods of armed hostility. More than that: in spite of terrible failures to understand one another, there has been a will to exchange goods and to suspend views, to compromise and very often to collaborate – though frequently the collaboration was against a common enemy. From fear, greed or indifference, men often accepted such compromises, and evaded the obligations that arose either from Christian or Muslim holy war. Passions of a common and lowly sort were more effective than religious holiness in discouraging holy warfare: St Francis went to Egypt, and probably saw the Sultan, but he did not call for the crusade's discontinuance, and his followers became some of its most effective propagandists.

There has never been pure religious purpose in holy war. The notion that this is so makes a basic error in accepting the vocabulary of religion as an instrument for the assessment of acts committed in its name. Purity is an immensely important religious concept, and an immensely important religious weapon. There have been no holy wars fought for an exclusively idealistic motive, and the historiography that sets up purity of intention as a criterion for holy war is mistakenly moralistic in its methods. It is also mistaken about the ways in which holy wars occur, and the motives for which they are fought.

Because Saladin and Richard I of England waged holy war with motives that included all sorts of temporal objectives, but principally their own dynastic aggrandizement, neither was deviating from an ideal norm. T.S. Eliot was only poeticizing the myth when he wrote:

> But our King did well at Acre.
> And in spite of all the dishonour,
> The broken standards, the broken lives,
> The broken faith in one place or another,
> There was something left that was more than the tales
> Of old men on winter evenings.
> Only the faith could have done what was good of it,
> Whole faith of a few,
> Part faith of many.[7]

Similarly, the contrast that often used to be made between the supposed idealism of the First Crusade and the 'political' nature of its successors is absurd. The First Crusade did indeed differ from its successors, but not on these grounds.

For centuries, the Ottoman Empire exercised holy war in a spirit that was, in the sense of Islamic law, on the whole correct, but also opportunist and pragmatic. Holy wars were proclaimed against enemies like the Safavi Shi'a rulers of Persia that clearly reflected political and dynastic interest. Alliances and truces were made with Christian states on the basis of political and economic convenience. Holy war was a part of Islamic statecraft, that at one stage of dynastic development was opportune, at another less so. Babur, the founder of the Mughal dynasty, was a Turkish Central Asian ruler with the usual concept of holy war, who celebrated his own achievement, as he saw it, of *ghazi* status. The later Mughal ruler Akbar, also in the sixteenth century, found it expedient to abandon the following of strict Islamic law and to adopt a religious ideology that gave a quasi-divine status to the ruler, making it easier for him to patronize a ruling class of mixed Muslim and Hindu allegiance. A century later the return of Aurangzeb to the old *ghazi* ethic turned out to be a sign of the decadence of the dynasty, not of its resurgence.

One of the most penetrating observations on holy war was made by a learned Muslim clerk of the western Sudan who could see the historic progression that the *jihad* states made in his area of Africa: 'You know the power of *jihad*. But *jihad* leads to kingship, and kingship leads to oppression.'

In modern terms holy war is most likely to be invoked when religious fervour and radical nationalism converge. Today, as in the eleventh century, Palestine is a place where religious and political passions can take fire, with effects that are felt in very distant lands. People have recently begun to realize, after the renewed struggles to control the holiest places of the city of Jerusalem and of other sites like Hebron, that the call to holy war is not confined to Islamist terrorist fanatics, but can also arise among extremist Jews.

The history of holy war teaches us that we cannot escape the moral responsibilities of our human condition. A pious or correct way of life, or entry into a religious fraternity or a closed religious community, do not excuse us from the common responsibility for the violence of one human being to another. The call to kill has sounded as often from the monastery or the *ribat* as from the quarters of statesmen or generals. Christian protests that their religion forbids the offering of violence in return for violence are entirely in vain: the whole history of Christianity testifies against them. Labelling our enemies as terrorists or fanatics, and holy war a peculiarly wicked form of conflict, is just as vain as the attempt to make it seem peculiarly virtuous.

War is more or less just according to its occasion. Four and a half centuries ago the Spanish cleric Francisco de Vitoria wrote that there is a single and only just cause for commencing a war, namely a wrong received: 'Nothing else warrants the use of force in international society – above all, not any difference in religion or politics.'[8] Men may decide to assume the identity of holy warriors in good faith, when the true motives for their wars are only indirectly connected with religious belief. That does not mean that some holy wars have not been, and perhaps at this moment are, just wars. But holiness of intention does not supplant the requirement for justice.

GLOSSARY

(References are to explanatory or relevant passages in the text)

aman protection pp. 73, 87

'ayyar scoundrels p. 123

ba'th [ba'ath] rebirth [political party] pp. 237, 263

bay'a treaty of allegiance p. 224

bughat civil offence p. 46

dar al-harb abode of war, area outside the control of Muslims p. 47

dar al-Islam abode of peace, Islamic-controlled area p. 47

da'wa mission work, proselytism pp. 262, 305

devshirme seizure of subject Christian male children for Ottoman military service p. 199

dhimmis 'people of the book', i.e. Christians and Jews resident in Muslim lands p. 136

fakkak ransomer [of prisoners] p. 150

fard 'ayn duty incumbent upon the Islamic community pp. 42, 91, 258–9

fard kifaya duty incumbent upon individual Muslims pp. 42, 258–9

fasad mischief, vice p. 34

fatwa formal juridical opinion concerning Islamic law p. 125

fay public property of the Islamic community p. 42

fiqh Islamic law pp. 244–5, 247

fitna persecution, oppression, idolatry pp. 32–3

funduq trading post p. 135

futuwwa medieval organization of armed youths p. 123

ghazi; ghuzan; ghaziyah raider; raiders; raiding pp. 32–3, 50

ghazw; al-maghazi raid, campaign; the campaigns [of the Prophet] p. 35

hadith reported saying of the Prophet p. 46

hajj [see *hijra*] pilgrimage p. 87

hakimayya sovereignty, dominion p. 236

hijra emigration for the sake of Allah pp. 32–3, 252

hizbullah party of Allah p. 32

hudna truce p. 87

imam prayer leader, religious leader p. 216

infitah openness [economic policy] p. 268

jahili: jahiliyah ignorant; state of ignorance about religous truth p. 239

jama'at association p. 225

jihad struggle in the way of Allah, holy war pp. 32, 43, 260

jihad al-akbar higher or better holy war p. 43

jizya Muslim property tax p. 211

kafar unbeliever, heretic p. 267

khadira civilization p. 235

kharaj land tax p. 141

kufr unbelief, infidelity see *kafar*

madrasa Muslim religious school p. 154

maghlub defeated, vanquished condition p. 267

Maghreb Islamic western regions

mawali non-Arabian converts to Islam p. 42

minbar pulpit for the Friday prayer p. 92

mujahid; mujahidin fighter; fighters in the holy war p. 51

muluk al-tawa'if kings of the factions p. 68

munafiq hypocrite p. 34

Murabitun [see *ribat*] people of the ribat p. 68

mustaman, see *aman* protected person

muthla exemplary punishments p. 148

muwa'ada agreement p. 135

muwahhid person who affirms the unity of God p. 99

naskh doctrine concerning abrogation of Qur'anic pronouncements on the same subject, made by the Prophet at an earlier date than the later revelation p. 43

qanun secular legislation p. 257

razzia [see *ghazw*] raid p. 35

ribat [see *Murabitun*] frontier post pp. 50, 52–3

ridda apostasy p. 34

salafiyya doctrines attributed to the '[venerable] ancestors' pp. 232, 234

shahada Islamic confession of faith p. 240

shahid confessor, martyr pp. 37, 51

shari'a corpus of Islamic law p. 231

sheikh elder, chief; alternatively, person trained in traditional religous doctrine p. 248

shi'a branch of Islam pp. 242–3

sufi follower of religious group p. 123

sunna; sunni rules of right conduct; historical division of Islamic believers pp. 239, 243

tafarnuj Westernization ['Frankification'] p. 233

takfir unbelief p. 240

tanzimat Ottoman reformist p. 233

taqlid 'imitation', slavish following of religious authority p. 232

'ulama community of men learned in Islamic law p. 44

umma Islamic community p. 235

'uzla break, rupture p. 240

vilayat-i-faqih [see *fiqh*] governance by the learned in the law pp. 244–5

waqf Islamic charitable foundation p. 154

zahara prevail, conquer p. 38

CHRONOLOGICAL TABLE

1230BC Tribe of Israel mentioned as one of those subdued in Palestine by Egyptian armies

c.925BC Death of Solomon

c.930BC Egyptian invasion affects Judah

853–838BC Assyrian campaigns in Syria and Palestine

805–796BC Renewed Assyrian pressure on Syria and Palestine

c.730BC Assyrian domination of Syria-Palestine begins

701BC Siege of Jerusalem by Assyrian Sennacherib

612BC Fall of Assyrian capital of Nineveh to Babylonians

597BC Babylonian King Nebuchadnezzar (reigned 605–562) takes Jerusalem. First Israelite deportations to Babylon

c.587BC Second fall of Jerusalem to Babylonians; sack of city and captivity of inhabitants

539BC Fall of Babylon to Cyrus of Persia. Return of Israelites to Judah. Persian domination begins

c.333–323BC Campaigns of Alexander the Great; fall of Persian Empire. Hellenistic supremacy in Near East

c.323–301BC Civil wars of Alexander's generals (the Diadochi)

301–198BC Rule of Ptolemies in Palestine

c.201BC Seleucid rule in Palestine

c.165BC Beginning of 'Maccabaean' revolt against Seleucid rule under Mattathias. Roman influence in Palestine begins

164BC Fall of Temple area in Jerusalem to Maccabaeans

c.142–63BC Hasmonaean dynasty in Judaea

64BC Syria becomes Roman province

63BC   Roman General Pompey conquers Jerusalem

60–53BC   Triumvirate of Pompey, Crassus and Caesar over Rome

c.55BC   Idumaean dynasty in power in Roman Palestine

37–4BC   Herod the Idumaean King in Roman Palestine

17BC–14AD   Principate of Octavian Augustus

30 or 33AD   Trial and condemnation of Jesus

54–68   Nero Emperor

58   Paul arrested in Jerusalem

66–74   Jewish Revolt in Palestine

69–79   Vespasian Emperor

70   Fall of Jerusalem and destruction of the Temple by Titus

74   Fall of fortress of Masada

79–81   Titus Emperor

305–11   Persecution of Christians under emperors Diocletian and Galerius

311   Religious toleration conceded by Galerius

312   Emperor Constantine's victory over Maxentius at Milvian Bridge outside Rome

313   Constantine grants religious toleration (Edict of Milan), as does Licinius

321–81   Arian schism in the Christian church

323   Constantine unseats Licinius from imperial rule

324   Defeat of Licinius by Constantine at Adrianople

330   Constantinople (Byzantium) becomes capital of the Empire

337   Death of Constantine

354–430   St Augustine, Bishop of Hippo 396–430

397   Death of St Ambrose, Bishop of Milan

476   Deposition of last titular Emperor of the Latin West

481–511   Clovis King of Franks, baptized 503

525–75   Abyssinian rule in Yemen

527–65	Justinian I Emperor of the East and of many of the Roman lands of the West
539–94	Gregory, Bishop of Tours 573–94
590–604	St Gregory the Great, Pope
597	St Augustine of Canterbury lands in Britain
613–19	Persian conquests from Byzantium in Syria and Egypt
622	Flight (*hijra*) of Muhammad from Mecca to Medina
625	Battle of Uhud
628	Treaty of al-Hudaybiyah between Muhammad and the Meccans
629	Byzantine Emperor Heraclius recovers Jerusalem
630	Entry of Muhammad into Mecca
631	Military expedition of Muslims to northern Hijaz (Tabuk)
632	Death of Muhammad. Abu Bakr Caliph (632–4)
633	Wars of the *ridda* against apostasy in Arabia
634–44	'Umar Caliph
635	Fall of Damascus to Khalid ibn-al-Walid
636	Khalid defeats Byzantines on River Yarmuk
638	Fall of Jerusalem: city is granted a treaty by Caliph 'Umar
642	Fall of Egypt to Muslims. Foundation of old Cairo (al-Fustat)
656	'Ali elected Caliph
659	Arbitration between 'Ali and Mu'awiyah about their claims to the caliphate
661	Murder of 'Ali and succession of 'Umayyad Mu'awiyah to uncontested caliphate
669	First siege of Constantinople by Muslims
680	Defeat and death of Husayn, son of 'Ali, at hands of 'Umayyad force at Karbala, Iraq
685–705	'Abd-al-Malik Caliph: zenith of 'Umayyad dynasty
717–18	Unsuccessful siege of Constantinople by Muslims

717–41	Leo III the Iconoclast, Emperor in Constantinople
732	Defeat of 'Abd al-Rahman by Charles Martel of Francia at Poitiers
750	Massacre of eastern 'Umayyads by partisans of Abu-al-'Abbas, founder of 'Abbasid dynasty (750–1258)
756–1031	'Umayyad Caliphate in Spain
786–809	Harun al-Rashid Caliph in Baghdad
800	Charlemagne crowned Emperor by Pope Leo III
800–909	Aghlabid dynasty in Qayrawan, North Africa
827	Aghlabid army land in Sicily under Asad ibn al-Furat
846	Rome sacked by Aghlabid force
909	Fatimid Shi'a Caliphate in Qayrawan
915	Pope John X leads Christian army to disperse Muslim base on River Garigliano
962–1186	Ghaznawid dynasty in Afghanistan and Punjab
969–1171	Fatimid Caliphs in Egypt
981–1002	Hajib al-Mansur ('Almanzor') ruler of Muslim Spain
1027	Fragmentation of Muslim Spain under the 'party kings'
1038–1194	Seljuq dynasties in Central Asia, Asia Minor, Iraq, Iran etc.
1061–1147	Almoravid dynasty rules in North Africa and (from 1090) in Spain
1071	Byzantine Emperor Romanus IV defeated by Seljuqs at Manzikert
1073–85	Gregory VII Pope
1081–1118	Alexius Comnenus Byzantine Emperor
1086	Spanish defeat at Zallaqa by Almoravid army
1088–99	Urban II Pope
1092	Death of Seljuq Sultan, Malikshah
1094–9	El Cid (Rodrigo Díaz de Bivar) holds Valencia
1095	Urban II summons crusade at Council of Clermont

1096   Failure of first crusading expedition under Peter the Hermit. Main crusading army leaves

1098   Crusading army takes Antioch

1099   Fall of Jerusalem

1100–18   Baldwin I King of Jerusalem

1144–7   Defeat and suppression of Almoravid dynasty by Almohads (Muwahhids)

1144   'Imad al-Din Zangi captures Edessa

1147–9   Second Crusade

1167–8   Frankish army in Fatimid Egypt

1171   Saladin proclaims 'Abbasid Sunni Caliphate of Baghdad in Egypt

1174   Death of Zangid ruler Nur al-Din

1187   Battle of Hattin and fall of Jerusalem

1189–93   Third Crusade

1189–91   Siege of Acre

1193   Death of Saladin (Salah al-Din ibn-Ayyub)

1193–1249   Ayyubi dynasty in Egypt and Syria

1195   Alfonso VIII of Castile defeated at battle of Alarcos by Almohad Ya'qub al-Mansur

1197–1216   Innocent III Pope

1198   Innocent III authorizes Jean de Matha to organize 'Trinitarian' group of friars for the redemption of captives from unbelievers. Innocent authorizes crusading taxation throughout Christendom

1202–4   Fourth Crusade

1204   Fall of Constantinople

1204–61   Latin Empire of Constantinople

1207   Albigensian Crusade

1212   Final defeat of Almohads in Spain at battle of Las Navas de Tolosa

1217–21   Fifth Crusade. Mission of St Francis in Egypt

1229	Jaffa Treaty of Holy Roman Emperor Frederick II with Ayyubi Sultan al-Kamil. Frederick crowns himself King of Jerusalem in Jerusalem
1229–30	Aragonese conquest of Majorca
c.1230	Teutonic Knights begin their eastern advance into Prussia
1239	Pope Gregory IX declares crusade against the Emperor Frederick II
1246	Nasir uddin Mahmud Sultan of Delhi
1250–1517	Mamluk rulers supplant Ayyubi dynasty in Egypt and Syria
1248–54	Sixth Crusade led by St Louis of France
1258	Fall of Baghdad to Mongols under Hulagu
1260	Mongol army in Syria defeated at Ain Jalud by Mamluks, Qutuz and Baybars
1266	Ghiyas uddin Balban Sultan of Delhi
1270	Tunis crusade of St Louis of France
1291	Fall of Acre to Sultan al-Ashraf Khalil and end of crusading settlement in Syria
c.1300	Treatise on the recovery of the Holy Land by French royal official Pierre Dubois
1303	Venetian treaty with Mamluk government to protect the Venetian trading settlement in Alexandria
1321	Crusade proclaimed against political enemies of the papacy in Italy
1324	Meccan pilgrimage of King of Mali
1340	Castilian-Aragonese-Portuguese army defeats Moroccan Marinids and Granadan Nasrid Muslims at battle of Rio Salado
1344	Capture of Smyrna by papal-sponsored crusading alliance
1349	Turkish embassy received by Pope Clement VI in Avignon
1352	Genoese commercial treaty with Ottomans

1365	Crusading raid by King Peter of Cyprus against Alexandria
1389	Serbs defeated by Ottomans at first battle of Kossovo
1396	Ottoman victory over Western crusading army at Nicopolis
1398	Mongol ruler Timur (Tamerlane) takes Delhi
1400–1	Timur conquers Syria
1402	Timur defeats Ottomans at Ankara and captures Sultan Bayazid. End of Tughlug Sultanate of Delhi
1404	Death of Timur
1415	Portuguese conquest of Ceuta in Morocco
1420–31	Crusades against Hussite heretics of Bohemia
1444	Mamluk siege of Rhodes. Ottoman victory over Western crusading army at Varna
1453	Fall of Constantinople to Ottoman Mahmud the Conqueror
1455	Pope Nicholas V concedes to Portugal the African ports, islands and seas lying to the south of Capes Nun and Bojador
1456	Ottomans repulsed from Belgrade by Janos Hunyadi and Giovanni Capistrano. Portuguese take Alcazar in northern Morocco
1464	Pope Pius II dies at Ancona in central Italy while waiting to embark on crusade
1470	Fall of Venetian Negroponte in Greece to Ottomans
1471	Tangier, Arsila and Arache in Morocco fall to Portuguese. Portuguese ships reach La Mina on Gold Coast of West Africa
1492	Fall of Granada to Spanish kingdom of Castile and Aragon. First Atlantic expedition of Columbus
1493	Partition bulls of Pope Alexander VI demarcate seas and regions to east and west of the Azores and Cape Verde islands between Spain and Portugal

1494	Modification of Alexander VI's awards negotiated between Spain and Portugal in Treaty of Tordesillas
1497–1510	Spaniards occupy Melilla, Mers el-Kebir, Oran, Bougie and other North African *presidios*
1499–1500	Fall of Lepanto, Coron and Modon in Greece to Ottomans
1502–1736	Safavid dynasty of Iran
1514	Spanish colonial policy defined in royal *Requerimiento*
1516–17	Ottoman conquest of Syria and Egypt
1520	Hernando Cortés entertained by Aztec Emperor Montezuma, whom he arrests and executes
1521	Belgrade falls to Ottomans
1522	Capture of Rhodes by Ottomans
1525	Hungarians defeated by Ottomans at battle of Mohácz
1526	Babur establishes Mughal dynasty at Delhi (1526–1761)
1529	Ottoman siege of Vienna
1535	Habsburg Emperor Charles V takes Tunis
1541	Buda falls to Ottomans
1556–1605	Akbar Mughal Emperor
1565	Ottoman siege of Malta
1571	Capture of Cyprus by Ottomans. Victory of Catholic naval alliance over Ottoman fleet at Lepanto
1578	Defeat and death of King Sebastian of Portugal in Morocco at battle of Alcazar
1578–1603	Ahmad el-Mansur Sultan of Morocco
1586–1628	Abbas Shah of Iran
1588	Crusading status granted to Spanish forces taking part in Armada sent against England
1606	Peace of Zsitva-Torok between Habsburg Empire and Ottomans
1627	Missionary College *De Propaganda Fide* founded in Rome
1659–1707	Aurangzeb Mughal Emperor

1669	Crete falls to Ottomans
1673–4	*Jihad* of Nasir al-Din (Awbek b. Ashfaga) to impose orthodox Islam in Senegal area
1683	Ottoman siege of Vienna
1686	Buda falls to Charles of Lorraine
1687	Ottoman defeat at battle of Mohácz
1699	Peace of Karlowitz between Habsburgs, Poland, Venice and Ottomans; cession by the Ottomans of Hungary, Transylvania, Croatia, Slavonia, Podolia, Ukraine and Morea
1717	Austrian capture of Belgrade
1736	Nadir Khan Shah of Iran
1739	Nadir Khan sacks Delhi
1757	Clive wins battle of Plassey
1785	Warren Hastings returns to England
1793	'Permanent settlement' of Bengal
1798	French expedition to Egypt
1799	Napoleon held by British at Acre; leaves Egypt. Tippo Sahib defeated and killed at Seringapatam
1803–4	Wahhabi capture of Mecca and Medina
1804–12	Holy war of 'Uthman dan Fodio ('the Shehu') in Hausaland
1806	Deposition of reformist Sultan Selim III
1811	Massacre of Mamluks in Cairo by Muhammad 'Ali
1818	Muhammad 'Ali's campaign against Wahhabis in Arabia
1822	Muhammad 'Ali subdues Sudan
1826	Holy war of Said Ahmad against Sikhs of Punjab. Sultan Mahmud II blows up Janissary barracks ('the auspicious event')
1829	Peace of Adrianople ends Russo–Turkish War
1830	French conquest of Algiers
1831	Said Ahmad killed near Peshawar

1833–43	Holy wars of 'Abd al-Qadir in Algeria, ending in his defeat and exile
1837–46	Holy wars of Shamyl against Russians in Daghestan and Chechnia
1839–42	British fight First Afghan War
1839–76	*Tanzimat* (reform) period in Ottoman Empire
1849	British annexation of Punjab
1857–8	Indian Mutiny
1858	Sir Sydney Cotton destroys *mujahidin* base in Sittana. Government of India Act
1859	Chechnia subdued: Shamyl exiled to Kaluga and subsequently to Mecca
1861–4	Holy War of 'Umar Tal in Senegalia
1869	Suez Canal opened
1876	First Turkish Constitution granted. Bulgarian massacres. Balkan Wars of Serbia and Montenegro with Turkey
1877–8	Russo–Turkish War
1878	Congress of Berlin partitions much of the Ottoman Balkans. Closure of Ottoman Parliament marks start of absolutist rule of Sultan Abdülhamid II (1878–1908)
1881–2	Nationalist regime of Ahmad 'Urabi in Egypt
1881–3	French occupation of Tunisia
1881–5	Holy War of Muhammad Ahmad (the Mahdi) in the Egyptian Sudan
1882	British occupation of Egypt
1885	Deaths of General Gordon and Muhammad Ahmad
1889	Defeat of Mahdist forces by Anglo-Egyptian army
1897	Jamal al-Din al-Afghani dies in Constantinople
1898	Kitchener's expedition destroys Mahdist Sudan and enables Anglo-Egyptian condominium of Sudan
1900–20	Holy War of Muhammad Abdille Hasan ('the mad mullah') in Somalia
1906	Constitution granted by Mazaffar ad Din Shah to Iran

1907   Anglo–Russian Agreement for division of Iran into Russian and British spheres of influence

1908   Second Turkish Constitution

1911   Sanusi holy war against Italians in Libya begins

1912   Treaty of Fez establishes French protectorate over most of Morocco. Spanish occupation of northern Morocco. Libya ceded to Italy by Ottoman government. Wahhabi Brotherhood (Ikhwan) established in Arabia

1914   Ottoman Empire enters First World War as ally of Central Powers and declares holy war on Britain, France and Russia. British end Ottoman sovereignty in Egypt

1916   Sykes–Picot Agreement for partition of Ottoman Empire

1917   Balfour Declaration promising to favour the establishment in Palestine of a national home for the Jewish People. Allenby enters Jerusalem. Palestine under British administration

1919   Peace of Paris

1920   Iraq established under Hashemite monarchy (British mandate until 1927). Treaty of Sèvres rejected by revolutionary government of Turkey

1920–6   Holy war of 'Abd al-Karim al Khattabi in northern Morocco

1921   Principality of Transjordan set up (British mandate 1923–46). Soviet–Iranian Treaty

1923   French Mandate (1923–46) established for Syria. Treaty of Lausanne recognizes Turkish government and its boundaries

1925   Riza Khan sets up Pahlavi dynasty in Iran

1926   French Mandate (1924–46) established for Lebanon. Ibn Saud recognized as King of Hejaz by Soviet Union

1928   Red Line Agreement allots oil interests in Middle East to British, French and American groups

1929   Suppression of tribes of Ikhwan by Ibn Saud

1932   Ibn Saud proclaimed King of Saudi Arabia

1936 Anglo–Egyptian agreement ends British military occupation except in the Suez Canal zone. Arab Revolt in Palestine

1940 Muslim League calls for separate state for Muslims (Pakistan)

1941 Government of Rashid 'Ali al-Gaylani overturned by British force in Iraq. British and Russian forces occupy Persia: Riza Shah exiled

1942 Britain imposes government of Nahas Pasha on Egypt

1945 Arab League established in Cairo. Zionist Revolt in Palestine

1947 UN resolution determines partition of Palestine. Britain leaves India; states of India and Pakistan established

1948 End of British mandate in Palestine; Israel proclaimed; first Arab–Israeli War

1949 Arab–Israeli armistice signed in Rhodes

1951 Nationalization of Anglo-Iranian Oil Company by Prime Minister Mosaddegh

1952 Egyptian Revolution brings government of Free Officers into power

1954 Gamal 'Abdul Nasser in sole power in Egypt; Muslim Brotherhood dissolved. Outbreak of Algerian rebellion against France

1955 Baghdad Pact between Turkey, Iraq, Britain, Pakistan and Iran. Return of Sultan Sidi Muhammad Ibn Yusuf to Morocco from exile; Moroccan independence from France

1956 Suez crisis and Second Arab–Israeli War; Anglo-French military action in Egypt. Independence of Sudan. Independence of Tunisia. Pakistan proclaimed an Islamic republic

1957 Independence of Ghana

1958 Formation of United Arab Republic of Egypt and Syria. Iraqi revolution brings Abdul Karim Qassem to power. Russian aid for Aswan High Dam in Egypt. First American intervention in the Lebanon

1959   Independence of Senegal and Mali (Soudan)

1960   Independence of Mauritania. Breakup of federation of Senegal and Mali

1961   Dissolution of United Arab Republic of Syria and Egypt. Independence of Kuwait

1962   Independence of Algeria. 'Freedom, socialism and unity' proclaimed as objectives of Nasser's Arabism

1963   Independence of Nigeria

1964–75   Modernization of Saudi Arabia by King Faysal

1965   India–Pakistan war

1967   Third Arab–Israeli war; Israeli occupation of Arab Jerusalem and the West Bank. British withdrawal from Aden; South Yemen Republic established

1969   Mu'ammar al-Qadhafi seizes power in Libya

1971   East Pakistan (Bangladesh) secedes from Pakistan. British withdrawal from most of Gulf states

1973   Fourth Arab–Israeli war. Republic proclaimed in Afghanistan

1975   Beginning of Lebanese civil war

1976   First military intervention of Syria in Lebanon

1977   Egyptian President Sadat in Israel

1978   Camp David Agreements between Egypt and Israel. Outbreak of Iranian Revolution

1979   Islamic republic established in Iran. Occupation of part of Prophet's Mosque in Mecca by Islamists. Soviet intervention in Afghanistan

1980–8   Iraqi–Iranian War

1981   Murder of President Sadat of Egypt by member of al-Jama'at al-Islamiya

1982   Israeli invasion of Lebanon; siege of Beirut; multinational force in Lebanon; Israeli security zone set up in south Lebanon. Syrian military suppression of Muslim Brotherhood in Homs and Hama

1983   Hizbullah attacks on US forces in Beirut

1987	Outbreak of Intifada resistance to Israel in Gaza
1988–9	Soviet withdrawal from Afghanistan
1989	Multi-party law in Algeria; electoral victories of Islamic Salvation Front. Taif agreements lay down preliminaries for end of Lebanese civil war
1990	Sudan proclaimed an Islamic state
1991	Gulf War fought by US-led alliance of Western and Arab states against Iraq. Armed insurrection of Islamist parties in Algeria
1993	Oslo negotiations on Israeli–Palestinian relationship lead to Declaration of Principles in Washington. Hekmatyar Hizb-i-Islami government formed in Afghanistan
1994	Palestine National Authority established
1996	Head of Islamist Rifah party in Turkey, Necmettin Erbakan, Prime Minister of coalition government. Taliban party enters Kabul

NOTES

INTRODUCTION

1 Revelation 9:19.

CHAPTER 1: *Holy Wars of the Ancient Near East*

The bibliography on Yahweh as a war god is given by Cohn, C., *Cosmos, Chaos and the World to Come: The Ancient Roots of Apocalyptic Faith* (New Haven and London, 1993), pp. 246–7. Kang, S.-M., *Divine War in the Old Testament and the Ancient Near East* (Berlin, 1987) is especially helpful. I also used: Cogan, M., *Imperialism and Religion: Assyria, Judah and Israel in the Eighth and Seventh Centuries BC* (Missoula, 1974); Albright, W.F., *Yahweh and the Gods of Canaan: A Historical Analysis of the Two Contrasting Faiths* (London, 1968); Cross, F.M. and Freedman, D.N., *Studies in Ancient Yahwistic Poetry* (Missoulla, 1975); Jagersma, H., *History of Israel to Bar Kochba* (London, 1994); Ringgren, H., *Israelite Religion*, trans. Green, D. (London, 1966); Fohrer, G., *History of Israelite Religion*, trans. Green, D. (London, 1973).

1 *Iliad* 4:128.
2 Exodus 15.
3 Psalm 78:13–14.
4 Psalm 77:16–19. Cross, F.M., *Canaanite Myth and Hebrew Epic: Essays in the History of the Religion of Israel* (Cambridge, Mass., 1973), p. 136.
5 Joshua 10:11–13.
6 Psalms 24, 47.
7 Genesis 14:14.

8 2 Samuel 5:17–25.
9 Exodus 17:15–16.
10 1 Samuel:4–11.
11 Exodus 15:1–21.
12 Judges 5.
13 Judges 20:18.
14 2 Samuel 11:10–11.
15 Numbers 31:7–18; Deuteronomy 2:34.
16 1 Samuel 18:27.
17 See Weippert, M., ' "Heilige Krieg" in Israel und Assyrien: Kritische Anmerkungen zu G. von Rads Konzept', *Zeitschrift für alttestamentliche Wissenschaft*, 84 (1972), pp. 460–93, at.488–9.
18 Exodus 18:16.
19 2 Kings 19:32–5; Isaiah 37:33–6; 2 Kings 18:14–16.
20 Isaiah 30:27,30.
21 Deuteronomy 32:41–2.
22 Ezekiel 39:6,20.
23 Qur'an 18:93.
24 Ezekiel 21:5.

CHAPTER 2: *Jewish Sects in the Hellenistic World*

Cohn, C., *Cosmos, Chaos and the World to Come: The Ancient Roots of Apocalyptic Faith* (New Haven and London, 1993), pp. 163ff; Hengel, M., *Judaism and Hellenism: Studies in their Encounter in Palestine During the Early Hellenistic Period* (London, 1974); Collins, J.J., 'The Mythology of Holy War in Daniel and the Qumran War Scroll: A Point of Transition in Jewish Apocalyptic', *Vetus Testamentum*, 25 (1975), pp. 596–612; Dimant, D., 'Qumran Sectarian

Literature', Stone, M.E. (ed.), *Jewish Writings of the Second Temple Period (Compendia Rerum Iudaicarum ad Novum Testamentum 2/2* (Philadelphia, 1984), pp. 483–550; Hengel, M., *The Zealots: Investigations into the Jewish Freedom Movement in the Period from Herod I until 70 AD* (Edinburgh, 1989), p. 387; Millar, F., 'Background to the Maccabaean Revolt', *Journal of Jewish Studies,* 29 (1978), pp. 1ff; Jagersma, H., *History of Israel to Bar Kochba* (London, 1994), especially pp. 53–4, 104–5, 188–9; Stone, M.E., *Scriptures, Sects and Visions: A Profile of Judaism from Ezra to the Jewish Revolt* (Oxford, 1982); Yadin, Y., *The Art of Warfare in Biblical Lands* (Jerusalem, 1963), pp. 2, 275–7; Bauckham, R., *The Climax of Prophecy: Studies in the Book of Revelation* (Edinburgh, 1993).

1 Zechariah 9:13–14; 10:3–5.
2 See 2 Enoch; also the Qumran War Scroll.
3 See Cohn, N., *Cosmos, Chaos and the World to Come: The Ancient Roots of Apocalyptic Faith* (New Haven and London, 1993), at.222. The symbolism of the four metals in the Book of Daniel, representing four world-ages, could have had a Zoroastrian origin.
4 On Mark 13:14, which speaks of the 'abomination of desolation'.
5 Qur'an 27:82.
6 *Inferno* 14:94–114.
7 Bickermann, E., *Der Gott der Makkabäer: Untersuchungen über Sinn und Ursprung der Makkabäischen Erhebung* (Berlin, 1937; English trans. Leiden, 1979).
8 Numbers 25:7–8.
9 Qur'an 2:191.
10 2 Maccabees 6, 7.
11 1 Maccabees 5:27–36.
12 *Paradiso* 18:40–2.
13 Gaster, T.H., *The Scriptures of the Dead Sea Sect* (London, 1957), p. 291.
14 Mark 15:7–8; John 18:40.
15 Hengel, M., *The Zealots: Investigations into the Jewish Freedom Movement in the*

Period from Herod I until 70 AD (Edinburgh, 1989), p. 387.
16 Qur'an 2:154; 9:111.
17 Qur'an 9:111. Muslim commentators sometimes refer to Matthew 10:39, but no such reference can be found in the Torah.
18 'Do you take me for a robber?' Matthew 26:55.
19 Matthew 26:52; 5:38–46.
20 Matthew 24, 25. See below.
21 Matthew 24:3–51; 25:1–46.
22 Job 39:30. Quoted in Matthew 24:28.
23 Matthew 5:39.
24 There is a useful discussion in Johnson, J.T., *The Quest for Peace: Three Moral Traditions in Western Cultural History* (Princeton, 1987), pp. 3–47. See also the classic statement of a more pacifist position, that of Bainton, R.H., *Christian Attitudes Towards War and Peace: A Historical Survey and Critical Re-Evaluation* (New York and Nashville, 1960).
25 See Johnson, J.T., *The Quest for Peace: Three Moral Traditions in Western Cultural History* (Princeton, 1987). Tertullian's reference is to Matthew 26:52.
26 Howard, M., *War and the Liberal Conscience* (London, 1978).
27 Howard, M., in a sermon delivered on 11 November 1984 at St Mary's Church, Oxford, and quoted in Harris, R., *Christianity and War in a Nuclear Age* (Oxford, 1986), pp. 158–9.

CHAPTER 3: *Islam and War*

Crone, P., *Meccan Trade and the Rise of Islam* (Oxford, 1987); Watt, W.M., *Muhammad at Medina* (Oxford, 1956); Watt, W.M., *Muhammad, Prophet and Statesman* (Oxford, 1961); Wansbrough, J., *The Sectarian Milieu: Content and Composition of Islamic Salvation History* (Oxford, 1978); Tyan, E., *Encyclopaedia of Islam,* 2 (Leiden and London, 1965), p. 538; Kennedy, H.N., *The Prophet and the Age of the Caliphates* (London, 1986);

Creswell, K.A.C., *A Short Account of Early Muslim Architecture* (Harmondsworth, 1958), pp. 43–4, 49; Hourani, A.H., *A History of the Arab Peoples* (London, 1991), chapters 1–5; Canard, M., 'La Guerre sainte dans le monde islamique et dans le monde chrétien', *Byzance et les musulmans du Proche Moyen Orient* (London, 973), pp. 605–23; Grünebaum, G.E. von, 'Eine poetische Polemik zwischen Byzanz und Bagdad im X. Jahrundert', *Analecta Orientalia*, 14 (1937), pp. 43–64; Partner, P., *The Lands of St Peter: The Papal State in the Middle Ages and the Early Renaissance* (London and Los Angeles, 1972), pp. 50–9; Collins, R., *The Arab Conquest of Spain* (Oxford, 1989); Bosworth, C.E., 'Political and Dynastic History of the Iranian World 1000–1217', *Cambridge History of Iran*, 5 (1968), pp. 1–202; Goldziher, I., *Muslim Studies*, ed. Stern, S.M., 2 (London, 1971), pp. 52, 57, 350; Peters, R. and Vries, G.J.J., 'Apostasy in Islam', *Welt des Islams*, n.s. 17 (1976/77), pp. 1–25; Khadduri, M., *The Law of War and Peace in Islam: A Study in Muslim International Law* (London, 1940); *Bell's Introduction to the Qur'an*, ed. Watt, W.M. (Edinburgh, 1970); Al-Mawardi, A.H., *Al-Ahkam as-sultaniyah. Les statuts gouvernmentaux ou règles de droit public et administratif*, ed. Fagnan, L. (Algiers, 1915), pp. 109ff, 114; Ibn Ishaq, K. al-J., *Il Muhtasar o sommario del diritto malechita di Halil [Khalil] ibn Ishaq*, trans. Guidi, I. and Santillana, D., 2 (Milan, 1919), p. 391; Al-Quduri, 'Le Livre de la guerre sainte [Kitab as-siyar]', ed. Bercher, L., *Revue tunisienne de droit*, 2 (Tunis, 1954), pp. 123–4.

1 Qur'an 42:52.
2 Qur'an 53:19. For the subsequent correction by Muhammad of what had been falsely suggested to him by Satan, Qur'an 22:51. The story that Muhammad had in the first instance referred to the three Meccan goddesses as some kind of angelic beings who assumed the form of birds is related by the annalist

Muhammad ibn Jarir al-Tabari (died 923 AD). The alleged incident furnished the point of departure for Salman Rushdie's 1988 novel.

3 Qur'an 25:52.
4 Qur'an 2:191; 47:5.
5 Qur'an 8:17; 9:25.
6 Qur'an 3:166–7.
7 Qur'an 4:97.
8 Qur'an 48:20.
9 Qur'an 5:33.
10 Peters, R., *Islam and Colonialism* (The Hague, 1979), pp. 152–3.
11 Qur'an 4:75; 2:216.
12 Gaudefroy-Demombynes, M., *Mahomet* (Paris, 1957), p. 122.
13 Qur'an 9:5.
14 Qur'an 8:72.
15 Qur'an 8:60.
16 Qur'an 9:29.
17 Qur'an 9:111.
18 Qur'an 2:154.
19 Qur'an 9:1–28 (excluding some verses).
20 Qur'an 9:33; 48:28; 61;9.
21 Erdmann, C., *Die Enststehung des Kreuzzuggedankens* (Berlin, 1935), p. 1. And see Nöth, A., *Heiliger Krieg und heiliger Kampf in Islam und Christentum: Beiträge zur Vorgeschichte und Geschichte der Kreuzzüge* (Bonn, 1966), pp. 21, 147.
22 Crone, P., *Meccan Trade and the Rise of Islam* (Oxford, 1987), p. 241.
23 Qur'an 2:256: 'You shall not be compelled, though truth will be distinguished from error.'
24 Bulliet, R.W., *Conversion to Islam in the Medieval Period: An Essay in Quantitative History* (Cambridge, Mass. and London, 1979). For the question of property rights, see Wansbrough, J., *The Sectarian Milieu: Content and Composition of Islamic Salvation History* (Oxford, 1978), p. 96.
25 e.g. Qur'an 2:177.
26 Qur'an 61:11.
27 Qur'an 25:52.
28 Qur'an 49:9.
29 Qur'an 5:33.
30 See El Fadl, K.A., ''*Ahkam al-Bughat*: Irregular Warfare and the Law of

Rebellion in Islam', *Cross, Crescent and Sword: The Justification and Limitation of War in Western and Islamic Tradition*, ed. Johnson, J.T. and Kelsay, J. (New York, Westwood and London, 1990), pp. 149–76.

31 Khadduri, M., *The Law of War and Peace in Islam: A Study in Muslim International Law* (London, 1940), p. 37.

32 Qur'an 85:1–11.

33 Qur'an 2:109; 3:99–100.

34 Hourani, A.H., *A History of the Arab Peoples* (London, 1991), p. 187.

35 Gibb, H.A.R., *Dumbarton Oaks Papers*, 12 (Georgetown DC, 1958).

36 Bosworth C.E., in *Cambridge History of Iran*, 5 (Cambridge, 1968), p. 43.

37 Ibid., pp. 62–4.

CHAPTER 4: *Christianity and War*

Bringman, K., 'Die Konstantinische Wende: Zum verhältnis von politischer und religiöser Motivation', *Historische Zeitschrift*, 260 (1995), pp. 21–47; Partner, P., *Lands of St Peter*, chapters 1, 4; Morisi, A., *La Guerra nel pensiero cristiano dalle origini alle crociate* (Florence, 1963); Cahen, C., *Orient et Occident au temps des croisades* (Paris, 1983); Barthold, W. (Vasily V.), *Turkestan Down to the Mongol Invasion* (3rd edn, E.J.W. Gibb Memorial ser., n.s., V, London, 1968); Bonner, M., 'Some Observations Concerning the Early Development of Jihad on the Arab-Byzantine Frontier', *Studia Islamica*, 75 (1992); Marçais, G., *La Berbérie Musulmane et l'Orient au Moyen Age* (Paris, 1946); Gilchrist, J., 'The Papacy and War Against the Saracens, 795–1216', *International Historical Review*, 10 (1988), pp. 174–97; Mayer, H.E., *Geschichte der Kreuzzüge* (6th revised edn, Stuttgart, 1985; English trans. Oxford, 1988); Riley-Smith, J., *The First Crusade and the Idea of Crusading* (London, 1986); Blake, E.O. and Morris, C., 'A Hermit Goes to War: Peter and the Origins of the First Crusade', Sheils, W.J., *Studies in Church History*, 22 (Oxford, 1985), pp. 79–107; Cahen, C.,

'L'Islam et la croisade', *Relazioni del X Congresso internazionale di scienze storiche* (Florence, 1955); Riley-Smith, J., 'Crusading as an Act of Love', *History*, 65 (1980), pp. 177–92; Proceedings of the Fourth International Conference of the Society for the Study of the Crusades and the Latin East, 'The First Crusade and its Consequences', Clermont-Ferrand, 22–25 June 1995 (awaiting publication).

1 Eusebius, *The History of the Church from Christ to Constantine*, trans. Williamson, G.A. (Rickmansworth, 1965), pp. 192–3.

2 Morisi, A., *La Guerra nel pensiero cristiano dalle origini alle crociate* (Florence, 1963), p. 119.

3 Partner, P., *The Lands of St Peter: The Papal State in the Middle Ages and the Early Renaissance* (London and Los Angeles, 1972), p. 5.

4 Falco, G., *The Holy Roman Republic: A Historic Profile of the Middle Ages* (London, 1964), p. 140.

5 Partner, *The Lands of St Peter*, p. 103.

6 Ibid., p. 114

7 Diehl, C. and Marçais, G., *Le Monde oriental de 395 à 1081* (Paris, 1944), p. 466.

8 Ibid, p. 461.

9 Luke 1:51, quoting Isaiah 51:9.

10 Holder-Egger, O. (ed.), *Lamperti Monachi Hersfeldensis Opera* (Hanover and Leipzig, 1914), pp. 93–9.

11 Riley-Smith, J., 'Crusading as an Act of Love', *History*, 65 (1980), pp. 177–92.

12 Hill, R. (ed.), *Gesta Francorum et aliorum Hierolimitanorum* (London and New York, 1962), p. 17.

13 Qur'an 8:17.

14 Cited by Cowdrey, H.E.J., in *Crusade and Settlement* (ed. Edbury, P.W.), (Cardiff, 1985), p. 52.

15 *The Letters of St Bernard of Clairvaux*, trans. James, B.S. (London, 1953), p. 464.

16 Gilchrist, J., in 'The Papacy and War Against the Saracens, 795–1216', *International Historical Review*, 10

(1988), pp. 174–97; and in 'The Lord's War as the Proving Ground of Faith: Pope Innocent III and the Propagation of Violence', Shatzmiller, M. (ed.), *Crusaders and Muslims in Twelfth-Century Syria* (Leyden, 1993), pp. 65–83.

CHAPTER 5: *Muslim and Christian Holy War*

Nöth, A., *Heiliger Krieg und heiliger Kampf in Islam und Christentum: Beiträge zur Vorgeschichte und Geschichte der Kreuzzüge* (Bonn, 1966); Holt, P.M., *The Age of the Crusades: The Near East from the Eleventh Century to 1517* (London and New York, 1986); Cahen, C., *Pre-Ottoman Turkey: A General Survey of the Material and Spiritual Culture and History c.1071–1330* (London, 1968); Edbury, P.W. and Rowe, J.G., *William of Tyre: Historian of the Latin East* (Cambridge, 1988); Schwinges, R.C., *Kreuzzugsidee und Toleranz: Studien zu Wilhelm von Tyrus* (Stuttgart, 1977); Gabrieli, F., 'The Arabic Historiography of the Crusades', *Historians of the Middle East*, ed. Lewis, B. and Holt, P.M., pp. 98–107 (London, New York and Toronto, 1962), pp. 98–107, at 103–4; Richards, D.S., 'Ibn al-Athir and the Later Parts of the Kamil: A Study in Aims and Methods, *Medieval Historical Writing in the Christian and Islamic Worlds*, ed. Morgan, D.O. (London, 1982), pp. 76–108; Sivan, E., 'Le Caractère sacre de Jérusalem dans l'Islam aux XII-XIIIe siècles', *Studia Islamica*, 27 (1967), pp. 149–82; Sivan, E., *L'Islam et la croisade: Idéologie et propagande dans les réactions Musulmanes aux croisades* (Paris, 1968); Willemart, P., *Pour Jérusalem: Croisade et djihad, 1099–1187* (Paris, 1988); Eliséef, N., *Nur ad-Din, un grand prince musulman de Syrie aux temps des croisades (511–569 H./ 1118–1174)* (Damascus, 1967); Prawer, J., *The Latin Kingdom of Jerusalem: European Colonization in the Middle Ages* (Oxford, 1972); Gibb, H.A.R., *The Life of Saladin from the Works of 'Imad ad-din and Baha 'ad-din* (Oxford, 1973);

Mohring, H., 'Der andere Islam: Zum Bild vom toleranten Sultan Saladin und neuen Propheten Shah Ismail', *Die Begegnung des Westen mit dem Osten*, ed. Engels, O. and Schreiner, P. (1993), pp. 131–55; Mohring, H., 'Heilige Krieg und politische Pragmatik: Salahadinus tyrannus', *Deutsches Archiv*, 39 (1983), pp. 417–66; Mohring, H., *Saladin und der dritte Kreuzzug: Aiyubidische Strategie und Diplomatie im Vergleich vornehmlich der arabischen mit den lateinischen Quellen* (Wiesbaden, 1980); Daiber, H., 'Die Kreuzzüge im Lichte islamischer Theologie bei Abu Samu', *Orientalische Kultur und europaisches Mittelalter*, ed. Zimmermann, A. etc. (Berlin and New York, 1985), pp. 77–86; Partner, P., 'Guerra santa, crociate e "Jihad": Un tentativo di definire alcuni problemi', *Studi Storici*, 39 (1995), pp. 945–55; Burns, R.I., *The Crusader Kingdom of Valencia: Reconstruction of a Thirteenth-Century Frontier* (Cambridge, Mass., 1967); Burns, R.I., *Islam under the Crusaders: Colonial Survival in the Thirteenth-Century Kingdom of Valencia* (Princeton, 1973); Barber, M., *The New Knighthood: A History of the Order of the Temple* (Cambridge, 1994); Riley-Smith, J., *The Knights of St John in Jerusalem and Cyprus* (London, 1967).

1 Hageneder, O. and Haidacher, A. (eds), *Die Register Innocenz III* (Graz-Cologne, 1964), p. 430.
2 Riant, P., *Archives de l'Orient Latin*, 1 (1881), p. 2.
3 Usamah Ibn-Munqidh, *Memoirs of an Arab-Syrian Gentleman*, trans. Hitti, P.K. (Beirut, 1964), pp. 94–5.
4 Kedar, B.Z., *Crusade and Mission: European Approaches Toward the Muslims* (Princeton, 1984), p. 35.
5 William of Tyre, *Historia rerum in partibus transmarinis gestarum*, lib. 1, cap. 9. A more favourable view of William's tolerance is taken in Schwinges, R.C., *Kreuzzugsidee und Toleranz: Studien zu Wilhelm von Tyrus* (Stuttgart, 1977), esp. pp. 116–17, 124.

6 Qur'an 17:1.

7 Gibb, H.A.R., *The Life of Saladin from the Works of 'Imad ad-din and Baha 'ad-din* (Oxford, 1973), p. 6.

8 Ibid., pp. 14–15

9 e.g. Professor W. Montgomery Watt, reported in Murphy, T.P. (ed.), *The Holy War* (Columbus, 1976), p. 198.

10 Hitti, P.K., 'The Impact of the Crusades on Moslem Lands', *History of the Crusades*, 5, ed. Zacour, N.P. and Hazard, H.W. (Madison, 1985), pp. 33, 49. No equivalent to this view was expressed by another Lebanese Christian historian, Albert Hourani, in his *A History of the Arab Peoples* (London, 1991).

11 Darwish, M., 'Memory for Forgetfulness: August, Beirut, 1982' (Los Angeles, New York and London, 1995), ll.114-15.

12 See Richards, D.S., 'Ibn al-Athir and the Later Parts of the Kamil: A Study in Aims and Methods, *Medieval Historical Writing in the Christian and Islamic Worlds*, ed. Morgan, D.O. (London, 1982), pp. 76–108.

13 Qur'an 6:43.

14 Cited by Holt, P.M., in *Medieval Historical Writing in the Christian and Islamic Worlds*, ed. Morgan, D.O. (London, 1982), pp. 22–3.

15 Quoted by Little, D.P., 'The Fall of Akka in 690/1291: The Muslim Version', *Studies in Islamic History and Civilization Presented to Professor David Ayalon* (Jerusalem, 1986), pp. 159–81.

16 In *Omne datum optime*, 29 March 1139.

17 *Liber ad milites Templi de laude novae militiae*, in *Sancti Bernardi opera*, ed. Leclerq, J., 3 (Rome, 1963).

18 Usamah Ibn-Munqidh, *Memoirs of an Arab-Syrian Gentleman*, trans. Hitti, P.K. (Beirut, 1964), pp. 163–4.

19 Quoted by Southern, R.W., *The Making of the Middle Ages* (London, 1959), p. 57.

CHAPTER 6: *Two Societies Organized for Holy War*

Daniel, N., 'Legal and Political Theories of the Crusade', *History of the Crusades*, 6 (Madison, 1989); Russell, F.H., *The Just War in the Middle Ages* (Cambridge, 1975); Muldoon, J., *Popes, Lawyers, and Infidels* (Liverpool, 1979); Bonet, H., *The Tree of Battles*, trans. Coopland, G.W. (Cambridge, Mass., 1949), pp. 126–8; Holt, P.M., 'Qalawun's Treaty with Acre in 1283', *English Historical Review*, 91 (1976), pp. 802–12; Holt, P.M., 'The Treaties of the Early Mamluk Sultans with the Frankish States', *Bulletin of the School for Oriental and African Studies*, 43 (1980), pp. 67–76; Wansbrough, J., 'The Safe-Conduct in Muslim Chancery Practice', *Bulletin of the School for Oriental and African Studies*, 34 (1971), pp. 20–35; Tyerman, C.J., 'The Holy Land and the Crusades of the Thirteenth and Fourteenth Centuries', *Crusade and Settlement*, ed. Edbury, P.W. (Cardiff, 1985), pp. 105–12; Setton, K.M., *The Papacy and the Levant (1204–1571)*, 1–2 (Philadelphia, 1976–8); Housley, N., *The Later Crusades, 1274–1580: From Lyons to Alcazar* (Oxford, 1992); Housley, N., *The Italian Crusade: The Papal–Angevin Alliance and the Crusades against Christian Lay Powers* (Oxford, 1982); Housley, N., *The Avignon Papacy and the Crusades, 1305–1378* (Oxford, 1986); Christiansen, E., *The Northern Crusades: The Baltic and the Catholic Frontier 1100–1525* (London, 1980); Little, D.P., 'The Fall of Akka in 690/1291: The Muslim Version', *Studies in Islamic History and Civilization Presented to Professor David Ayalon* (Jerusalem, 1986), pp. 159–81; Ayalon, D., 'Preliminary Remarks on the Mamluk Military Institution in Islam', *The Mamluk Military Society: Collected Studies* (London, 1979); Irwin, R., *The Middle East in the Middle Ages: The Early Mamluk Sultanate 1250–1382* (London and Sydney, 1986); Pipes, D., *Slaves, Soldiers and Islam: The Genesis of a Military System* (New Haven

and London, 1981); Inalcik, H., *The
Ottoman Empire: The Classical Age
1300–1600* (London, 1973); Abun-
Nasr, J.M., *A History of the Maghrib in
the Islamic Period* (Cambridge, 1987);
Gervers, M. and Bikazi, R.J., *Conversion
and Continuity: Indigenous Christian
Communities in Islamic Lands, Eighth to
Eighteenth Centuries* (Toronto, 1990);
Vryonis, S., *The Decline of Medieval
Hellenism in Asia Minor and the Process of
Islamization from the Eleventh through the
Fifteenth Century* (Los Angeles and
London, 1971); Arié, R., *L'Espagne
Musulmane aux temps des Nasrides
(1239–1492)* (Paris, 1973).

1 *The Letters of St Bernard of Clairvaux*,
  trans. Scott James, B. (London, 1953),
  p. 461.
2 Gilchrist, J., 'The Lord's War as the
  Proving Ground of Faith: Pope
  Innocent III and the Propagation of
  Violence', Shatzmiller, M. (ed.),
  *Crusaders and Muslims in Twelfth-
  Century Syria* (Leyden, 1993),
  pp. 65–83. There is a much wider
  discussion in Cipollone, G.,
  *Cristianità–Islam: Cattività e
  liberazione in nome di Dio: Il Tempo di
  Innocenzo III dopo il '1187'* (Rome,
  1992).
3 Pope Paschal II to the Emperor
  Alexius I (1112), quoted by Southern,
  R.W., *Western Society and the Church
  in the Middle Ages* (Harmondsworth,
  1970), p. 76. The quotation is from
  Jaffé, P., *Regesta Pontificum
  Romanorum*, 1 (Leipzig, 1885),
  no.6334.
4 See Russell, F.H., *The Just War in the
  Middle Ages* (Cambridge, 1975),
  pp. 204–5.
5 Notably by Professor Norman
  Housley, whose views are
  conveniently presented in his *The
  Later Crusades, 1274–1580: From
  Lyons to Alcazar* (Oxford, 1992).
6 *Inferno* 27:85.
7 Quoted by Little, D.P., 'The Fall of
  Akka in 690/1291: The Muslim
  Version', *Studies in Islamic History and*

*Civilization Presented to Professor
David Ayalon* (Jerusalem, 1986),
pp. 159–81.
8 Quoted by Inalcik, H., *The Ottoman
  Empire: The Classical Age 1300–1600*
  (London, 1973), p. 14
9 Ibid.
10 See Repp, R.C., *The Müfti of Istanbul:
  A Study in the Development of the
  Ottoman Learned Hierarchy* (London,
  1986), pp. 212–17.
11 Aeneas Sylvius, *Opera* (various
  editions), Ep. 127.
12 Ibid., Ep. 162.
13 cf. Abun-Nasr, J.M., *A History of the
  Maghreb in the Islamic Period*
  (Cambridge, 1987), pp. 102–3. For
  the weakness of the ideal of Islamic
  holy war in Islamic Spain at this time,
  see Rosenberger, B., *Annales,
  Économies, Sociétés, Civilisations*, 49
  (1994), p. 118.

CHAPTER 7: *Outside the Holy Wars*

Dufourcq, C.-E., *L'Espagne catalane et le
Maghrib aux XIIIe et XIVe siècles* (Paris,
1966); Dufourcq, C.E., 'Chrétiens et
musulmans durant les derniers siècles du
moyen âge', *Anuario de estudios medieváles*,
10 (Barcelona, 1980), pp. 207–26;
Scalia, G., 'Contributi pisani alla lottanel
mediterraneo centro-occidentale durante
il secolo xi e nei primi decenni del xii',
Anuario de estudios medievales, 10
(Barcelona, 1980), pp. 135–41; Heers, J.,
'Gênes et l'Afrique du Nord vers 1450:
Les Voyages percosteriam', *Anuario de
estudios medievales*, 21 (Barcelona, 1991),
pp. 233–45; Urbani, R., 'Genova e il
Maghrib tra il '400 e '500', *Genova, la
Liguria e l'oltremare tra Medioevo e eta
moderna*, 2 (Genoa, 1976), pp. 185–206;
Ashtor, E., 'Il Retroscena economico
dell'urto genovese-pisano alla fine del
duecento', *Genova, Pisa e il Mediterraneo
tra due e trecento* (Genoa, 1984),
pp. 51–81; Richard, R., 'Le Royaume de
Chypres et l'embargo sur le commerce
avec l'Egypte', *Comptes rendus de
l'Académie des Inscriptions et Belles-Lettres*
(Paris, 1984), pp. 120–34; Balard, M.,

'Genois et Pisans en Orient (fin du
13e–début du 14e siècle)', *Genova, Pisa e
il Mediterraneo tra due e trecento* (Genoa,
1984), pp. 181–208; Allmendiger, K.,
'Die Beziehungen zwischen der
Kommune Pisa und Aegypten im hohen
Mittelalter', *Vierteljahrschrift für Sozial-
und Wirtschaftsgeschichte*, 54 (1967);
Abulafia, D., 'The Role of Trade in
Muslim–Christian Contact in the
Middle Ages', in 'The Arab Influence in
Medieval Europe', *Folia Scholastica
Mediterranea*, ed. Agius, D.A. and
Hitchcock, R. (Reading, 1994), pp. 1–24;
Abulafia, D., *Commerce and Conquest in
the Mediterranean, 1100–1500*
(Aldershot, 1993); Zachariadou, E.A.,
*Trade and Crusade: Venetian Crete and the
Emirates of Menteshe and Aydin
(1300–1415)* (Venice, 1983),
pp. 112–14; Inalcik, H. and Quataert,
D., *An Economic and Social History of the
Ottoman Empire 1300–1914* (Cambridge,
1994); Verlinden, C., 'Le Recrutement
des esclaves à Venise aux xive et xve
siècles', *Bulletin de l'institut historique belge
de Rome*, 39 (1968), pp. 83–102;
Verlinden, C., 'La Crète, débouche et
plaque tournante de la traite des esclaves
au xive et xve siècles', *Studi in onore di
Amintore Fanfani*, 3 (Milan, 1962),
pp. 593–69; Verlinden, C., 'La Traite
des esclaves et traitants italiens à
Constantinople (xiiie–xive siècles)', *Le
Moyen Age*, 69 (1963), pp. 791–804;
Verlinden, C., 'Aspects quantitatifs de
l'esclavage méditerranéen au bas moyen
age, *Anuario de estudios medievales*, 10
(Barcelona, 1980), pp. 769–90; Gioffré,
D., *Il Mercato degli schiavi a Genova nel
secolo xv* (Genoa, 1967); Balard, M.,
'Remarques sur les esclaves à Gênes dans
la seconde moitié du xiiie siècle', *Mélanges
d'Archéologie et d'histoire de l'Ecole française
de Rome*, 80 (1968), pp. 627–80; Delort,
R., 'Quelques précisions sur le commerce
des esclaves à Gênes vers la fin du xv e
siècle', *Mélanges d'Archéologie et d'histoire
de l'Ecole française de Rome*, 78 (1966),
pp. 215–50; Pistarino, G., 'Tra liberi e
schiave a Genova nel Quattrocento',
Anuario de estudios medievales, 1

(Barcelona, 1964), pp. 353–74;
Brodman, J., *Ransoming Captives in
Christian Spain: The Order of Merced on
the Christian–Islamic Frontier*
(Philadelphia, 1986); Cipollone, G.,
*Cristianità–Islam: Cattività e liberazione in
nome di Dio: Il Tempo di Innocenzo III dopo
il '1187'* (Rome, 1992); Meyerson, M.D.,
*The Muslims of Valencia in the Age of
Fernando and Isabel: Between Co-existence
and Crusade* (Los Angeles, 1991); Boswell,
J., *The Royal Treasure: Muslim
Communities under the Crown of Aragon
in the Fourteenth Century* (New Haven,
1977).

1 Braudel, F., *The Mediterranean and the
Mediterranean World in the Age of
Philip II* (London, 1973), pp. 759–60.
Cited by Ajami, F., 'The
Summoning', *Foreign Affairs*, 72
(1993), pp. 2–9.
2 See Dufourcq, C.-E., *L'Espagne
catalane et le Maghrib aux XIIIe et XIVe
siècles* (Paris, 1966), pp. 556 ff, 571.
3 Braudel, F., *The Mediterranean and the
Mediterranean World in the Age of
Philip II* (London, 1973), p. 342.
4 Dufourcq, C.-E., 'Chrétiens et
Musulmans durant les derniers siècles
du moyen-âge', *Anuario de estudios
medievales*, 10 (Barcelona, 1980),
pp. 207–26. See also Dufourcq's
major work, *L'Espagne catalane et le
Maghrib aux XIIIe et XIVe siècles*
(Paris, 1966).
5 e.g. Lewis, A.R., 'The Islamic World
and the Latin West, 1350–1500',
Speculum, 65 (1990), pp. 833–44, esp.
841.
6 Quoted by Tenenti, A., 'The Sense
of Space and Time in the Venetian
World in the Fifteenth and Sixteenth
Centuries', *Renaissance Venice*, ed.
Hale, J.R. (London, 1973),
pp. 17–46, at.26.
7 Hourani, A.H., *A History of the Arab
Peoples* (London, 1991), pp. 215–16.
8 Valensi, L., *The Birth of the Despot:
Venice and the Sublime Porte* (Ithaca and
London, 1993), p. 55.
9 Braudel, F., *The Mediterranean and the*

Mediterranean World in the Age of
Philip II (London, 1973).

10 There is an illustration in Father
Giulio Cipollone's sensitive and
enormously learned book
*Cristianità–Islam: Cattività e
liberazione in nome di Dio: Il Tempo di
Innocenzo III dopo il '1187'* (Rome,
1992). He has also published *Il
Mosaico di S. Tommaso in Formis a Roma
(ca 1210)* (Rome, 1984).

11 Hourani, A.H., *A History of the Arab
Peoples* (London, 1991), p. 118.

12 Qur'an 4:100.

13 de Bartholomaeis, V., *Poesie
provenzali storiche relative all'Italia*, 2
(Rome, 1931), pp. 222–4.

14 Annales Herbipolenses, *Monumenta
Germaniae Historiae, Scriptores*, 16
(Hanover, 1859), p. 3.

15 Revelation 13.

16 Revelation 13:10.

17 *The Complete Works of John Gower*, ed.
Macaulay, G.C. (Oxford, 1901),
pp. 293–4.

CHAPTER 8: *Holy War, Colonies and
Conversion*

Richard, J., 'Les États féodaux et les
consequences de la croisade', Balard, M.
(ed.), *État et colonisation au moyen âge et à
la Renaissance* (Paris, 1989), pp. 181–91;
Richard, J., *La Papauté et les missions
d'Orient au moyen âge, XIIIe–XVe siècles*
(Rome, 1977); Santamaria, A., 'La
Reconquista de las vias maritimas',
Anuario de estudios medievales, 10
(Barcelona, 1980), pp. 41–133;
Magalhaes-Godinho, V., *L'Economie de
l'empire portugais au XVe et XVIe siècles*
(Paris, 1969); Zavala, S., *New Viewpoints
on the Spanish Colonization of the New
World* (Philadelphia, 1943); Brooks, F.J.,
Xocoyott, M., Cortes, H. and del Castillo,
B.D., 'The Construction of an Arrest',
Hispanic-American Historical Review, 75:2
(1995), pp. 149–84; Fernandez-Armesto,
F., *Before Columbus: Exploration and
Colonisation from the Mediterranean to the
Atlantic 1229–1492* (London, 1987);
Hanke, L., *The Spanish Struggle for Justice*

in the Conquest of America (Philadelphia
and Oxford, 1949); de Witte, C.-M., 'Les
Bulles pontificales et l'expansion
portugais au xve siècle', *Revue d'Histoire
Ecclesiastique*, 48 (1953), 49 (1954), 51
(1956), 53 (1958); Prosperi, A., 'New
Heaven and New Earth: Prophecy and
Propaganda at the Time of the Discovery
and Conquest of the Americas', Reeves,
M. (ed.), *Prophetic Rome in the High
Renaissance Period* (Oxford, 1992),
pp. 279–303; Prosperi, A., 'L'Europa
cristiana e il mondo: Alle origini dell'idea
di missione', Zorzi, R. (ed.), *L'Epopea delle
scoperte* (Florence, 1994), pp. 327–58.

1 Ranke, L., *History of the Latin and
Teutonic Nations (1494 to 1514)*, trans.
Dennis, G.R. (London, 1909), p. 17;
*Geschichte der romanischen und
germanischen Völker von 1494 bis 1514*
(Leipzig, 1885), pp.xxix–xxx.

2 See the introduction by Michel
Balard to *État et colonisation au Moyen
Age et à la Renaissance* (Lyon, 1989).
The essay by Charles Verlinden on
'The Transfer of Colonial
Techniques from the Mediterranean
to the Atlantic', translated in his *The
Beginnings of Modern Colonization*
(Ithaca and London, 1970), is the
classic exposition of this point of
view.

3 See Ashtor, E., *Levant Trade in the
Later Middle Ages* (Princeton, 1983),
pp. 511–12.

4 *The Complete Works of John Gower*, ed.
Macaulay, G.C. (Oxford, 1901),
pp. 345–6.

5 Erasmus, D., *Adagia*, 2, 1161E.

6 Doughty, C., *Travels in Arabia
Deserta*, 1 (1936 edn, London),
pp. 141–2.

7 Hakluyt, R., *The Principall
Navigations, Voiages and Discoveries of
the English Nation*, 3 (1965 edn,
London), p. 677.

8 See the symposium proceedings,
'The Crusading Kingdom of
Jerusalem: The First European
Colonial Society?' published in

Kedar, B.Z. (ed.). *The Horns of Hattin* (London, 1992), pp. 341–66.

CHAPTER 9: *Decay and Transformation of Holy War*

Schwoebel, R., *The Shadow of the Crescent: The Renaissance Image of the Turk 1453–1517* (Nieuwkoop, 1967); Halecki, O., 'The Defense of Europe in the Renaissance Period', *Didascalia: Studies in Honor of Anselm M. Albereda*, ed. Prete, S. (New York, 1961), pp. 123–46; Inalcik, H., 'State and Ideology under Sultan Suleiman I', *The Middle East and the Balkans under the Ottoman Empire* (Bloomington, 1993), pp. 55, 56, 188; Repp, R.C., *The Müfti of Istanbul: A Study in the Development of the Ottoman Learned Hierarchy* (London, 1986), pp. 212–17; Faroqhi, S., 'The Venetian Presence in the Ottoman Empire 1600–30 in Islamoglu-Inan', Huri, H. (ed.), *The Ottoman Empire and the World Economy* (Cambridge, 1987); Van Baumer, F., 'England and the Turk and the Common Corps of Christendom', *American Historical Review*, 50 (1944/45), pp. 26–48; Walsh, J.B., 'The Historiography of Ottoman–Safavid Relations in the Sixteenth and Seventeenth Centuries', Holt, P.M. and Lewis, B., *Historians of the Middle East* (London, New York and Toronto, 1962), pp. 197–210; Lewis, G.L., 'The Utility of Ottoman Fethnames', Holt, P.M. and Lewis, B., *Historians of the Middle East* (London, New York and Toronto, 1962), pp. 192–6; Valensi, L., *The Birth of the Despot: Venice and the Sublime Porte* (Ithaca and London, 1993); Lutz, H., 'Friedensideen und Friedensprobleme in der frühen Neuzeit', Heiss, G. and Lutz, H., *Friedensbewegungen: Bedingungen u. Wirkungen* (Munich, 1984), pp. 28–54; Pannier, J., 'Calvin et les Turcs', *Revue Historique*, 180 (1937), pp. 268–86; Repgen, K., 'Kriegslegitimationen in Alteuropa: Entwurf einer historischen Typologie', *Historische Zeitschrift*, 241 (1985), pp. 27–49; Repgen, K., 'What is a Religious War?', in Kouri, E.J. and Scott, T.S. (eds), *Politics and Society in Reformation Europe: Essays for Sir Geoffrey Elton on his Sixty-Fifth Birthday* (London, 1987), pp. 311–28; Guilmartin, J.F., 'Ideology and Conflict: The Wars of the Ottoman Empire, 1453–1606', in Rotberg, R.I. and Rabb, T.K. (eds), *The Origin and Prevention of Major Wars* (Cambridge, 1989), pp. 149–75; Buchanan, H., 'Luther and the Turks', *Archiv für Reformationsgeschichte*, 47 (1956), pp. 145–59; Setton, K.M., 'Lutheranism and the Turkish Peril', *Balkan Studies*, 3 (1962), pp. 132–67; Setton, K.M., 'Pope Leo X and the Turkish Peril', *Proceedings of the American Philosophical Society*, 113 (1969), pp. 367–424; Setton, K.M., *Western Hostility to Islam and Prophecies of Turkish Doom* (Philadelphia, 1992); Fischer-Galati, S.A., *Ottoman Imperialism and German Protestantism 1521–1555* (Cambridge, 1959); Mantran, R. (ed.), *Histoire de l'empire Ottoman* (Paris, 1989); Pannier, J., 'Calvin et les Turcs', *Revue Historique*, 180 (1937), pp. 268–86; Erasmus, D., *Opera Omnia Desiderii Erasmi Roterodami, 5:3. Utilissima consultatio de bello Turcis inferendo*, ed. Weiler, A.G. (Amsterdam, 1986); Heath, M.J., *Crusading Commonplaces: La Noue, Lucinge and Rhetoric Against the Turks* (Geneva, 1986); Heath, M.J., 'Erasmus and the War Against the Turks', *Acta conventus neo-latini Turonensis*, ed. Margolin, J.C. (Paris, 1980), pp. 991–9; Johnson, J.T., *The Quest for Peace: Three Moral Traditions in Western Cultural History* (Princeton, 1987); Johnson, J.T., *Ideology, Reason and the Limitation of War: Religious and Secular Concepts, 1200–1740* (Princeton, 1975); Walzer, M.L., *The Revolution of the Saints: A Study in the Origins of Radical Politics* (London, 1966); Lange, C.L., *Histoire de l'internationalisme* (Kristiana, 1919–63); Hinsley, F.H., *Power and the Pursuit of Peace: Theory and Practice in the History of Relations Between States* (Cambridge, 1963).

1 Braudel, F., *The Mediterranean and the Mediterranean World in the Age of Philip II* (London, 1973), pp. 842–5, 897–9.

2 Daniel 4:14 (Luther and Authorized Version), 4:18 (Vulgate). See also Proverbs 8:15.

3 See Buchanan, H., 'Luther and the Turks 1519–1529', *Archiv für Reformationsgeschichte*, 47 (1956), p. 155.

4 Repgen, K., 'What is a Religious War?', Kouri, E.J. and Scott, T.S. (eds), *Politics and Society in Reformation Europe: Essays for Sir Geoffrey Elton on his Sixty-Fifth Birthday* (London, 1987), pp. 311–28; Repgen, K., 'Kriegslegitimationen in AltEuropa: Entwurf einer historischen Typologie', *Historische Zeitschrift*, 241 (1985), pp. 27–49.

5 Johnson, J.T., *Ideology, Reason, and the Limitation of War: Religious and Secular Concepts 1200–1740* (Princeton, 1975), p. 115.

6 Ibid.

7 Gouge, W., *God's Three Arrows* (London, 1631).

8 Judges 5:23.

9 *The Faithful Testimony of that Antient Servant of the Lord and Minister of the Everlasting Gospel William Dewsbery in his Books, Epistles and Writings, Collected and Printed for Further Service* (London, 1689), pp. 48–9.

10 There is a fine essay on Erasmus's pacifism by Otto Herding in *Erasmus und Europa* (ed. Buck, A.) (Wiesbaden, 1988), pp. 13–32. See also Heath, M.J., 'Erasmus and the War Against the Turks', Margolin, J.C (ed.), *Acta conventus neo-latini turonensis* (Paris, 1980), pp. 991–9, at.993.

11 Heath, M.J., 'Erasmus and the War Against the Turks', *Acta conventus neo-latini Turonensis*, ed. Margolin, J.C. (Paris, 1980).

12 *Grammatica arabica* (1538), Preface, cited by Febvre, L., *Le Problème de l'incroyance au xvie siècle: La Religion de Rabelais* (Paris, 1947), pp. 124–5.

13 *Negotiations of Sir Thomas Roe in his Embassy to the Porte, 1621–28* (London, 1740), p. 22.

14 *Henry V*, Act V, Scene ii.

15 Hair, P.E.H., 'Protestants as Pirates, Slavers, and Protomissionaries: Sierra Leone 1568 and 1582', *Journal of Ecclesiastical History*, 21 (1970), pp. 203–24.

16 *Orlando Furioso* 17:73–9.

17 'The Third Universitie of England', in Stowe, J., *Annales, or a Generall Chronicle of England* (London, 1631).

18 Ashmole, B., *Institutions, Laws and Ceremonies of the Most Noble Order of the Garter* (London, 1672).

19 Cited by Van Baumer, F., 'England and the Turk and the Common Corps of Christendom', *American Historical Review*, 50 (1944/45).

20 Ibid.

21 Hinsley, F.H., *Power and the Pursuit of Peace: Theory and Practice in the History of Relations Between States* (Cambridge, 1963), pp. 30–1. I am much indebted to this work.

22 Ibid., p. 34.

CHAPTER 10: *Holy War and the European Empires*

Richards, J.F., *The New Cambridge History of India*, ov.1, Pt 5, *The Mughal Empire* (Cambridge, 1993); Peters, R., *Islam and Colonialism: The Doctrine of Jihad in Modern History* (The Hague, 1979); Holt, P.M., *The Mahdist State in the Sudan 1881–1898* (Oxford, 1958); Robinson, D., *The Holy War of Umar Tal* (Oxford, 1985); Brenner, L., 'The Jihad Debate Between Sokoto and Borno: An Historical Analysis', *People and Empires in African History: M. Crowder Memorial Essays* (London and New York, 1992), pp. 21–43; Hiskett, M., *The Development of Islam in West Africa* (London and New York, 1984); Levtzion, N., *Cambridge History of Africa*, ed. Gray, R., 4 (Cambridge, 1975), pp. 199–216; Batran, A., 'The Nineteenth-Century Islamic Revolutions in Africa', *UNESCO General History of Africa*, 6 (London and

Los Angeles, 1989), pp. 537–54; Last, M., 'The Sokoto Caliphate and Borno', *UNESCO General History of Africa*, 6 (London and Los Angeles, 1989), pp. 538–99; Laroui, A., 'African Initiatives and Resistance in North Africa and the Sahara', *UNESCO General History of Africa*, 7 (London and Los Angeles, 1985), pp. 87–113; Harrison, C., *France and Islam in West Africa 1860–1960* (Cambridge, 1988); Clancy-Smith, J.A., *Rebel and Saint: Muslim Notables, Populist Protest, Colonial Encounters (Algeria and Tunisia, 1800–1904)* (Los Angeles, 1994); Ageron, C.R., *Histoire de l'Algérie contemporaine*, 2 (Paris, 1979); Abun-Nasr, J.M., *The Tijaniya: A Sufi Order in the Modern World* (Oxford, 1965); Mallick, A.R., *British Policy and the Muslims in Bengal 1757–1856* (2nd edn, Dacca, 1977).

1 *Memoirs of Zehir-ed-Din Muhammad Babur Emperor of Hindustan Written by Himself*, trans. Leyden, J. and Erskine, revised by King, Sir L., 2 (Oxford, 1921, p. 307).
2 Jalal al-Din al-Suyuti (d.1505), quoted by Hiskett, M., *The Development of Islam in West Africa* (London and New York, 1984), p. 37.
3 Robinson, D., *The Holy War of Umar Tal* (Oxford, 1985), p. 305.
4 Lovejoy, P. and Hogendorn, J.S., 'Revolutionary Mahdism and Resistance to Colonial Rule in the Sokoto Caliphate 1905–6', *Journal of African History*, 31 (1990), pp. 217–44.
5 Hiskett, M., *The Development of Islam in West Africa* (London and New York, 1984), p. 236.
6 Mallick, A.R., *British Policy and the Muslims in Bengal 1757–1856* (2nd edn, Dacca, 1977), pp. 162–3.
7 The great French historian Jacques Berque had wise things to say about this in his *L'Intérieur du Maghreb xve–xixe siècle* (Paris, 1978), pp. 142–9, 162–90.
8 Latif, S.M., *History of the Punjab from Remotest Antiquity to the Present Time* (Calcutta, 1891), pp. 437–43.

CHAPTER 11: *Modernity and Political Islam*

Hourani, A.H., *Arabic Thought in the Liberal Age, 1798–1939* (London, New York and Toronto, 1962); al-Afghani, J., *Réfutation des matérialistes* (trans. Goichon, A.-M.) (Paris, 1942); Cleveland, W.L., *Islam Against the West: Shakib Arslan and the Campaign for Islamic Nationalism* (London, 1985); Choueiri, Y.M., *Islamic Fundamentalism* (London, 1990); Al-Azmeh, A., *Islams and Modernities* (London and New York, 1993); Kepel, J. and Richard, Y., *Intellectuels et militants de l'Islam contemporain* (Paris, 1990); Qutb, S., *Milestones* (Delhi, 1988); Qutb, S., *In the Shade of the Qur'an*, vol. 30 (trans. Salahi, M.A. and Shamis, A.A.) (Delhi, 1990); Carré, O., *Mystique et politique: Lecture révolutionnaire du Coran par Sayyid Qutb Frère musulman radical* (Paris, 1984); Alavi, H., 'Pakistan and Islam: Ethnicity and Ideology', Halliday, F. and Alavi, H., *State and Ideology in the Middle East and Pakistan* (Basingstoke, 1988), pp. 64–111; Nasr, S.V.R., *The Vanguard of the Islamic Revolution: The Jama'at-i Islami of Pakistan* (Los Angeles, 1994); Momen, M., *An Introduction to Shi'i Islam: The History and Doctrines of Twelver Shi'ism* (New Haven and London, 1985); Mottadeh, R., *The Mantle of the Prophet: Learning and Power in Modern Iran* (London 1986); Abrahamian, E., *Iran Between Two Revolutions* (Princeton, 1982); Abedi, M., and Leghausen, G., *Jihad and Shahadat: Struggle and Martyrdom in Islam* (Houston, 1986).

1 'Se moderniser, pour un peuple, ce n'est pas seulement accéder à de nouvelles instances. C'est rallumer en soi le combat de l'antique et du neuf.' Berque, J., *L'Intérieur du Maghreb xve–xixe siècle* (Paris, 1978), pp. 15–16. Berque's approach, that can also be found in his other books, was welcomed in Britain by the influential Anglo-Lebanese historian Albert Hourani (1915–93).

2 Mardin, S., 'Religion and Secularism in Turkey', *The Modern Middle East: A Reader*, ed. Hourani, A., Khoury, P.S., Wilson, M.C. (London and New York, 1993), pp. 347–74.

3 Ahmed, J.M., *The Intellectual Origins of Egyptian Nationalism* (London, 1960), p. 109.

4 Abrahamian, E., *Iran Between Two Revolutions* (Princeton, 1982), p. 465.

5 Islamists after Qutb have relied much upon the legal opinion of Ibn Taymiyya (1262–1327 AD), who was most concerned to refuse recognition of their status as Muslims to Mongol rulers who were still making war upon the Mamluks. Ibn Taymiyya therefore denounced the Mongol princes as feigning and not true Muslims.

6 Qur'an 13:11.

7 Qutb, S., *Milestones* (Delhi, 1988), esp. p. 245.

8 Kotb, S. (trans. Hardie, J.B.), *Social Justice in Islam* (Washington, 1953), pp. 38, 40, 135.

9 Qutb's Indian source was Asad, M., *Islam at the Crossroads* (Lahore, 1937). The circumstances of Allenby's entry into Jerusalem are explained in James, L., *Imperial Warrior: The Life and Times of Field Marshal Viscount Allenby 1861–1936* (London, 1993), pp. 143ff. James quotes the Cabinet Paper reference.

10 Mitchell, R.P., *The Society of the Muslim Brothers* (Oxford, 1969), pp. 234–5. Mitchell thought that the political demands of al-Banna and his successor as leader of the Muslim Brothers, Hudaybi, would have been satisfied if the existing parliamentary constitutional framework of Egypt had been reformed.

11 Nasr, S.V.R., *The Vanguard of the Islamic Revolution: The Jama'at-i Islami of Pakistan* (Los Angeles, 1994), p. 219.

CHAPTER 12: *Faith, Government and Dissent*

Owen, R., *State, Power and Politics in the Making of the Modern Middle East* (London and New York, 1992); Zubaida, S., *Islam, the People and the State* (London and New York, 1993); Piscatori, J.P. (ed.), *Islam in a World of Nation States* (Cambridge, 1986); Mitchell, R.P., *The Society of the Muslim Brothers* (Oxford, 1969); Kepel, G., *The Prophet and Pharoah: Muslim Extremism in Egypt* (Los Angeles, 1985); Ibrahim, S.E., 'Egypt's Islamic Activism in the 1980s', *Third World Quarterly*, 10/2 (London, 1988), pp. 632ff; Ansari, H.N., 'The Islamic Militants in Egyptian Politics', *International Journal of Middle East Studies*, 16 (Cambridge, 1984), pp. 123–44; Guenena, N., 'The "Jihad": An Islamic Alternative in Egypt', *Cairo Papers in Social Science*, vol. 9, monograph 2 (Cairo, 1986); Abdel-Fattah, N., *Veiled Violence: Islamic Fundamentalism in Egyptian Politics in the 1990s* (Cairo, 1994); Batatu, H., 'Syria's Muslim Brethren', Halliday, F. and Alavi, H. (eds), *State and Ideology in the Middle East and Pakistan* (Basingstoke, 1988), pp. 112–33; Shadid, M.K., 'The Muslim Brotherhood Movement in the West Bank and Gaza', *Third World Quarterly*, 10 (London, 1988); Schiff, Z. and Ya'ari, E., *Intifada* (New York, 1990); Mayer, T., 'Pro-Iranian Fundamentalism in Gaza', *Religious Radicalism and Politics in the Middle East*, ed. Sivan, E. and Friedman, M. (Albany, 1990), pp. 143–56; Johnson, N., *Islam and the Politics of Meaning in Palestinian Nationalism* (London, 1982); Bakhash, S., *The Reign of the Ayatollahs* (London, 1984); Kechichian, J.A., 'Islamic Revivalism and Change in Saudi Arabia: Juhayman al-'Utaybi's "Letters" to the Saudi People', *The Muslim World*, 80 (1990), pp. 1–16; Bligh, A., 'The Saudi Religious Elite (Ulama) as Participants in the Political System of the Kingdom', *International Journal of Middle East Studies*, 17 (Cambridge, 1985), pp. 37–50; Roy, O., *Islam and Resistance in Afghanistan* (Cambridge, 1986); Rouadjia, A., *Les Frères et la mosquée: enquête sur le mouvement islamiste en Algérie* (Paris, 1990); Moussaoui, A., 'De la violence au Djihad', *Annales*, 49, no.6 (Paris, 1994), pp. 1315–33; Tapper, R. (ed.), *Islam in Modern Turkey: Religion, Politics and Literature in a Secular State* (London and New York, 1991).

1 el-Bisri, D., 'Mouvement islamiste et guerre du Golfe, ou l'éclatement de deux concepts', *Peuples Méditerranéens*, 58–9 (1992), pp. 23–38. See also Roy, O., *The Failure of Political Islam* (London, 1994), pp. 121–2. Other references in Halliday, F., *Islam and the Myth of Confrontation: Religion and Politics in the Middle East* (London and New York ~~96), p. 228.

2 Guenei, N., 'The "Jihad": An Islamic Alternative in Egypt', *Cairo Papers in Social Science*, vol. 9, monograph 2 (Cairo, 1986), p. 37.

3 Roy, O., *The Failure of Political Islam* (London, 1994), pp. 84–106. Also his important *Islam and Resistance in Afghanistan* (Cambridge, 1986).

4 Report of interview near Damascus with Robert Fisk, *Independent* (London), 30 January 1995.

CHAPTER 13: *Western Dreams, Memories and Fears*

Said, E.W., *Orientalism* (London, 1978); Said, E.W., *Culture and Imperialism* (London, 1993); Gellner, E., *Muslim Society* (Cambridge, 1981); Partner, P., *The Murdered Magicians: The Templars and their Myth* (Oxford, 1982), part 2; Friedmann, J., 'Jihad in Ahmadi Thought', *Studies in Islamic History and Civilization Presented to Professor David Ayalon*, ed. Sharon, M. (Jerusalem, 1986), pp. 221–35.

1 Vaughan, C.E. (ed.), *Du Contrat social, ou principes du droit politique* (Manchester, 1926), book 4, chapter 8.

2 Voltaire, 'Essai sur les moeurs et l'esprit des nations', *Oeuvres complètes*, 2 (Paris, 1819), pp. 166–7, 103ff.

3 Ibid.

4 *The Koran, Commonly Called the Alkoran of Mohammed* (trans. Sale, G.) (London, n.d.), Preliminary Discourse, p. 111.

5 Gibbon, E., *The History of the Decline and Fall of the Roman Empire*, chapter 50. See also Hourani, A., *Islam in European Thought* (Cambridge, 1991), pp. 15–16.

6 Gibbon, E., *The History of the Decline and Fall of the Roman Empire*, chapter 58.

7 Discussed in Partner, P., *The Murdered Magicians: The Templars and their Myth* (Oxford, 1982), pp. 103–5.

8 Chateaubriand, F.-R. de, *Itinéraire de Paris à Jérusalem et de Jérusalem à Paris* (Paris, 1963), pp. 219–20. Edward Said draws on this passage in his *Orientalism* (London, 1978), pp. 171–5.

9 Poujoulat, J.J.-F., biography of Michaud in the *Biographie Universelle* (Paris, 1843 and 1852–66).

10 Michaud, J.-F. and Poujoulat, J.J.-F., *Correspondance d'Orient 1830–1*, 4 (Brussels, 1841), p. 249.

11 Raffles, Lady Stamford, *Memoir of the Life and Public Service of Sir Thomas Stamford Raffles, FRS & C* (London, 1830), p. 78, quoted by Hammer, J., *Geschichte des osmanisches Reiches*, 9 (Pest, 1831), p.xxxix.

12 Rey, E., *Les Colonies Franques de Syrie aux XIIme et XIIIme siècles* (Paris, 1883), introduction.

13 Ranke, L. von, *Weltgeschichte* (4th edn, Leipzig, 1898), part 8, p. 239: 'die einst so blühende Colonie'.

14 Kugler, B., *Geschichte der Kreuzzüge* (Berlin, 1880), p. 5.

15 Riant, P., 'Inventaire critique', *Archives de l'Orient Latin*, 1 (1881), p. 18. Bréhier, L., *L'Eglise et l'orient au moyen age: Les Croisades* (Paris, 1921), p. 26, maintained that

Charlemagne's position was like that of the capitulations between France and the Ottoman Empire in the sixteenth and seventeenth centuries, which is unlikely. He had expressed this view also at the Congrès français de la Syrie, held at Marseille in 1919.

16 Setton, K.M., *The Papacy and the Levant (1204–1571)*, 2 (Philadelphia, 1978), pp. 337, 397.

17 Hyman, A.M., *The Rise and Fall of Horatio Bottomley* (London, 1972), p. 154.

18 Bryant, K. and Wilkes, L., *Would I Fight?* (Oxford, 1935), p. 43.

19 Friedmann, J., 'Jihad in Ahmadi Thought', *Studies in Islamic History and Civilization Presented to Professor David Ayalon*, ed. Sharon, M. (Jerusalem, 1986), pp. 221–35.

20 Storrs, R., *Orientations* (London, 1945), p. 84.

CHAPTER 14: *Assumed Identities*

Roy, O., *The Failure of Political Islam* (London, 1994); Esposito, J.L., *The Islamic Threat: Myth or Reality?* (New York and Oxford, 1992); Kepel, G., *The Revenge of God: The Resurgence of Islam, Christianity and Judaism in the Modern World* (London, 1994); Halliday, F., *Islam and the Myth of Confrontation: Religion and Politics in the Middle East* (London and New York, 1996); Howard, M., *War and the Liberal Conscience* (London, 1978), pp. 115–16; Harris, R., *Christianity in a Nuclear Age* (London and Oxford, 1986); Johnson, J.T., *Just War Tradition and the Restraint of War: A Moral and Historical Inquiry* (Princeton, 1981); Kelsay, J. and Johnson, J.T. (eds), *Just War and Jihad: Historical and Theoretical Perspectives on*

War and Peace in Western and Islamic Traditions (New York, Westport and London, 1991); Kelsay, J. and Johnson, J.T. (eds), *Cross, Crescent and Sword: The Justification and Limitation of War in Western and Islamic Tradition* (New York, Westport and London, 1990); Mayer, A.E., *Islam and Human Rights: Tradition and Politics* (Boulder, San Francisco and London, 1991); al-Sayyid, R., 'Contemporary Muslim Thought and Human Rights' (unpublished paper, Beirut, 1994).

1 Ranke, L. von, *Serbien und die Türkei im neunzehnten Hundert* (Leipzig, 1879), p. 61. The book had been written in Vienna in 1828, and was first published in the following year.

2 Michaud, J.F. and Poujoulat, J.J.-F., *Correspondance d'Orient 1830–1*, 6 (Brussels, 1841), p. 179.

3 Cromer, E.B., *Modern Egypt*, 2 (London, 1908), p. 179.

4 Huntington, S.P., 'The Clash of Civilizations?', *Foreign Affairs*, 72 (1993), pp. 22–49.

5 Mayer, A.E., *Islam and Human Rights: Tradition and Politics* (Boulder, San Francisco, London, 1991), p. 147.

6 El Fadl, K.A., ''*Ahkam al-Bughat*: Irregular Warfare and the Law of Rebellion in Islam', *Cross, Crescent and Sword: The Justification and Limitation of War in Western and Islamic Tradition*, ed. Johnson, J.T. and Kelsay, J. (New York, Westwood and London, 1990).

7 Eliot, T.S., Choruses from 'The Rock' (*Collected Poems 1909–35*, London, 1936).

8 Walzer, M., *Just and Unjust Wars: A Moral Argument with Historical Illustrations* (London, 1978), p. 62.

A SHORT READING LIST

This is not a bibliography, but a list of books that may be useful to someone without specialized knowledge who wishes for more information about some of the topics treated in this book. Fuller lists of books and articles – still only those that seemed most important to my argument – are given in the sections preceding the notes to each chapter. The volume of writings on most of these subjects is enormous, and anyone seriously interested will have their own ideas on what are the most important books.

Holy War in Ancient Times

Bickermann, E., *The God of Maccabees*, Leiden, 1979
Cohn, C., *Cosmos, Chaos and the World to Come: The Ancient Roots of Apocalyptic Faith*, London, 1994
Jagersma, H., *History of Israel to Bar Kochba*, New Haven–London, 1993

Muhammad and Islam

Kennedy H.N., *The Prophet and the Age of the Caliphates*, London, 1986
Rodinson, M., *Mohammed*, London, 1971
Ruthven, M., *Islam in the World*, Harmondsworth, 1984
Watt, W.M., *Muhammad: Prophet and Statesman*, Oxford, 1961

Christianity, Islam and War

Bainton, R.H., *Christian Attitudes Towards War and Peace: A Historical Survey and Critical Re-Evaluation*, New York–Nashville, 1960
Harris, R., *Christianity and War in a Nuclear Age*, Oxford, 1986
Johnson, J.T., *The Quest for Peace: Three Moral Traditions in Western Cultural History*, Princeton, 1987
Johnson, J.T. and Kelsay, J. (eds), *Cross, Crescent and Sword: The Justification and Limitation of War in Western and Islamic Tradition*, New York–Westwood –London, 1990
Johnson, J.T. and Kelsay, J. (eds), *Just War and Jihad: Historical and Theoretical Perspectives on War and Peace in Western and Islamic Traditions*, New York–Westwood–London, 1991

The Crusade and Christian Society in the Middle Ages

Housley, N., *The Later Crusades 1274–1580*, Oxford, 1992
Kedar, B.Z., *Crusade and Mission: European Approaches Toward the Muslims*, Princeton, 1984
Mayer, H.E., *The Crusades*, Oxford, 1988
Morris, C., *The Papal Monarchy: The Western Church from 1050 to 1250*, Oxford, 1989
Riley-Smith, J., *The Crusades: A Short History*, London, 1987
Southern, R.W., *The Making of the Middle Ages*, London, 1953

Islamic Culture and Society

Burns, R.I., *Islam under the Crusades: Colonial Survival in the Thirteenth-Century Kingdom of Valencia*, Princeton, 1973
Hodgson, M.G.S., *The Venture of Islam*, Chicago, 1974
Hourani, A., *A History of the Arab Peoples*, London, 1991
Inalcik, H., *The Ottoman Empire: The Classical Age, 1300–1600*, London, 1973

Trade and Cultural Exchange in the Mediterranean

Abulafia, D., *Commerce and Conquest in the Mediterranean, 1100–1500*, Aldershot, 1993
Ashtor, E., *Levant Trade in the Later Middle Ages*, Princeton, 1983
Braudel, F., *The Mediterranean and the Mediterranean World in the Age of Philip II*, London, 1973
Goitein, S.D., *A Mediterranean Society*, Berkeley, 1967–1988
Inalcik, H. and Quataert, D., *An Economic and Social History of the Ottoman Empire 1300–1914*, Cambridge, 1994

The Mentalities and Techniques of European Colonizers

Fernandez-Armesto, F., *Before Columbus: Exploration and Colonization from the Mediterranean to the Atlantic 1229–1492*, London, 1987
Verlinden, C., *The Beginnings of Modern Colonization*, Ithaca and London, 1970

Internationalism and Pacifism

Hinsley, F.H., *Power and the Pursuit of Peace: Theory and Practice in the History of Relations Between States*, Cambridge, 1963
Johnston, J.T., *Ideology, Reason and the Limitation of War: Religious and Secular Concepts, 1200–1740*, Princeton, 1975
Walzer, M., *Just and Unjust Wars: A Moral Argument with Historical Illustrations*, London, 1978

Short Reading List

Islamic Peoples and Western Imperialism

Abun-Nasr, J.N., *The Tijaniya: A Sufi Order in the Modern World*, Oxford, 1965

Berque, J., *Egypt: Imperialism and Revolution*, London, 1972

Hiskett, M., *The Development of Islam in West Africa*, London and New York, 1984

Holt, P.M., *The Mahdist State in the Sudan 1881–1898*, Oxford, 1958

Park, Mungo, *Travels into the Interior of Africa* (published 1815–1816), reprint London, 1983

Peters, R., *Islam and Colonialism: The Doctrine of Jihad in Modern History*, The Hague, 1979

Robinson, D., *The Holy War of Umar Tal*, Oxford, 1985

Islamic Peoples and Modernity

Al-Azmeh, A., *Islam and Modernities*, London and New York, 1993

Gilsenan, M., *Recognizing Islam: An Anthropologist's Introduction*, London and Canberra, 1982

Hourani, A.H., *The Emergence of the Modern Middle East*, London and Basingstoke, 1981

Laroui, A., *The Crisis of the Arab Intellectual*, Berkeley and Los Angeles, 1976

Mitchell, R.P., *The Society of the Muslim Brothers*, Oxford, 1969

Mottadeh, R., *The Mantle of the Prophet: Learning and Power in Modern Iran*, London, 1986

Rahman, F., *Islam and Modernity*, Chicago, 1982

Zubaida, S., *Islam, the People and the State: Essays on Political Ideas and Movements in the Middle East*, London and New York, 1993

Islamic History and Modern History

Gellner, E., *Muslim Society*, Cambridge, 1981

Hourani, A.H., *Islam in European Thought*, Cambridge, 1991

Lewis, B., *Islam in History: Ideas, Men and Events in the Middle East*, London, 1973

Lewis, B., *History Remembered, Recovered, Invented*, Princeton, 1975

Said, E., *Orientalism*, New York and London, 1979

INDEX